D0198174

Science, Religion, and
the Human Experience

RENEWALS 458-4574

Acknowledgments

We wish to acknowledge the gracious support of the University of California, Santa Barbara, for sponsoring our Science, Religion, and the Human Experience lecture series from January 2001 through May 2003, and the generosity of the John Templeton Foundation in providing primary financial assistance for this three-year adventure in ideas. Public institutions of higher education and private philanthropic organizations serve quite different agendas, but the successful collaboration of UCSB and the John Templeton Foundation is evidenced by the consistently strong university and community participation our lecture series enjoyed, and the wide range of scholarly viewpoints that were presented and discussed.

Special thanks are due to Billy Grassie and the Metanexus Institute for ably administering the Templeton Research Lectures Series on the Constructive Engagement of Science and Religion, of which UC Santa Barbara was an initial awardee. Charles Harper, executive director of the John Templeton Foundation, Pamela Thompson, vice president for communications, and Paul Wason, director of science and religion programs, provided frequent and abundant support.

We were grateful to receive dedicated and high-quality administrative and logistic support at UCSB via the College of Letters and Science, the Office of Institutional Advancement (in particular, the Public Affairs Office, Office of Public Events, and Office of Development), the Office of Instructional Resources, and the Institute for Social, Behavioral, and Economic Research. Support spanned the entire campus, from the Institute for Theoretical Physics to the Interdisciplinary Humanities Center, and included a diverse faculty steering committee drawn from the physical and life sciences, social and behavioral sciences, and humanities. In all, over sixty UCSB faculty participated in some significant way during the three-year period of the lecture series. UCSB's Chancellor Henry Yang deserves special recognition for his sustained and enthusiastic commitment to what must have appeared to be a rather unorthodox scholarly venture taking place on his campus.

The editor, Jim Proctor, offers appreciation to the distinguished guest scholars who visited UCSB and presented lectures as a part of our series, then carefully revised their lectures into publishable essays for the present volume. It has been my joy to work with each one of them and get to know the person behind the intellect. My hope is that our collective efforts will mark a watershed in the scholarly study of science and religion, one where the human experience is welcomed as an equal partner.

Finally, I wish to acknowledge continued support and love from my daughters, Joy and Elise, who mostly heard of our Science, Religion, and the Human Experience series secondhand through discussions at home, but finally showed up for a lecture when it was their daddy's turn! I look forward to seeing how your many dreams unfold: all the activities culminating in this volume were once just a wild dream as well.

Contents

Contributors

Pascal Boyer, Henry Luce professor of individual and collective memory, Washington University in St. Louis, and author of *The Naturalness of Religious Ideas* (1994) and *Religion Explained* (2001).

John Hedley Brooke, Oxford University historian of religion and science, and author of *Science and Religion: Some Historical Perspectives* (1991) and *Reconstructing Nature: The Engagement of Science and Religion* (Oxford University Press, 1998).

Thomas A. Carlson, professor of religious studies at UC Santa Barbara, and author of *Indiscretion: Finitude and the Naming of God* (1999), as well as numerous translations of French philosopher Jean-Luc Marion.

Anne Harrington, historian of science at Harvard University, and author of *Medicine, Mind and the Double Brain* (1987) and *Reenchanted Science: Holism and German Culture from Wilhelm II to Hitler* (1997).

Bruno Latour, sociologist of science at Centre de Sociologie de l'Innovation, École des Mines de Paris, and author of *We Have Never Been Modern* (1993) and *Pandora's Hope: Essays on the Reality of Science Studies* (1999).

Daniel C. Matt, scholar of Jewish mysticism and author of *The Essential Kabbalah* (1995) and *God and the Big Bang* (1996).

Ronald L. Numbers, University of Wisconsin historian of American science and religion, and author of *The Creationists* (1993) and *Darwinism Comes to America* (1998).

Harold H. Oliver, professor emeritus of theology, Boston University, and author of *A Relational Metaphysic* (1981).

James D. Proctor, professor of geography at UC Santa Barbara, director of the Science, Religion, and the Human Experience lecture series, and editor of *Geography and Ethics: Journeys in a Moral Terrain* (1999).

Hilary Putnam, professor emeritus of philosophy, Harvard University, and author of *Reason, Truth, and History* (1981) and *Realism with a Human Face* (1990).

Michael Ruse, philosopher of science, Florida State University, and author of *Mystery of Mysteries: Is Evolution a Social Construction?* (1999) and *Can a Darwinian Be a Christian? The Relationship between Science and Religion* (2000).

Jeffrey Burton Russell, professor emeritus of history at UC Santa Barbara, and author of seventeen books, including *The Devil: Perceptions of Evil from Antiquity to Primitive Christianity* (1987) and *A History of Heaven* (1998).

Evan Thompson, philosopher of mind, York University, and author of *The Embodied Mind: Cognitive Science and Human Experience* (1993) and *Colour Vision: A Study in Cognitive Science and the Philosophy of Perception* (1995).

B. Alan Wallace, former professor of religious studies at UC Santa Barbara and author of *Choosing Reality: A Buddhist View of Physics and the Mind* (1996) and *The Taboo of Subjectivity: Toward a New Science of Consciousness* (Oxford University Press, 2001).

Science, Religion, and
the Human Experience

I

Introduction: Rethinking Science and Religion

James D. Proctor

Science without religion is lame, religion without science is blind.
—Albert Einstein

Prolegomenon: "Science"? "Religion"?

Is science without religion lame, and religion without science blind? Einstein's famous statement[1] finds many supporters: here, at last, the conflict between science and religion is laid to rest, and both are upheld for their different yet complementary roles. Others, however, may be less enthusiastic with Einstein's proposition that religion is necessary to give legs to science, or science to give eyes to religion. For them, the issue is indeed one of science versus religion, reason versus faith, realism versus idealism, matter versus spirit. Still others may wish Einstein had made the stronger statement that science and religion are parallel quests revealing similar truths. To this group of people, declaring science and religion to be separate but equal is to miss their metaphysical common ground. Reminiscent of "Goldilocks and the Three Bears," then, some may find Einstein's position to be just right, while others may find it to be too hot or too cold.

This volume reconsiders these and other major positions on the relationship between science and religion. But a fundamental question underlies any such position: what is meant by science and by religion? Einstein's argument is illustrative. In the same text where the above statement is found, Einstein defines science as "the century-old endeavor to bring together by means of systematic thought the perceptible phenomena of this world into as thoroughgoing an association as possible."[2] Yet, he argues, "The scientific method can teach us nothing else beyond how facts are related to, and conditioned by, each other. . . . [K]nowledge of what is does not open the door directly to what should be."[3] And this is how Einstein conveniently defines religion, stating "To make clear these fundamental ends and valuations, and to set them fast in the emotional life of the individual, seems to me precisely the most important function which religion has to perform in the social life of man."[4]

The literature on defining science and religion is immense and not amenable to concise review—certainly not within the space of this introduction. As one would imagine, there are lumpers and splitters, those who discover a unity to science or to religion and those who stridently dispute such a unity. What is important here is to note that Einstein's argument is utterly dependent on his definitions: if, indeed, science and religion are defined as unitary (science is about this; religion is about that) and complementary (in this case, science is about facts, religion about values, and the two need each other), then there is no other possible way to imagine their relationship.

Definitions of science and religion are inextricably bound to any position one encounters concerning the relationship between science and religion. There is no such thing as some neutral point of beginning from which we may compare alternative arguments, as these arguments necessarily concern not only the relationship between science and religion, but their essential identity as well. We thus hope the fresh perspectives we offer in this volume on the relationship between science and religion will reinvigorate discussion over fundamental questions concerning the nature of science and of religion—questions that go far beyond their relevance here.

Science and Religion: One or Two?

The range of possible positions regarding the relationship between science and religion has been formalized by Ian G. Barbour in a well-known typology.[5] Barbour identifies four types: Conflict, Independence, Dialogue, and Integration. Conflict theorists would find Einstein's position too "hot" (i.e., too supportive of science/religion compatibility). Einstein's position itself may be read as Independence, with science and religion understood as separate enterprises, or stronger interpretations of this position may lead to Dialogue, examining the mutual dependence between science and religion. Lastly, Integration theorists would read Einstein as much too "cold" for their tastes, which desire an essential similarity between science and religion.

Though useful, Barbour's typology has been criticized as static, overgeneralized, and ahistoric—a limitation of many typologies.[6] One could perhaps improve upon Barbour by moving toward greater complexity, as does Willem Drees in a ninefold schema;[7] but I would like to suggest an even simpler typology into which many positions on science and religion could be placed. It derives from Barbour's typology as well as the work of Harold Oliver,[8] and focuses not on science and religion per se, but rather the assumed domains onto which they map.

There are two underlying models for many positions on science and religion: a one-domain, or monistic, model, and a two-domain, or dualistic, model. In the one-domain model, science and religion either vie for the same turf (following Barbour's Conflict type and Oliver's Conflict Theory) or work harmoniously in the same arena (Barbour's Integration type). In the two-domain model, science and religion occupy distant worlds (Barbour's Independence type, or Oliver's Compartment Theory) or close but different worlds (Barbour's Dialogue type); in both cases science and religion are at peace because they are somewhat separable. Let us call the one-domain models conflict and convergent monism, respectively, and the two-domain model conciliatory dualism.

The story often begins with conflict monism, a battle between science and religion built on the one-domain model. Here science and religion play the role of dueling outlaws in a Wild West town that's not big enough for the both of 'em. Conflict monism has its modern roots in late-nineteenth-century publications such as J. W. Draper's 1875 *History of the Conflict between Religion and Science* and A. D. White's 1895 *History of the Warfare of Science with Theology in Christendom*,[9] yet retains continued popularity among those who feal religion is treading on the toes of science or vice versa. Perhaps the best contemporary example, at least in the case of the United States, involves competing accounts of the origin of life: the evolution versus creation controversy.[10] Here, as the caricature goes, theistic and naturalistic accounts are inevitably at odds over how living things—especially humans—came to be.

The broader issue in many accounts of conflict monism is the validity of religion in its claims on reality. Consider the biologists Paul and Anne Ehrlich, in their book *Betrayal of Science and Reason*:

> In the United States today, a surprising number of people believe in horoscopes, "out-of-body" experiences, the magical powers of crystals, and visitors from space. Our society is also witnessing a resurgence of creationism. . . . Such beliefs, and the activities they inspire, threaten rational scientific inquiry by rejecting the methods and procedures . . . that characterize modern science.[11]

Yet conflict monism can equally challenge the validity of science and scientific rationalism. Consider the statement of Prince Charles:

> The idea that there is a sacred trust between mankind and our Creator, under which we accept a duty of stewardship for the earth, has

been an important feature of most religious and spiritual thought throughout the ages. . . . It is only recently that this guiding principle has become smothered by almost impenetrable layers of scientific rationalism. . . . If literally nothing is held sacred anymore—because it is considered synonymous with superstition or in some other way "irrational"—what is there to prevent us treating our entire world as some "great laboratory of life" with potentially disastrous long term consequences?[12]

How can it be that the Ehrlichs strongly support rationalism and Prince Charles strongly opposes it? Perhaps the issue is not with rationalism per se, but rather with the domain onto which rationalism is applied. Prince Charles' speech addressed sustainable development and the fate of the earth; but his primary concern was with our attitudes toward nature, and where we should turn for moral guidance in these matters. Perhaps Prince Charles would agree that science and scientific rationalism are fine methods to get at the structure of the objective world; but when we get to our subjective selves, our values and attitudes, then science is ill-equipped to help, and can in fact hurt if it displaces spirituality as a moral resource. In its claims on the objective world, science is fine, but in the domain of the self, religion and spirituality are crucial. We hear in Prince Charles' assertion the broader, well-known religious critique of secularism and its threat to the soul.

If this is how the battle is perceived, if religion treads on science's domain when it makes pronouncements on the nature of reality, whereas science treads on religion's domain when it becomes the preeminent guide for the self, then there is a ready solution to conflict monism: separate the two. It is thus in the context of conflict monism that Einstein's statement makes sense. His characterization of science, religion, and their relationship is a familiar one, built on a quasi-metaphysical distinction between the continent of Facts on the one hand, which point directly to reality, and the continent of Values on the other, which point back to the self. This is precisely the path taken by the late Harvard paleontologist Stephen Jay Gould, who in his book *Rocks of Ages* argues that science and religion are noble, valid, but essentially different paths distinguished by their respective fact- and value-based domains of authority, which Gould terms "non-overlapping magisteria" or NOMA.[13] (The title of his book comes from the old joke: science tells us about the ages of rocks, whereas religion tells us about the Rock of Ages.)

Einstein and Gould represent conciliatory dualism, an attempt to reconcile science and religion, to grant them both validity, by casting each into its own separable domain. Let the scientists deal with facts about the world; let the religious leaders help us to clarify the values by which we live in the world. Perhaps they need each other (as Einstein admits more forthrightly than Gould), but they are certainly different.

But there is another approach that repudiates both conflict monism and conciliatory dualism by seeking a solution where science and religion, reality and self, come into harmony. Indeed, perhaps the biggest business in science and religion today builds on the theme of convergent monism, where science and religion offer coherent claims on reality and the self. Consider new-age thinkers such as Ken Wilber, who promises in his book *The Marriage of Sense and Soul: Integrating Science and Religion*:

> From the depths of a Kosmos too miraculous to believe, from the heights of a universe too wondrous to worship, from the insides of an astonishment that has no boundaries, an answer begins to suggest itself, and whispers to us lightly. If we listen very carefully, from within this infinite wonder, perhaps we can hear the gentle promise that, in the very heart of the Kosmos itself, both science and religion will be there together to welcome us home.[14]

Wilber's cosmology reconnects matter and spirit—and hence, the realities to which science and religion point—in a manner hearkening back to the Great Chain of Being.[15] Other convergence accounts have a more mainstream ring and respectability, but at minimum suggest a belief in the unity of science and religion in their claims on reality, if not a new vision of self. Mathematical physicist Paul Davies introduces his *Mind of God*, for instance, by stating:

> Through my scientific work I have come to believe more and more strongly that the physical universe is put together with an ingenuity so astonishing that I cannot accept it merely as a brute fact. There must, it seems to me, be a deeper level of explanation. Whether one wishes to call that deeper level "God" is a matter of taste and definition.[16]

Convergent monism has captured the attention of many people looking for a resolution to the cognitive dissonance of conflict monism without separating science from religion as in conciliatory dualism. A brief glance at science and religion titles in bookstores suggests the huge popularity of this convergence message. In my hometown of Santa Barbara, a recurrent lecture series called Mind/Supermind features many of these authors: one recent series ended with Fritjof Capra of *Tao of Physics* fame.[17]

This approach to science and religion thus elides the distinction between the universe and the self: here, science speaks to the soul, and religion speaks of deeper truths about reality. In this sense, convergent monism is a thoroughgoing monism, whereas conflict monism is a sort of inattentive monism, one that has placed the whole battle onto the domain of either the object or the subject, but never both.

How are we to make sense of monistic and dualistic treatments of science and religion? What should be apparent after brief reflection is that both offer a naïve taxonomy of the underlying domains upon which science and religion are founded. Consider dualism: can the domains of science and religion be so easily separated? Anyone who tries to assert that facts and values are readily separable, and that science has nothing to do with the latter and religion nothing to do with the former, is conjuring purified apparitions of both. So, then, is monism vindicated? Only by a similar simplification of science and religion—in this case with unificationist aspirations—and by the creation of a single domain stretching from you to the universe, one so vast as to be arguably meaningless. Perhaps, indeed, the universe and the self are one at some level, but only by squinting out all the important and interesting details.

Enter the Human Experience

With only two entities under consideration, it is perhaps understandable that science and religion are often discussed in terms of monistic or dualistic models: after all, the basic logic of comparison between two entities is sameness and difference, one or two. Yet, what if a third element is added? This is, analogically, the very problem Henri Poincaré entertained in the classic statement of chaos in celestial mechanics.[18] The relative orbits of two celestial bodies—say, the Earth and the Sun—are stable and the solution predictable (indeed, it was completely worked out centuries ago by Newton). When a third body is introduced (e.g., the classic problem of Jupiter, Earth, and the Sun), however, the situation was shown by Poincaré to be enormously complex and mathematically insoluble. Poincaré, a genius in several mathematical and scientific fields, had entered a contest sponsored by the king of Sweden that began in 1887, in which one question necessitated demonstrating that the solar system's dynamic stability could be proven by means of Newtonian mechanics. Poincaré's failure to do so nonetheless so impressed the judges that he was declared the winner: what Poincaré effectively demonstrated was the impossibility of solving the three-body problem, or in other words the inevitability of chaotic behavior. The well-known characteristic of sensitivity to initial conditions in chaotic systems can be attributed to Poincaré, as he explains, "It may happen that small differences in the initial conditions produce very great ones in the final phenomena. A small error in the former will produce an enormous error in the latter. Prediction becomes impossible, and we have the fortuitous phenomenon."[19]

So, working from a strictly Newtonian perspective, one can obtain mathematical chaos—a complex, beautiful, but unpredictable phenomenon—simply by moving from two to three celestial bodies. Such may be the result of considering the human experience in treatments of science and religion. By the human experience, we mean the unfolding of human life in its historical, political, geographical, psychological, and other contexts. Just as the three-body problem grants each of its entities de facto validity in exerting a "pull" on the others, so in considering science, religion, and the human experience we intend to take all three realms seriously and respectfully, and not simply collapse one onto another to produce some ready Newtonian solution. One could, for instance, conceive of science as pointing to objective reality, but religion as simply a human construct, a projection (as Freud would have it) of childhood neurosis, something made-up. In this case, there are but two bodies: science (understood more or less as knowledge of reality) and the human experience, of which religion is a part. Or, we could even further simplify the system, and declare both science and religion to be human constructs, citing history as ample evidence that both have feet of clay. Then we have a system of one body: the human experience.

But we are not seeking a simple solution in bringing the human experience into the science-and-religion equation: we are seeking something more faithful to life. The three-body-problem analogy implies that the realities toward which science and religion point, and the forms of human experience in which they are grounded, may all interrelate in complex and unpredictable ways. Too often, science and religion become a shorthand for physical reality and for God (or the sacred), as if science were some transparent window onto reality and religion a similarly transparent window onto the realm of the sacred. The opposite position is to understand science and religion in terms of their human face. Both have some justification. Yet how can science and religion be a part of the human experience, yet transcend it? This is the central question considered in different ways by this volume's essays.

The Essays

These essays derive from a research lecture series that took place at UC Santa Barbara between January 2001 and May 2003, with generous funding provided by the John Templeton Foundation. They have been grouped into four thematic sections: Theory, Cosmos, Life, and Mind. Theory concerns broad ways of understanding science and religion; Cosmos considers the ultimate nature of the universe; Life entertains the question of origins so prominent in science and religion discussion; and Mind concerns topics running from religious concepts to human consciousness. These four themes represent much of the current literature on science and religion; yet the perspective of the human experience casts each in a new light.

Theory

The Theory section begins with a brilliant essay by Bruno Latour, which aims to subvert typical assumptions about science and religion as a necessary preface to rethinking their relationship. Latour likens religion to love as a performative (versus merely referential) manner of speech that brings immediacy, not the distant God as is generally assumed; and he similarly flips general assumptions about science upside down in arguing that science is concerned not with the immediate stuff of life but with largely invisible worlds (the supposed domain of religion). Latour then addresses representation in science and religion, suggesting that science is not a simplistic matter of corresponding words to world, but an unending process of cascading chains of transformation by which matter becomes form. Latour also critiques the traditional notion of religious images as pointing toward the invisible and not being sacred in themselves. Rather, he argues that religious images work to distort and confuse general notions of direct apprehension of the distant and invisible, thus placing a reemphasis on the immediate, a (literal) re-presentation. In both cases, then, Latour argues for a dynamic notion of truth, cautioning against "freeze-framing" truth as either a static world of scientific reference or a static incarnation of the sacred in historical time.

The next essay, by Thomas Carlson, similarly questions common assumptions about science and religion. Carlson notes the intimate and practically inseparable connection between science and technology, arguing how "techno-science" is involved in producing not only knowledge of the world but also a sense of what it means to be human. This sense of humanness involves a connection of techno-science, and modernity in general, with the mystical realm usually associated with religion. Techno-science generally is understood precisely in the opposite sense as eliminating ignorance, of knowing (and mastering) all. Building upon the work of Weber and Heidegger, Carlson argues that this "will to mastery" is framed in the positing of an objective reality that the knowing subject masters, based on the certainty of the knowing subject as framed historically in Protestant theology and the philosophy of Descartes. Yet, given the inaccessibility of much of the actual process of techno-science to most people, there is an important component of faith: Carlson cites the argument of Derrida that any authority is hence grounded on a "mystical foundation." Indeed, similar to mystical systems of old, the aim of techno-science becomes to transcend time and space and attain a position of omniscience, much in the way that navigating the World Wide Web renders one everywhere and nowhere at once. Carlson emphasizes that this act of human self-creation is based on an essential un-knowing of oneself, in particular one's destiny. The result, via our participation in increasingly powerful networks of knowledge and power, is a type of omniscience without comprehension of where we are heading—a sense of the human experience as conveying not finitude but infinitude, instability.

Where Latour and Carlson took science and religion as their point of departure, Hilary Putnam's essay focuses on the dimension of human experience. Putnam seeks to dispense with the shallow notion of experience (including, but not limited to, religious experience) as something utterly reduced to sensations. He does so by carefully comparing the shallow Humean conception of experience, based on impressions or "pictures" formed on the senses, to the Kantian conception, which combines perception and conceptual ideas in a continuous self which fuses these experiences over time. Putnam then extends this Kantian notion of experience to discuss Kant's aesthetic argument concerning "indeterminate concepts," those that both involve and extend the creative imagination. Putnam applies Kant's treatment of indeterminacy to morality as a means of suggesting its relevance to religious experience. He also extends this notion to science, arguing that the technological and aesthetic process of scientific knowledge production is far more complex than a sense-data view would suggest. Putnam then returns to religious experience, specifically the problem of skepticism, which may seem to result from a rejection of immediate sense-impression and an embrace of indeterminacy. He discusses several responses, ultimately siding with the existentialist approach, which stresses a responsibility to live (and hence make choices) despite what cannot be fully proven following "reasonable" means. Putnam concludes by noting the symmetry between atheists and fundamentalists, because for both groups religious belief (or nonbelief) is obvious; this obviousness, in his mind, betrays a simplistic notion of experience, again pointing to the centrality of rethinking human experience prior to deep consideration of science and religion.

In the final essay of this section, Jim Proctor considers science and religion as major institutions of epistemic and moral authority. Proctor argues that authority is at the heart of most discussions related to science and religion, given the ways these discussions generally compare their authoritative claims. Both the ideological means by which scientific and religious authority are constructed and defended, and the different patterns of trust in authority among ordinary individuals and communities, are relevant to understanding science and religion. In the former case, a common tendency is to elide the humanness of scientific and religious institutions and base their authority on some notion of objectivity or transparency, such that science points directly to reality and religion to God (or the sacred). This claim, however, ignores the ways both are fully enmeshed in the human experience. In the case of peoples' differing trust of authority, Proctor refers to his recent survey and interviews of adult Americans regarding their trust in four major domains of authority: science, religion, nature, and the state. The results suggest two primary models of authority that Americans decide whether or not to trust: theocracy, with God (religion) as the ultimate authority and the state as the mediating human authority; and ecology, with nature as the ultimate authority and science as the mediating human authority. Though problems exist in both of these models, Proctor notes that some measure of trust in authority is unavoidable—and, as representing a commitment to life, potentially beneficial as well. Proctor ultimately argues that both commitment and critique must be present if trust in authority is to lead to meaningful epistemological and moral guidance in our lives.

Cosmos

The section on Cosmos begins with an essay by Jeffrey Russell. Russell commences by distinguishing between universe and cosmos, the human understanding of the universe. Cosmos etymologically implies order and purpose, in contrast to chaos; to Russell, both science and religion are concerned with cosmos or meaning. Yet cosmos, Russell claims, is seriously fragmented in modern times; he proposes an exploration of history and metaphor to heal cosmos. The history of concepts allows one a cultural memory to consider worldviews or notions of cosmos distant in space and time. Augustine understood that God's creation of the universe was a creation of meaning (cosmos), as well as substance, and biblical truths were understood in a symbolic as well as overt sense. Dante's *Paradiso* culminated this rich tradition of cosmos; yet by the sixteenth century religious reformation led to an overemphasis on literal truth and a deemphasis on symbolism. Thus began the decline of meaningful cosmos, of conflation of cosmos with universe, suggested in the infamous Galileo affair. With the growth of a concept of science in the seventeenth and eighteenth centuries, the reduction of cosmos to universe was secured. The loss of cosmos can, however, be healed by considering the importance of metaphor. Metaphor opens up, versus closing down, the meaning of reality. Russell introduces the term "metaphorical ontology" to suggest how deep meanings of things—cosmos—can be suggested in language, and claims that the proper language of religion is thus metaphor. The healing of cosmos will be aided by metaphorical ontology as it is enacted through religion, science, and other vistas on the ultimate nature of reality, leading humankind along paths yet unknown.

The next Cosmos essay, by Daniel Matt, considers possible resonances between contemporary physical cosmology and the kabbalistic tradition of Jewish mysticism. Matt begins by suggesting that common views of science and religion as distinct or separable are themselves limited in not suggesting possibilities for fruitful interaction. Religion, for example, gives science wonder; and science gives religion a view of knowledge as provisional, thus leading to humility in light of realities such as the nature of God. Matt then recapitulates the scientific theory of the big bang, but echoes Jeffrey Russell in bemoaning the loss of "myth" necessary to give meaning to life. Yet perhaps in the big bang one can recapture mythic depth and meaning, as the big bang indicates that we are made out of the same stuff as all creation; we all come from the cosmic seed. The kabbalistic tradition of Jewish mysticism, for instance, sometimes refers to God as nothingness, as a oneness that animates all things.

Kabbalah and physical cosmology, in fact, make parallel statements as to the singularity of the origin of the universe and its resultant unfolding. Other physical theories such as broken symmetry find kabbalistic parallels, in spite of their widely differing methodologies, and suggest that science and spirituality are complementary. Ultimately, this fractured world needs mending, argues Matt, and God needs us to mend it. But, as science may contend and kabbalah confirm, this God is no white-haired man in the sky; God is best understood as infinite and hidden, yet as close to us as is our connection with the big bang.

Harold Oliver closes the Cosmos section with an essay that addresses cosmos at the level of metaphysics and hearkens back to the Theory section in his reconception of science and religion. Oliver's essay focuses on the notion of complementarity between science and religion: Oliver grounds complementarity in relativity theory and quantum theory. More generally, Oliver appeals to metaphysics as the basis for his relational paradigm, reassessing its Aristotelian legacy, which assumed the subject/object structure of the Greek language and produced the substantialist thesis that reality ultimately consists of things whereas relations between things are accidental. To Oliver, the cosmos is a grand unity of relations, with subject and object, mind and brain, and ultimately God and World, existing as derivatives of this fundamental relatedness. Oliver then proceeds to argue that religious language is not referential, but symbolic of relational reality; it is when this relational reality is reduced to its derivatives that religious language is changed from mythical to referential discourse. In the case of science, Oliver argues that science aims for the most economical way of speaking of the world, versus the rich metaphorical language of religion. Ultimately, though, religion and science are about the same domain of human experience. Oliver then considers the question of science, religion, and truth. He cautions against saying that certain scientific theories may be "true," arguing that it is preferable to consider that well-established scientific theories add to our experience of reality. In the case of religion, Oliver cautions even more strongly against the subject-object notion of truth, in which it is seen to refer to the independent existence of an object; religious "truth," rather, is a realization or experience of relational reality.

Life

The third section, Life, consists of three essays which present different interpretations of Darwin and evolutionary theory, one of the most central topics in the study of science and religion. The section is launched with an essay by historian John Hedley Brooke, who focuses on the idea of the unity of nature, which has been important in both scientific and religious discourse. Brooke notes that the unity of nature thesis, so central to Christian theology, was not simply an epistemological assertion, but one that was intended to demonstrate the beauty of God and creation. In the case of Darwin, the unity of nature thesis would seem to pose a threat to his religious belief, as a naturalistic explanation of the origin of life would leave no need for God. Yet Brooke notes that Darwin's personal beliefs about God were complex, arguing that it was ultimately a series of incidents, both personally experienced and impersonally witnessed, which led Darwin to thoroughly question the idea of God as a caring, guiding Creator. Darwin's own theory of evolution did not seem to uphold any tidy unity of nature—since nature competes against itself in a struggle for existence!—and among some Christian leaders it had similarly challenging implications as well. But what greater unification could be imagined than Darwin's theory? In particular, his inclination toward the view that all of life had been derived from a single proto-life form suggests his striving toward unification. Brooke concludes by noting the important political ends to which the unity of nature thesis has been applied after Darwin, suggesting that it could remain as a meeting-ground between science and religion.

Michael Ruse's essay examines, and ultimately dispenses with, philosophical arguments that claim Darwinism leads to the rejection of religious belief. Ruse considers the arguments of three scholars who maintain that there is, indeed, a contradiction between Darwinism and religion. The first is entomologist and sociobiologist Edward O. Wilson. Wilson, Ruse argues, is quite sympathetic to religion as an ethical system, yet maintains that its existence can be explained on evolutionary grounds. Yet Wilson considers religion to be a necessary illusion, hardly true in its own right. In the second case, Ruse considers biologist Richard Dawkins, who argues that, until Darwin, no one could reasonably dismiss the "God hypothesis" of design. Ruse considers the thesis, popular among early Christian Darwinians, that God designed life through the process of evolution. One problem with this thesis is the very random, seemingly undesigned nature of evolution; yet Dawkins himself is not worried by random variation. As his third example, Ruse considers his own argument that the biblical injunction to love one's neighbor as oneself does not seem to be based on biological fitness, as much as on a near-neighbor form of love. Yet Ruse counters himself by arguing that perhaps Jesus' injunction did not admonish one to love everyone equally; alternatively, Christianity could be reaching out to extend a system of morality that biology has attuned to only near-neighbor forms of concern. Ultimately, Ruse argues that the conflict between Darwinism and religion was initiated for social and political, not scientific, reasons, and though challenges still exist in reconciling the two viewpoints, there is no necessary contradiction.

Ronald Numbers's essay also examines Darwinian theory and religious belief, but takes a different tack from that of the philosopher Ruse, examining in some detail a range of positions people have adopted in coming to personal terms with evolution. Numbers focuses on four individuals, all from the United States with scientific backgrounds, who struggled with reconciling evolutionary theory and theistic faith. He begins with Joseph LeConte, well-known in the late nineteenth century for his efforts at harmonizing theism and evolution. LeConte's deep personal struggles over the loss of a two-year-old daughter and his rejection of the atheistic "dragon of materialism" formed a powerful emotional thrust toward an espousal of evolution that avoided materialism, supported the hope of immortality, and maintained a resolute if not altogether traditional theism. Numbers's second and third examples, J. Peter Lesley and George Frederick Wright, both were trained in geology and had deep religious backgrounds; both also accepted modified forms of Darwinism yet rejected full-bore evolutionary thought. Lesley's and Wright's beliefs are understandable via life events and quite different forms of engagement with Christianity, Lesley rejecting much of it though not in turn embracing evolution, and Wright growing more fundamentalist with time. His final example, early-twentieth-century creationist George McCready Price, found personal and professional satisfaction in well-publicized rejections of evolution. Numbers candidly recounts his own life story, in which an emotional crisis, precipitated in part by a reconsideration of evolutionary theory, eventually led to his rejection of a fundamentalist upbringing. Numbers closes by reiterating his belief that "feelings count—often more than facts" and suggests that this is why so many Americans continue to call themselves creationists rather than evolutionists.

Mind

The fourth section, Mind, begins with an essay by Pascal Boyer, who follows up on the spirit of the preceding section by providing an evolutionary explanation of religion, in particular religious mental concepts. The human "mind-brain," Boyer argues, consists of multiple systems that guide understanding and action in different realms; though none of these systems are specific to religion, several may be connected to religious concepts, and some concepts may be more successful at cultural transmission via these systems than others. The first important feature of religious concepts to Boyer is that they are supernatural concepts, defined by their violation of some, but not all, normal domain-level expectations. Boyer then further clarifies that religious concepts tend to build on our templates of persons, yet emphasize their intentional agency, which can be evolutionarily explained either in terms of the mind-brain's need to understand the complex social interactions characteristic of humans, or as an asset in predator-prey interactions. Religious concepts are also about social interaction; yet, in contrast to ordinary people, supernatural agents have "perfect access" to all strategic (socially relevant) information relevant to a given social situation. Boyer cites research that suggests people who believe in the Christian God combine features of omniscience with a human-like mind; for instance, one must pray in order for God to hear you. Finally, Boyer argues that religious concepts prey upon common intuitions about misfortune: gods that do not matter much to peoples' daily lives, no matter how powerful they are otherwise, are not that religiously important. These concepts focus not on how, but why, the supernatural agents cause misfortune, the reason tracing back to some mishap of social interaction with these agents.

The section continues with an essay by Evan Thompson, who considers empathy as a central feature of the human experience, one which grounds both science and religion. Thompson draws upon cognitive science, contemplative psychology, and phenomenological philosophy in considering empathy the dynamic coupling of self and other, as a basic intersubjective dimension that precludes the distinction of inner and outer realities. Phenomenological inquiry suggests four aspects to empathy: involuntary coupling of self and other, imaginary transposition of oneself to the place of the other, interpretation of oneself as Other to the other and vice versa, and moral perception of other as person. These capacities exist wholly or in part in specific instances; all of these elements are found in human developmental psychology and come together in the lived bodily experience and via language. Thompson then turns to Buddhist contemplative psychology as a means of discussing implications for nonduality of self and other. Thompson analyzes the eighth-century Way of the Bodhisattva, which argues that notions of "self" and "other" have no independent existence, but are conceptually based; Buddhism, as a middle way, negotiates between the conventional truth that we have bounded selves and the ultimate truth that self has no bounds. Thompson finally turns to consider implications for cognitive science, arguing that it tends to rely on third-person theories and models, whereas for Thompson, the very fact of experience suggests the importance of adding first-person models to develop scientific accounts of consciousness. These first-person methods not only provide authentic experience, but trained, disciplined first-person methods afford the kind of reflective distancing necessary to process the complex set of interactions that intersubjective experience affords.

In the third essay of this section, Anne Harrington explores the overlap between faith and science in the context of medicine. Does the mind, or do higher powers accessed by the mind, have power to heal the body? Harrington considers four related claims, all offering some scientific validation. The first is that participation in religious services is good for one's health, which can apparently be explained only in part by religious communities serving as high-quality social networks. The second is that meditation reduces physical stress and aids healing, whether or not the meditator has any knowledge of or connection with a religious tradition. The third, larger claim is that religious belief of any sort can heal the body; this claim has strong roots in American religious history, but seems to derive more from the belief that the mind has innate healing capacities, rather than that healing comes from any sort of divine power. The fourth claim, in contrast, is that prayer conveys healing benefits, whether or not it is the patient or an intercessor who prays. This fourth claim is bolstered by certain controversial studies and differs from the other three in its implicit support for divine power, and thus divinity, whereas the other claims are exceedingly pragmatic in their overtones: religion is important because it works. All four claims, however, are somewhat distinct, and hardly form a coherent package. Overall, Harrington is concerned with the broad assertion that religion heals the body, due to its insistence that science has provided conclusive proof, as well as its utilitarian emphasis on medicinal therapy versus any other benefits conveyed by religion. To Harrington, what may result is not the spiritualization of medicine, but the medicalization of religion.

The final essay is by Alan Wallace and revisits the Theory section while connecting it with Mind. Wallace aims to present an alternative to metaphysical realism on the one hand, and to relativism and constructivism on the other, by exploring the possibility of intersubjective truth in science and religion. Wallace gives a summary of objectivism, the view that there is a world separate from human perceptions and concepts. As scientific naturalism proceeded to build knowledge of the objective world, religion recoiled against this naturalism as insufficient to account for God or the soul, thus maintaining a sort of mind/matter dualism. Wallace argues that the science of mental phenomena has been largely speculative and not systematically empirical, due in large part to the strong emphasis of science on external phenomena. Thus contemporary cognitive science focuses on the mechanics of mental phenomena, instead of the dynamics of the mind. Wallace discusses the pioneering work of William James, suggesting that science could consider the ways that brain and mind influence each other rather than taking mind to be simply an outcome of brain processes. He asserts that science works with the world of experience, not a world independent of human experience. Yet truth-claims can be organized according to their intersubjective invariance across multiple frames of experience-based reference. Wallace then discusses how one may validate scientific and religious claims made by those who are highly trained and have opportunities for extraordinary experiences of consciousness—those that outsiders cannot share nor perhaps understand. Yet both apply intersubjective empirical and pragmatic criteria to determine the utility of their truths. Wallace closes with a quote by William James that asserts the need for an empiricism of religious experience.

The Upshot: Between One and Two

Fourteen essays, each with a particular take on science, religion, and the human experience. Is there any overarching message one can bring home from these essays? To offer a tidy package to the reader would cheapen these great thinkers and their diverse thoughts: read the essays for yourself and see what you get from them.

But there may be some broad lesson we can gain by bringing the human experience into our discussions of science and religion. On one level, these discussions are simply about how scientific and religious people could get along, which is an important problem to resolve. But on a deeper level, science and religion have served as semiotic representatives, as binary code words pointing to longstanding philosophical tensions between the Great Domains of matter and spirit, truth and meaning, fact and value, transcendence and immanence, autonomy and constructedness, nature and culture. As suggested earlier, positions typically taken on science and religion concern not only science and religion, but also these Great Domains. Of course the easiest solutions are to either separate these Domains (and science and religion) or to unify them: dualism and monism are thus unsurprisingly popular options. But, just as Poincaré suggests how a third body forever disrupts any tidy solution to two-body planetary motion, here the human experience forever disrupts these two tidy solutions to the relationship between science and religion.

So have we simply made things more complex? Yes, but that is not all: indeed, many of the essays in this volume suggest an alternative approach to science and religion as informed by the human experience. A classic formulation of this approach is the early-twentieth-century work of Alfred North Whitehead. Whitehead, a brilliant mathematician-turned-metaphysician, was himself quite interested in science and religion: as he states, "When we consider what religion is for mankind, and what science is, it is no exaggeration to say that the future course of history depends upon the decision of this generation as to the relations between them."[20]

Whitehead's seminal contribution, one that resonates with many of the essays in this volume, amounts to a fundamental reexamination of the Great Domains that science and religion are assumed to signify, whether as separate (following conciliatory dualism) or unified (following convergent monism). What Whitehead suggests is that underlying these Great Domains is a supposed substratum of two substances, Object and Subject, a belief in "the concept of matter as the substance whose attributes we perceive. . . . Namely we conceive ourselves as perceiving attributes of things, and bits of matter are the things whose attributes we perceive."[21]

This is known as Whitehead's account of the bifurcation of nature:

What I am essentially protesting against is the bifurcation of nature into . . . two divisions, namely into the nature apprehended in awareness and the nature which is the cause of awareness. The nature which is the fact apprehended in awareness holds within it the greenness of the trees, the song of the birds, the warmth of the sun, the hardness of the chairs, and the feel of the velvet. The nature which is the cause of awareness is the conjectured system of molecules and electrons which so affects the mind as to produce the awareness of apparent nature.[22]

How is this bifurcation of nature, this fundamental bifurcation underlying all related bifurcations into Great Domains, bifurcations to which science and religion rush and declare them either separate but equal or one and the same, how is this bifurcation to be conceptually healed? This is precisely where many of the essays in our volume make a similar claim to that of Whitehead. As Isabelle Stengers and Bruno Latour note, Whitehead's dismissal of the bifurcation of nature into Object and Subject, primary (real) versus secondary (perceived) qualities of things, is supported by (surprise!) none other than our trilogy's third player, the human experience.[23] A world of human experience is a world that precedes objects and subjects; in other words, object and subject are derivative of experience. Experience points forward to objects as much as it points backward to subjects; experience thus annuls the hard dichotomy between subjects and objects, since it is from experience that the very meaning of "subject" and "object" is obtained.

There is much more to human experience, however, than what may appear to be a mere semantic point that it precedes objects and subjects. Significantly, experience is best evidenced in life, far different from the cold substantialist bias in much philosophy. Life is about experiences, not primarily about substances, and certainly not primarily about some Great Domains of reality and perception that categorically exclude the possibility of life. Latour summarizes Whitehead's argument, and Stengers' commentary, thus:

> The modernist philosophy of science implies a bifurcation of nature between primary and secondary qualities; however, if nature had really bifurcated, no living organism would be possible given that being an organism implies to ceaselessly blur the difference between primary and secondary qualities. Since we are organisms surrounded by many other organisms, nature has not bifurcated.[24]

Or, as Latour remarks, "an organism can't learn anything from the bifurcation of nature except that it should not exist. In that sense, philosophies that accept the bifurcation of nature are so many death-warrants."[25]

Important implications follow for Latour and Stengers concerning science and religion. For starters, science is no longer trapped in subjectivist skepticism—though certainly naïve empiricism is gone too, following the demise of the object-world. Another, perhaps more startling implication, is that Whitehead's argument for the necessity of God is not something to be conveniently excised, but plays a well-deserved role in his new cosmology. Though Latour reminds us that "[Whitehead's] God is there to solve very precisely a technical problem of philosophy not of belief,"[26] and though the involved explications

Latour and Stengers provide of Whitehead's extremely involved account of God are, perhaps unsurprisingly, dense, the broad point is unmistakable: science, religion, and the human experience are each refashioned, then each upheld and respected in a manner that denies anything fundamental to the Procrustean beds of Object and Subject, on which their living limbs are so often lopped off.

One way of putting Whitehead's philosophy in different terms is that, given its emphasis on process and experience, it finds relations to be more fundamental than things. This is a theme you will find in many contributions to this volume. "Relationality," "complementarity," "intersubjectivity," "experience": these are different terms than monism—we are not solving the problem of Two by retreating to the simple world of One. By bringing the human experience into science and religion, we have not so much gone from two to three or two to one, but rather have found a point somewhere between one and two, somewhere between the denial of difference (and hence the possibility of relation) that so bedevils monism and the metaphysical gap that defines dualism.

If there is no inherent subject, no object, but only as derivative of the relational human experience, then one can answer the central question of this volume, "Are science and religion a part of, or apart from, the human experience?" by eliminating a priori the subjectivist and objectivist options. The nature of human experience suggests that no longer can science or religion be dismissed as subjective constructions, nor can they be exalted as conduits for direct access to the objective reality of the universe and/or God. Yet we could equally say that the relationship between science, religion, and the human experience is a curious one in which *both* the subjectivist and the objectivist positions are upheld. Science and religion are both fully human enterprises, yet illuminate—however dimly at times—a reality that transcends human understanding.

The relational character of the worlds of human experience revealed by science and religion, then, is perhaps unavoidably expressed in conventional subject/object language as paradox, an admission of two seemingly contradictory truths. Science and religion as neither subjective nor objective, or in another way of speaking, as both subjective and objective. How can they be both subjective and objective? How can they be both and be neither at the same time? A multilayered paradox indeed. Yet the deepest human truths by which we live are the same: these truths can be fully historical products of a given culture in a given location and yet somehow provide brilliant glimpses of our ultimate realities. Paradox is much harder to grasp than a simple dualist statement that science is this, religion is that, or the monist assertion that science and religion are ultimately one and the same. But paradox, that elusive space somewhere between one and two, is certainly a part of our human experience of life. And how could we expect anything less in the relationship between science and religion?

NOTES

1. This statement from Albert Einstein, *Ideas and Opinions*, trans. Sonja Barg-mann (New York: Crown Publishers, Inc., 1954), 46. Einstein invoked several formulations of the relationship between science and religion, of which this is but one. In another passage, for instance, Einstein adopts the historical argument that "While it is true that scientific results are entirely independent from religious or moral considerations, those individuals to whom we owe the great creative achievements of science were all of them imbued with the truly religious conviction that this universe of ours is something perfect and susceptible to the rational striving for knowledge"; see Einstein, *Ideas and Opinions*, 52.

2. Ibid., 44.

3. Ibid., 41 42.

4. Ibid., 42.

5. Barbour's taxonomy is most recently presented in scholarly format in Ian G. Barbour, *Religion and Science: Historical and Contemporary Issues* (San Francisco: HarperSanFrancisco, 1997), and used as an organizing framework for Ian G. Barbour, *When Science Meets Religion* (San Francisco: HarperSanFrancisco, 2000).

6. See Geoffrey Cantor and Chris Kenny, "Barbour's Fourfold Way: Problems with His Taxonomy of Science-Religion Relationships," *Zygon* 36.4 (2001): 765–781. Barbour's reply is found in Ian G. Barbour, "Response Ian Barbour on Typologies," *Zygon* 37.2 (2002): 345 359. For other critiques of Barbour, see, e.g., William A. Stahl, Robert A. Campbell, Yvonne Petry, and Gary Diver, *Webs of Reality: Social Perspectives on Science and Religion* (New Brunswick, N.J.: Rutgers University Press, 2002); Willem B. Drees, *Religion, Science, and Naturalism* (Cambridge: Cambridge University Press, 1996).

7. See Drees, *Religion, Science, and Naturalism*.

8. See, e.g., Harold H. Oliver, "The Complementarity of Theology and Cosmology," *Zygon* 13.1 (1978): 19–33, where he discusses "conflict" (one-domain) and "compartment" (two-domain) positions as a preliminary to his argument on complementarity. See also Oliver's essay in this volume.

9. See John Hedley Brooke, *Science and Religion: Some Historical Perspectives*, Cambridge History of Science (Cambridge: Cambridge University Press, 1991), 33ff., for a discussion of these and other historical publications supporting the conflict thesis.

10. See, for instance, Robert T. Pennock, *Intelligent Design Creationism and Its Critics: Philosophical, Theological, and Scientific Perspectives* (Cambridge, Mass.: MIT Press, 2001); Michael Ruse, *The Evolution Wars: A Guide to the Debates* (Santa Barbara, Calif.: ABC-CLIO, 2000).

11. Paul R. Ehrlich and Anne H. Ehrlich, *Betrayal of Science and Reason: How Anti-Environmental Rhetoric Threatens Our Future* (Washington, D.C.: Island Press, 1996), 25.

12. Prince Charles, Millenium Reith Lecture, April–May 2000. Available online at http://news.bbc.co.uk/hi/english/static/events/reith_2000/lecture6.stm.

13. Stephen Jay Gould, *Rocks of Ages: Science and Religion in the Fullness of Life*, The Library of Contemporary Thought (New York: Ballantine Publishing Group, 1999).

14. Ken Wilber, *The Marriage of Sense and Soul: Integrating Science and Religion* (New York: Random House, 1998), xii.

15. Arthur O. Lovejoy, *The Great Chain of Being: A Study of the History of an Idea* (Cambridge: Harvard University Press, 1936).

16. P. C. W. Davies, *The Mind of God: The Scientific Basis for a Rational World* (New York: Simon & Schuster, 1992), 16.

17. Fritjof Capra, *The Tao of Physics: An Exploration of the Parallels between Modern Physics and Eastern Mysticism* (Berkeley: Shambhala, 1975).

18. I am grateful to Walter Kohn for suggesting this analogy.

19. Henri Poincaré, *Science and Method*, trans. Francis Maitland (New York: Dover Publications, Inc., 1952), 68.

20. Alfred North Whitehead, *Science and the Modern World* (New York: Macmillan, 1925), 260.

21. Alfred North Whitehead, *The Concept of Nature: Tarrner Lectures Delivered in Trinity College, November, 1919* (Cambridge: The University Press, 1920), 26.

22. Ibid., 30–31.

23. Isabelle Stengers, *Penser avec Whitehead: Une libre et sauvage création de concepts* (Paris: Gallimard, 2002); Bruno Latour, "What Is Given in Experience? A Review of Isabelle Stengers's *Penser avec Whitehead: Une libre et sauvage création de concepts*," *Boundary 2* 32.1 (forthcoming).

24. Latour, "What Is Given in Experience?"

25. Ibid.

26. Ibid.

BIBLIOGRAPHY

Barbour, Ian G. *Religion and Science: Historical and Contemporary Issues*. San Francisco: HarperSanFrancisco, 1997.

———. "Response: Ian Barbour on Typologies." *Zygon* 37.2 (2002): 345–359.

———. *When Science Meets Religion*. San Francisco: HarperSanFrancisco, 2000.

Brooke, John Hedley. *Science and Religion: Some Historical Perspectives*. Cambridge History of Science. Cambridge: Cambridge University Press, 1991.

Cantor, Geoffrey, and Chris Kenny. "Barbour's Fourfold Way: Problems with His Taxonomy of Science-Religion Relationships." *Zygon* 36.4 (2001): 765–781.

Capra, Fritjof. *The Tao of Physics: An Exploration of the Parallels between Modern Physics and Eastern Mysticism*. Berkeley: Shambhala, 1975.

Davies, P. C. W. *The Mind of God: The Scientific Basis for a Rational World*. New York: Simon & Schuster, 1992.

Drees, Willem B. *Religion, Science, and Naturalism*. Cambridge: Cambridge University Press, 1996.

Ehrlich, Paul R., and Anne H. Ehrlich. *Betrayal of Science and Reason: How Anti-Environmental Rhetoric Threatens Our Future*. Washington, D.C.: Island Press, 1996.

Einstein, Albert. *Ideas and Opinions*. Trans. Sonja Bargmann. New York: Crown Publishers, Inc., 1954.

Gould, Stephen Jay. *Rocks of Ages: Science and Religion in the Fullness of Life*. The Library of Contemporary Thought. New York: Ballantine Publishing Group, 1999.

Latour, Bruno. "What Is Given in Experience? A Review of Isabelle Stengers' *Penser avec Whitehead: Une libre et sauvage création de concepts*." *Boundary 2* 32.1 (forthcoming).

Lovejoy, Arthur O. *The Great Chain of Being: A Study of the History of an Idea*. Cambridge: Harvard University Press, 1936.

Oliver, Harold H. "The Complementarity of Theology and Cosmology." *Zygon* 13.1 (1978): 19–33.

Pennock, Robert T. *Intelligent Design Creationism and Its Critics: Philosophical, Theological, and Scientific Perspectives*. Cambridge, Mass.: MIT Press, 2001.

Poincaré, Henri. *Science and Method*. Trans. Francis Maitland. New York: Dover Publications, Inc., 1952.

Ruse, Michael. *The Evolution Wars: A Guide to the Debates*. Santa Barbara, Calif.: ABC-CLIO, 2000.

Stahl, William A., et al. *Webs of Reality: Social Perspectives on Science and Religion*. New Brunswick, N.J.: Rutgers University Press, 2002.

Stengers, Isabelle. *Penser avec whitehead: Une libre et sauvage création de concepts*. Paris: Gallimard, 2002.

Whitehead, Alfred North. *The Concept of Nature, Tarrner Lectures Delivered in Trinity College, November, 1919*. Cambridge: The University Press, 1920.

———. *Science and the Modern World*. New York: Macmillan, 1925.

Wilber, Ken. *The Marriage of Sense and Soul: Integrating Science and Religion*. New York: Random House, 1998.

PART I

Theory

2

"Thou Shall Not Freeze-Frame," or, How Not to Misunderstand the Science and Religion Debate

Bruno Latour

I have no authority whatsoever to talk to you[1] about religion and experience because I am neither a predicator, nor a theologian, nor a philosopher of religion—nor even an especially pious person. Fortunately, religion might not be about authority and strength, but exploration, hesitation, and weakness. If so, then I should begin by putting myself in a position of most extreme weakness. William James, at the end of his masterpiece, *The Varieties of Religious Experience*,[2] says his form of pragmatism possesses a "crass" label, that of pluralism. I should better state at the beginning of this talk that my label—should I say my stigma?—is even crasser: I have been raised a Catholic; and worse, I cannot even speak to my children of what I am doing at church on Sunday. It is from this very impossibility of speaking to my friends and to my own kin about a religion that matters to me, that I want to start tonight: I want to begin this essay by this hesitation, this weakness, this stuttering, by this speech impairment. Religion, in my tradition, in my corner of the world, has become impossible to enunciate.[3]

But I don't think I could be allowed to talk only from such a weakened and negative position. I have also a slightly firmer ground that gives me some encouragement in addressing this most difficult topic. If I have dared answering the invitation to speak, it is also because I have been working for many years on offering other interpretations of scientific practice than common ones.[4] It is clear that in an argument on "science and religion," any change, however slight, however disputed, in the way science is considered, will have some consequences on the many ways to talk about religion. Truth production in science, religion, law, politics, technology, economics, and so on is what I have been studying over the years in my program to advance toward an anthropology of the modern (or rather nonmodern) world. Systematic comparisons of what I call "regimes of enunciation" is what I am after, and if there is any technical argument in what follows, it is this rather idiosyncratic comparative anthropology from which they will come. In a sort of weak analogy with speech-act theory, I've devoted myself to mapping out the "conditions of felicity" of the various activities that, in our cultures, are able to elicit truth.

I have to note at the beginning, that I am not trying to make a critique of religion. That truth is in question in science, as well as in religion, is not for me in question. Contrary to what some of you who might know my work on science (most probably by hearsay) could be led to believe, I am interested mainly in the practical conditions of truth-telling and *not* in debunking religion after having, so it is said, disputed the claims of science. If it was already necessary to take science seriously without giving it some sort of "social explanation," such a stand is even more necessary for religion: debunkers simply would miss the point. Rather, my problem is how to become attuned to the right conditions of felicity of those different types of truth-generators.

And now to work. I don't think it is possible to speak of religion without making clear the form of speech that is adjusted to its type of predication. Religion, at least in the tradition I am going to talk from, namely the Christian one, is a way of preaching, of predicating, of enunciating truth in a certain manner—this is why I have to mimic in writing the situation of an oration given from the pulpit. It is literally, technically, theologically, a form of news, of "good news," what in Greek was called *evangelios,* what has been translated into English as "gospel." Thus, I am not going to speak of religion in general, as if there existed some universal domain, topic, or problem called "religion" that could allow one to compare divinities, rituals, and beliefs from Papua New Guinea to Mecca, from Easter Island to Vatican City. A person of faith has only one religion, as a child has only one mother. There is no point of view from which one could compare different religions and *still* be talking in the religious fashion. As you see, my purpose is not to talk *about* religion, but to talk to you *religiously,* at least religiously enough so that we can begin to analyze the conditions of felicity of such a speech act, by demonstrating in vivo, tonight, in this room what sort of truth-condition this speech-act requests. Since the topic of this series implies "experience," experience is what I want to generate.

Talking of Religion, Talking from Religion

What I am going to argue is that religion—again in the tradition which is mine—does not speak *of* things, but *from* things, entities, agencies, situations, substances, relations, experiences, whatever is the word, which are highly sensitive to the ways in which they are talked about. They are, so to speak, manners of speech—John would say Word, Logos, or *Verbum*. Either they transport the spirit from which they talk and they can be said to be truthful, faithful, proven, experienced, self-verifiable, or they don't reproduce, don't perform, don't transport what they talk from, and immediately, without any inertia, they begin to lie, to fall apart, to stop having any reference, any ground. Either they elicit the spirit they utter and they are true; or they don't and they are worse than false, they are simply irrelevant, parasitical.

There is nothing extravagant, spiritual, or mysterious in beginning to describe religious talk in this way. We are used to other, perfectly mundane forms of speech that are evaluated not by their correspondence with any state of affairs either, but by the quality of the interaction they generate from the way they are uttered. This experience—and experience is what we wish to share—is common in the domain of "love-talk" and, more largely, personal relations. "Do you love me?" is not assessed by the originality of the sentence—none are more banal, trivial, boring, rehashed—but rather by the *transformation* it manifests in the listener, as well as in the speaker. Information talk is one thing, transformation talk is another. When the latter is uttered, something happens. A slight displacement in the normal pace of things. A tiny shift in the passage of time. You have to decide, to get involved: maybe to commit yourselves irreversibly. We are not only undergoing an experience among others, but a change in the pulse and tempo of experience: *kairos* is the word the Greeks would have used to designate this new sense of urgency.

Before going back to religious talk, in order to displace our usual ways of framing it, I wish to extract two features from the experience we all have—I hope—in uttering or listening to love-carrying sentences.

The first one is that such sentences are not judged by their *content*, their number of bytes, but by their performative abilities. They are mainly evaluated by only this question: do they produce the thing they talk about, namely *lovers*? (I am not so much interested here in love as "eros," which often requires little talk, but in love as "agapè," to use the traditional distinction.) In love injunction, attention is redirected not to the content of the message, but to the container itself, the person-making. One does not attempt to decrypt it as if it transported a message, but as if it transformed the messengers themselves. And yet, it would be wrong to say that they have no truth-value simply because they possess no informational content. On the contrary, although one could not tick p's and q's to calculate the truth table of those statements, it is a very important matter—one to which we devote many nights and days—to decide whether they are truthful, faithful, deceitful, superficial, or simply obscure and vague. All the more so, because such injunctions are in no way limited to the medium of speech: smiles, sighs, silences, hugs, gestures, gaze, postures, everything can relay the argument—yes, it is an argument and a tightly knit one at that. But it is an odd argument that is largely judged by the *tone* with which it is uttered, its tonality. Love is made of syllogisms whose premises are persons. Are we not ready to give an arm and a leg to be able to detect truth from falsity in this strange talk that transports persons and not information? If there is one involvement in truth-detection, in trust-building that everyone shares, it is certainly this ability to detect right from wrong love talk. So, one of the conditions of felicity we can readily recognize is that there exist forms of speech—and again it is not just language—that are able to transfer *persons* not information, either because they produce in part personhood, or because new states, "new beginnings," as William James would say, are generated in the persons thus addressed.

The second feature I wish to retain from the specific—and totally banal—performance of love talk is that it seems to be able to shift the way space is inhabited and time flows. Here, again, the experience is so widespread that we might overlook its decisive originality. Although it is so common, it is not often described, except in a few movies by Ingmar Bergman, or in some odd novels, because eros, Hollywood eros, usually occupies the stage so noisily that the subtle dynamic of agapè is rarely noticed. But we can share, I think, enough of the same experience to capitalize on it later for my analysis: what happens to you, would you say, when you are thus addressed by love-talk? Very simply put: you were *far*, you are now *closer*—and lovers seem to have a treasure of private lore to account for the subtle reasons of those shifts from distance to proximity. This radical change concerns not only space, but also time: you just had the feeling of inflexible and fateful destiny, as if a flow from the past to the ever-diminishing present was taking you straight to inertia, boringness, maybe death; and suddenly, a word, an attitude, a query, a posture, *un je ne sais quoi*, and time flows again, as if it were starting from the present and had the capacity to open the future and reinterpret the past: possibility arises, fate is overcome, you breathe, you feel enabled, you hope, you move. In the same way as the word "close" captured the different ways space is now inhabited, it is the word "present" that now seems the best way to capture what happens to you: you are present again and anew to one another. And, of course, you might become absent and far again in a moment—this is why your heart beats so fast, why you are at once so thrilled and so anxious: a word badly uttered, a clumsy gesture, a wrong move and, instantly, the terrible feeling of estrangement and distance, this despondency that comes from the fateful passage of time, all of that boredom falls over you again, intolerable, deadly. You suddenly don't understand what you are doing with one another: unbearable, simply unbearable.

Have I not sketched a very common experience, the one acquired in the love crisis, on both sides of this infinitely small difference between what is close and present and what is far and absent? This difference that is marked so vividly by a nuance, sharp as a knife, both subtle and sturdy: a difference between talking rightly and talking wrongly about what make us alive to the presence of one another?

If we now take together the two features of love-addressing I have just outlined, we may convince ourselves that there exists a form of speech that (a) is concerned by the transformation of messengers instead of the transport of information, and (b) is so sensitive to the tone in which it is uttered that it can abruptly shift, through a decisive crisis, from distance to proximity—and back to estrangement—and from absence to distance and, alas, back again. Of this form of talk, I will say that it "re-presents" in one of the many literal meanings of the word: it presents anew what it is to be present in what one says. And (c) this form of talk is at once completely common, extremely complex, and not that frequently described in detail.

How to Redirect Attention?

Such is the atmosphere I want to benefit from, in order to start again my predication—since to talk, nay, to preach religion is what I want to attempt, so as to obtain enough common experience that it can be analyzed afterwards. I want to use the template of love-addressing so as to rehabituate ourselves to a form of religious talk which has been lost, unable to represent itself again, to repeat itself because of the shift from religion to belief; more on this later. We now know that the competence we are looking for is common, that it is subtle, that it is not very much described, that it easily appears and disappears, tells the truth and then gives the lie. The conditions of felicity of my own talk are thus clearly outlined: I will fail if I cannot produce, perform, educe what it is about. Either I am able to re-present it to you again, that is to present it in its renewed and olden presence, and I speak in truth; or I don't, and although I might have pronounced the same words, it is in vain that I speak, I have lied to you, I am nothing but an empty drum that beats in the void.

Three words are important, then, in respect to my risky contract with you: "close," "present," and "transformation." To give me some chance to succeed in re-enacting the right way to say religious things—in the Word tradition I have been raised in—I need to redirect your attention away from topics and domains thought to pertain to religion, but which might render you indifferent or hostile to my way of talking. We have to resist two temptations in order for my argument to stand a chance of representing anything—and thus to be truthful. The first temptation would be to abandon the transformation necessary for this speech-act to function; the second would be to direct our attention to the far away instead of the close and present.

To put it simply, but I hope not too provocatively: if, when hearing about religion, you direct your attention to the far away, the above, the supernatural, the infinite, the distant, the transcendent, the mysterious, the misty, the sublime, the eternal, chances are that you have not even begun to be sensitive to what religious talk tries to involve you in. Remember, I am using the template of love-addressing, to speak of different sentences with the same spirit, the same regime of enunciation. In the same way as those love-sentences should transform the listeners in being close and present or else are void, the ways of talking religion should bring the listener, and also the speaker, to the same closeness and to the same renewed sense of presence—or else they are worse than meaningless. If you are attracted to the distant, by religious matters, to the far away, the mysteriously encrypted, then you are *gone*, you are literally not *with me*, you remain absentminded. You make a lie of what I am giving you a chance to hear again tonight. Do you understand what I am saying? The way I am saying it? The Word tradition I am setting into motion again?

The first attempt at redirecting your attention is to make you aware of the pitfall of what I will call "double-click communication." If you use such a benchmark to evaluate the quality of religious talk, it will become exactly as meaningless, empty, boring, and repetitive as misaddressed love-talk, and for the same reason: because they carry no messages, but rather a transport and transform the messengers themselves, or fail. And yet, such is exactly the yardstick of double-click communication: it wants us to believe that it is feasible to transport without any deformation whatsoever of some accurate information about states of affairs which are not presently here. In most ordinary cases, what people have in mind when they ask "Is this true?," or "Does this correspond to a state of affairs?" is just such a double-click gesture allowing immediate access to information: tough luck, because this is also what gives the lie to ways of talking that are dearest to our heart. On the contrary, to disappoint the drive toward double-click, to divert it, to break it, to subvert it, to render it impossible, is just what religious talk is after. Speakers of religious talk want to make sure that even the most absentminded, the most distant gazers, are brought back to attention so that they don't waste their time ignoring the call to conversion. To disappoint, first, to disappoint. "What has this generation in requesting a sign? No sign will be given to them!"

Transport of information without deformation is not, *no* it is not one of religious talk's conditions of felicity. When the Virgin hears the angel Gabriel's salutation, she is so utterly transformed, says the venerable story, that she becomes pregnant with the Savior, rendered through her agency present again to the world. Surely this is not a case of double-click communication! On the other hand, asking "who was Mary?" checking whether or not she was "really" a Virgin, imagining some pathway to impregnate her with spermatic rays, deciding whether Gabriel is male or female, *these* are double-click questions. They want you to abandon the present time and to direct your attention away from the meaning of the venerable story. These questions are not impious, nor even irrational, they are simply a category mistake. They are so irrelevant that no one has even to bother answering them. Not because they lead to unfathomable mysteries, but because their idiocy makes them generate uninteresting and utterly useless mysteries. They should be broken, interrupted, voided, ridiculed—and I will show later how this interruption has been systematically attempted in one of the Western Christian iconographic traditions. The only way to understand stories such as that of the Annunciation is to *repeat* them, that is to utter again a Word which produces into the listener the same *effect*, which impregnates *you*, because it is you I am saluting, I am hailing tonight, with the same gift, the same present of renewed presence. Tonight, I am your Gabriel! Or else you don't understand a word of what I am saying—and I am a fraud.

Not an easy task—I will fail, I know, I am bound to fail, I speak against all odds—but my point is different because it is a little more analytical: I want you to realize through which sort of category mistake belief in belief is being generated. Either I repeat the first story because I retell it in the same efficient mode in which it was first told, or I hook up a stupid referential question to a messenger-transfer one and I do more than a crass stupidity. I make the venerable story lie because I have distorted it beyond recognition. Paradoxically, by formatting questions in the procrustean bed of information transfer so as to get at "exactly" what it meant, I would have *deformed* it, transmogrified it into an absurd belief, the sort of belief that weighs religion down and lets it slide toward the refuse heap of past obscurantism. The truth-value of those stories depends on us tonight, exactly as the whole history of two lovers depends on their ability to re-enact the injunction to love again in the minute they are reaching for one another in the darker moment of their estrangement: if they fail (present tense), it was in vain (past tense), that they have lived so long together.

Note that I did not speak of those sentences as being either irrational or unreasonable, as if religion had somehow to be protected against an irrelevant extension of rationality. When Ludwig Wittgenstein writes: "I want to say 'they don't treat this as a matter of reasonability.' Anyone who reads the Epistles will find it said: not only that it is not reasonable, but that it is a folly. Not only it is not reasonable, but it doesn't pretend to be,"[5] he seems to deeply misunderstand what sort of folly the Gospel is writing about. Far from not pretending to be reasonable, it simply applies the same *common* reasoning to a *different* kind of situation: it does not try to reach a distant state of affairs, but bring the locutors closer to what they say of one another. To suppose that, in addition to rational knowledge of what is graspable, there exists also some sort of nonrea-sonable and respectable belief of things too far away to be graspable, seems to me a very condescending form of tolerance. I'd rather like to say that rationality is never in excess, that science knows no boundary, and that there is absolutely nothing mysterious, or even unreasonable in religious talk—except the artifi-cial mysteries generated, as I just said, by asking the wrong questions, in the wrong mode, in the wrong *key*, to perfectly reasonable person-making argu-mentations. To seize something by talk, or to be seized by someone else's talk might be different, but the same basic mental, moral, psychological, and cog-nitive equipment is necessary for both.

More precisely we should differentiate two forms of mystery: one that refers to the common, complex, subtle ways in which one has to pronounce love-talk for it to be efficacious—and it is indeed a mystery of ability, a knack, like good tennis, good poetry, good philosophy, maybe a sort of "folly"—and another mystery, totally artificial, that is caused by the undue short-circuit of two different regimes of enunciation colliding with one another. The confusion between the two mysteries is what makes the voice of people quiver when they talk of religion, either because they wish to have no mystery at all—good, there is none anyway!—or because they believe they are looking at some encrypted message they have to decode through the use of some special and esoteric grid only initiates know how to use. But there is nothing hidden, nothing encrypted, nothing esoteric, nothing odd in religious talk: it is simply difficult to enact, it is simply a little bit subtle, it needs exercise, it requires great care, it might save those who utter it. To confuse talk that transforms messengers with talk that transports messages—cryptic or not—is not a proof of rationality, it is simply an idiocy doubled by an impiety. It is as idiotic as if a lover, asked to repeat whether she loves her partner or not, simply pushed the "play" button of a tape recorder to prove that five years ago she had indeed said "I love you, darling." It might prove something, but certainly *not* that she has renewed her pledge to love presently—it is a valid proof, to be sure, a proof that she is an absentminded and probably lunatic woman.

Enough for double-click communication. The two other features—close-ness and presence—are much more important for our purpose, because they will lead us to the third term of our lecture series, namely "science." It is amazing that most speakers, when they want to show generosity toward reli-gion, have to couch it in terms of its necessary irrationality. I sort of prefer those who, like Pascal Boyer, frankly want to explain—to explain away—reli-gion altogether, by highlighting the brain loci and the survival value of some of its most barbarous oddities.[6] I always feel more at home with purely natu-ralistic accounts than with this sort of hypocritical tolerance that ghettoizes religion into a form of nonsense specialized in transcendence and "feel good" inner sentiment. Alfred North Whitehead had put an end, in my views, to those who wish religion to "embellish the soul" with pretty furniture.[7] Religion, in the tradition I want to render present again, has nothing to do with subjectivity, nor with transcendence, nor with irrationality, and the last thing it needs is tolerance from open-minded and charitable intellectuals who want to add to the true but dry facts of science, the deep and charming "supplement of soul" provided by quaint religious feelings.

Here, I am afraid I have to disagree with most, if not all, of the former speakers on the science-religion confrontation because they are talking like Camp David diplomats drawing lines with a felt pen over some maps of the Israel/Palestine territories. They all try to settle disputes as if there was one single domain, one single kingdom to share in two, or, following the terrifying similarity with the Holy Land, as if two "equally valid claims" had to be established side by side, one for the natural, the other for the supernatural. And some speakers, like the most extremist zealots of Jerusalem and Ramallah—the parallel is uncanny—rejecting the efforts of diplomats, want to claim the whole land for themselves, either by driving the obscurantist religious folks to the other side of the Jordan River or, conversely, by drowning the naturalists in the Mediterranean Sea. I find those disputes—whether there is one or two domains, whether it is hegemonic or parallel, whether polemical or peaceful—equally moot for a reason that strikes at the heart of the matter: they all suppose that science and religion have similar but divergent claims to reach and settle a territory, either of this world, or of this other world. I believe, on the contrary, that there is no point of contact between the two, no more, let's say than nightingales and frogs have to enter into any sort of direct ecological competition

I am not saying that science and religion are incommensurable because one grasps the objective visible world of here and there, and the other grasps the invisible subjective or transcendent world of beyond, but rather that even their incommensurability would be a category mistake. The reason is that neither science nor religion fits even this basic picture that would put them face-to-face, or enough in relation to be deemed incommensurable! Neither religion nor science are much interested in the visible: it is science that grasps the far and the distant; as to religion, it does not even try to *grasp* anything.

Science and Religion: A Comedy of Errors

My point might appear at first counterintuitive because I wish to draw simultaneously on what I have learned from science studies about scientific practice and what I hope you have experienced here in reframing religious talk with the help of a love argument. Religion does not even try, if you have followed me until now, to reach anything beyond, but to represent the presence of that which is called in a certain technical and ritual idiom the "Word incarnate"—that is to say again that it is here, alive, and not dead over there far away. It does not try to designate something, but to speak from a new state that it generates by its ways of talking, its manner of speech. Religion, in this tradition, does everything to constantly redirect attention by systematically breaking the will to go away, to ignore, to be indifferent, blasé, bored. Conversely, science has nothing to do with the visible, the direct, the immediate, the tangible, the lived world of common sense, of sturdy "matters of fact." Quite the opposite, as I have shown many times, it builds extraordinarily long, complicated, mediated, indirect, sophisticated paths so as to reach the worlds—like William James I insist on the plural—that are invisible because they are too small, too far, too powerful, too big, too odd, too surprising, too counterintuitive, through concatenations of layered instruments, calculations, models. Only through the laboratory and instrument networks can you obtain those long referential chains that allow you to maximize the two contrary features of mobility (or transport) and immutability (or constant) that both make up information— what I have called for this reason "immutable mobiles."

And notice here that science in action, science as it is done practically, is even further from double-click communication than religion: distortion, transformation, recoding, modeling, translating, all of these radical mediations are necessary to produce reliable and accurate information. If science was information *without* transformation, as good common sense would like to have it, we would still be in complete obscurity about states of affairs distant from here and now. Double-click communication does even less justice to the transformation of information in scientific networks than to the strange ability of some speech-acts to transform the locutors in religion.

What a comedy of errors! When the debate between science and religion is staged, adjectives are almost exactly reversed: it is of science that one should say that it reaches the invisible world of beyond, that she is spiritual, miraculous, soul-fulfilling, uplifting.[8] And it is religion that should be qualified as being local, objective, visible, mundane, unmiraculous, repetitive, obstinate, sturdy.

In the traditional fable of a race between the scientific rabbit and the religious tortoise, two things are totally unrealistic: the rabbit *and* the tortoise. Religion does not even attempt to race to know the beyond, but attempts at breaking all habits of thoughts that direct our attention to the far away, to the absent, to the overworld, in order to bring attention back to the incarnate, to the renewed presence of what was before misunderstood, distorted and deadly, of what is said to be "what was, what is, what shall be," toward those words that carry salvation. Science does not *directly* grasp anything accurately, but slowly gains its accuracy, its validity, its truth-condition by the long, risky, and painful detour through the mediations of experiments not experience, laboratories not common sense, theories not visibility, and if she is able to obtain truth it is at the price of mind-boggling transformations from one media into the next. Thus, to even assemble a stage where the deep and serious problem of "the relationship between science and religion" could unfold is already an imposture, not to say a farce that distorts science and religion, religion and science beyond all recognition.

The only protagonist who would dream of the silly idea of staging a race between the rabbit and the tortoise, to put them face-to-face so as to decide afterward who dominates whom—or to invent even more bizarre diplomatic settlements between the two characters—the only Barnum for such a circus, is double-click communication. Only he, with this bizarre idea of transportation *without* transformation to reach a far away state of affairs, could dream of such a confrontation, distorting the careful practice of science, as well as the careful repetition of religious, person-giving talk. Only he can make both science and religion incomprehensible, first by distorting the mediated and indirect access of science to the invisible world through the hard labor of scientists, into a direct, plain, and unproblematic grasp of the visible; and then, in giving the lie to religion by forcing her to abandon her goal of representing anew what it is about and making all of us gaze, absentmindedly toward the invisible world of beyond which she has no equipment nor competence nor authority nor ability to reach—even less to grasp. Yes, what a comedy of errors, a sad comedy, one that has made it almost impossible to embrace rationalism, because it would mean to ignore the workings of science even more than the goals of religion.

Two Different Ways of Linking Statements to One Another

Those two regimes of invisibility, which have been so distorted by the appeal to the dream of instant and unmediated communication, might be made more demonstrative by appealing to visual documents. My idea, as I hope it is now clear, is to move the listener from one opposition between science and religion, to another one between two types of objectivities. The first traditional fight has pitted science, defined as the grasp of the visible, the near, the close, the impersonal, the knowable, against religion, which is supposed to deal with the far, the vague, the mysterious, the personal, the uncertain, and the unknowable.

To this opposition, which is, in my view, an artifact, I want to substitute another opposition between, on the one hand, the long and mediated referential chains of science that lead to the distant and the absent, and, on the other, the search for the representation of the close and present in religion. As I have shown elsewhere, science is in no way a form of speech-act that tries to bridge the abyss between words and *the* world—in the singular. That would be amounting to the *salto mortale* so ridiculed by James; rather, science as it is practiced, attempts to "deambulate"—James' expression again—from one inscription to the next by taking each of them in turn for the matter out of which it extracts a form. "Form" here has to be meant very literally, very materially: it is the paper in which you place the "matter" of the stage just preceding.

Because an example is always better to render visible the invisible path that science traces through the pluriverse, let's take the case of Jean R's laboratory in Paris, where they try to gain information on the releasing factors of a single isolated neuron. Obviously, there is no unmediated, direct, unartificial way to render one neuron visible out of the billions that make up the brain's gray matter. So they have to begin with rats, which are first guillotined. Then the brain is extracted, then cut (thanks to a microtome) in very fine slices. Then each slice is prepared in such a way that it remains alive for a couple of hours, then put under a powerful microscope. And then, on the screen of the television, a microsyringe and a microelectrode are delicately inserted into one of the neurons on which the microscope is able to focus among the millions that are simultaneously firing—and this may fail because focusing on one neuron and bringing the microsyringe in contact with the same neuron to capture the neurotransmitters while recording the electric activity is a feat few people are able to achieve. Then the activity is recorded, the chemical products triggered by the activity are gathered through the pipette, and the result is written into an article that presents synoptically the various inscriptions. I don't want to say anything about neuron firing—no matter how interesting—but to attract your attention to the movement, the jump from one inscription to the next.

It is clear that without the artificiality of the laboratory, none of this path through inscriptions, where each plays the role of matter for the next that put it into a new form, would produce a *visible* phenomenon. Reference is not the gesture of a locutor pointing with a finger to a cat purring on a mat, but a much riskier affair and much dirtier business, which connects a published literature—outside the lab, to published literature—from the lab, through many intermediations, one of them, of course, being the rats, those unsung heroes of much biology.

The point I want to make is that these referential chains have very interesting contradictory features: they are producing our best source of objectivity and certainty, yet they are artificial, indirect, multilayered. There is no doubt that the reference is accurate, yet this accuracy is not obtained by any two things mimetically resembling one another, but, on the contrary, through the whole chains of artificial and highly skilled *transformations*. As long as the chain obtains these transformations, the truth-value of the whole reference is calculable. But if you isolate one inscription, if you extract one image, if you freeze-frame the continuous path of transformations, then the quality of the reference immediately deteriorates. Isolated, a scientific image has no truth-value, although it might trigger, in the mythical philosophy of science that is being used by most people, a sort of shadow referent that will be taken, by a sort of optical illusion, to be the model of the copy—although it is nothing but the virtual image of an isolated "copy"!

This proves, by the way, that matters of fact, those famous matters of fact that are supposed by some philosophers to be the stuff out of which the visible commonsense world is made, are actually nothing but a misunderstanding of the artificial but productive process of scientific objectivity, which has been derailed by freeze-framing a referential path. There is nothing primitive or primeval in matters of fact; they are not the ground of mere perceptions.[9] It is thus entirely misguiding to try to *add* to the objective matters of fact some sort of subjective state of affairs that, in addition, would occupy the mind of the believers.

Although some of what I said here, much too briefly, might still be controversial, I need to have it taken as an undisputed background because I want to use it to shed a new light on the religious regime of invisibility. In the same way that there is a misunderstanding on the path traced by the deambulation of scientific mediations, there is, I think, a common misunderstanding on the path traced by religious images.[10] The traditional defense of religious icons in Christianity has been to say that the image is not the object of a "latry" (as in ido*latry*), but of a *duly*, a Greek term that says a worshipper, at the occasion of the copy—whether it be a Virgin, a crucifix, or the statue of a saint—has turned his or her mind to the prototype, the only original worth adoring. This is, however a weak defense that never convinced the Platonist, the Byzantine, the Lutheran or the Calvinist iconoclasts—not to mention Mullah Omar when he had the Damian Buddhas put to the gun.

In effect, the Christian regime of invisibility is as different from this traditional meek defense, as the scientific reference path is from the glorified matters of fact. What imageries have tried to achieve through countless feats of art is exactly the opposite of turning the spectator's eyes to the model far away: on the contrary, incredible pain has been taken to *break* the habitual gaze of the viewer so as to attract his or her attention to the *present* state, the only one which can be said to offer salvation. Everything happens as if painters, carvers, patrons of the works of art had tried to break the images inside so as to render them unfit for normal informative consumption; as if they wanted to begin, to rehearse, to start a rhythm, a movement of conversion that is understood only when the viewer—the pious viewer—takes upon herself to repeat the same tune in the same rhythm and tempo. This is what I call, with my colleague (and co-curator of *Iconoclash*) Joseph Koerner, "inner iconoclasm," compared to which the "external iconoclasm" looks always at least naïve and moot—not to say plain silly.[11]

A few examples will be enough: in the Fra Angelico fresco in San Marco, Florence, the painter has multiplied ways of complicating our direct access to the topic. Not only is the tomb empty—first a great disappointment to the women—but the angel's finger points to an apparition of the resurrected Christ, which is not directly visible to the women because it shines behind them. What can be more disappointing and surprising than the angel's utterances: "He is no longer here, he has risen"? Everything in this fresco is about the emptiness of the usual grasp. However, it is not *about* emptiness, as if one's attention was directed toward nothingness, it is, on the contrary, slowly bringing us back to the presence of presence: but for that we should not look at the painting, and what the painting suggests, but at what is now there present for us. How can one evangelist and then a painter like Brother Angelico better render vivid again the redirection of attention: "You look in the wrong place . . . you have misunderstood the scriptures." And in case we are dumb enough to miss the message, a monk placed on the left—the representant of the occupant of the cell—will serve as a *legend* of the whole story in the etymological sense of the word "legend," that is, he will show us how we should see. What does he see? Nothing at all, there is nothing to see *there*. But you should look *here* through the inward eye of piety to what this fresco is supposed to mean: elsewhere, not in a tomb, not among the dead but among the living.

Ever more bizarre is the case studied by Louis Marin of an annunciation by Piero della Francesca in Perugia.[12] If you reconstruct the picture in virtual reality—and Piero was such a master at this first mathematization of the visual field that it can be done very accurately with a computer—you realize that the angel actually remains invisible to the Virgin! He—or she?—is hidden by the pillar! And with such an artist this cannot be just an oversight. Piero has used the powerful tool of perspective to recode his interpretation of what an invisible angel is, so as to render impossible the banal, usual, trivial *view* that this is a normal messenger meeting the Virgin in the normal space of daily interactions. Again, the idea is to avoid as much as possible the normal transport of messages, even when using the fabulous new space of visibility and calculation invented by quattrocento painters and scientists—this same space that will be put to use so powerfully by science to multiply those immutable mobiles I defined a minute ago. The aim is not to add an invisible world to the visible one, but to distort, to render the visible world opaque enough, so that one is not led to misunderstand the scriptures but to reenact them truthfully.

To paint the disappointment of the visible without simply painting another world of the invisible—which would be a contradiction in terms—no painter is more astute than Caravaggio. In his famous rendering of the Emmaus pilgrims who do not understand at first that they have been traveling with the resurrected Savior and recognize him only when he breaks the bread at the inn table, Caravaggio re-produces in the painting this very invisibility, just by a tiny light—a touch of paints—that redirects the attention of the pilgrims when they suddenly realize what they had to see. And, of course, the whole idea to paint such an encounter without adding any supernatural event is to redirect the attention of the viewer of the *painting*, who suddenly realizes that he or she will never see more than those tiny breaks, these paint strokes, and that the reality they have to turn to is not absent in death—as the pilgrims were discussing along the way coming to the inn—but present now in its full *and veiled* presence. The idea is not to turn our gaze away from this world to another world of beyond, but to realize at last, at the occasion of this painting, this miracle of understanding: what is in question in the Scriptures is now realized, is realized now, among the painter, viewers, and patrons, among you: have you not understood the scriptures? He has risen, why do you look far away in death, it is here, it is present anew. "This is why our heart burnt so much while he was talking."

Christian iconography in all its forms has been obsessed by this question of representing anew what it is about and to make visually sure that there is no misunderstanding in the messages transmitted, that it is a really a messenger that is transforming what is in question in the speech-act—and not a mere message transfer wrongly addressed. In the venerable and somewhat naïve theme of the St. Gregory Mass—banned after the Counter-Reformation—the argument seems much more crude than in Caravaggio, but it is deployed with the same subtle intensity. Pope Gregory is supposed to have suddenly seen, while celebrating the Mass, the host and the wine replaced in three dimensions by the real body of the suffering Christ with all the associated instruments of the Passion. Real presence is here represented yet again and then painted in two dimensions by the artist to commemorate this act of re-understanding by the Pope *realizing*, in all the sense of the verb, what the venerable ritual meant.

This rather gory imaging became repulsive to many after the Reformation, but the point I want to make is that each of those pictures, no matter how sophisticated or naïve, canonical or apocryphal, always sends a double injunction: the first one has to do with the theme they illustrate, and most of those images, like the love-talk I began with, are repetitive and often boringly so (the resurrection, the Emmaus encounter, the Gregory's Mass) but then they send a second injunction that traverses the boring repetition of the theme and forces us to remember what it is to understand the presence that the message is carrying. This second injunction is equivalent to the tone, to the tonality that we have been made aware of in love-talk: it is not what you say that is original, but the movement that renews the presence through the old sayings.

Lovers, religious painters and their patrons have to be careful to make the usual way of speaking vibrate in a certain way if they want to make sure that the absentminded locutors are not led far away in space and time. This is exactly what happens suddenly to poor Gregory: during the repetition of the ritual, he is suddenly struck by the very speech-act of transforming the host into the body of Christ, by the realization of the words under the shape of a suffering Christ. The mistake would be to think that this is a naïve image that only backward papists could take seriously: quite the opposite, it is a very sophisticated rendering of what it is to become aware again of the real presence of Christ in the Mass. But for that you have to listen to the two injunctions at once. This is not the painting of a miracle, although it is also that: rather this painting also says what it is to understand the word "miracle" literally and not in the habitual, blasé sense of the word—"literal" here meaning not the opposite of spiritual, but of ordinary, absentminded, indifferent.

Even an artist so brilliant as Philippe de Champaigne in the middle of the seventeenth century, was still making sure that no viewer ignore that repeating the face of Christ—literally printing it on a veil—should *not* be confused with a mere photocopy (see Figure 2.1). This extraordinary meditation on what is to hide and to repeat is revealed by the presence of three different linens: the cloth out of which the canvas is made, doubled by the cloth of what is called a "veronica," tripled by another veil, a curtain, this one in trompe l'œil, which could dissimulate the relic with a simple gesture of the hand if one was silly enough to misunderstand its meaning. How magnificent to call *vera icona*, meaning "true image" in Latin, what is exactly a *false* picture thrice veiled: it is so impossible to take it as a photography that, by a miracle of reproduction, a *positive* and not a negative of Christ's face is presented to the viewer—and those artists, printers, engravers knew everything about positive and negative. So again, as in the case of Piero, this cannot be an oversight. But of course this is a "false positive"—if I can use this metaphor—because the *vera icona*, the true picture, is precisely not a reproduction in the referential meaning of the world, but a reproduction, in the re-presentational sense of the world: "Beware! Beware! To see the face of Christ is not to look for an original, for a true referential copy that would transport you back to the past, back to Jerusalem, but a mere surface of cracking pigment a millimeter thick that begins to indicate how you yourself, now, in this Port Royal institution, should look at your Savior." Although this face seems to look back at us so plainly, it is even more hidden and veiled than the one that God refused to reveal to Moses. To show *and to hide* is what true reproduction does, on the condition that it should be a false reproduction by the standard of photocopies, printing, and double-click communication. But what is hidden is not a message beneath the first one, an esoteric message disguised in a banal message, but a tone, an injunction for you, the viewer, to redirect your attention and to turn it away from the dead and back to the living.

This is why there is always some uncertainty to be felt when a Christian image has been destroyed or mutilated (see Figure 2.2). This pietà was broken to be sure by some fanatic—we do not know if it was during the Reformation or during the Revolution, as France has no lack of such episodes. But whoever he was, he certainly never realized how ironic it could be to add an *outside* destruction to the *inner* destruction that the statue itself represented so well. What is a pietà if not the image of the heartbroken Virgin holding on her lap

FIGURE 2.1.

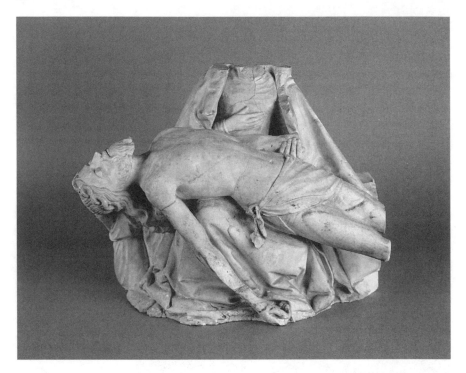

FIGURE 2.2.

the broken corpse of her Son, who is the broken image of God, his father—although, as the scripture is careful to say, "none of his bones have been broken"? How could you destroy an image that is already that much destroyed? How would you want to eradicate belief in an image that has already disappointed all beliefs to the point that God himself, the God of beyond and above lies here, dead on his mother's lap? Can you go further into the self-critique of all images than what theology explicitly says? Rather, should it not be better to argue that the outside iconoclast does nothing but add a naïve and shallow act of destruction to an extraordinary and deep act of destruction? Who is more naïve, the one who sculpted this pietà of the kenosis of God, or the one who believes there are believers naïve enough to grant existence to a mere image instead of turning spontaneously their gaze to the true original God? Who goes further? Probably the one who says there is *no* original.

How to Continue the Movement of Truth-Making Statements?

One way to summarize my point, in conclusion, is to say that we have probably been mistaken in defending the images by their appeal to a prototype they simply alluded to, although this is, as I showed above, the traditional defense of images. Iconophily has nothing to do with looking at the prototype, in a sort of Platonician stair-climbing. Rather, iconophily is in *continuing* the process begun by an image, in a prolongation of the flow of images. St. Gregory continues the text of the Eucharist when he sees the Christ in his real and not symbolic flesh, and the painter continues the miracle when he paints the representation in a picture that reminds us of what it is to understand really what this old mysterious text is about; and I, now, today, continue the painter's continuation of the story reinterpreting the text, if, by using slides, arguments, tones of voices, anything, really anything at hand, I make you aware again of what it is to understand those images without searching for a prototype, and without distorting them in so many information-transfer vehicles. Iconoclasm or iconolatry, then, is nothing but freeze-framing, interrupting the movement of the image and isolating it out of its flows of renewed images to believe it has a meaning by itself—and because it has none, once isolated it should be destroyed without pity.

By ignoring the *flowing* character of science and religion we have turned the question of their relations into an opposition between "knowledge" and "belief," opposition that we then deem necessary either to overcome, to politely resolve, or to widen violently. What I have argued in this essay is very different: *belief is a caricature of religion exactly as knowledge is a caricature of science*. Belief is patterned after a false idea of science, as if it was possible to raise the question "Do you believe in God?" along the same pattern as "Do you believe in global warming?" Except the first question does not possess any of the instruments that would allow the reference to move on, and the second is leading the locutor to a phenomenon even more invisible to the naked eye than that of God, because to reach it we have to travel through satellite imaging, computer simulation, theories of earth atmospheric instability, high-stratosphere chemistry, and so forth. Belief is not a quasi-knowledge question *plus* a leap of faith to reach even *further* away; knowledge is not a quasi-belief question that would be answerable by looking directly at things close at hand.

In religious talk, there is indeed a leap of faith, but this is not an acrobatic *salto mortale* in order to do even better than reference with more daring and risky means, it is a somersault yes, but one which aims at jumping, dancing toward the present and the close, to redirect attention away from indifference and habituation, to prepare oneself to be seized again by this presence that breaks the usual, habituated passage of time. As to knowledge, it is not a direct grasp of the plain and the visible against all beliefs in authority, but an extraordinarily daring, complex, and intricate confidence in chains of nested trans-formations of documents that, through many different types of proofs, lead toward new types of visions that force us to break away from the intuitions and prejudices of common sense. Belief is simply immaterial for any religious speech-act; knowledge is not an accurate way to characterize scientific activity. We might move forward a bit, if we were calling "faith" the movement that brings us to the close and to the present, and retaining the word "belief" for this necessary mixture of confidence and diffidence with which we need to assess all the things we cannot see directly. Then the difference between sci-ence and religion would not be found in the different mental competencies brought to bear on two different realms—"belief" applied to vague spiritual matters, "knowledge" to directly observable things—but in the *same* broad set of competences applied to *two* chains of mediators going in two *different* direc-tions. The first chain leads toward what is invisible because it is simply too far and too counterintuitive to be directly grasped—namely, science; the second chain, the religious one, also leads to the invisible but what it reaches is not invisible because it would be hidden, encrypted, and far, but simply because it is difficult to renew.

What I mean is that in the cases of both science and religion, freeze-framing, isolating a mediator out of its chains, out of its series, instantly forbids the meaning to be carried in truth. Truth is not to be found in correspon-dence—either between the word and the world in the case of science, or be-tween the original and the copy in the case of religion—but in taking up again the task of *continuing* the flow, of elongating the cascade of mediations one step further. My argument is that, in our present economy of images, we might have made a slight misunderstanding of Moses's Second Commandment and thus lacked respect for mediators. God did not ask us not to make images—what else do we have to produce objectivity, to generate piety?—but he told us not to freeze-frame, not to isolate an image out of the flows that only provide them with their real (their constantly re-realized, re-represented) meaning.

I have most probably failed in extending the flows, the cascade of media-tors to you. If so, then I have lied, I have not been talking religiously; I have not been able to preach, but I have simply talked *about* religion, as if there was a domain of specific beliefs one could relate to by some sort of referential grasp. This then would have been a mistake just as great as that of the lover who, when asked "do you love me?" answered, "I have already told you so many years ago, why do you ask again?" Why? Because it is no use having told me so in the past, if you cannot tell me again, now, and make me alive to you again, close and present anew. Why would anyone claim to speak religion, if it is not in order to save me, to convert me, on the spot?

NOTES

1. Editor's note: In the spirit of Latour's argument, the essay is presented in the form of a direct verbal address.

2. William James, *The Varieties of Religious Experience* (New York: Penguin, [1902] 1987).

3. For an extension of this argument and of its practical demonstration, see Bruno Latour, *Jubiler ou les tourments de la parole religieuse* (Paris: Les Empêcheurs de penser en rond, 2002). I have turned around those questions in C. Jones and P. Galison, "How to Be Iconophilic in Art, Science and Religion?" in *Picturing Science, Producing Art* (London: Routledge, 1998), 418–440, and Bruno Latour, "Thou Shall Not Take the Lord's Name in Vain—Being a Sort of Sermon on the Hesitations of Religious Speech," *Res* 39 (spring 2002): 215–235. For a general inquiry into the background of the comparison between science and religion, see Bruno Latour and Peter Weibel, eds., *Iconoclash—Beyond the Image Wars in Science, Religion, and Art* (Cambridge, Mass.: MIT Press, 2002).

4. See, for instance, my *Pandora's Hope: Essays on the Reality of Science Studies* (Cambridge: Harvard University Press, 1999).

5. Cited in Putnam essay in this volume, pp. 80–81.

6. See Boyer essay, this volume, pp. 237–259, and his book *Religion Explained: The Evolutionary Origins of Religious Thought* (New York: Basic Books, 2001). Evolutionary theology shares with the old natural theology of the eighteenth century the admiration for the "marvelous adjustment" of the world. It does not matter much if this leads to an admiration for the wisdom of God or of evolution, because in both cases it is the marvelous fit that generates the impression of providing an explanation Darwin, of course, would destroy the natural theology of old as well as this other natural theology based on evolution: there is no fit, no sublime adaptation, no marvelous adjustment. But the new natural theologians have not realized that Darwin dismantled their church even faster than the church of their predecessors, whom they despise so much.

7. Alfred North Whitehead, *Religion in the Making* (New York: Fordham University Press, 1926).

8. Under William James's pen, science is a "she"—a nice proof of political correctness before its time.

9. For a much more advanced argument about visualization in science, see Peter Galison, *Image and Logic: A Material Culture of Microphysics* (Chicago: University of Chicago Press, 1997); Carrie Jones and Peter Galison, eds., *Picturing Science, Producing Art* (London: Routledge, 1998); and Latour and Weibel, *Iconoclash*.

10. See the catalog of the exhibition, Latour and Weibel, *Iconoclash*.

11. See Joseph Koerner, "The Icon as Iconoclash," in Latour and Weibel, *Iconoclash*, 164–214.

12. Louis Marin, *Opacité de la peinture: Essais sur la représentation* (Paris: Usher, 1989).

BIBLIOGRAPHY

Galison, Peter. *Image and Logic: A Material Culture of Microphysics*. Chicago: University of Chicago Press, 1997.

James, William. *The Varieties of Religious Experience*. New York: Penguin, [1902] 1987.

Latour, Bruno. How to Be Iconophilic in Art, Science and Religion? In *Picturing Science, Producing Art*, edited by Jones, Carrie, and Peter Galison. London: Routledge, 1998.

———. *Pandora's Hope: Essays on the Reality of Science Studies*. Cambridge: Harvard University Press, 1999.

———. *Jubiler ou les tourments de la parole religieuse*. Paris: Les Empêcheurs de penser en rond, 2002.

———. "Thou Shall Not Take the Lord's Name in Vain—Being a Sort of Sermon on the Hesitations of Religious Speech." *Res* 39 (Spring 2002).

Latour, Bruno, and Peter Weibel, eds. *Iconoclash—Beyond the Image Wars in Science, Religion, and Art*. Cambridge, Mass.: MIT Press, 2002.

Marin, Louis. *Opacité de la peinture: Essais sur la représentation*. Paris: Usher, 1989.

Whitehead, Alfred North. *Religion in the Making*. New York: Fordham University Press, 1926.

3

Modernity and the Mystical: Technoscience, Religion, and Human Self-Creation

Thomas A. Carlson

Introductory Remarks on Technoscience and Its Re-Definition
of the "Human": A Sign of the Mystical in the Modern?

While not the same thing, science and technology do nevertheless
prove today, both conceptually and practically, inseparable. The reality we come to know scientifically appears to us thanks only to technology, by means of the framing or mediation, the computation and
memory, even the cognition and imagination, exercised by technological instruments that function as indispensable faculties—and
science itself finds support in our culture largely, if not primarily, to
the degree that it yields (or is believed to yield) knowledge having a
demonstrably practical value, which is to say an instrumental or a
technological application. This intimate tie between scientific research and "practical" application, quite complex both historically
and theoretically, would go a long way in helping to explain the
striking discrepancies in support—financial and otherwise—enjoyed
today by scientific research and teaching, on the one hand, and by
humanistic inquiry and education, on the other. The practical application or "real-life" value of humanistic study is rarely presupposed
as it is for scientific study (and this is so even when the latter takes
the most theoretical and esoteric forms). To understand, then, both
the actual work of scientists and the place of science in our culture
more broadly—and it will be mainly this latter issue that concerns
me here—one needs to speak about science in its intimate and complex cooperation with technology, which I will signal here by the
term "technoscience."

In what follows, I want to suggest that we think and act everyday, unavoidably and increasingly, by means of technoscientific systems whose operation does not simply open access to an independent, objective reality "out there" but rather plays a fundamental role in constructing and sustaining what we see and know as reality. Furthermore, I want to argue that by means of this technoscientific construction of the worlds we inhabit, we continually shape and reshape not only what counts as nature or reality "out there" but also, at the same time, what it means at bottom to be "human." Indeed, in our technoscientific thinking and practice today, we are engaged concretely and at bottom in a project of human self-creation. Such a project, as I'll suggest, remains necessarily open, incomplete, and always to a certain degree blind—and for this reason it engenders both our greatest hopes and our deepest anxieties concerning technoscience, whose promise and danger can indeed seem to grow in direct proportion.

We can quickly gain a sense of the logic and the stakes of such human self-creation if we think for a moment about the ways that technoscience reshapes our relations to life and death "themselves," which it does, for example, by means of bioengineering and the thermonuclear bomb. As French philosopher Michel Serres puts it, in the second half of the twentieth century, we managed in some new and decisive sense to assume responsibility for "the end and the beginning, creation and annihilation":

> Through the double mastery of DNA and the bomb, we ourselves
> have become actively responsible for our birth and our death. Where
> will we come from? From ourselves. Where are we going? Toward
> an end prescribed by ourselves. . . . This sudden hold that we as-
> sume over the two poles of our destiny, that of the species as well as
> the individual, changes our status. Remaining human [hommes], but
> becoming our own works, we are no longer the same humans
> [hommes].[1]

To change fundamentally the way that we humans experience even life and death, Serres rightly asserts, is to alter the "human" "itself." Thanks to technoscience, the nuclear bomb concretely forms a new, global humanity—insofar as August of 1945 undeniably transposed the global extinction of humanity from the realm of apocalyptic myth to the realm of material possibility. Likewise, with our mapping of the genome and related achievements in biotechnology and bioengineering, the generation and manipulation of human (and other) life promises to fall within our grasp. A kind of destruction and creation that remained previously the sole privilege of gods or, even more, of God Himself become more and more our own responsibility—and we thereby become, like that God, our own cause (HM, 50).[2]

As these examples should suggest, our technoscientific redefinition of humanity signals enormously complex and far-reaching questions about the relation between science and religion. I'd like here to frame our discussion of that relation by focusing on the categories of the "modern" and the "mystical," and I choose this focus because it is perhaps the mystical dimension of religious thought and experience that is most often and almost automatically assumed to exclude religion from the rationality and practice of a truly modern science or technology. I will, of course, want to challenge such an assumption, and I will do so on the basis of my suspicion that we are in the course of witnessing not only a period of extraordinary technoscientific change but also a reemergence of something resembling or resonating with the mystical in just those rationalized, technoscientific contexts that have long been thought by scholars and theorists to exclude any trace of the mystical from our modern experience. As I'll suggest, such a reemergence or resonance of the mystical in the modern should leave us vigilant to the senses in which technological science today, like the history of mystical religion, can render the "human" fundamentally unstable—and hence leave it irreducibly open—both as a category of thought and as a form of "experience."

Modernity and the Mystical at Odds: "Disenchanted" Rationality and the Will to Mastery

The common assumption that modernity stands at odds with the mystical goes back in decisive ways, of course, to those Enlightenment traditions according to which the human subject would achieve his freedom—which here means his individual autonomy or self-determination—through the exercise of a rationality or science that yields a full and accurate understanding of the natural and social worlds we inhabit. To comprehend the rational order and operation of our natural and social worlds is, from this perspective, to acquire the means to manipulate or master those worlds.

Central to this search for practical control by means of rational comprehension would be the ongoing attempt to eliminate from our relation to reality any form of "ignorance" or "unknowing." The best scientists are, indeed, those who can most thoroughly and most precisely define and measure the boundaries of their ignorance—which they do, of course, not at all in the hope of reaching the kinds of "mystical unknowing" or "learned ignorance" sought and cultivated by mystics throughout the history of religions but rather in the hope of overcoming their ignorance by subjecting all of the hitherto unknown to the power and reach of a purely rational and purely human comprehension. By contrast to those mystical traditions that one might trace in the Christian world, for example, from Pseudo-Dionysius (ca. 500) to Nicholas of Cusa (1401–1464) and beyond, the celebration or cultivation of "unknowing" or "ignorance" as a good and a goal in itself simply does not belong to the attitude that defines modern scientific approaches to reality—and at this level, despite an often overlooked diversity amidst the sciences, all science today would stand on the same ground: to a scientific perspective, the unknown appears never as unknowable but always and only as not-yet-known. Scientific ignorance, in other words, is the space and time of scientific knowledge just waiting to happen, an indispensable provocation to the quest for a knowledge that would be complete.

We can find a powerful and still widely echoed analysis of this scientific attitude in sociologist Max Weber's classic 1918 lecture titled "Science as a Vocation,"[3] in which Weber emphasizes that the rationalized attitude defining modern science (and modern culture more broadly) implies both a "disenchantment" (Entzauberung) of the world and, correlatively, a calculated attempt to master that world technologically. As Weber very famously puts it, our world would be "disenchanted" when we approach it in "the knowledge or belief" that "there are no mysterious incalculable forces that come into play" in the world and hence "that one can, in principle, master all things by calculation."[4] While the "savage" or religious believer as Weber imagines him would implore mysterious powers by magical means, those of us moderns shaped by the processes of rationalization find rather that "technical means and calculations perform the service."[5] Now, as Weber notes in discussing an individual's use of the streetcar whose workings the individual cannot in fact understand or explain, the individual agent within a disenchanted world does not need actually to possess or to command the scientific knowledge that grounds the technological powers upon which that individual nevertheless counts daily; he needs rather to know—or more precisely to believe—that such knowledge is, in principle, at all times available or at least possible.

From Weber's perspective, then, the type of rationality governing the intersection of science and technology in modern culture is one that aims to secure both conceptual and practical control over our natural and social worlds by means of a thinking that is calculative and instrumental, concerned primarily with understanding and manipulating means-ends relations. As is well known, in order to function as it does, such thinking attempts to frame reality in terms of an "objectivity" that would stand open to the comprehension, manipulation, and eventual mastery of a rational human subject who can analyze such an objective reality in value-neutral terms—which means in terms that say nothing about the purpose or meaning of such reality or about the direction we ought to take in our manipulations of it. (One might note here that, if a good deal of the rhetoric within and around science today still clings to this pretense of value-neutrality, such pretense becomes increasingly difficult to maintain as scientific knowing is bound ever more intimately and powerfully with technological activity that does always have a direction and effect—hence blurring the boundary between nature and culture, and introducing the question of final causes, traditionally associated with the artifact, into our exploration of nature, which turns increasingly artifactual.[6] When our investigation of "natural" reality thus alters that reality itself, epistemology and ethics are no longer clearly separable.)

With a similar emphasis on the will to mastery that one might see operative in the technologies of an instrumental and calculative rationality, one of the most influential European philosophers of the twentieth century, Martin Heidegger, will argue (already in his 1938 essay "The Age of the World Picture")[7] that modern science is built on the foundation of a distinctively modern understanding of reality or being that implies a distinctively modern attitude concerning the nature and purpose of the human subject who would seek to know "the truth" about that reality or being. Within these modern perspectives as Heidegger analyzes them, the nature of "being" itself, the character of the real, is framed primarily in terms of "objectivity," and the essence of "truth" is located in subjective certainty or security with respect to the knowledge and control of objectified being. Operating according to its preestablished ground rules, science will count as "real" only that realm of being which can be defined objectively, which means observed empirically and measured quantitatively according to consistent method, and it ranks degrees of truth or knowledge according to the level of rational certainty that the human subject can reach through such methodical definition, observation, and measurement—in short, through what Heidegger later calls "calculative" thinking.[8] Certainty, in other words, is sought through the calculative or predictive power of science, and that power derives from the possibility of verification through methodic regulation and repetition. As Heidegger puts it, "knowing, as research, calls whatever is to account with regard to the way in which it lets itself be put at the disposal of representation. Research has disposal over anything that is when it can either calculate it in its future course or verify a calculation about it as past."[9]

This emphasis on subjective certainty within modern science and its culture has a lineage, both religious and philosophical, that is important to any understanding of how we tend to associate certainty with "freedom." The religious lineage would be seen notably in Protestant conceptions of faith as the inward, individual certainty of salvation, and the philosophical lineage would be seen notably in René Descartes's decisive attempt in the early seventeenth century to re-ground philosophy in the self-certainty of the thinking subject. The religious and, especially, philosophical obsessions with certainty in the modern world imply a conception of freedom that in significant ways shapes both science and our attitudes about science:

> Liberation *from* the revelational certainty of salvation [was] intrinsically a freeing *to* a certainty [*Gewissheit*] in which man makes secure for himself the true as the known of his own knowing [*Wissens*]. That was possible only through self-liberating man's guaranteeing for himself the certainty of the knowable. Such a thing could hap-

pen, however, only insofar as man decided, by himself and for himself, what, for him, should be "knowable" and what knowing and the making secure of the known, i.e., certainty, should mean. Descartes's metaphysical task became the following: to create the metaphysical foundation for the freeing of man to freedom as the self-determination that is certain of itself.[10]

This philosophical conception of freedom as the subjective self-determination that is certain of itself, a conception that will stand at the heart also of modern science, involves, Heidegger wants to insist, a kind of imperialistic thinking and practice within which the world as a whole becomes the object of human conquest—"conquered" by the human subject who, in representing the world to himself rationally, becomes the "relational center"[11] of all that is and thereby secures, both conceptually and practically, a hold or control over all that is. From this perspective, the key to modern man's conquest of the world is the mental activity through which the rational human subject "represents" the world to himself—and in this context "to represent" (vorstellen) would mean "of oneself to set something before oneself and to make secure what has been set in place, as something set in place."[12] Within the modern age, Heidegger argues, by means of the subjective representation of objects, by means of this attempt to put all things in their place, "man contends for the position in which he can be that particular being who gives the measure and draws up the guidelines for everything that is,"[13] and through such contention "man brings into play his unlimited power for the calculating, planning, and molding of all things."[14]

Reemergence of the Mystical in Technoscientific Contexts

If major theorists like Weber and Heidegger in the earlier twentieth century can see in modern science and its technologies primarily a project of human mastery over reality, a project that would, as heir to distinctive tendencies of the Enlightenment, seem to exclude any operation of the mystical from our world, more recent thinkers are beginning to glimpse a persistence or a reemergence, a shadow or resonance of something like the mystical in precisely those forms of technoscientific practice that are so often taken to exclude the mystical.

For example, in a 1995 text titled "Faith and Knowledge: The Two Sources of Religion at the Limits of Reason Alone," French philosopher Jacques Derrida suggests that our everyday experience of technoscience takes on an increasingly mystical quality as the technological and scientific systems we inhabit and navigate reach a scale and complexity that would set those systems beyond our actual comprehension and control. In making use of those systems, then, we inevitably exercise a kind of faith or trust in powers for which we cannot account in terms of our own knowledge or reasoning. Hence, while according to Max Weber's analysis of the rationalized and disenchanted worldview, any apparent gap between technological know-how and the science that makes such know-how possible would remain, in principle, reducible if not always actually reduced (in other words, even if I don't really know how the streetcar works, I can, in principle, always find out), for Derrida technoscientific performance takes place more and more today within a gap that proves irreducible between a high level of technological power or manipulative competence and a relatively low level of actual knowledge or scientific comprehension on the part of those agents—both individual and, increasingly, collective—who exercise such manipulative power: ". . . because one increasingly *uses* artifacts and prostheses of which one is totally ignorant, in a growing disproportion between knowledge [*savoir*] and know-how [*savoir-faire*], the space of such technical experience tends to become more animistic, magical, mystical."[15] A major part of humanity, Derrida notes, lives today by means of technoscientific systems whose effectiveness is exploited and taken for granted even in face of the absence—or the impossibility—of actual comprehension or mastery by any single, stable, self-identical subject.

As Derrida will emphasize, the faith involved in my use of technological powers whose ground and logic I do not comprehend serves to highlight, more broadly, the kind of faith or trust that proves indispensable, in fact, for any system of authority—including that of a modern, rational science. The authority of any system, Derrida insists, requires what he calls a "mystical foundation," by which he means a founding moment of decision that could not be dictated or justified by the system it founds, a ground, then, that is itself groundless; the decision, for example, to accept science and its rationality as authoritative, the decision that leads me to begin thinking scientifically, could not itself be dictated or justified by science; it could not be based on the authority of science itself, for, precisely, it alone gives that authority its force. Hence, from this perspective, even science requires faith, and all knowledge, practical or otherwise, necessarily involves an element of belief.[16]

This disproportion that Derrida emphasizes between scientific knowledge and technological power, which itself would highlight a kind of mystical faith at the heart of any technoscientific performance, proves operative today within immeasurably complex networks whose most evident, even clichéd, symbol is perhaps the Internet—a global technoscientific network whose striking resemblances to traditional mystical worlds have been noted recently not only by leading philosophers and theorists like Derrida or Michel Serres, but also by important fiction writers such as Don DeLillo, and even by a major public institution such as the Getty Center in Los Angeles.

Indeed, by exploring the complex intersections among science, technology, and popular culture, a 2001–2002 show at the Getty, entitled "Devices of Wonder: From the World in a Box to Images on a Screen," succeeded nicely in highlighting an often overlooked tension—and hence a coexistence—in modern thought and culture "between a disenchanted rationality and an obsession with mystifying metamorphoses,"[17] that is, quasi-religious metamorphoses that are achieved in and through the very technologies often taken to realize or embody modernity's "disenchanted" rationality. Tracing the logic and legacy of the early-modern "cabinet of wonders" into contemporary cyberspace, the "Devices of Wonder" show was able convincingly to argue that "the typically modern 'Enlightened' association of technology with secularization tends to overlook its historical role in materializing the sacred"[18]—and in making such an argument, the show managed to signal and illustrate with particular force a mystical tendency in the human effort to frame reality, to capture all time and space, the cosmos as a whole, in and through technoscientific media. Such media—from the sorcerer's mirror through the lenses of the telescope and microscope to the desktop processor—can indicate the operation or even the realization *in* technology and science of a desire, much like that found throughout the mystical traditions, to transcend space and time, to achieve an omniscience and omnipotence in which the limited self would surpass itself, moving ecstatically into a cosmic totality that, much like the mystical God and his cosmic body, could never be objectively defined, discretely located, fully comprehended, or finally controlled.

Taking a similar perspective on technoscientific media in his 1993 book titled (in the English translation) *Angels: A Modern Myth*, Michel Serres is able to interpret our global communication and transportation networks as concretely angelic systems in whose light our contemporary world can seem to resemble a mystical cosmos. Figures for the complexity and flux of message-bearing systems, Serres's technoscientific angels would comprise, through their infinite interconnectivity, a global technoscientific city that Serres names "Newtown" (recalling in striking ways the "the gigantic" and the "monstrous" in Heidegger's analyses of modern science and technology).[19] A kind of realized utopia, or a place that is "no-place," this technoscientific "Newtown" would constitute "an unimaginable mediator, invisible and all-embracing, informatic, pedagogic, stable in its rapid intercommunications . . . realizing intimate proximities across immense distances . . . [It] has its center everywhere and its circumference nowhere."[20]

If one can glimpse a shadow or image of the mystical cosmos in the philosopher's words here, so might one see such a cosmos in Don DeLillo's recent novel *Underworld*, which, itself haunted by angels, will imagine the encounter between an old-school nun and the "miracle" of the Internet, "where everybody is everywhere at once"[21]: "She is not naked exactly but she is open—exposed to every connection you can make on the world wide web," and she discovers that "there is no space or time out here, or in here, or wherever she is. There are only connections. Everything is connected. All human knowledge gathered and linked, hyperlinked, this site leading to that, this fact referenced to that, a keystroke, a mouse-click, a password—world without end, amen."[22]

What do these cultural signals point to? What are we to think when French philosophers, American novelists, and Californian museums all find themselves moved, in similar ways, to note and reflect on apparent resemblances between our highly rationalized technoscientific networks, on the one hand, and, on the other, historically distant mystical worlds?

The resemblances can be striking, for by means of their seemingly infinite connectivity and comprehensive memory, which can seem through their interplay to unsettle any clear division between the local and the global or between the temporal and the timeless, our technoscientific networks can seem to realize a ubiquity and a simultaneity that recall the mystical God; they can seem to constitute, indeed, an infinitely variable, combinatorial, and perspectival cosmos whose center is everywhere and circumference nowhere—a cosmos, in this sense, much like that thought to embody the mystical God in speculative mystics and writers throughout the West from John Scotus Eriugena in the ninth century or Alain de Lille in the eleventh, through Nicholas of Cusa (1401–1464) and Giordano Bruno (1548–1600) on the eve of modernity,[23] perhaps even into the late-modern reception and reworking of these same thinkers in the cosmic vision of James Joyce's *Finnegans Wake*.[24]

Even more striking, perhaps, than this quasi-mystical ubiquity and simultaneity would be another point of resemblance between our technoscientific networks and more traditional mystical worlds—namely, the point at which both can be seen as related intimately to processes of self-creation. Just as we human subjects can be thought constantly to re-create ourselves in and through the technoscientific networks we build and inhabit, so for key mystical thinkers, the cosmos itself constitutes the space and time of God's own self-creation. Any number of writers, including those we've just mentioned, will note the senses in which our technoscientific systems constitute very concretely the means of our own ongoing self-creation. As art historian and cultural theorist Barbara Maria Stafford indicates in the "Devices of Wonder" catalog, the history of technology teaches us that "subjectivity is creatively modifiable, reaching outward and inward, to other beings and to the mechanisms we continually fabricate,"[25] or as Don DeLillo puts it in his haunting essay on 9/11, noting more explicitly the religious resonance of our technological self-assertion, "the materials and the methods we devise make it possible for us to claim our future. We don't have to depend on God or the prophets or other astonishments. We are the astonishment. The miracle is what we ourselves produce, the systems and networks that change the way we live and think."[26] But while various writers and thinkers will thus emphasize the fact that our technoscientific networks constitute a means for human self-creation, and while some will also note a kind of religious resonance in such self-creation, no writer to my knowledge has noted or explored the sense in which both our self-creation in technoscientific contexts and divine (as well as human) self-creation in certain mystical traditions might be understood to constitute processes founded on an essential ignorance or unknowing—and it is the important function of just such ignorance or unknowing *within* the process of self-creation that I would like to emphasize in my reflections here on the modern and the mystical.

In other words: just as the infinitely incomprehensible God of certain mystical thinkers (Eriugena is a decisive example) is himself created in and through the world that he creates, and just as that same God never fully comprehends himself in and through the creation where alone he comes to know himself,[27] so might it be that we ourselves are created and re-created today by those technoscientific networks that we fabricate, even as we remain, in and through that self-creation, unable fully or finally to comprehend ourselves— perhaps above all because we are unable to foresee what we are becoming.[28]

Human Self-Creation and the Logic
of Technoscientific Networks

In order to suggest the role of such ignorance or unknowing within our own self-creation, and in order to recognize the senses in which such a role might unsettle the modern model of subjectivity tied by thinkers like Weber and Heidegger to the modern project of technoscientific mastery, we would need to recognize the ways in which the operation of networks such as those evoked in Serres or DeLillo can unsettle the founding oppositions upon which that modern model of subjectivity rests—above all the opposition between the knowing or representing subject and its known or represented object, but also many related oppositions, such as that between culture and nature and that between the human and the machine.

In this direction, among religious studies scholars, some of the more far-reaching analyses are to be found in the recent work of Mark C. Taylor. Emphasizing especially the relational and interactive quality of our technoscientific networks, Taylor elucidates both the ways in which they allow "subjectivity" to extend itself by means of "objective" devices and the ways in which seemingly "objective" devices come to act or even to think more and more like "subjects." Departing from a straightforwardly instrumental conception of technology, according to which a discrete, self-contained or self-sustaining subject would manipulate some independent, objective reality by means of instrumental technologies that would leave both subject and object standing apart in their apparent independence, the relational and interactive conception of technology that becomes unavoidable in today's "network culture" highlights the senses in which technology itself perceives and reacts to our thought and behavior, understands and speaks to us through a kind of interaction that breaks down

MODERNITY AND THE MYSTICAL   59

the clear distinction between subject and object, rendering it "virtually impossible to be sure where the human ends and the machine begins."[29]

Drawing on information and complexity theory in order to elaborate the logic of these networks that break down the border between subject and object, or human and machine, Taylor argues that informational networks would be themselves "neither subjective nor objective" but rather constitute "the matrix in which all subjects and objects are formed, deformed, and reformed."[30] Within his analyses of networks as complex adaptive systems, Taylor's emphasis on relation and interaction will yield two insights that are especially important to our concerns here. The first insight is that subjectivity is not discrete, self-contained, or self-sustaining but rather emerges and evolves within distributed and fluid systems that exceed the individual and unsettle any clear and fixed boundaries between individual and environment:

> The self—if indeed this term any longer makes sense—is a node in a complex network of relations. In emerging network culture, *subjectivity is nodular*. Nodes, we have discovered, are knots formed when different strands, fibers, or threads are woven together. As the shifting site of multiple interfaces, nodular subjectivity not only screens the sea of information in which it is immersed, but is itself the screen displaying what one is and is not. . . . In the midst of these webs, networks, and screens, I can be no more certain where I am than I can know when or where the I begins and ends. I am plugged into other objects and subjects in such a way that I become myself in and through them, even as they become themselves in and through me.[31]

The second and related insight is that a subject so constituted by means of networks that exceed the individual is a subject haunted by unconscious operations that are realized concretely in the technological prostheses through which informational currents flow. Taylor develops this insight by exploring the logic of "distributed" mind or intelligence. Recalling, to powerful effect, G. W. F. Hegel's understanding of "objective spirit,"[32] Taylor emphasizes that information processing is something that goes on constantly throughout our natural and sociocultural worlds—and in such a way that "it is no longer clear where to draw the line between mind and matter, self and other, human and machine. *Mind is distributed throughout the world*" (MC, 230).[33] From this perspective, we come to be shaped by informational currents that circulate "through us" and that "bind self and world in increasingly complex relations."[34] Today, of course, these informational currents are mediated, these relations binding self and world are embodied, by ever more sophisticated and pervasive technologies, so that "in network culture," technology becomes "an indispensable prosthesis through which body and mind expand."[35]

If understood according to the relational and interactive logic of techno-scientific interfacing, thinking and acting "subjects" are never wholly self-contained or self-identical, to the degree that they realize themselves in and through the various technological prostheses that always already extend subjective intelligence and agency "beyond" the subject, or embody the apparently "subjective" in the apparently "objective"; and likewise, as constituted relationally within technoscientific networks, "objects" are never simply or only "objects" insofar as they themselves come to act with their own kind of intelligence—which does not simply *extend* but also, at the same time, reshapes or transforms the subjective itself. As Taylor emphasizes, "this relationship is always two-way: as the body and mind extrude into the world, world intrudes into body and mind."[36] by means of technological prostheses and the informational currents flowing through them. Our technologies, then, act or even think on and through us just as much as we act or think on and through them—and in such a way that "the networks extruding from and into our bodies and minds form something like a *technological unconscious*, which, like conscious mental processes, screens information."[37] In other words, we think and act through technological and informational systems—and they through us—without our being wholly conscious or in control of such thought and action. Much as Sigmund Freud argued that the operations of psychic life as a whole are far more complex and extensive than the relatively limited sphere of the conscious ego's awareness and command, so Taylor argues that the individual subject of network culture never thinks and acts as a purely self-contained or self-determining entity but rather thinks and acts only by means of complex and evolving systems, networks of distributed intelligence and agency over the whole of which no subject could ever claim comprehension or mastery.

What Taylor understands here in terms of nodular subjectivity and the technological unconscious has also been taken recently by theorist N. Katherine Hayles to signal the emergence of a "posthuman" subjectivity that would render untenable modern models of the subject as a self-contained, self-possessed, or self-determining individual.[38] Whereas modern Western thought, especially in its liberal humanist forms, would tend to presuppose an autonomous, independent subject who might seek to assume responsibility for technological mastery over its world by means of conscious agency, the posthuman perspective that Hayles elaborates would insist that "conscious agency has never been 'in control.' . . . Mastery through the exercise of autonomous will is merely the story consciousness tells itself to explain results that actually come about through chaotic dynamics and emergent structures."[39] Along with feminist critics of science like Donna Haraway and Sandra Harding, and echoing the Heideggerian analysis of science that we noted above, Hayles highlights the intimate ties "among the desire for mastery, an objectivist account of science, and the imperialist project of subduing nature"[40]—and she will seek to offer an alternative account within which "emergence replaces teleology; reflexive epistemology replaces objectivism; distributed cognition replaces autonomous will; embodiment replaces a body seen as a support system for the mind; and a dynamic partnership between humans and intelligent machines replaces the liberal humanist subject's manifest destiny to dominate and control nature."[41] From this posthuman perspective, Hayles emphasizes, "subjectivity is emergent rather than given, distributed rather than located solely in consciousness, emerging from and integrated into a chaotic world rather than occupying a position of mastery and control removed from it."[42]

Decisive to this reconception of subjectivity in terms of emergence and distribution will be the sense in which the partnership between human and machine, or between individual and environment, involves an insurmountable gap of unknowing for the human subject, a gap recalling and perhaps extending what Derrida points to under the category of the mystical, or what Taylor names the "technological unconscious." Because "the distributed cognition of the emergent human subject correlates with . . . the distributed cognitive system as a whole, in which 'thinking' is done by both human and nonhuman actors,"[43] each shaping the other, we humans participate everyday, Hayle rightly emphasizes, "in systems whose total cognitive capacity exceeds our individual knowledge."[44] From this perspective, thinking occurs through us perhaps more than within us, for it occurs by means of networks in which we are only limited—and always shifting –points of intersection. More than thinking about or knowing the world as an "object," then, we always think within the world as a network—which itself cannot be circumscribed or defined in terms of any fixed objectivity.[45]

Self-Creation and In-Definition of the Human

In his philosophical insistence that relation and communication are more fundamental than substance or being, Michel Serres emphasizes a dimension of unknowing similar to that which Hayles and Taylor highlight within our technoscientific self-creation, and through his treatment of such unknowing Serres points us toward an understanding of the human that would help to account for the mystical resonance in such self-creation: the human proves at once creative and self-creative in just the measure that it lacks definite boundaries (or vice versa), which is to say also in the measure that it cannot fully or finally comprehend itself.

From a perspective much like that of Hayles on the "posthuman," Serres coins the term "hominescence" to name and describe the fundamentally relational and interactive technoscientific process that, while actually bringing forth a new humanity, "does not yet know what humanity [homme] it is going to produce"[46] and, likewise, cannot know exactly what humanity "does" that producing.[47] As Serres elaborates both in the 2001 book titled *Hominescence* and in its 2003 follow-up *L'Incandescent*,[48] we now inhabit humanly constructed and global systems whose cognitive and agentive capacities not only exceed us but also transform us—and in such a way that the self-creation we realize by means of those systems transpires always in conjunction with an insurmountable ignorance or unknowing concerning both producer and produced.

Much in line with Taylor and Hayles, Serres argues that such ignorance proves operative in technoscientific networks that alter not only human relations to time and space, as occurs through the various media associated with digital technologies, satellite networks, mobile communications, cyberspace, cybernetics, and so on, but also to death and life, as occurs through technoscientific achievements like the thermonuclear bomb and bioengineering, wherein we assume concretely a responsibility for life and death that is distinctly new because of its global scale, one that eludes and defies our grasp both conceptually and practically. In light of such achievements, we would need to see ourselves no longer as passive recipients or even as vigilant observers of a nature "out there" but rather as nature's "active architects and workers."[49] Taking "nature" as a verb, one could say not only that we "are natured," as given over to the given, but also that we "nature," by actively interfacing with the given so as to shape and transform it—only then to be, in turn, reshaped once more by our own creation, and so on: "we are causing to be born, in the etymological sense of the term, an entirely new nature, in part produced by us and reacting upon us."[50] Assuming, then, a kind of "omni-responsibility"[51] or even "omnipotence"[52] known formerly only by God, we are becoming in concrete ways "our own cause, the continuous creator of our world and of ourselves,"[53] but we do so in such a way that "through new and unexpected loops, we ourselves end up depending on the things that depend globally on us."[54]

Such looping between that which we create and that which, in turn, recreates us takes place notably by means of what Serres calls "world-objects" (*objets-monde*), which is to say, humanly fabricated devices or systems whose scale reaches that of a world, technoscientific creations of ours that finally exceed us in such a way that, instead of relating to them from a stance of distance and independence (as with the "representational" relation between subject and object in Heidegger's account of modern Western metaphysics), we actually live and move within them and find ourselves shaped by them: "We dwell in them as in a world."[55] At this level, the "object" of human thought and action, much like Hayles's distributed systems or Taylor's networks, would differ from any object that might be set apart and placed securely in front of a subject, defined discretely, circumscribed and hence *located*[56] in such a way as to fall under the conceptual or practical hold, mastery, or possession of that subject. The "world-object," in short, puts us "in the presence of a world that we can no longer treat as an object,"[57] a world no longer passive but actively— interactively—engaged with us.

The emergence of such "world-objects," which goes hand in hand with today's irreducibly technoscientific processes of globalization, yields a "new universe" that would challenge the modern philosophy of domination and possession insofar as that philosophy is founded on a clear and stable division of the subject from the object—a division thanks to which alone the subject might hope finally to comprehend and thereby control an objectified reality. And just as the character of "object" here changes fundamentally, so too does that of "subject"; the subject emerging in Serres's thought is no longer the self-grounding or self-possessed individual subject of modern thought (Descartes, Locke, etc.) but rather a thoroughly relational and interactive "we," an irreducibly collective and emergent subject whose distributed intelligence and agency make impossible any discrete or punctual *location* of the subject. From this angle, philosophy would need to reexamine its basic categories and concepts:

> The subject, objects, knowledge, action . . . all [were] constructed for millenia under the condition of localities whose divisions defined, among other things, a subject-object distance along which knowledge and action played themselves out. The measure of that [subject-object] distance conditioned [knowledge and action]. Divisions, proximities, distance, measure . . . these finitudes that were preconditions to our theories and practices are being undone today, where we are passing into a larger theater and where we are losing our finitude.[58]

If, as Serres argues, we are losing our finitude today in demonstrable ways, if we are indeed undoing the kinds of spatial and temporal limit that have long defined us, the boundaries of subject and object, then the human "itself" likewise grows increasingly difficult or even impossible to locate clearly or define securely. The category of the human, indeed, can seem to prove endlessly plastic, open-ended, or indeterminate—and it would be in this sense especially that our technoscientific re-creation of the human recalls the thinking of mystical tradition, where the human subject, like the God in whose image the subject is created, can prove at bottom incomprehensible because unbounded or indefinite.[59]

An indeterminacy or in-definition of the human, then, would seem inextricably bound to its creative and self-creative capacities, and in this direction, as Serres suggests, the human would move always within a constitutive gap between self-knowledge and practical power—a gap recalling at once the deepest traditions of mystical reflection and the most contemporary disjunction, noted above with Derrida, between our scientific knowledge and our technological know-how:

> What is man? That beast who refuses to know who it is, because all of its fortune consists precisely in not knowing this [*à l'ignorer*]. For

the first time, finally, a speculative non-knowing [*non-savoir*] seems to free us in relation to a practical knowledge, about which we always affirm that it can, and knows how to, free us. For this meta-knowledge [*métasavoir*] would be our own unhappiness and that of our children; it would put us back at the level of brute beasts and of fixed plants, which themselves are something defined. We discover the horror of any ontology. We therefore leave open the indetermination of the answer. What is man? Answer: A possibility within a range of powers, potency, omnipotence, because he can become all. What is man? This range itself, this omnipotence.[60]

From this perspective, the power of technoscientific humanity, its virtually endless creative potential, must be understood to depend on its relative lack of definition or determination: the more programmed the creature, the less open in its potential; the less programmed, the more open and adaptable. Human "nature"—and eventually "nature" more broadly—would come then to signal not fixed law or the closure of any determinism but rather the open and incalculable potentiality of a birth (*nascor*) whose freedom stems from a deprogramming or forgetting, a kind of poverty or blankness that leaves the human specifically adapted to little or nothing and therefore open to virtually all. Echoing mystical thinkers dating back at least to Gregory of Nyssa (c. 332–395), who associate the creative power both of God *and* of the human subject with an infinitude that defies definition or conception, Serres argues that technoscientific humanity proves to be endlessly inventive and adaptive in the measure that it lacks, at bottom, any fixed essence. As human, we cannot in essence be defined—or we are defined by our essential lack of definition, and we might understand this relation between our indetermination and self-creation in two directions: on the one hand, through the kind of self-creation unfolding by technoscientific means today, we constantly undo the limits that might ever be taken to define us, but also, even more, we become self-creative in the first place thanks only to such indetermination.

Hence, from a perspective that might apply as much to modern technoscience as to traditional mystical religion, the crux of "human experience" could turn out to be less the question of human finitude—and what may turn to have been its many comforts—and more the question of human "infinitude," where we would confront the irreducible instability or indetermination of the human "itself." Insofar as such instability or indetermination would be tied to a virtually boundless possibility that "grounds" human experience, it would be tied also to the complex anxieties engendered by such possibility.

One can witness the work of such anxieties in the multifaceted and often violent responses being made on the world stage today in reaction against a technoscience that can, as we've clearly suggested here, threaten the boundaries of categories that may once have seemed (or that only now, on the verge of their collapse and disappearance, begin to seem) fundamental—categories such as "nature," "life," and "the human" "themselves," which for many in the contemporary world begin to appear all the more "sacred" in the measure that they are all the more deeply called into question. As Serres writes (in a passage that could be read quite productively in relation to the analyses that Derrida develops in "Faith and Knowledge"), "the diffuse anxieties today surrounding chemistry or biotechnologies, for example, bring back the old abandoned figures of 'Nature,' of 'Life,' and of 'Man,' [which prove] all the less defined and all the more sacred in the measure that these fears grow. Let's not touch 'Man,' say these fears, let us not violate 'Life' or 'Nature,' whose myths reappear, like so many ghosts."[61]

According to the positions I have sketched out in this paper, we might suspect that current efforts to resecure such categories within their fixed limits and stable definitions will be bound to fail, yielding, indeed, figures whose spectral quality could not but disappoint the desires—and aggravate the anxieties—driving them. Both technoscience and mystical religion as we've sketched them here would compel us to recognize the degree to which, in fact, we cannot but "touch man" today—that is, work and rework, in a process of continuous creation, "the human" "itself," in its very "life" and "nature." The "human experience," from this perspective, would prove, both in traditions of mystical religion and in contemporary technoscience, irreducibly open and emergent—a function of that self-creation whose ground and result alike would be the irreducible instability of any limit or definition to the "human" and its "experience."

NOTES

1. Michel Serres, *Hominescence* (Paris: Le Pommier, 2001), 50. Translations are mine.

2. Serres, *Hominescence*, 50.

3. In *From Max Weber: Essays in Sociology*, H. H. Gerth and C. Wright Mills, eds, (New York: Oxford University Press, 1946).

4. Weber, "Science," 139.

5. Weber, "Science," 139.

6. On this, see Serres, *Hominescence*, 55–57. See also the related arguments in Serres' subsequent work *L'Incandescent* (Paris: Le Pommier, 2003).

7. In Heidegger, *The Question Concerning Technology and Other Essays*, trans. William Lovitt (New York: Harper and Row, 1977).

8. For a brief introduction to "calculative" thinking and its defining contrast with "meditative" thinking, see Heidegger's 1955 "Memorial Address," in *Discourse on Thinking*, trans. John Andersen and E. Hans Freund (New York: Harper and Row, 1966).

9. Heidegger, "Age," 127.

10. Heidegger, "Age," 148.

11. Heidegger, "Age," 128.

12. Heidegger, "Age," 149.

13. Heidegger, "Age," 134.

14. Heidegger, "Age," 135.

15. Jacques Derrida, "Faith and Knowledge: The Two Sources of 'Religion' at the Limits of Reason Alone," in Derrida and Gianni Vattimo, eds., Religion (Stanford: Stanford University Press, 1998), 56. A more thorough and careful discussion than we can develop here would attempt to identify and elaborate, in both historical and theoretical terms, the important distinctions and relations among these three categories.

16. On this "mystical foundation" of authority, see especially Derrida's much discussed essay "The Force of Law: 'The Mystical Foundations of Authority,'" in Deconstruction and the Possibility of Justice, ed. Drucilla Cornell (New York: Routledge, 1992).

17. Barbara Maria Stafford, "Revealing Technologies/Magical Domains," in Devices of Wonder: From the World in a Box to Images on a Screen (Los Angeles: Getty Publications, 2001), 79.

18. Stafford, Devices, 53. As I will suggest in my conclusion, it may well be that we would need to draw distinctions here between the sacred and the mystical, such that the rationalized technologies under discussion here might prove to realize the "mystical" while threatening the "sacred."

19. On "the gigantic" (das Riesige) see "Age of the World Picture," in Martin Heidegger, The Question Concerning Technology and Other Essays, trans. William Lovitt (New York: Harper and Row, 1977), 135: "A sign of this event is that everywhere and in the most varied forms and disguises the gigantic is making its appearance. In so doing, it evidences itself simultaneously in the tendency toward the increasingly small. We have only to think of numbers in atomic physics. The gigantic presses forward in a form that actualy seems to make it disappear—in the annihilation of great distances by the airplane, in the setting before us of foreign and remote worlds in their everydayness by a flick of the hand." To this one might compare the later essay "The Question Concerning Technology" (1953), where Heidegger signals the "monstrousness" that reigns when nature—above all in the form of energy—is ordered and approached in terms of the availability and manipulability of "standing reserve." See "The Question Concerning Technology," in Basic Writings, ed. David F. Krell (New York: Harper and Row, 1977), esp. 297–303.

20. Serres, Angels, 71.

21. Don DeLillo, Underworld (New York: Scribner, 1997), 808.

22. Ibid., 824–825.

23. Compare, for example, the Serres or DeLillo passages just quoted to Nicholas of Cusa's description of the cosmos whose center and circumference are an incomprehensible God (itself echoing Alain de Lille echoing the Corpus Hermeticum): "Since it is not possible for the world to be enclosed between a corporeal center and circumference, the world, whose center and circumference are God, is not comprehended"; "the world and its motion and shape cannot be grasped, for it will appear as a wheel in a wheel and a sphere in a sphere, nowhere having a center or circumference," from "On Learned Ignorance" in Nicholas of Cusa: Selected Spiritual Writings, trans. Lawrence Bond (New York: Paulist Press, 1997), 158, 160.

24. On the resonance of Eriugena et al. in *Finnegans Wake*, see my essay "And Maker Mates with Made: World- and Self-Creation in Eriugena and Joyce," in *Secular Theology: American Radical Theological Thought*, ed. Clayton Crockett (New York: Routledge, 2001).

25. Stafford, *Devices*, 114.

26. Don DeLillo, "In the Ruins of the Future: Reflections on Terror and Loss in the Shadow of September," *Harper's*, December 2001, 37.

27. For a fine discussion of divine self-creation in Eriugena, see Don Duclow, "Divine Nothingness and Self-Creation in John Scotus Eriugena," in *Journal of Religion* 57.2 (April 1977).

28. Whether in the unexpectedly modern vision of a medieval mystic like Eriugena or in the strikingly mystical vision of a late-modern like James Joyce, in both directions we might locate a quasi-Hegelian conception of world and history as the self-embodiment and self-education of rational Spirit—but a conception that also fundamentally unsettles the secure self-grounding and the final self-comprehension of the rationality that fully recollects or comprehends itself in Hegel's Absolute Knowing (see, e.g., *Phenomenology of Spirit*, sect. 808).

29. Mark C. Taylor, *Hiding* (Chicago: University of Chicago Press, 1997), 273.

30. Ibid., 325.

31. Mark C. Taylor, *The Moment of Complexity: Emerging Network Culture* (Chicago: University of Chicago Press, 2001), 231.

32. Taylor, *Moment*, 230.

33. Taylor, *Moment*, 230. In a fairly unexpected way, Taylor's understanding of mind in terms of distribution can seem, from a technophilic perspective, to resemble the conception of mind that Wendell Berry elaborates from a more technophobic perspective. See, for example, Berry's *Life Is a Miracle: An Essay against Modern Superstition* (Washington, D.C.: Counterpoint, 2000), 48–49: "To have one mind you have got to have at least two (and undoubtedly many more) and a world. We could call this the Adam and Eve theory of the mind. The correct formula, in fact, is more like this: mind = brain + body + world + local dwelling place + community + history . . . Mind in this definition has become hard to locate in an organ, organism, or place. It has become an immaterial presence or possibility that is capable of being embodied and placed."

34. Taylor, *Moment*, 230.

35. Taylor, *Moment*, 230.

36. Taylor, *Moment*, 230–231.

37. Taylor, *Moment*, 231.

38. In this direction, both Taylor and Hayles can be seen to extend the insights that Donna Haraway brings to her much discussed analysis of the "cyborg." See especially "A Cyborg Manifesto: Science, Technology, and Socialist-Feminism in the Late Twentieth Century," in Haraway, *Simians, Cyborgs, and Women: The Reinvention of Nature* (New York: Routledge, 1991).

39. N. Katherine Hayles, *How We Became Posthuman: Virtual Bodies in Cybernetics, Literature, and Informatics* (Chicago: University of Chicago Press, 1999), 288.

40. Hayles, *Posthuman*, 288.

41. Hayles, *Posthuman*, 288.

42. Hayles, *Posthuman*, 291.

43. Hayles, *Posthuman*, 290.

44. Hayles, *Posthuman*, 289. Hayles finds one of the most striking explications of this logic in Edwin Hutchins' rereading of John Searle's "Chinese room," which Searle intended as an argument against the notion that machines can think: "In Hutchins' neat interpretation, Searle's argument is valuable precisely because it makes clear that it is not Searle but the entire room that knows Chinese. In this distributed cognitive system, the Chinese room knows more than do any of its components, including Searle. The situation of modern humans is akin to that of Searle in the Chinese room."

45. In this direction, the positions developed by thinkers such as Hayles and Taylor might be seen as extensions of Heidegger's approach to worldhood in *Being and Time*, where the irreducibly relational—and pragmatic—character of worldhood would prevent its reduction to an object of representation.

46. Serres, *Hominescence*, 14.

47. From this perspective, our relation to the task of human self-creation is much like the writer's relation to his work in Maurice Blanchot's understanding of literature: "Either: as an interior project [the work] is everything it ever will be, and from that moment the writer knows everything about it that he can learn, and so will leave it to lie there in its twilight, without translating it into words, without writing it— but then he won't ever write: and he won't be a writer. Or: realizing that the work cannot be planned, but only carried out, that it has value, truth, and reality only through the words which unfold it in time and inscribe it in space, he will begin to write, but starting from nothing and with nothing in mind—like a nothingness working in nothingness, to borrow an expression of Hegel's" ("Literature and the Right to Death," in *The Station Hill Blanchot Reader: Fiction and Literary Essays*, ed. George Quasha [Barrytown, NY: Station Hill Press, 1999], 362).

48. Michel Serres, *L'Incandescent* (Paris: Le Pommier, 2003).

49. Serres, *Hominescence*, 49.

50. Serres, *Hominescence*, 182.

51. Serres, *Hominescence*, 164.

52. Serres, *Hominescence*, 163.

53. Serres, *Hominescence*, 165.

54. Serres, in Michel Serres and Bruno Latour, *Conversations on Science, Culture, and Time* (Ann Arbor: University of Michigan Press, 1995), 172.

55. Serres, *Hominescence*, 180.

56. It is worth noting here that the association of location with definition or circumscription is decisive to the mystical insistence that God cannot be located. On this, see my essay "Locating the Mystical Subject," in *Mystics: Presence and Aporia*, eds. Michael Kessler and Christian Sheppard (Chicago: University of Chicago Press, 2003).

57. Serres, *Hominescence*, 181.

58. Serres, *Hominescence*, 183.

59. On this theme in Gregory of Nyssa, one of the first to formulate the issue, and in Eriugena, who transports the theme into the Latin West, see, again, my "Locating the Mystical Subject."

60. Serres, *Hominescence*, 63.
61. Serres, *L'Incandescent*, 29.

BIBLIOGRAPHY

Berry, Wendell. *Life Is a Miracle: An Essay Against Modern Superstition.* Washington, D.C.: Counterpoint, 2000.

Blanchot, Maurice. "Literature and the Right to Death." In *The Station Hill Blanchot Reader: Fiction and Literary Essays,* edited by George Quasha. Barrytown, N.Y.: Station Hill Press, 1999.

Carlson, Thomas A. "And Maker Mates with Made: World- and Self-Creation in Eriugena and Joyce." In *Secular Theology: American Radical Theological Thought,* edited by Clayton Crockett. New York: Routledge, 2001.

———. "Locating the Mystical Subject." In *Mystics,* edited by Michael Kessler and Christian Sheppard. Chicago: University of Chicago Press, 2003.

DeLillo, Don. *Underworld.* New York: Scribner, 1997.

———. "In the Ruins of the Future: Reflections on Terror and Loss in the Shadow of September." *Harper's,* December 2001.

Derrida, Jacques. "The Force of Law: The Mystical Foundations of Authority." In *Deconstruction and the Possibility of Justice,* edited by Drucilla Cornell. New York: Routledge, 1992.

———. "Faith and Knowledge: The Two Sources of 'Religion' at the Limits of Reason Alone." In *Religion,* edited by Jaques Derrida and Gianni Vattimo. Stanford: Stanford University Press, 1998.

Duclow, Don, "Divine Nothingness and Self-Creation in John Scotus Eriugena." *Journal of Religion,* 57.2 (April 1977).

Haraway, Donna. "A Cyborg Manifesto: Science, Technology, and Socialist-Feminism in the Late Twentieth Century." In *Simians, Cyborgs, and Women: The Reinvention of Nature.* New York: Routledge, 1991.

Hayles, N. Katherine. *How We Became Posthuman: Virtual Bodies in Cybernetics, Literature, and Informatics.* Chicago: University of Chicago Press, 1999.

Hegel, G. W. F. *Phenomenology of Spirit.* Translated by A. V. Miller. Oxford: Oxford University Press, 1977.

Heidegger, Martin. *Being and Time.* Translated by J. Macquarrie and E. Robinson. Oxford: Basil Blackwell, 1962.

———. "Memorial Address." In *Discourse on Thinking.* New York: Harper and Row, 1966.

———. "The Age of the World Picture." In *The Question Concerning Technology and Other Essays.* Translated by William Lovitt. New York: Harper and Row, 1977.

———. "The Question Concerning Technology." In *Basic Writings,* edited by David F. Krell. New York: Harper and Row, 1977.

Nicholas of Cusa. "On Learned Ignorance." In *Nicholas of Cusa: Selected Spiritual Writings.* Translated by Lawrence Bond. New York: Paulist Press, 1997.

Serres, Michel. *Hominescence.* Paris: Le Pommier, 2001.

———. *L'Incandescent.* Paris: Le Pommier, 2003.

Stafford, Barbara Maria. "Revealing Technologies/Magical Domains." In *Devices of*

Wonder: From the World in a Box to Images on a Screen. Los Angeles: Getty Publications, 2001.

Taylor, Mark C. *Hiding.* Chicago: University of Chicago Press, 1997.

———. *The Moment of Complexity: Emerging Network Culture.* Chicago: University of Chicago Press, 2001.

Weber, Max, "Science as a Vocation." In *From Max Weber: Essays in Sociology,* edited by H. H. Gerth and C. Wright Mills. New York: Oxford University Press, 1946.

4

The Depths and Shallows of Experience

Hilary Putnam

No one who has the temerity to address such broad themes as "science, religion, and the human experience," can hope to hide behind an academic façade of professional expertise. To be sure, there are issues here that can benefit from being treated with scientific or philosophical sophistication, I believe—otherwise, what am *I* doing in this volume? But the big issues: to believe in God or not to believe in God; to engage in such religious practices as prayer, attending services, studying religious texts or not to do so (I am *not* equating this with the issue of believing or not believing in God, by the way); to look for proof of God's existence, if one is religious (or thinking of being religious), or to regard such a quest as misguided; to be pluralistic in one's approach to religion, or to regard one religion as truer than all the rest—these are deeply personal choices, choices of who to be, not just what to do or what to believe. I do not believe that philosophical or scientific discussion can provide compelling reasons for making these choices one way rather than another, although such discussion can help us make whichever choices we make more reflectively. (Avi Sagi once told me that, in a still unpublished fragment of—I think it was a diary of Kierkegaard's—he found the words "Leap of faith—yes, but only after reflection.")

I did say, however, that there are aspects of these issues that a philosophically sophisticated discussion (as well as a scientifically sophisticated discussion) could illuminate. The intentionally broad phrase "the human experience" that the editors adopted in the title of this volume raises the issue of what is meant by "experience" in the context of discussions of science and religion (as well, perhaps, as the issue of what it means to be "human" in our age, or in any age). In this essay, it is the question of how we should understand "experience" that I shall address.

Both in life and in philosophical reflection, experience is sometimes seen as intrinsically shallow, as mere surface, and sometimes as deep. I want particularly to investigate the origins of our Western notion of experience in Cartesian and post-Cartesian philosophy and explore with you the relevance of the long-standing philosophical disputes about experience to our broad themes of "science, religion, and the human experience."

The Depths and Shallows

When I speak of "religious experience" in what follows, I will not mean experience that purports to be of supernatural beings or of "revelation" conceived of on the model of having words dictated to one by a divine being. (One can find a very different model—the model of revelation as the ongoing connection between the individual and God—in the writing of Franz Rosenzweig.)[1] Rather, I will have in mind the way in which a religious person may, at any time, experience something or some event—whether it be an obviously significant one, say the birth of a child or the sort of deep crisis in one's life that William James describes in *The Varieties of Religious Experience,* or whether it be a superficially ordinary one—as full of religious significance. Speaking for myself, I cannot imagine being religious in any sense, theistic or not theistic, unless one has had and cherished moments of religious experience in this latter sense. Yet the concept of experience that we have operated with, from Descartes and Hume to today's cognitive scientists, has a troubled history, and it will repay us, I believe, to reflect on that history.

What I shall be talking about for the most part will not be what I just called "religious experience." Rather, I am going to spend a few minutes trying to explain why so many people have (and from where they got) a concept of experience that leaves literally no room for *depth,* a conception of experience as, so to speak, all psychological *surface,* one traditionally summed up in the conception of experiences as sensations, and after that I shall try to explain why that conception is wrong, drawing especially on Kant's profound analysis of experience.

We all know that the philosophers of the seventeenth and eighteenth centuries are classified by the standard texts as "empiricists" and "rationalists." While the classification is in many ways a procrustean bed, it certainly captures a broad divide between, say, the British philosophers Locke, Berkeley, and Hume, and the continental philosophers Descartes, Spinoza, and Leibniz, and while the pattern of disagreements is by no means as tidy as the labels "empiricism" and "rationalism" suggest, it is certainly true that we find very different conceptions of experience in the two groups, and especially in Hume and Leibniz. (What is not often remarked is that Hume, the empiricist who makes experience—under the name "impressions and ideas"—the be-all and end-all of his philosophy, and who prides himself on being a sort of Newton of psychology,[2] is, in fact, far less subtle in his description of experience than Leibniz.)[3] Be that as it may, the line that came to be recognized is between conceptions of experience that go back to Hume, and conceptions that go back to Kant (who hoped, of course, to sublate the categories "empiricism" and "rationalism").[4] I shall briefly sketch these two conceptions, because they epitomize the idea of experience as shallow, and the idea of experience as deep.

Hume and the Shallow Conception

For Hume, the very paradigm of an "impression" is a visual image; (the other sort of experience—"ideas"—was defined by him as "faint copies" of impressions. Similarly, Descartes and Berkeley both tried to read the nature of visual impressions directly from the newly investigated nature of retinal images.[5] The result of this approach was a tendency to think of all "impressions" on the model of *pictures*—not necessarily visual, of course—there were also tactile, olfactory, and so on, representations; but like pictures, these, and the "ideas" or faint copies that corresponded to them, were thought by Hume to refer only to what they *resembled*.[6] Content, on this resemblance semantics, is a rather primitive affair.[7] The very idea of a fact that cannot be *sensorily pictured* was rejected by Hume. The only other sort of content arises from "association"—especially the association of "passions" (feelings and emotions) with images.

Today there are very few, if any, old-fashioned empiricists in philosophy. But what survives of the older view is the very influential idea that experience (still identified by empiricists with sensory inputs) is nonconceptual. Quine's idea that, for philosophical purposes, experience-talk could simply be replaced with talk of "surface irritations" (stimulation of the nerves on or near the surface of the body) in many ways foreshadowed this influential idea.

Kant and the Deep Conception

In Kant's writings one can find a response to the empiricist view of experience as consisting of sensory images, a response so deep that even today few philosophers who are not primarily Kant specialists have fully appreciated it (Strawson, Sellars, and more recently John McDowell and James Conant being among the happy exceptions). In the few minutes I can afford to devote to it this evening, I cannot, of course, do justice to it, but I hope to point out at least some of the leading ideas of the Kantian conception. It is important, however, to realize that no one book of Kant contains all of it. From *The Critique of Pure Reason* to *Religion Within the Bounds of Mere Reason*, Kant constantly broadens and deepens the presentation of his view, if not the view itself. The account in *The Critique of Pure Reason* is, nonetheless, the basis on which the deeper and broader reflections in Kant's subsequent writings depend.

Hume, as we just saw, conceives of experiences on the model of pictures and their cognitive content as contained and communicated via (sensory) *resemblance*. Only sensory qualities are, thus, properly cognizable at all. If one accepts this, then many of Hume's other famous doctrines readily follow: for example, Hume's claim that we don't "observe" causal connection depends both on Hume's limitation of what we can observe to sensory qualities and on his very narrow inventory of sensory qualities: since causal connection is not a sensory quality for Hume, it is evident to him that casual connection is never *observed*. On the other hand, although objective time hardly consists of sensory qualities either, Hume never worries about the question, "How and why are we able to think of impressions and 'ideas' as succeeding one another in an objective time?"

Kant did, however, worry about this question, and he concluded that our notions of objective time, causality, and lawful connection are *interdependent*. For example, our awareness of a boat sailing down a river (coming, let us say, to a certain bridge) as *earlier* than the boat sailing *beyond* the bridge, even though we think of a building's back as existing at the same time as the front even if we look at the front *before* we look at the back, are internally related to our beliefs that we could have chosen to experience the front before the back, but we could not, conditions being as they were, have chosen to experience the boat sailing beyond the bridge *before* we experienced it approaching the bridge, and these beliefs are in turn related to the system of causal connections we accept.[8] The notion of time is inextricably connected with the notions of space and causality. This is not just a fact about Newton's physics, or Einstein's, but about our ordinary conceptual scheme as well. Imagine, just as a thought-experiment, that there is a (more or less instantaneous) world-state, call it "A," consisting of a sense-impression as of a cat chasing a mouse; a world-state, call it "B," consisting of a sense-impression as of a twelve-foot cat singing "Yankee Doodle"; and a world-state, call it "C," consisting of a sense-impression as of a purple tidal wave sweeping over a field of flowers with heads like Charlie Chaplin. What sense would it have to say that these are *states of one and the same world*, let alone to speak of them as temporally ordered, if there are no causal connections of any kind between them?[9] Hume's argument depends upon our thinking of the concepts "experiences A and B [think of experiences at different times here] lie in one and the same phenomenal world" and "A is earlier than B" as *presuppositionless*.

Our question, however, concerns how we *experience* things, and not how we *conceive* them. But—long before modern psychology—Kant questioned the coherence of such a dichotomy. We do not experience familiar objects and events—a cat drinking milk, a tree swaying in the wind, someone hammering a nail into a wall—as collections of color points on a spatial grid. As James put it (in the case of a "presented and recognized material object"), "sensations and apperceptive idea fuse . . . so intimately that you can no more tell where one begins and the other ends, than you can tell, in those cunning circular panoramas that have lately been exhibited, where the real foreground and the painted canvas join together."[10] To employ Kant's language, in the sort of perception James described (or—an example Kant himself uses—in the case of experiencing something as a boat sailing down a river), we have not mere unconceptualized sensations, whatever those might be, but a *synthesis* of experiences and conceptual ideas, the ideas of space, time, and causation. This is something that the phenomenological school, beginning with Husserl, likewise emphasized: I see a building as something which *has* a back, Husserl pointed out, even when I don't see the back. Such perception is fallible, to be sure; but so is the perception that something is red or circular. And the retreat to "sense data" in the hope that *there* we can find something "incorrigible" has long been recognized to be a "loser."

A second issue that plays a large role in *The Critique of Pure Reason*, and one that figures into contemporary attacks on what postmodernists consider to be the metaphysical illusion of the "ego," is the issue of right and wrong ways to think about what it means to be or have a *self*. (As Nicholas Doyle has observed, postmodernist doubts about whether there is such a thing as a self, or an "author," never stop the postmodernist from cashing a royalty check.) Here again, paying more attention to Kant would help to clear our heads.

For Kant, rational thought itself depends on the fact that I regard my thoughts, experiences, memories, and so on, as *mine*. To illustrate Kant's point, imagine yourself going through a very simple form of reasoning, say, "Boiling water hurts if you stick your finger in it; this is boiling water; so it will hurt if I stick my finger in this." If the time-slice of me that thought "Boiling water hurts if you stick your finger in it" was one person, person A, and the time slice that thought the minor premise, "This is boiling water," was a different person, person B, and the person that thought the conclusion, "It will hurt if I stick my finger in this," was yet a third person, person C, then that conclusion was not warranted, indeed, the sequence of thoughts was not an argument at all, since the thoughts were thoughts of different thinkers, none of whom had any reason to be bound by what the others thought or had thought. We are *responsible* for what we have thought and done in the past, responsible *now*, intellectually and practically, and that is what makes us *thinkers*, rational agents in a world, at all. Kant, like Locke before him, can be seen as making the point that the thinking of my thoughts and actions at different times as *mine* does not depend on a metaphysical premise about "self-identical substances," and is nonetheless a form of conceptualization that we cannot opt out of when we are engaged in judgment in action.

As before, to say that Kant's point is valid for conceptualization but not for experience would be to miss the way in which experiences and concepts interpenetrate, the way in which they are synthesized. When I reason (say, about the boiling water), I *experience* my successive thoughts as "mine." Hume is right in holding that this is not a sensory quality; there is no "impression" of "my-ownness"; and Kant would emphasize this just as much as Hume. But whereas Hume concludes that the self is an *illusion*, Kant sees that experience transcends Humean "impressions." Whereas for Hume, experiences are sheer psychological surface, for Kant even the simplest perception links us to and interanimates such deep ideas as the ideas of time, space, causality, and the self. And this is something that Kant does not just claim, but that he argues in detail, and with incomparable brilliance. That experience is intrinsically *deep* is the heart of the Kantian conception. It is not something that was overthrown by the collapse of Kant's "synthetic apriori" and the metaphysics Kant tried to base upon it.

Kant on Aesthetic Experience

I said above that Kant deepens the presentation of his views (and perhaps the views themselves) in successive books, and, I should add, not only in books. For example, a wonderful (and sadly neglected) discussion of what is right and wrong in mysticism may be found scattered in Kant's writing.[11] But no where is this more true than in *The Critique of the Power of Judgment*.

I cannot, of course, even sketch the complex and rewarding aesthetic theory of that *Critique*. Fortunately, that is not my goal. What I want to do is extract one item from that complex discussion, although to do that I will have to say a little about the ideas that surround it.[12] The item in question is the fascinating notion of an "indeterminate concept." When we experience a work of art, Kant tells us, we experience it as escaping capture by "determinate concepts," but we do perceive it as—not being captured by, but evoking—a kind of concept, an indeterminate concept, one which is deeply connected with what Kant calls "the free play of the faculties" (imagination and reason, under the guidance of the former).

Here I do have to interpret the aesthetic theory I said I wouldn't discuss, to the extent of warning my readers against two common misinterpretations. The first, which I am indebted to Paul Guyer for pointing out, is the assumption that when Kant speaks of "pure" aesthetic experience he is using "pure" as a value-term. The reverse is the case; the art that Kant values and thinks we should all value, Guyer has conclusively shown, is mixed, impure. "Pure aesthetic experience" in Kant's sense is concerned only with form; but to value, say, a painting which moves us both on account of its subject matter and its formal properties, or a novel or a poem, is to respond not only to the "purely aesthetic" features in this technical sense, but to the *interplay* of description, valuation, and purely formal experience.[13] The second misunderstanding is that it is only "the concept of beauty" that Kant has in mind by the term "indeterminate concept."

To illustrate what I believe Kant actually had in mind, think of a painting by Vermeer (pick your favorite!). It is not indescribable; a great deal about it can be described. The notorious Vermeer-forger, Van Meegeren, could undoubtedly have given a precise (determinate) description of a great many features of this painting or of Vermeer paintings in general. But the description, although it might teach us a lot, and even add to our appreciation of such a painting, would not answer the question: "Why is this painting so beautiful?" Indeed, as Van Meegeren's rather unpleasant forgeries testify, a painting could satisfy this "determinate" description and *not be beautiful*. What Kant, interestingly, says about the discussion of works of art is not that it is impossible to describe what it is that strikes us as beautiful (which it would be, if the only alternatives were either to apply to them determinate concepts of the kind a Van Meegeren—or an art historian—might offer, or to apply the *single* indeterminate concept "beautiful"). What he says is that the aesthetic ideas that are the content of works of artistic genius evoke so much thought that language cannot fully attain them or make them intelligible.[14] (He also says that we add to a determinate concept "a representation of the imagination that belongs to its presentation, but which . . . aesthetically enlarges the concept itself in an unbounded way).[15] In short, certain concepts seek—and manage—less to *finish* a discussion or answer a determinate question, as to further provoke both thought and imagination and to raise an unbounded number of further questions. And these are the concepts we need and have to use to talk meaningfully about art.

What connects the notion of an indeterminate concept with my topic of experience is that it is precisely in the context of discussing how we perceive works of art in which Kant invokes this notion. Indeterminate concepts are not purely intellectual concepts; they require both a *sensible* subject matter and the application of an active imagination. That perception is fused with conceptual content is something we learned from *The Critique of Pure Reason*; that some of the perceptions we value most are fused with *indeterminate*, open-ended, conceptual content, content in which imagination and reason cooperate under the leadership of imagination, is something we learn from *The Critique of the Power of Judgment*.

The notion of an indeterminate concept, understood in this way, naturally extends to moral notions. If Kant does not use it in the area of morals, it is because, I think, of a desire to keep morality rigorous and transparent. But morality, good morality, cannot always be rigorous and transparent, and a thinker who has seen that something like the notion of an indeterminate concept that I just described applies also to the highest type of moral awareness is Iris Murdoch, even if she does not cite Kant or use his terminology. (Thus, in her philosophical masterpiece, *The Sovereignty of Good*, she writes, "Moral tasks are characteristically endless not only because 'within,' as it were, a given concept our efforts are imperfect, but also because as we move and as we look our concepts themselves are changing. . . . We do not simply, through being rational and knowing ordinary language words, 'know' the meaning of all necessary moral words. We may have to learn the meaning; and since we are human historical individuals the movement of understanding is onward into increasing privacy, in the direction of the ideal limit, and not backwards towards a genesis in the ruling of an impersonal public language."[16])

Beyond both aesthetics, in the sense of the open-ended appreciation and discussion of works of art, and morality, in the sense of Murdoch's "loving attention," to the whole complexity of human beings and human moral life, it should be obvious, I think, that religious experiences are both guided by and spontaneously give rise to indeterminate concepts in a way analogous to the ways in which aesthetic and moral experiences do. And if we see religious, aesthetic, and moral experiences in this way, as I have been urging we should, we will avoid Hume's mistake of trying to analyze them as a chemist analyzes a compound, analyze them into so much of this factor ("ideas and impressions"), so much of that factor ("passions"), and so much of this other factor ("beliefs"). In the deepest human experiences, ways of perceiving things that are inseparable from those experiences but nonetheless conceptual, at least in the way indeterminate concepts are conceptual, fuse so intimately that you cannot tell where one begins and the other ends, to mimic William James's words quoted earlier.

Although the phenomenological school of philosophy which began with Husserl inherited and extended the Kantian insights I have been describing, the most influential twentieth-century phenomenologist, Heidegger, had a contemptuous attitude toward science, which, for him, was merely an aspect of technological civilization (which he regarded as intrinsically evil). In Heidegger's writing, everything I have been saying about the depth of religious experience (including the experiences of "being" and of being "thrown" into the world and of finding a destiny that is one's "ownmost," which are Heidegger's versions of or substitutes for religious experience), as well as of artistic experience (especially experience of poetry), and even of our everyday experiences with artifacts is recognized and phenomenologically interpreted; but science is denigrated.

But by default, if we do not examine the impact of science on our ways of experiencing the world in a more sympathetic spirit than Heidegger was capable of, we are likely to fall back into the empiricist picture of science as consisting of deductive and inductive inferences from simple sense-data (or Machian *Empfindungen*). To find a sustained critique of this way of thinking, we have to turn to the American pragmatists, and especially John Dewey. Extending the line of thought that William James had begun with his talk of apperceptive ideas and sensations as "fusing," Dewey saw that science endlessly and inventively creates new observation-concepts, and that by so doing it institutes new *kinds* of data.[17] A scientist with a cloud chamber may now *observe* a proton colliding with a nucleus (without being able to answer the question "Exactly what visual sensations did you have when you observed it?" except by saying "It looked like a proton colliding with a nucleus"), or *observe* a virus with the aid of an electron microscope, or *observe* a DNA sequence, and so on. And the impact of science on the conceptualization of experience is not confined to specialists; the way in which all of us experience the world was changed by Darwin, and was changed by Freud (whether one thinks this or that claim of Freud's was well- or ill-founded) as the notion of the unconscious became part of our vocabulary, and is being changed today by computer science and the concepts and metaphors it adds to the language.

On the metalevel, the level of the methodological appraisal of scientific theories, we also find something in science analogous to the indeterminate concepts involved in aesthetic judgment, indeterminate concepts that figure in judgments that are internal to scientific inquiry itself: judgments of coherence, simplicity, plausibility, and the like. The similarity of such judgments to aesthetic judgments has, indeed, often been pointed out. Dirac was famous for saying that certain theories should be taken seriously because they were "beautiful," and Einstein talked of the "inner perfection" of a theory as an "indispensable criterion."[18]

But it is time to say something of the wider relevance of this picture of experience, the picture of experience as deep, for the concerns of the present volume, for reflections on "science, religion, and the human experience."

Conceptuality and Skepticism

At first blush, recognizing that perception (and experience that purports to be perception or resembles perception) is always conceptualized, may seem to make the problem of skepticism much worse, especially when religion is the issue. From Kant to John McDowell, philosophers who point out that experience is conceptualized have been told that they are problematizing our access to reality. Concepts can, after all, mislead as well as lead, conceal as well as reveal.

The fact that religious concepts are no longer intersubjectively shared within Western culture, and have not been for a long time, makes this more than a purely theoretical issue, as skepticism about the existence of houses and rocks happily has become. (For the ancient Greek skeptics, it is often pointed out, it was anything but a "purely theoretical issue," but that is another story, and not one I need to tell today.) While no one can say that there are only so many possible answers a religious person can give to the atheist or to the religious skeptic, three main approaches are familiar to all of us.

The traditional approach, and the one that is still that of the Roman Catholic Church, is to continue (albeit with contemporary sophistication) the medieval attempt to prove the existence of God (neo-Thomism). This is not an approach I find possible for myself, at any rate, for the following reasons:

First, in order to understand talk about God, whether or not that talk takes the form of a proof, one must be able to understand the concept "God." But there are very different possible conceptions of what it is to understand the concept "God," in a way that has no analogue in the case of, say, a mathematical proof. Secondly, even if one understands the concept "God," to accept any of the traditional proofs, one has to find a connection between that concept and the highly theoretical philosophical principles involved in those proofs, premises about conditioned and unconditioned existence, and about what sorts of necessity there are. Some of the most profound religious thinkers of the last two hundred years (particularly the religious existentialists from Kierkegaard to Rosenzweig and Buber) have had no use at all for this sort of philosophizing; and I would be the last to say that they lacked the concept "God." What the traditional proofs of the existence of God in fact do is *connect* the concerns of two different salvific enterprises: the enterprise of ancient and medieval philosophy,[19] which, after all, is the source of the materials for these proofs, and the enterprise of monotheistic religion. While it is certainly possible to have a deeply worthwhile religious attitude that combines these two elements—indeed, the effort to do so has contributed profoundly to Judaism as well as to Christianity and Islam—it is also possible to have a deeply fulfilling religious attitude while keeping far away from metaphysics.

A second familiar response to religious skepticism is that of the dogmatists: "my religion is true and every other belief is wicked (especially atheism), or no better than witch doctoring (other religions)." (A friend remarked, "I understand this is very popular among people philosophers don't talk to.")[20] Not only is this response a denial of the very raison d'etre of philosophy itself, which John Dewey so well defined as "criticism of criticisms,"[21] but, in a marvelous discussion of the psychology of "fanaticism" in The Critique of the Power of Judgment, Kant argues that this is, at bottom, not religion but a disease of religion.[22]

Part of Kant's point is that the "fanatic" (his term for what I just called "the dogmatist") treats religious beliefs as if they were as sure as ordinary perceptual beliefs. I remarked a few moments ago that skepticism about the existence of houses and rocks has happily become a purely theoretical issue. In practice, as Kant pointed out in The Critique of Pure Reason, perception of such objects is passive; we have no real choice about whether to believe that there is a house in front of us when we see one. Nor do we have to "take responsibility" for believing that there is a house there when we see one or walk into one. For the fanatic, it is as if he had as simply (and as unproblematically) seen God, or seen Jesus (or, in Kantian language, seen the unconditioned). For the fanatic, those who do not accept what is so obvious are wicked or stupid or both, or, in the best case, waiting for the fanatic to enlighten them. Such an attitude, Kant believes, misses the essence of true religious faith, which (for him) involves the recognition that what one believes is not simply forced on one passively. The uncertainty, the unprovability, of religious propositions is, Kant believed, a *good* thing; for if religious propositions could be proved, there would be nothing to take responsibility for. To put it in present-day language, the fanatic is unconsciously *fleeing responsibility*. I find that my perceptions are in accord with Kant's here: I find that both his psychology of fanaticism and the phenomenology of faith presupposed by that psychology are very deep.

A third approach to skepticism, often associated with existentialism, is to accept responsibility for believing what cannot be proved. I already mentioned the note Avi Sagi found in an unpublished bit of Kierkegaard's *Nachlass* which reads: "Leap of faith—yes, but only after reflection." In this approach, the role of religious experience is not to *prove* something but to confront one with an existential choice, to make "believe or don't believe" a "live option," in William James's words. A fine, but deeply challenging, account of this third option can be found in Wittgenstein's "Lectures on Religious Belief."[23] (Wittgenstein described himself as not a believer, "although I cannot help seeing every question from a religious point of view.")

Here is what Wittgenstein says:

> These [religious] controversies look entirely different from normal controversies. Reasons look entirely different from normal reasons. They are, in a way, quite inconclusive. The point is that if there were evidence, this would in fact destroy the whole business.[24]

Several paragraphs later, Wittgenstein discusses a "Father O'Hara"[25] who, he tells us "is one of those people who make it a question of science." And he continues:

> Here we have [religious] people who treat this evidence in a different way. They base things on evidence which taken in one way would seem exceedingly flimsy. They base enormous things on this evidence. Am I to say they are unreasonable? I wouldn't call them unreasonable. I would say they are certainly not *reasonable*, that's obvious. "Unreasonable" implies, with everyone, rebuke. I want to say: they don't treat this as a matter of reasonability. Anyone who reads

the Epistles will find it said: not only that it is not reasonable, but that it is folly. Not only is it not reasonable, but it doesn't pretend to be. What seems to me ludicrous about O'Hara is his making it appear to be *reasonable*.[26]

The question Wittgenstein's remarks invite is the obvious one: is it ever *justified* to believe what is not "reasonable." This is the question that William James dealt with in his celebrated essay, "The Will to Believe" (which he considered calling "The Right to Believe," which is what the essay actually defends). That often misrepresented and misinterpreted essay, it seems to me, gives exactly the right answer to this question, but it would take a much longer essay than this one to interpret and discuss it. I want, however, to make just one point about it, namely that James emphasizes that saying there is a right to believe is by no means to say that there is a right to be intolerant,[27] and that too seems to me exactly right.

Why Did I Focus on Experience, Then?

In view of what I just said, it will be clear that I did not focus on experience in this essay because I wish to argue that religious experience *answers* skeptical questions. But I did have a reason for focusing on it, just as Wittgenstein had a reason for focusing on the complexity of the phenomenon of religious belief. Wittgenstein began his lectures on religious belief by pointing out that believers and atheists regularly talk past each other. If you search the Web under "atheism," you will find a great deal of intelligent and painstaking proof that the Bible contains errors, that it is silly to think that every word of the Bible was literally dictated by God, and so on, but precious little recognition that most religious people are not fundamentalists, and many do not believe in the idea of divine *dictation* at all. It is as if atheists too were "fanatics," in Kant's sense; for atheists, too, their [negative] religious belief is, it seems, akin to a perceptual certainty, something that involves no responsibility. Wittgenstein, if I interpreted him correctly,[28] did not want to make us believers (he was not religious himself), but he felt an enormous respect for the literature and the spirituality contained in religious traditions, and he wished to combat this sort of simplistic stereotyping. One way of overcoming the idea—and we need to overcome it!—that it is simply *obvious* what having a religious faith consists in, is to overcome the idea that it is simply obvious (or if not obvious, obviously irrelevant) what the words "religious experience" refer to. In this essay, I have tried to suggest that what "experience" refers to is far more complicated a matter than we tend to think, and that understanding how deep experience can be is a necessary preliminary to any discussion of "science, religion, and the human experience."

NOTES

1. See, for example, F. Rosenzweig, "Revelation as the Ever-Renewed Birth of the Soul," *The Star of Redemption* (New York: Holt, Rinehart and Winston, [1921] 1971).

2. N. Kemp Smith, *The Philosophy of David Hume* (London: Macmillan, 1949).

3. For example, it is Leibniz and not Hume who sees that there is no sharp line between "conscious" and "unconscious" experience and who is aware of the ways in which experience and cognition shade into one another.

4. For a discussion of these two conceptions with major implications for contemporary philosophy of mind, see J. McDowell, *Mind and World* (Cambridge: Harvard University Press, 1994).

5. C. Wolf-Devine, "Descartes on Seeing: Epistemology and Visual Perception," *Journal of the History of Philosophy*, Monograph Series (Carbondale: Southern Illinois University Press, 1993).

6. D. Hume, *A Treatise of Human Nature*, edited by L. A. Selby-Bigge (Oxford: Clarendon Press, [1740] 1976).

7. E. Milgram, "Hume on Practical Reasoning: Treatise 463–469," *Iyyun: The Jerusalem Philosophical Quarterly* 46 (1997): 235–265; E. Milgram, "Was Hume a Humean?" *Hume Studies* 21.1 (1995): 75–93.

8. I. Kant, *The Critique of Pure Reason*, translated by Norman Kent Smith (Houndmills: Macmillan Press Ltd., [1787] 1965), B23//A192.

9. Even if one tries to reconstruct time-order phenomenalistically, à la R. Carnap, *Der Logische Aufbau der Welt* (Berkeley: University of California Press, [1928] 1967), by defining A to be earlier than B if a memory of A coincides with B, we are committed to there being a lot more in the world than an arbitrary sequence of sense impressions if there is to be time-order. For one thing, there have to be all those memories; and—although Carnap chooses to ignore this—a lot has to be in place before it makes sense to speak of an experience as a "memory."

10. W. James, *Essays in Radical Empiricism* (Cambridge: Harvard University Press, [1912] 1976), 16.

11. I. Kant, *Religion Within the Boundaries of Mere Reason and Other Writings: Immanuel Kant*, translated and edited by Allen Wood and George Di Giovanni (Cambridge: Cambridge University Press, [1793] 1998); and for a fine discussion, see P. W. Frank, *Kant and Hegel on the Esotericism of Philosophy* (unpublished doctoral dissertation, Harvard University, 1993).

12. I thank Paul Guyer for discussions and for access to unpublished papers, which enriched my understanding of Kant's aesthetics. I believe the interpretation offered here is thoroughly consonant with Guyer's reading of Kant, *Critique of the Power of Judgment* (Cambridge: Cambridge University Press, [1790] 2000).

13. In "The Origins of Modern Aesthetics: 1711–1735" (forthcoming), Paul Guyer speaks of "the common caricature of Kant's purported reduction of aesthetic re-

sponse, whether in the case of works of nature or works of art, to perceptual form apart from all content and significance." Guyer points out that "when Kant turns to his explicit discussion of the fine arts—buried in the sections following the "Analytic of the Sublime" and the "Deduction of Pure Aesthetic Judgments" without the benefit of a heading of its own—it becomes clear that artistic imagination and aesthetic response can play freely with content as well as form."

14. Kant characterizes the content of a work of artistic genius as "that representation of the imagination that occasions much thinking without it being possible for any determinate thought, i.e. *concept*, to be adequate to it, which, consequently, no language fully attains or can make intelligible." Ibid., 314.

15. In a work of artistic genius, Kant tells us, "we add to a concept a representation of the imagination that belongs to its presentation, but which *by itself stimulates so much thinking that it can never be grasped in a determinate concept*, hence which aesthetically enlarges the concept itself in an unbounded way . . . in this case the imagination is creative and sets the faculty of intellectual ideas (reason) into motion" [emphasis added]. Ibid., 317.

16. I. Murdoch, *The Sovereignty of Good* (New York: Schocken Books, 1971), 29.

17. J. Dewey, *Logic: The Theory of Inquiry*, vol. 12 of *The Later Works of John Dewey*, ed. Jo Ann Boydston (Carbondale: Southern Illinois University Press, [1938] 1986), 388–389; see also vol. 4, 60–86, 87–111, and 142–143.

18. A. Einstein, "Autobiographical Notes," in *Albert Einstein Philosopher-Scientist*, ed. P. A. Schilpp (LaSalle, Ill.: Open Court, 1949), 21–23.

19. For the reasons for seeing "philosophie antique" (ancient and medieval philosophy) as a group of salvific enterprises, see P. Hadot, *Philosophy as a Way of Life* (Oxford: Blackwell, 1995).

20. The friend is Philip Devine.

21. J. Dewey, *Experience and Nature*, vol. 1 in *The Later Works of John Dewey*, ed. Jo Ann Boydston (Carbondale: Southern Illinois University Press, [1925] 1981), 298.

22. E. Friedlander, "Kant and the Critique of False Sublimity," *Iyyun: The Jerusalem Philosophical Quarterly* 48 (1999): 69–93, is a beautiful analysis of Kant's discussion.

23. L. Wittgenstein, *Lectures and Conversations on Aesthetics, Psychology and Religious Belief: Compiled from Notes Taken by Yorick Smythies, Rush Rhees, and James Taylor*, ed. Cyril Barrett (Oxford: Basil Blackwell, 1966), 53–72.

24. Ibid., 56.

25. Father O'Hara, we are told by the editors, wrote a contribution to a symposium on Science and Religion. James Conant and Cora Diamond have come up with the following information, which has not been, as far as I know, previously published: Wittgenstein came across Father O'Hara's piece by hearing it delivered as a talk on a BBC radio broadcast. The piece was part of a series of twelve broadcasts, including ones by Huxley, Haldane, Malinowski, and Eddington. The title of the series was Science and Religion. The twelve talks were broadcast between September and December, 1930. O'Hara's piece was subsequently published along with all the other pieces in the series in M. Pupin, ed., *Science and Religion: A Symposium* (London: Gerald Howe, 1931), 107–116. None of the individual pieces in the volume are titled. It is almost impossible to lay hands on a copy of the original 1931 volume. But, fortunately,

it was reprinted in 1969 by an obscure outfit called Books for Libraries Press in Free-port, New York.

26. Wittgenstein, *Lectures and Conversations*, 57–58.

27. W. James, *The Will to Believe and Other Essays* (Cambridge: Harvard University Press, [1897] 1979), 33.

28. H. Putnam, *Renewing Philosophy* (Cambridge: Harvard University Press, 1992).

BIBLIOGRAPHY

Carnap, R. *Der Logische Aufbau der Welt* [The Logical Stucture of the World]. Trans-lated by Rolf George. Berkeley: University of California Press, [1928] 1967.

Dewey, J. *Experience and Nature*. Vol. 1 of *The Later Works of John Dewey*, edited by Jo Ann Boydston. Carbondale: Southern Illinois University Press, [1925] 1981.

———. *The Quest for Certainty*. Vol. 4 of *The Later Works of John Dewey*, edited by Jo Ann Boydston. Carbondale: Southern Illinois University Press, [1929] 1982.

———. *Logic: The Theory of Inquiry*. Vol. 12 of *The Later Works of John Dewey*, edited by Jo Ann Boydston. Carbondale: Southern Illinois University Press, [1938] 1986.

Einstein, A. "Autobiographical Notes." In *Albert Einstein Philosopher-Scientist.* edited by P. A. Schilpp. LaSalle, Ill.: Open Court, 1949.

Frank, P. W. "Kant and Hegel on the Esotericism of Philosophy." Unpublished doc-toral dissertation. Hollis Catalog, Harvard University Widener Library.

Friedlander, E. "Kant and the Critique of False Sublimity." *Iyyun: The Jerusalem Philo-sophical Quarterly* 48 (1999): 69–93.

Guyer, P. "The Origins of Modern Aesthetics: 1711–1735." Forthcoming in *Blackwell's Guide to Aesthetics,* edited by Peter Kivy.

Hadot, P. *Philosophy as a Way of Life*. Oxford: Blackwell, 1995.

Hume, D. *A Treatise of Human Nature*, edited by L. A. Selby-Bigge. Oxford: Clarendon Press, [1740] 1976.

James, W. *Essays in Radical Empiricism*. Cambridge: Harvard University Press, [1912] 1976.

———. *The Will to Believe and Other Essays*. Cambridge: Harvard University Press, [1897] 1979.

Kant, I. "On a Newly Arisen Superior Tone in Philosophy." In *Raising the Tone in Phi-losophy: Late Essays by Immanuel Kant, Transformative Critique by Jacques Derrida*. Translated by Peter Fenves. Baltimore: Johns Hopkins University Press, 1998.

———. *Religion Within the Boundaries of Mere Reason and Other Writings: Immanuel Kant*. Translated and edited by Allen Wood and George Di Giovanni. Cambridge: Cambridge University Press, [1793] 1998.

———. *Critique of the Power of Judgment*. Edited by Paul Guyer. Translated by Paul Guyer and Eric Mathews. Cambridge: Cambridge University Press, [1790] 2000.

———. *The Critique of Pure Reason*. Translated by Norman Kent Smith. Houndmills: Macmillan Press Ltd., [1787] 1965.

Kemp Smith, N. *The Philosophy of David Hume*. London: Macmillan, 1949.

McDowell, J. *Mind and World*. Cambridge: Harvard University Press, 1994.

Milgram, E. "Hume on Practical Reasoning: *Treatise* 463–469." *Iyyun: The Jerusalem Philosophical Quarterly* 46 (1997): 235–265.

Murdoch, I. *The Sovereignty of Good.* New York: Schocken Books, 1971.

Pupin, M. *Science and Religion: A Symposium.* London: Gerald Howe, 1931.

Putnam, H. *Renewing Philosophy.* Cambridge: Harvard University Press, 1992.

———. "Thoughts Addressed to an Analytical Thomist." *The Monist* 80.4 (1997): 487–499.

———. *The Collapse of the Fact/Value Dichotomy and Other Essays.* Cambridge: Harvard University Press, 2002.

Rosenzweig, F. *The Star of Redemption.* New York: Holt, Rinehart and Winston, [1921] 1971.

Wittgenstein, L. *Lectures and Conversations on Aesthetics, Psychology and Religious Belief: Compiled from Notes Taken by Yorick Smythies, Rush Rhees and James Taylor,* edited by Cyril Barrett. Oxford: Basil Blackwell, 1966.

Wolf-Devine, C. "Descartes on Seeing: Epistemology and Visual Perception." *Journal of the History of Philosophy,* Monograph Series. Carbondale, Ill.: Southern Illinois University Press, 1993.

5

In _____ We Trust: Science, Religion, and Authority

James D. Proctor

Background

When I first delivered the lecture[1] that led to this essay, I was up against some pretty stiff competition: the opening night of *The Matrix: Reloaded*, which not only had a slightly bigger special effects budget than I had, but was all about science and religion. Science, as both diabolical and redemptive technology, science as a seemingly real yet utterly virtual world of computer code in which people are unwittingly trapped like the prisoners in Plato's cave, science as the empowering tool of Morpheus and his band of high-tech freedom fighters.

Yet religion, too. Listen to the strong parallels one scholar draws between the original *Matrix* and the central story of Christianity:

> Neo, like Jesus, is the long-expected Messiah who is ultimately killed only to resurrect as a fully "divine" creature. The final scene even evokes the bodily ascent of Jesus to heaven. Also, Morpheus seems every bit the equivalent of John the Baptist, even to the point of baptizing Neo in a graphic scene in the liquid bowels of the human battery chambers. Trinity might be compared to Mary Magdalene and Cypher clearly parallels Judas.[2]

He also notes the very important Buddhist theme in *The Matrix*, stressing "our ignorance of existential reality" as the fundamental problem both in Buddhism and in the world depicted in the movie.

So we have science on both sides, but most significantly, science is the tool of the oppressor. And religion clearly is the source of insight and strength among Neo and his disciples. Science up against religion. And who wins? In the battle between diabolical science and religious insight, religion prevails. But the victory is short-lived: after all, the original *Matrix* grossed a measly $165 million, thus the imperative to produce sequels such as that competing with my lecture.

Science and religion: powerful stuff in our society, as revealed in *The Matrix* and countless other instances of popular culture. Here, I would like to examine one thread that winds its way through many of these discussions. This is the thread of authority in science and religion. The approach I will take can be clarified by means of a well-known Buddhist proverb, as represented in the early-nineteenth-century artwork by a Zen priest shown in Figure 5.1.

Here the childlike, rotund, enlightened figure, Hotei, points heavenward (note there is no actual moon) and asks: "Mr. Moon, how old are you: seventeen or three?" Doctrine and teachings, according to this proverb, are like a finger pointing to the moon, which represents ultimate reality, or more properly our experience of this ultimate reality. There is wisdom in this proverb, but a cursory reading would overlook how the moon and the finger are intertwined. Science and religion are often understood as mere fingers pointing transparently to reality and God, or the sacred; hence, a good deal of what you read about science and religion constitutes an attempt to harmonize reality and God, to bring these multiple moons together.

Our series has been based on an expanded premise: we are interested in the finger as well as the moon, the human experience of science and religion as well as the realities toward which science and religion point. We do this not because we don't believe in the moon, but because we wish to avoid the intellectual hypocrisy of making certain scientific or religious claims about the moon without acknowledging that this very act involves pointing a finger.

I want to help clarify science and religion by taking the next step. I am interested in the fingers pointing to the finger that points to the moon. When I was working for the Peace Corps in southern Africa in the early 1980s, I met a man who was once a teacher and now wandered the streets of the small border town nearby with a pencil and small notebook in hand. And each time he passed an object that caught his eye he would stop and take notes about it. This man's notebook was filled with glimpses of the moon. But no fingers pointed to him; most people thought he was crazy. There will never be a lecture series devoted to this man. Perhaps the difference is that science and religion offer such rich insights in comparison to the scribblings of a crazy man. But, at bottom, the ultimate reason is that many fingers point—rightly or wrongly— to science and/or religion, and no fingers ever pointed to him.

So if we want to make sense of science and religion, and the realities toward which science and religion point, we must also bring ourselves into the

FIGURE 5.1.

picture. It is our fingers, pointing toward or away from science and/or religion, that complete the picture sketched by the Zen priest. This is why authority, or more precisely trust in authority, matters fundamentally when considering science and religion.

If there is one overarching concern I have that motivates this talk, it's not primarily *what* we believe about the moon, nor even *whom* we trust as authorities, but rather *how* we trust these authorities, and what power these authorities wield over us as a result. I want to treat science, religion, and other major institutions of epistemic and moral authority with respect, but take them off their pedestal, in what I will call a blending of commitment and critique. I want to rebuild science and religion from the bottom up—that is, from the trust we place in them that gives them the right to command our attention. Trust places us in a position of openness to profound insights, but it also places us in a position of vulnerability. Blending commitment and critique recognizes that trust in authority is a good and necessary thing, but that these authorities are, after all, thoroughly human and finite entities. They are, in the truest sense of the old Buddhist proverb, the finger and not the moon, and we must never forget that both are implicated in the act of pointing.

Trust in Authority among Americans

The results of a National Science Foundation–sponsored research project I administered are relevant here.[3] Among other topics, the project concerned the trust Americans place in four domains of authority on matters of true and false, right and wrong. We know that there are different levels of public trust in institutions of science and religion. But science and religion do not stand alone as domains of epistemic and moral authority. Catherine Albanese has written extensively on what she calls "nature religion" in America, a phenomenon she traces from our contemporary environmental age back to the times of early European settlement.[4] As the famous American architect Frank Lloyd Wright once said, "I believe in God, only I spell it Nature." The case of nature religion suggests that many people place nature alongside science and religion as an important authority—think of, for instance, how much we tend to trust products that are natural, the ways many people regard nature as a source of spiritual insight, or the notion that a society based on the principles of nature would be in much better condition than it is now.[5] These notions build upon long-standing historical traditions: the tradition of natural law—descending at least from Saint Thomas Aquinas of the thirteenth century and arguably reaching back to Aristotle—in which standards of morality are related to the nature of the world and of humans, and the rather different tradition of naturalism, which regards nature as a substitute for God in explaining physical and human reality. Nature is thus an interestingly complex authority, spanning theism, spirituality, and antisupernaturalism alike. To this trilogy I add government or state as a fourth authority, based in part on the work of scholars of religion such as Robert Bellah[6] on a phenomenon they call civil religion, a veneration of state and national identity that implies a trust in government not simply as a political power, but also for larger epistemic and moral matters.

I, then, was interested in exploring the trust Americans place in these four authorities: science, religion, nature, and state.[7] There are important differences between, and complexities within, these authorities that must be acknowledged at the outset. For example, science, religion, and the state can readily be identified with human institutions, but nature is an elusive and abstract category, perhaps more of a subliminal authority than the others. Additionally, these authorities can mean different things to different people. Science, for instance, can mean technology to one person and a certain form of rationality to another, while religion could mean God or it could imply the thoroughly human institutions of religion that many Americans escape by calling themselves "spiritual, not religious."[8] Because of these and other complexities, I utilized a dual methodological strategy, involving a quantitative survey of over one thousand Americans administered between April and June, 2002,[9] and a follow-up set of in-depth qualitative interviews of roughly one hundred selected survey respondents over the summer of 2002.

Let's remember a few features of 2002 related to trust in authority. Perhaps the most important item was the continued U.S. response to the terror attacks of September 11, 2001: if we had delivered the survey and interviews just one year prior, the political climate would have been altogether different. Recall that, for at least some Americans, the election of George W. Bush to the presidency in late 2000 was mired in questionable legal practices stretching from Florida to the Supreme Court. September 11 gave the United States an enemy and thus a new authority to the president and the federal government. By spring 2002, the enemy was increasingly portrayed as Iraq, specifically Saddam Hussein, preparations were being finalized for the new Department of Homeland Security, terror alerts continued throughout the country, and in general, the issue of trust or distrust in government was perhaps never more timely, as Americans struggled to make sense of these sweeping changes affecting their country and their lives.

The status of other authorities was in the news as well: religion received both increased zeal and scrutiny in the light of September 11, and the connection between religion and government was highlighted in June 2002 as the U.S. 9th Circuit Court of Appeals ruled that the words "under God" in the Pledge of Allegiance amount to a government endorsement of religion, prompting leaders on all sides of the political fence to rush to decry the ruling, though—if political cartoons are any indication of the breadth of public opinion—Americans were more divided, expressing both trust and distrust in God, government, conservatives, and liberals in the context of this controversy.

Religion received attention for another reason in the spring of 2002: the sex scandals of Catholic priests and their apparent cover-up by the Roman Catholic Church. In comparison to the state and religion, science and nature received relatively less attention, though there was some concern over genetics and cloning, as well as the marked shift of the Bush administration on environmental policy. But trust and distrust were expressed in other realms as well, from baseball in the summer of 2002 to the revelations throughout the year of major corporate scandals and their possible connections with the Bush administration.

With all this bad news, you would think that Americans would have expressed high levels of distrust in authority. This refusal to accept authority at face value was an apparent feature of the country that so enamored one famous nineteenth-century European student of American democracy, the Frenchman Alexis de Tocqueville, that he envisioned a new model of authority emanating from the American experience. To de Tocqueville, the bonds of traditional authority were weak even in the American family:

> In America the family, in the Roman and aristocratic signification of the word, does not exist. . . . [As] soon as the young American approaches manhood, the ties of filial obedience are relaxed day by day; master of his thoughts, he is soon master of his conduct. . . . When the condition of society becomes democratic and men adopt as their general principle that it is good and lawful to judge of all things for oneself, using former points of belief not as a rule of faith, but simply as a means of information, the power which the opinions of a father exercise over those of his sons diminishes.[10]

Yet trust in authority in contemporary America is generally stronger than in European societies. Results from a 1998 survey conducted under the auspices of the International Social Survey Programme (ISSP) suggest that Americans display a much higher trust in religion than do people from European countries, and a somewhat higher trust in government.[11] An earlier ISSP survey from 1993 asked respondents to indicate their trust in science, and it also had an interesting question concerning sacredness in nature which we can use as a surrogate for some form of deep trust in nature. The results show that Americans tend to trust science more than people from other countries included in the survey, but do not trust nature as highly. Thus, on a relative scale, Americans are near the top in trust in religion, close to the top in trust in science, above average in trust in government, and below average in trust in nature.

Now let's examine the results of our survey of adult Americans. We gauged respondents' levels of concern for twelve categories of policy issues, and for those where a high level of concern was expressed, we asked respondents to rate science, religion, nature, and state as authoritative sources of information or guidance with respect to that policy issue. Then we calculated the average trust expressed for each of these authorities. We also included two questions for each of these four authorities that probed the possibility of what one could call "hypertrust," an extreme or exclusive trust in authority. Finally, toward the end of the survey, we asked respondents to give a summary rating of their overall trust in these authorities as sources of information or guidance for their lives.

I can give you some general statistics. In terms of overall trust in these four authorities on a scale of 0 to 10, with 5 as a midpoint, the average trust expressed by Americans was relatively comparable, ranging from 5.5 for government to 6.7 for science, with religion and nature in between. There was much more variability in the responses of Americans on religion than, for instance, science: religion is both trusted strongly and distrusted relatively strongly.

For the questions on hypertrust there was more variability between authorities. As examples, the mean response to the statement "Science will eventually answer all important questions about humans, the world, and the universe" was only 3.7 on a scale of 0 to 10, whereas "The Bible is the literal word of God" had an average of 5.8. "There would be more peace and harmony in society if we simply followed nature" had an average of 5.4, and—though one could argue that public opinion from 2002 contradicts this—the statement "Our American government can be trusted to tell the truth" had an average of only 3.5. Each of these statements elicited considerable variability among Americans, though few people showed strong hypertrust in science and in state.

What is more interesting than overall statistics, however, are the patterns in trust placed by individuals in these four authorities. Examining the overall trust responses, for instance, one sees a strong correlation between trust in religion and trust in state, and another strong correlation between trust in science and trust in nature. What this means is that people who tended to trust, or distrust, religion felt likewise about the government, and the same with nature and science. By applying a procedure called factor analysis to all sixteen trust variables, these patterns come into sharper focus, as two primary underlying factors or composite models of trust are revealed. The first involved a hypertrust (or distrust) in religion, including strong adherence to traditional theological tenets, and trust (or distrust) in state; this factor alone explains nearly a quarter of all the differences (i.e., variance) in the entire set of sixteen variables. A second model is close behind: the model of linked trust in science and nature. This model, too, has both adherents and detractors. Note that, following typical factor analysis procedure, these two models are assumed to be independent of each other: it's not that Americans choose either God and government *or* science and nature—they could choose both or neither.

Interestingly, there was relatively little association of these models with standard demographics; those who were young and old, male and female, rich and poor, educated and uneducated can be found supporting or opposing both models. However, in one strong difference between the two models, people who trust religion and state tend to identify as politically and morally conservative, whereas the opposite is true of those who trust in science and nature.

We also interviewed selected respondents in depth, and we asked those who scored in the top and bottom extremes of each of these models of trust in authority to say more about it. Among those who trust strongly in God and government, you do find some relatively pure cases of trust, as in respondent number 584, a 61-year-old, well-educated woman from Alabama:

> I was raised to trust in God and I do, and again I think that our government is better than anywhere else that we could be and I would like to think that people are trying to do right.

But just as often, those who scored the highest were reluctant to speak as if they trusted everything they heard, especially from the government; for instance, respondent 608, a 19-year-old Latina student from California, says:

> I believe in certain religious things . . . I don't know I believe in the government but I believe that they're not doing as much as they could be doing. So that's why I don't believe as highly in government as I do in religion because [with] religion I can have my own beliefs.

Those on the other end of the spectrum, however, were quite willing to characterize themselves as not trusting in religion and state, and some offered their own theories as to the linkage; for instance, respondent 466, a 56-year-old female from Michigan, says:

> I think it's accurate in so far as government and religion are hierarchies. . . . Religion is a hierarchy. An ecclesiastical hierarchy. Government is a bureaucracy. Those types of entities, with my relationship and my recent history with them—I'm talking about the last half a century—are not credible. They are not truth-tellers. They are at times, but they are not purveyors of truth as much as they are formers of opinion and modifiers of behavior.

In the case of the second model of trust in authority, those who scored the highest were quite willing to admit their trust in science and nature. Respondent 561, for instance, a 60-year-old man from Washington State, says:

> Well, I mean science brings us the truth, as best as they can, and nature *is* the truth, and we need both to have a balanced way. To survive.

On the other end, those who scored the lowest were similarly willing to express either strong distrust or irrelevance to their lives; for instance, respondent 28, a wealthy 44-year-old from Pennsylvania, says:

Science doesn't necessarily have all the answers, although they may think so. You look at some of the scientists, and they think we all evolved from some exploding dinosaur, but I don't think so. . . . I trust nature in the fact that nature's here and it's been provided by God, but I don't trust that for my source of being.

These responses raise the very important question: why the strong alliance between religion and state, and between nature and science? The interviews suggest lots of possible combinations, but the overall pattern is clear. I will venture two answers at this point. The first is probably obvious to you: this is, in part, how these authorities are packaged in contemporary American culture, especially the connection between God and government. We need look no further than the American president, who, as commentators have noted, frequently resorts to religious language and images. His 2003 State of the Union message, for instance, ended with an explicit linkage of God and American destiny:

> The liberty we prize is not America's gift to the world, it is God's gift to humanity. We Americans have faith in ourselves, but not in ourselves alone. We do not know . . . all the ways of Providence, yet we can trust in them, placing our confidence in the loving God behind all of life, and all of history. May He guide us now. And may God continue to bless the United States of America.

A second explanation is more speculative, but worth considering. There is an interesting structural similarity between these two models: each has an ultimate authority—religion, or ultimately God, on the one hand, and nature on the other—as well as an authoritative human institution—the state, or science—that represents and communicates the truths of their respective ultimate authority in the human realm. Now, of course, in the case of religion and government, this association is tantamount to theocracy, a violation of the U.S. constitutional separation of church and state. Yet support for a linkage of church and state is stronger in the United States than in many other countries, as revealed by 1998 ISSP results. The second model's linkage, between science and nature, is well represented in many people's views of ecology: here again—perhaps less problematically than with the theocracy model—the human institution of science is understood as an authoritative conduit for the ultimate authority of nature, following Enlightenment naturalism.

Trust in Authority: A Deeper Examination

Let's now think more deeply about trust in authority. I'll begin by making a few important points, which are perhaps self-evident yet are often forgotten.

(1) Trust in science and religion is prior to belief. Many studies of the popular uptake of science and/or religion focus on beliefs, such as theism, evolutionism, or materialism, as indicative of behavior. But ours is a highly plural world of meaning, in which diverse truths are proclaimed; to return to our former analogy, many fingers are pointing at a particular moon. Trust is the filter that commits us to certain of these beliefs and avoids others, based on the messenger as well as the message. We choose which authoritative finger to point our own fingers at, and based on this commitment, we open ourselves to understanding the moon as revealed by this or that authoritative finger. That's why I'm more concerned about trust than belief: trust is prior to belief.

(2) Trust in science and religion may be necessary, yet entails vulnerability. As in personal relationships, trust involves commitment without full under-standing or control, which we do not have over this world, not even our own lives. We cannot simply point our own finger to the moon in an act of defiant isolation; to some degree we must depend on those fingers we consider au-thoritative. But this commitment places us in a vulnerable position: we could be manipulated, or manipulate ourselves. Many people have blamed religion for preying upon vulnerable souls, but science, or more specifically a certain form of rationality associated with science, has come under scrutiny as well.

(3) Ultimately, what I'd like to argue is that, given their powerful roles as authorities, science and religion must encourage more mature forms of trust that blend commitment and critique. For better and for worse, many of us trust science and/or religion to guide our lives. We must choose wisely. But these authoritative fingers pointing to the moon have a duty to encourage a trust formed with both eyes open, a trust that blends the commitment of pointing our finger this way or that with the critical insight that we are, after all, only pointing our fingers at other fingers, and not at the moon itself.

Let's see how we could move toward this final point, by way of an expanded discussion of trust in authority.

What do I mean by "trust"? I distinguish trust from two related terms, "faith" and "confidence." Faith implies for many people a sort of blind convey-ance of trust, something unreasonable, irrational. It is a term many people reserve for religion. Yet physical chemist-turned-philosopher Michael Polanyi argued that faith is central to the scientist's commitment to the beliefs and norms of the scientific community,[12] and philosopher Mary Midgley has writ-ten that science is another form of religion, offering an alternative path to salvation for those who will put their faith in the scientific world-picture.[13] Indeed, Midgley defines faith much as I define trust, saying:

> Faith is not primarily a belief in particular facts. . . . The faith we live
> by is something that you must have before you can ask whether any-
> thing is true or not. It is basic trust. It is acceptance of a map, a
> perspective, a set of standards and assumptions, an enclosing vision

within which facts are placed. It is a way of organizing the vast jumble of data. In our age, when that jumble is getting more and more confusing, the need for such principles of organization is not going away. It is increasing.[14]

I will retain the term "trust" versus "faith" to avoid confusion over certain readings of faith, and also to emphasize the relational character of trust. If faith is an act on the part of the faithful, trust is both a premise for, and a desired outcome of, a relationship. This is where trust differs from confidence, a term often used in social surveys. What is your level of confidence in the economy? the media? and so on. But confidence is an instrumental, not a relational, property: one decides whether or not to invest in stocks based on confidence, but one decides whether or not to invest one's life in a relationship, or a meaningful network of relationships such as a religious organization, based on trust.[15]

Most of the literature on trust concerns its significance in interpersonal and professional relationships, regarding it anywhere from a mere social and economic lubricant,[16] to an intensely personal but inescapably political set of what Anthony Giddens calls "facework" commitments,[17] to the fundamental existential challenge in the first year of human life.[18] My interest lies in extending the capacity for trust learned from interpersonal relations to more distant authorities: this is similar to what Giddens calls "faceless" commitments and Niklas Luhmann calls "system trust," except trust in authority often takes forms that are quite personal and concrete rather than impersonal and abstract. When people say they trust in God, they do not generally imply some broad Platonic principle; even when people say their trust lies in scientific rationality and not God, the level of commitment and passion implied in this form of trust is often as deeply personal as that of the theist.

An important question concerns the "why" of trust in authority. As noted in the Mary Midgley quote earlier, it would be naïve to think that the necessity for trust in authority has diminished in modern times: perhaps our allegiances have shifted, and the decline in religious authority is evident especially in Europe, but trust appears to be here to stay. Luhmann argues that the very nature of modernity is its "unmanageable complexity," necessitating trust as the basis for the inevitable risk-taking behavior in which we all must engage.[19]

But trust in authority is not simply an individual act on our parts, as authority is both produced and consumed: institutions of authority expend considerable effort in achieving and maintaining legitimacy, that is, in securing our trust. To explore this two-way street of producing and consuming authority, the term "authority" requires further clarification. As with trust, authority is a relational concept: it does not exist unless it is recognized. Hannah Arendt distinguishes authority from relationships based on coercion on the one hand, and mere persuasion on the other; authority involves an agreed-upon hierarchy.[20] The *Oxford English Dictionary* distinguishes between two types of authority: involuntary authority, such as political and legal systems that demand our obedience whether or not we agree with them, and voluntary authority, that which concerns us here.[21]

My interest lies in authority as involving two forms of content: epistemic authority over what is true and false in how the world is, and moral authority over what is right and wrong in how the world ought to be. Authority is usually discussed in its political context, but assertions concerning epistemic and moral matters are arguably found in all contexts in which authority is exercised. It is convenient to think of science as a purely epistemic authority and religion as a purely moral authority; then they would be legitimate in their respective realms, and there is no possibility of conflict.

Such was the argument of the late Harvard paleontologist Stephen Jay Gould, who suggested that science and religion constitute NOMA or "nonoverlapping magisteria."[22] Gould's NOMA argument, though popular with many people and certainly conciliatory toward science and religion, nonetheless presents highly truncated notions of both scientific and religious authority. It is true that scientific authority is often grounded by reference to expert opinions on the facts, and religious authority is often claimed primarily over matters of value, but these schemes represent more of a political settlement worked out over the last few centuries than a reflection of some neat divide between facts and values, a commonly assumed schema with surprisingly little justification.[23]

This leads to an interesting challenge, what I call the "competing gods" problem: there are many claims to authority out there, which cannot be entirely ignored. As we discovered with religion and state, and with nature and science, a common answer to the competing gods problem is to forge alliances, to link up one's authority with another authority so as to declare an alignment of the constellations. This approach is exceedingly effective, perhaps because it addresses the discomfort most people experience with cognitive dissonance between two competing authoritative claims.[24] Thus the groundswell of interest in harmonizing science and religion, which seems primarily driven by a need to bring them into alliance.

Consider the imagined relations between science, religion, and state in the tragedy that took place over the skies of the United States, stretching from California to Texas, on the morning of February 1, 2003.[25] Here science and science-based technology provided both the underlying rationale and the source of protection for the one Israeli and six American crew members on board the U.S. space shuttle *Columbia* as they hurtled through space. Yet the comforting authority many people place on scientific expertise was shattered as the space shuttle itself, and its fragile occupants, were lost following heat buildup upon reentry. Many of the editorial cartoons of the time focused on— and generally justified—the issue at hand, namely scientific exploration. But many, many more resorted to highly anthropomorphic images of religion, as the God of what were apparently six Christians and one Jew served as the ultimate Protector. Others linked the tragedy directly to the American political identity.

These images contrasted sharply with the very technical reports emanating from NASA. The strategies available to NASA officials as they struggled to regain trust in their authority were limited: they could not build explicit alliances with state or with religion to share the blame. But NASA officials were aided nonetheless by a political and cultural climate in which God and government were closely allied with the space shuttle mission. Yes, science stumbled, but the very important scientific, economic, and moral questions that concern manned space research never found their way onto the editorial pages because of the distributed political and cultural effort to ensure that the broader authoritative network, this overarching alliance of religion, science, and state, was maintained.

There are certain philosophical meta-arguments common to science and religion in producing what appears to be convincingly legitimate authority. I'd like to mention one: objectivity, a claim to authoritative certainty on a reality separate from those claims, a moon far removed from the finger. Science is famous for this, but objectivity is not an inevitable feature of scientific institutions. Philosopher and historian Stephen Toulmin has argued that European modernity involved not one but two traditions: an earlier tradition of Renaissance humanism grounded in a tolerant blend of religion, science, and the arts, exemplified in the work of Erasmus, Montaigne, and Shakespeare; and what he calls the seventeenth-century Counter-Renaissance, when economic crisis and religious struggle resulted in an emphasis on the rational pursuit of abstract objectivity by key figures such as Descartes and Newton.[26] Scientific objectivity can, in Toulmin's view, be traced directly back to this seventeenth-century "struggle for certainty"; it is now, as it was then, epistemologically unnecessary to science, but politically advantageous in grounding claims of authority in uncertain times.

There are perhaps deeper reasons, and contradictions, underlying the premise of objectivity as well. Science studies scholar Evelyn Fox Keller invokes feminist and psychoanalytical theory in her attempt to fathom objectivity:

> The objectivist illusion reflects back a self as autonomous and objectified: an image of individuals unto themselves, severed from the outside world of other objects (animate as well as inanimate) and simultaneously from their own subjectivity.[27]

Objectivity is as much a feature of the transcendent God of certain Western religious traditions as the transcendent reality of Descartes. Yet religion, in claiming authority not just on matters about God but also on matters of the subject, the religious believer, necessarily adopts a divided stance on objectivity. Religion becomes, in essence, both "true" along objectivist lines and "true for me" in the subjectivist eyes of the believer, both a "fact" and a "value."

The problem with the whole scheme, as suggested in several essays in this volume, is that objects and subjects are not separable—in fact, as Harold Oliver argues in this volume, one can understand objects and subjects as derivative of relations. It is not that objects and subjects happen to relate, but that the very sense of object and subject assumes a prior relation between them. More concretely, there are profound ethical problems with the fact-value distinction implied in the object/subject dichotomy, where facts cling to objects and values cling to subjects: ethics becomes marginalized in a science devoid of values, yet amounts to moralizing among certain religious groups who claim to hold the truth on values.[28]

If you don't believe that claims to objectivity are central to scientific or religious authority, try challenging this philosophical premise among adherents and see what happens—I suggest you keep a safe distance when you do this. Thankfully, there are many devoted scientists and religious followers who have no problem admitting that objectivity is not the most accurate way to understand the truths they pursue or believe so passionately. But there are many who respond with mixed scorn and pity for the ignorance of those who cannot see the light: the story is repeated among scientists, for instance, of how physicist Alan Sokal proved the intellectual vacuity of would-be assailants of objectivity once and for all by publishing a parody of the movement in one of their very own journals, *Social Text*,[29] or, on the side of religion, how would-be doubters of the existence of a transcendent God have long been proven wrong.

So much for the production of authority; let us now consider its consumption, because that is where each of us comes in. One problem is what is known as authoritarianism, a mode of hypertrust in authority. Authoritarian personality theory was first suggested in the work of Erich Fromm.[30] To Fromm, freedom is the essential right and responsibility of being human, but with the evolution of individualism came not more freedom but less as people rushed away from its responsibilities and challenges.

This "escape from freedom," which Fromm witnessed in the aftermath of World War I, is primarily manifested in authoritarianism, founded on "the conviction that life is determined by forces outside of man's own self, his interest, his wishes. The only possible happiness lies in the submission to those forces."[31] Fromm's theory was applied in a major empirical study by Theodor Adorno and others,[32] who explained it developmentally in terms of child-parent relations, and postulated a number of features, including authoritarian aggression and submission, superstition, black-and-white views, destructiveness, and heightened prejudice. Adorno's theory has been criticized on both conceptual and empirical grounds, but one early finding that has been supported in more recent studies is that some sort of authoritarianism seems character-istic of the political right but not the political left.[33]

Related to authoritarianism or hypertrust is the problem of hyperobedi-ence, revealed in the classic but highly debated study by Stanley Milgram.[34] In this famous project from the early 1960s, Milgram devised an experiment whereby subjects were instructed to administer electric shocks to students when they missed answers on a verbally administered quiz, increasing the level of shock with each mistake. The shocks were not real, but the students acted as if they were in considerable pain. Nonetheless, on the stern urging of the experimenter, the majority of subjects raised the shock level to the maximum of 450 volts in spite of severe posted warnings on the device, the students' apparent pain, and the subject's own expressed doubts. Milgram says:

> This is . . . the most fundamental lesson of our study: ordinary peo-ple, simply doing their jobs, and without any particular hostility on their part, can become agents in a terrible destructive process. More-over, even when the destructive effects of their work become pat-ently clear, and they are asked to carry out actions incompatible with fundamental standards of morality, relatively few people have the re-sources needed to resist authority.[35]

Yet authoritarianism and obedience are complex. We found this by asking people if they had doubts about their trust in authority, which many of our respondents were quite willing to share with us. Respondent 195, a 33 year old woman from Texas, for instance, said of science:

> The distrust comes with thinking that they've got this report out on this now but ten years from now they're gonna realize they were wrong or there's more to it, and, so you wonder how much to believe.

And of religion:

> Just more and more I'm seeing that there's a lot of corruption in religious leaders as there are with anybody else in a position of power and it just makes me wonder if the organizational part of reli-gion is really necessary.

And of government:

> I'm never sure what to believe when one thing comes out because there's always gonna be something else, and half the time you're not getting the whole story.

And of nature:

> Not so much [struggle over trust] with that as with the others, I mean, nature in and of itself is not really trying to be deceptive. There may be mysteries, but it's not an intentional deception.

What does this all mean? In particular, is trust in science and/or religion necessarily linked with authoritarian obedience, or does it lead to more responsible forms? I could produce evidence supporting a favorable or harsh reading of both, but there are warning signs. For religion, think of the old standard hymn "Trust and Obey," and the injunction in the New Testament— one I often hear on patriotic Christian-radio talk shows—from Romans 13, which reads "Everyone must submit himself to the governing authorities, for there is no authority except that which God has established." Science has no equivalent sacred text with such explicit wording, and yet in its common claims to objectivity and universality, its common excuse that values are beyond the pale of science, there can be an implicit call to a similarly singular obedience. I suspect that authoritarianism is possible with any authority, but is certainly exacerbated if encouraged by that institution of authority.

Reenvisioning Science, Religion, and Trust

Consider, by way of conclusion, three alternatives for science, religion, and the webs of trusting relationships we spin with them. The first option, the authoritarian vision, is commitment without critique: science and/or religion possess insights to dazzling realities, and we would do well to follow them without question. The second is its opposite, critique without commitment, perhaps embodied in the paradigm of secularization with respect to religion. The third alternative is to explore ways of blending commitment and critique, to refuse to believe that these are zero-sum entities such that the more committed you are, the less your apparent capacity to think for yourself, and the more critical you become, the less bound you apparently are to communities that struggle for meaning.

I would like to reflect on these three options by closing, as I began, with reference to a major film on science and religion, one I suspect you may have seen. In 1890, an aspiring writer declared the following:

> The age of faith is sinking slowly into the past; our new unfaith
> gives us an eager longing to penetrate the secrets of Nature—an as-
> piration for knowledge we have been taught is forbidden. . . . The
> number of churchgoers is gradually growing less. The people are be-
> ginning to think that studying science . . . is the enemy of the
> church. Science, however, we know to be true.[36]

Ten years later this writer published a little book titled *The Wonderful Wizard of Oz*, and nearly fifty years later the movie we all know so well was released. Apparently, what the *Chronicles of Narnia* were for English literature scholar and Christian apologist C. S. Lewis, *The Wizard of Oz* was, perhaps in a quite different sense, for L. Frank Baum: a popular children's tale presenting a subtle yet sweeping statement about religion.

But what exactly was Baum trying to say? One interpretation, as suggested in his quote noted above, is the triumph of rational critique over religious commitment. This is from an essay entitled "*The Wizard of Oz* as the Ultimate Atheist Metaphor":

> In the film *The Wizard of Oz*, L. Frank Baum and Noel Langley have created the quintessential story of mankind's triumph over our primitive beliefs in the supernatural, in organized religion, and even in god.[37]

Well, well. Now let us consider a rather different interpretation, one that prefers the option of commitment by faith—without doubting, or certainly without critique—to God's path. This interpretation comes from a sermon entitled "Christian Themes in *The Wizard of Oz*":

> Very often, God will require that we step out in faith to do what would, to all appearances, seem to be impossible. The wizard says, "Bring me the broomstick of the Wicked Witch of the West. . . . Bring me her broomstick and I'll grant your requests." . . . To all outward appearances, to fetch the broomstick of the wicked witch would seem an impossible task. But with the help of God, all things are possible. , , , And so it is for those who follow the path of the Lord—the path of righteousness. . . . If we are obedient, God will get us through the frightening and evil things we encounter.[38]

I prefer the third option, of blending commitment and critique. As I have suggested earlier, commitment without critique is not only dangerous, it is ultimately irresponsible in the deepest sense of personal responsibility. But commitment without critique is at least an option; critique without commitment is not. To imagine that one is an entirely independent and free thinker, that one trusts no authority outside of oneself, is delusional. We can change our commitments, but we cannot cease to commit ourselves to some form of epistemic and moral authority. "Trust thyself," Emerson invoked; but if each of us trusted only what we directly experience and understand, our lives would grind to a halt.

We get, I believe, no better sense of the life of blending commitment and critique than as is revealed near the conclusion to *The Wizard of Oz*. Dorothy and her companions, who traveled far to find the Wizard and undertook a perilous assignment at his demand, have finally vanquished the Wicked Witch of the West and returned to the Wizard. And he is still a terrifying authority to them. Yet, as the Scarecrow points out to Dorothy, her humble dog, Toto, has revealed that the Great and Powerful Oz is just an ordinary man standing behind a curtain.

But the movie does not end there. The human face of authority does not necessarily deny its potential for wisdom, a far deeper form of authority than one based on power and inaccessibility. The Wizard of Oz is just a man, but he is a rather wise man, and imparts to Dorothy and her companions gifts that are far more profound than they had requested. Each comes with a sly twist: as, for example, the Wizard presents a diploma to the Scarecrow he confers on him the "honorary degree of Th.D."—not a doctorate in theology, but a doctorate in what the Wizard calls "Thinkology." By trusting this man even after his mystique has vanished, Dorothy and her companions are transformed. Dorothy ultimately learns that she must trust herself in order to get home, but by trusting the Wizard she and her companions have learned to trust themselves.

This is where blending commitment and critique come together, as both necessitate trust: trust in the wisdom that lies beyond oneself implied in commitment, and trust of one's own doubts and strengths implied in critique. Let us remember that, by pulling the curtains open on science, religion, nature, the state, or any other authority we trust to guide us, we will reveal the inescapable humanness of these institutions of authority. They are but the finger pointing to the moon.

There is, I would venture, no Great and Powerful Oz, at least in the form of a man up in the clouds, nor in the form of some scientifically tractable force out there guiding the unfolding of the universe. But there decidedly is something we experience called the Moon, and we make sense of that experience in part by trusting those authorities we deem wise.

My hope is to have suggested how commitment and critique can indeed get along, how both religious and scientific commitment can be big enough to embrace the hard questions the scholarly community—which itself embodies certain commitments it must acknowledge—will pose. It will take an effort from each one of us, but if we work at it we can collectively remove science and religion from their pedestals, invigorate them with humanity and humility, and ultimately develop a deeper trust and respect for them, and for each other, in the process.

NOTES

1. I would like to acknowledge the helpful comments of Catherine Albanese and Jon Cruz, who served as discussants for the original lecture presented on May 15, 2003.

2. James L. Ford, "Buddhism, Christianity, and *The Matrix*: The Dialectic of Myth-Making in Contemporary Cinema," *The Journal of Religion and Film* 4.2 (2000).

3. The project is discussed in more detail on a Web site, http://real.geog.ucsb .edu/esr. I would like to acknowledge the generosity of the National Science Foundation via research grant BCS-0082009. I'd especially like to acknowledge two graduate

students, Evan Berry of Religious Studies and Tricia Mein of Sociology, who worked alongside me.

4. Catherine L. Albanese, *Nature Religion in America: From the Algonkian Indians to the New Age*, Chicago History of American Religion (Chicago: University of Chicago Press, 1990); Catherine L. Albanese, *Reconsidering Nature Religion* (Harrisburg, Pa.: Trinity Press International, 2002).

5. See, for instance, Ian L. McHarg, *Design with Nature* (Garden City, N.Y.: Natural History Press, 1969).

6. Robert Neelly Bellah, *The Broken Covenant: American Civil Religion in a Time of Trial* (New York: Seabury Press, 1975).

7. We also were interested in trust in self, but discovered that few people were willing to admit they didn't trust themselves, so the notion of self as authority won't be included here.

8. Brian J. Zinnbauer, Kenneth I. Pargament, Brenda Cole, Mark S. Rye, Eric M. Butter, Timothy G. Belavich, Kathleen M. Hipp, Allie B. Scott, and Jill L. Kadar, "Religion and Spirituality: Unfuzzying the Fuzzy," *Journal for the Scientific Study of Religion* 36.4 (1997): 549–564; Penny Long and C. Kirk Hadaway Marler, " 'Being Religious' or 'Being Spiritual' in America: A Zero-Sum Proposition?," *Journal for the Scientific Study of Religion* 41.2 (2002): 289–300.

9. Thanks to Paolo Gardinali and UCSB's Social Science Survey Center for their assistance.

10. Alexis de Tocqueville, Henry Reeve, and John C. Spencer, *Democracy in America* (New York: J. and H. G. Langley, 1841), 2: Chapter 8.

11. Data available from ISSP Web site at www.issp.org; all analyses cited here and below, by author.

12. Michael Polanyi, *Science, Faith and Society*, Riddell Memorial Lectures (London: Oxford University Press, 1946).

13. Mary Midgley, *Science as Salvation: A Modern Myth and Its Meaning*, Gifford Lectures (London: Routledge, 1992).

14. Ibid, 57.

15. See Niklas Luhmann, *Trust and Power: Two Works* (New York: John Wiley and Sons, 1979).

16. Francis Fukuyama, *Trust: The Social Virtues and the Creation of Prosperity* (New York: Free Press, 1995).

17. Anthony Giddens, *The Consequences of Modernity* (Stanford. Stanford University Press, 1990).

18. Erik H. Erikson, *Childhood and Society* (New York: W. W. Norton, 1950).

19. Luhmann, *Trust and Power*.

20. Hannah Arendt, *Between Past and Future: Eight Exercises in Political Thought* (New York: Viking Press, 1968).

21. Sociologist Max Weber further distinguishes between rational, traditional, and charismatic appeals to legitimate authority. See Max Weber, *Economy and Society: An Outline of Interpretive Sociology* (New York: Bedminster Press, 1968).

22. Stephen Jay Gould, *Rocks of Ages: Science and Religion in the Fullness of Life*, The Library of Contemporary Thought (New York: Ballantine Publishing Group, 1999).

23. Hilary Putnam, *The Collapse of the Fact/Value Dichotomy and Other Essays* (Cambridge: Harvard University Press, 2002).

24. Leon Festinger, *A Theory of Cognitive Dissonance* (Stanford: Stanford University Press, 1957); Elliot Aronson, "The Theory of Cognitive Dissonance: The Evolution and Vicissitudes of an Idea," in *The Message of Social Psychology: Perspectives on Mind and Society*, eds. Craig McGarty and S. Alexander Haslam (Cambridge, Mass.: Blackwell Publishers, 1997), 20–35.

25. See http://www.nasa.gov/columbia/home/index.html.

26. Stephen Edelston Toulmin, *Cosmopolis: The Hidden Agenda of Modernity* (Chicago: University of Chicago Press, 1992).

27. Evelyn Fox Keller, *Reflections on Gender and Science* (New Haven: Yale University Press, 1995), 70.

28. See Hilary Putnam's excellent treatment in his *The Collapse of the Fact/Value Dichotomy and Other Essays* (Cambridge, Mass.: Harvard University Press, 2002).

29. Alan D. Sokal, "Transgressing the Boundaries: Towards a Transformative Hermeneutics of Quantum Gravity," *Social Text* 46/47 (spring–summer 1996): 217–252.

30. Erich Fromm, *Escape from Freedom* (New York: Rinehart and Company, Inc., 1941).

31. Ibid., 171.

32. Theodor W. Adorno, *The Authoritarian Personality*, Studies in Prejudice (New York: Harper and Row, 1950).

33. Jim Sidanius and Felicia Pratto, *Social Dominance: An Intergroup Theory of Social Hierarchy and Oppression* (Cambridge: Cambridge University Press, 1999).

34. Stanley Milgram, *Obedience to Authority: An Experimental View* (New York: Harper and Row, 1974).

35. Ibid., 6.

36. Quoted in William Leach, *Land of Desire: Merchants, Power, and the Rise of a New American Culture* (New York: Pantheon Books, 1993), 247.

37. Kevin Courcey, "*The Wizard of Oz* as the Ultimate Atheist Metaphor," *The Willamette Freethinker*, Corvallis Secular Society, Oregon, January 1998. Available online at http://css.peak.org.

38. Richard M. Riss, "Christian Themes in *The Wizard of Oz*," 1997. Available online at http://www.grmi.org/renewal/Richard_Riss/sermons/0003.html.

BIBLIOGRAPHY

Adorno, Theodor W. *The Authoritarian Personality*. Studies in Prejudice. New York: Harper and Row, 1950.

Albanese, Catherine L. *Nature Religion in America: From the Algonkian Indians to the New Age*. Chicago History of American Religion. Chicago: University of Chicago Press, 1990.

———. *Reconsidering Nature Religion*. Harrisburg, Pa.: Trinity Press International, 2002.

Arendt, Hannah. *Between Past and Future: Eight Exercises in Political Thought*. New York: Viking Press, 1968.

Aronson, Elliot. "The Theory of Cognitive Dissonance: The Evolution and Vicissitudes of an Idea." In *The Message of Social Psychology: Perspectives on Mind and Society,* edited by Craig McGarty and S. Alexander Haslam. Cambridge, Mass.: Blackwell Publishers, 1997.

Bellah, Robert Neelly. *The Broken Covenant: American Civil Religion in a Time of Trial.* New York: Seabury Press, 1975.

Courcey, Kevin. "*The Wizard of Oz* as the Ultimate Atheist Metaphor." *The Willamette Freethinker,* Corvallis Secular Society, Oregon, January 1998.

Erikson, Erik H. *Childhood and Society.* New York: W. W. Norton, 1950.

Festinger, Leon. *A Theory of Cognitive Dissonance.* Stanford: Stanford University Press, 1957.

Ford, James L. "Buddhism, Christianity, and *The Matrix*: The Dialectic of Myth-Making in Contemporary Cinema." *The Journal of Religion and Film* 4.2 (2000).

Fromm, Erich. *Escape from Freedom.* New York: Rinehart and Company, Inc., 1941.

Fukuyama, Francis. *Trust: The Social Virtues and the Creation of Prosperity.* New York: Free Press, 1995.

Giddens, Anthony. *The Consequences of Modernity.* Stanford: Stanford University Press, 1990.

Gould, Stephen Jay. *Rocks of Ages: Science and Religion in the Fullness of Life.* The Library of Contemporary Thought. New York: Ballantine Publishing Group, 1999.

Keller, Evelyn Fox. *Reflections on Gender and Science.* New Haven: Yale University Press, 1995.

Leach, William. *Land of Desire: Merchants, Power, and the Rise of a New American Culture.* New York: Pantheon Books, 1993.

Luhmann, Niklas. *Trust and Power: Two Works.* New York: John Wiley and Sons, 1979.

Marler, Penny Long, and C. Kirk Hadaway. "'Being Religious' or 'Being Spiritual' in America: A Zero-Sum Proposition?" *Journal for the Scientific Study of Religion* 41.2 (2002): 289–300.

McHarg, Ian L. *Design with Nature.* Garden City, N.Y.: Natural History Press, 1969.

Midgley, Mary. *Science as Salvation: A Modern Myth and Its Meaning.* Gifford Lectures. London: Routledge, 1992.

Milgram, Stanley. *Obedience to Authority: An Experimental View.* New York: Harper and Row, 1974.

Polanyi, Michael. *Science, Faith and Society.* Riddell Memorial Lectures. London: Oxford University Press, 1946.

Putnam, Hilary. *The Collapse of the Fact/Value Dichotomy and Other Essays.* Cambridge: Harvard University Press, 2002.

Riss, Richard M. "Christian Themes in *The Wizard of Oz*." 1997. Available online at http://www.grmi.org/renewal/Richard_Riss/sermons/0003.html.

Sidanius, Jim, and Felicia Pratto. *Social Dominance: An Intergroup Theory of Social Hierarchy and Oppression.* Cambridge: Cambridge University Press, 1999.

Sokal, Alan D. "Transgressing the Boundaries: Towards a Transformative Hermeneutics of Quantum Gravity." *Social Text* 46/47 (spring–summer 1996): 217–252.

Tocqueville, Alexis de, Henry Reeve, and John C. Spencer. *Democracy in America.* Vol. 2. New York: J. and H. G. Langley, 1841.

Toulmin, Stephen Edelston. *Cosmopolis: The Hidden Agenda of Modernity*. Chicago: University of Chicago Press, 1992.

Weber, Max. *Economy and Society: An Outline of Interpretive Sociology*. New York: Bedminster Press, 1968.

Zinnbauer, Brian J., et al. "Religion and Spirituality: Unfuzzying the Fuzzy." *Journal for the Scientific Study of Religion* 36.4 (1997): 549–564.

PART II

Cosmos

6

Science, Religion, Metaphor, and History

Jeffrey Burton Russell

Universe and Cosmos

Massive wounds have been torn in the cosmos during the past few centuries, but now in the new century, history and metaphor can help bring the patient into a new, cooperative vitality that is whole, holy, and healed (they are related words). I distinguish between "universe" and "cosmos." "Universe," as here defined, is the entire set of being and relativities external to or beyond humanity: Universe exists, and we dwell in it, whether we like it or not, and whatever our view of it may be. This chapter is more concerned with "cosmos," defined as the human understanding of universe, the human worldview. It is cosmos that needs healing.

Before addressing cosmos, there is a simple, but easily misunderstood, point to make about universe. All of us live in the same universe. this universe that we are in. We have no choice: thinking that the universe is one way or another does not change the universe. If, for example, there is no God, then thinking that there is does not make it so. If there is God, then thinking that there is not does not make it so. Now, it may be that the universe is exclusively physical (including not only matter and energy in the classical senses but also dark matter and dark energy and any other component that science may one day identify). Such a universe, the product of randomness and causation, is without inherent meaning or purpose. Or it may be that the universe includes both the physical *and* the spiritual and ideational entities that exist, relate, or occur; these are not limited by space-time, and they are not exhaustible by physical explanations. Such a universe has intrinsic order and meaning. We have no certain knowledge whether the universe is one or the other. Yet there is no reason to assume (as many contemporaries do) that we live in an entirely physical universe. In fact, there are enough indications to the contrary to encourage minds to open up again. But what is certain is that we can *not* choose for ourselves whether the universe has purpose or whether it is wholly physical. As opposed to "universe," "cosmos" (or "worldview") is *human* understanding of the universe.

At present it is widely assumed that science and religion are distinct entities with little if any overlap or common concern. Certainly the terms "science" and "religion" can be distinguished from one another in ways that are proper and useful. But we tend wrongly to reify the terms—that is, to imagine that "science" and "religion" are entities external to the human invention and use of the terms.

The root meaning of "cosmos" is "order and purpose," as opposed to the root meaning of "chaos," which is "gaping void." Order and purpose imply intelligence. No purpose, no cosmos. The Greek *kosmos*, means "order"; *chaein*, "to gape." Thus the question of purpose is basic to both science and religion. Logically, the propositions "nothing in the universe has inherent meaning and purpose" and "everything in the universe has inherent meaning and purpose" are contradictory. Some modern scientists and philosophers are attempting a middle way: the universe *may* have meaning and purpose. Observations of the universe are *compatible with* meaning and purpose in the universe. This cuts through Hume's argument against natural theology.[1]

It is unlikely that we have clear and present understanding of anything, but it is even more unlikely that the universe is mere illusion. It is best to assume that actual external events (external to us personally or to society or to human understanding in general) occur that our understanding, however wan, is attempting to grasp. A "moderate realist" view is that our ideas of externals have some relation to the external events, but that our understanding of externals is never entirely clear, so that cosmos changes through time. Cosmos is in a way always less than universe because it can never plumb or exhaust ultimate reality; yet it is also always more than a universe that lacks consciousness and creativity.

In fact, the dichotomy—the gap—often assumed between science and religion is neither logical nor inevitable. The gap expresses itself in stresses that are sometimes obvious (such as constitutional struggles over "church and state") and sometimes deeply tectonic (the growing sense of meaninglessness and futility in life). The dichotomy itself is a metaphor and has a history. Cosmos (that is, our worldview today) is severely wounded, not only split between science and religion but pulled apart in many directions. This chapter suggests that a deep understanding of history and metaphor can help transcend dichotomies and heal the injured cosmos.

Cosmos is made out of concepts. Concepts are intellectually and socially constructed over time by a fusion of personal constructs. A cosmos is a world-view based in *both/and* thinking more than *either/or* thinking: it is synthetic more than analytic, expansive more than reductionist. It understands by opening out wider and wider, rather than closing down narrower and narrower. The preference for narrowing-down understanding as opposed to opening-up understanding is a matter of psychology (the vain, sad, frightened desire to be certain), and of history.

History of Concepts

The history of concepts is a peculiarly effective way of describing religion and science. Religion and science are not rigid, eternal ideas. They are concepts that change through time. Therefore history can explain how science and religion came to be what they are today. History works differently from either science or religion. History has its own epistemology, working through events by narrative, relating how we got from point A to point C by going through process B.[2] History assumes the reality of persons in the past, including their thoughts and their feelings: their whole personalities. Some historians today have become part of the problem by ignoring the meaningful reality of persons and societies with a cosmos different from their own. No one is a "dead" anybody. To think so is to misunderstand the nature of time. When is "now"? As we reflect on our lives back to say, our tenth birthday, did we think at age 10 that we were really in the past and that the real "now" is reading this article today? Will we think tomorrow that we are at last in the future? On the contrary, when we were 10 is "now"; when we are reading this is "now"; when we are dying is "now." "Now" is an infinitesimal point moving across time, so that all moments are "now." It follows that Bach, Confucius, and Galileo are no less alive than we are today. History is never concerned with the dead past, always with the living encounter with persons living *now*.

History, properly understood, means opening up minds to understanding other cultures rather than imposing current assumptions on them. History takes the worldviews of other cultures seriously, whether in modern Papua, ancient Babylonia, or traditional Christianity. A worldview—a cosmos—is based in its society; on the other hand, a society is formed by its worldview. People's ideas are more important for the way they speak and even act than the economic and social structures that support them. Ideas *are* events: the history of concepts takes ideas seriously, as having real consequences.[3] Terms such as "concept" have a variety of meanings among philosophers, psychologists, mathematicians, and others. But they do not lack definition. "Definition" or "range" can best be understood in terms of the way words and concepts have been used over time. Etymologists have long understood this in terms of words: a word does not have a single meaning through spacetime but has developed and will continue to develop. Words vary in concreteness—from the solid "beech tree" to the conceptual "democracy," for example. They are also seldom directly translatable into other languages, where connotations are different: compare "beech forest" with *Buchenwald*. My use of the term "concept" is but one of many possible uses.[4]

We all gradually form our own personal constructs, not only of such relatively simple things as trees, but also, through interaction with others, of much more complex things such as democracy, or witchcraft.[5] Constructs even of concrete objects can vary widely. Consider "tree." Trees are different to physicists, poets, biochemists, taxonomists, painters, ecologists, loggers, and even more different to birds, dogs, and any possible extraterrestrials.[6] Concepts vary among societies in time and place and within societies. Further, there are a vast number of subsets of concepts in any given society—depending on whether you are on the baseball field, in corporate management, on the city desk of a newspaper, or whatever context. Within any of the subsets, concepts tend to be rigidified by social suasion, including force, propaganda, peer and professional pressure, and ridicule. Such subgroups may vary so much as to appear not even to belong to the same culture, yet there is something beyond their economic and environmental situation that unites them, however tenuously, and that is a tradition with ancient and pervasive roots.

Reasonable men and women may approximately agree on what a beech tree is, but no such agreement can exist on words that lack clear, immutable, external referents. Their meaning is best described in terms of their development, their history. "History" itself has such a history: though often used as a synonym for "the past," it originally meant "investigation" and was applied up to the twentieth century in this broad sense, as in the term "natural history," which meant something like "life sciences." The word "history" used as a synonym for "the past" gives an unwarranted impression of factual solidity. It is best understood as "investigation of the human past."

A number of things can happen to a concept: extinction; amalgamation with others; diffusion to the point of losing its discernable shape and so breaking into separate concepts; exchange by contact with other societies; becoming unchanging and mummified; encountering strong ideological opposition; having a long, rich, and traceable life. I take terms such as "truth," "reality," and "rationality" seriously, though I understand that their meaning is fluid, like that of all concepts. Tradition is essential to meaning, whether one likes that fact or not. Putnam points out that concepts are fluid and to be understood in terms of "continuity through change," and that "meanings have an identity through time but no essence."[7] The assumption of physicalism is that human minds can grasp outside realities in themselves; actually, we can know securely only what we have made ourselves—what is in our minds: our ideas and concepts. That point was first clearly made by Giambattista Vico (1668–1744).[8]

Concepts also vary along a spectrum from concrete to abstract and from simple to complex: compare the relatively concrete "beech tree" with the relatively abstract "Christianity," "Marxism," "science," and "religion." Concepts are inextricably bound up with words: both can develop through time. The prime contemporary example of the difficult connections between words and concepts is "democracy," a word that has a wide spectrum and a concept so blurry as almost to lack meaning.

It is sometimes assumed that there is a close correlation between word and fact. When one attempts to discern "facts" about abstract concepts, one encounters tenuous shapes. One changes the shape by one's own approach. Much hash has been made of the uncertainty principle by nonscientists; here I refer to history, not physics: every historian changes the past by writing or speaking about it. "Murder" is an example. Does "murder" have an immutable essence? Or does it have no meaning at all because it lacks a clear external referent? Or does it mean exactly what the laws of our particular state or our particular religion at this particular time say? Is capital punishment murder? Is feticide murder? Is killing in war murder? Is infanticide murder? They have all been considered so. For that reason an effort at a history of whatever everyone has meant by the term is manifestly impossible. The most interesting concepts are those that have a long tradition, a tradition showing both the underlying strength of the concept and its developments and modifications.

The history of concepts serves a purpose for culture similar to that served by memory for an individual. We cannot be a person without memory, and we cannot be a culture without the history of concepts. The history of concepts is the best method for understanding any human idea because it integrates the development of the concept in areas as diverse as philosophy, psychology, religion, mythology, art, and folklore. It denies nothing except the currently fashionable delusion that when people in other societies talk about ideas that are real to them what they "really" mean are things that seem "real" to our contemporary mode of perceiving reality. It is an odd conceit that although people (whether contemporary al-Qaeda or medieval Londoners) believe that they are thinking about religion, what they are really thinking about is what contemporary social scientists decide is "real": power. This pervasive delusion is "chronocentrism," a variety of bad old ethnocentrism quite insulting to its subjects.

The great Christian bishop Augustine (354–451) did more to construct a cosmos integrating religion and science than anyone before Dante.[9] Augustine strongly encouraged natural philosophy. God creates the cosmos; in Greek, he "makes" it. Greek *poiein*, "to make," means to create not only in a physical sense, but also in a metaphorical sense. A "poet" is a "maker" as much as an engineer is. (Old English *makar* means "maker" or creator of a poem, an object, or a universe.) Since God made everything, everything has meaning and purpose, including time. We have access to two great Books of Revelation: one is the Bible, and the other is the Book of Nature. The two, far from being incompatible, are both given us for our understanding. To understand God, we do three basic things: we look within ourselves; we look to God as revealed in the Bible; we look at the Book of Nature as revealed in the physical world around us. Augustine thought what we call "science" to be a holy activity.

Because of its openness to misunderstanding, I avoid using the term "literal" and instead contrast the "overt" sense of a text to its "symbolic" sense. The simplistic idea that "the ideal rational language is literal and univocal and has a unique relation to truth" underlies both biblical and scientific "literalism."[10] For example, the statement that God has a throne in heaven, or the statement that Christ sits at the "right hand of the Father" are seldom intended in the overt sense (there is a physical place called heaven where there is a physical elaborate chair, and so on) but rather in the symbolic sense, where God's throne represents his power throughout the cosmos or where the "right hand" expresses closeness and honor. Educated people have always understood that when Jesus warns people who have logs in their eyes not to judge others who have specks in their eyes (Matthew 7.3–5), he is not suggesting that people were walking around with pieces of cedar jutting out of their sockets. Traditional thinkers recognized that metaphor expresses a deeper reality than can be obtained through a reductionist reading. Since they regarded the Bible as revealed, they regarded everything in it as meaningful. This almost forced the growth of metaphor, as it was clear that everything in it does not have an overt meaning. Multiple levels of meaning were established by Origen (about 185–254) and then by Augustine.[11] They read the Bible on at least four levels, the overt, the allegorical, the moral, and the eschatological (referring to the end of the world), all of the latter three being generally metaphorical. Their intention was to open out meaning through "depth-metaphor."

By the middle of the twelfth century, Abelard's (d. 1142) critiques of Bible and tradition had led to a new method known as "dialectic."[12] A thesis was stated; then its antithesis; and then, through the use of reason, its synthesis. This dialectic, without which much of modern philosophy would have been impossible, was the core of the "scholastic method." No longer could a question be answered by simply citing a traditional view from the Church Fathers or Aristotle. On the other hand, a number of bishops feared that a principle vital to the life of the Christian Church was at stake: Apostolic Succession. The truth of Christianity was based on the authority that the bishops held as successors to the Apostles. The bishops feared that university professors would often (unsurprisingly) prefer their own rational expositions to apostolic authority. There was also an honest theological worry. When academics argued that academic formulas were true in the sense that they expressed absolute reality, they were skirting an equation of cosmos and universe. This problem would underlie the Galileo affair later.

At the end of the Middle Ages appeared a perfect cosmos, incorporating then-current ideas of philosophy and theology: Dante's *Paradiso*, the least appreciated but most intellectually and aesthetically satisfying book of his *Divine Comedy*. Uniting the Bible with Christian tradition and natural philosophy, Dante's work reveals how both theology and science permeated the thought of highly educated people in the fourteenth century. His geographical and astronomical accuracy is astounding: for example, it was no small feat in his day to calculate the exact position of the Sun at the same moment in latitudes and even longitudes as different as Italy and Jerusalem. But for Dante, the truest picture and deepest meaning of cosmos was ethical, not physical: Dante's physical universe is a metaphor for the ethical cosmos rather than the other way around.[13]

Dante's universe was arranged in an Aristotelean series of concentric spheres, the Earth being the sphere at the center. Above and around the Earth was the sphere of the Moon, and then, in order, those of Mercury, Venus, the Sun, Mars, Jupiter, Saturn, the fixed stars, and the primum mobile. The primum mobile, moved only by God, moves all the spheres below it down to the tiny Earth at the center, but it has no depth itself: it is the dimensionless skin of the entire cosmos.

Dante and his readers progress upward from the center of the universe (the Earth) through a series of concentric spheres, to the outermost and highest sphere, the primum mobile. Dante now "stands" at a point on the primum mobile, looking down at the tiny Earth far below. Beyond the primum mobile is nothing—nothing at all—yet beyond it is God. And Dante, thrillingly, metaphorically turns his head away from all those spheres and the tiny Earth at their center. Thrillingly, he turns and looks through the primum mobile to the other side. As soon as he puts his head through the skin of the primum mobile to look at God's heaven, a great inversion occurs. Now he can, by looking "in the other direction," see "down" through the spheres that circle the Blazing Point that is God. This direction is down, up, out, and in, all at once. Where is the Blazing Point? Nowhere: that is, nowhere in spacetime. Everywhere. It is beyond the cosmos, yet it is the source and ground of being of the whole cosmos. Dante is looking into a "place" where there is no dimension, time, or space. Physically it is not the universe at all, yet morally it is the center of the universe. It both contains and exceeds all time and space: it is everywhere and everywhen.

In the sixteenth century, cracks in Dante's cosmos appeared. The religious Reformers often emphasized the overt reading of the Bible, which narrowed its meaning down instead of opening it out to the rich multiplicity of understanding. For overt literalists, the scriptures must be read as true in every sense, including the historical and the scientific. The metaphorical was virtually eliminated, closing down meaning, and insistence on the overt meaning of scripture led eventually to many unnecessary conflicts.

The case of Galileo (1564–1642), often a proof text in the alleged war between science and religion, is vastly more complex and nuanced than usually believed. The problem for Galileo's opponents was not supplanting Aristotle and Ptolemy's views of the physical universe with the Copernican heliocentric system, but rather Galileo's view that natural reason applied through mathematics to observation of phenomena could provide a truth independent of that of theology. Galileo was implicitly proposing the creation of a natural philosophy independent of theological philosophy.

The implications of the views of Galileo and his contemporaries became manifest in the eighteenth century, especially the shift from looking at natural phenomena as an overlay on the universe to seeing the phenomena as being the universe itself. In the late seventeenth and eighteenth centuries occurred a slow passing of the cloak of certainty from religion to science. As sides formed, neither side understood that their language was metaphorical; both claimed to have the true, overt access to "objective reality." Both sides used power to impress: theologians used the authority of the Bible enforced by the churches; scientists used practical technology funded by corporations and governments.[14] Both sides set aside deep knowledge and asserted the overt, the literal, the reduced, the defined.

Science is at present seen as an effort to understand the universe through theory, mathematics, and especially rigorous experimentation. The first citation of the English word "science" occurs in 1340, at which time it meant learning or knowledge in general, as did its Latin root *scientia*, from *scire*, "to know." Not before 1725 did "science" mean an orderly, systematic system based on observation and mathematics. The history of the language is not just a curiosity; it is a strong clue to concepts—the way we look at things. The human mind is constructed in such a fashion that once we have a concept, a word for it very quickly follows. The lack of a word may mean that there is as yet no concept to express. The concept of science as distinct from other knowledge could not have much predated the appearance of the *word* "science" in that sense. But were Galileo and Newton not scientists? In an important way they were not. The word "scientist" does not occur before 1834. Although there were people doing things that look like what is usually called science today, they did not think of themselves as being in the category of "scientist." They thought of their subject as "natural philosophy" instead.

The distinction is important, because they thought of "natural philosophy" as an integral part of philosophy, a system for understanding the whole, in other words, a cosmos. The title of Newton's key work is *The Mathematical Principles of Natural Philosophy* (1686–1687). When the term "physics" first appears in 1589, it meant all knowledge of nature; not before 1715 did it mean knowledge specifically of matter and energy. No one called himself a "physicist" before 1840. In some senses there were physicists before then but in other, equally important, senses there were not. There is no divine, Platonic, or im-

mutable category "physicist" into which individuals in history may be loaded,
especially when they do not understand the term themselves.

Whatever the intent of Galileo or his opponents, the affair had unbounded
effect upon subsequent thought. The seventeenth and eighteenth centuries
produced a real revolution in thought that amounted to the replacement of a
coherent, organic world by "a mechanical world of lifeless matter, incessant
local motion, and random collision."[15] The assumption that we live in an entirely physical universe rather than in a more diverse universe became more
and more frequently the common opinion of philosophers and eventually of
the general population. Although many philosophers from Francis Bacon
(1561–1626) through the eighteenth-century Enlightenment believed that religion and science were incompatible, religion has usually supported rather than
resisted science, and the very idea of a warfare between science and religion
was invented in the mid-nineteenth century.[16] The declaration of war came
from John W. Draper (1811–1882), who wrote in *History of the Conflict between
Religion and Science*:

> The antagonism we thus witness between Religion and Science is
> the continuation of the struggle that commenced when Christianity
> began to attain political power. . . . The history of Science is not a
> mere record of isolated discoveries; it is a narrative of the conflict of
> two contending powers, the expansive force of the human intellect
> on one side, and the compression arising from traditionary [sic] faith
> and human interests on the other   [The fall of Rome] left reli-
> gious affairs to take their place, and accordingly those affairs fell
> into the hands of ignorant and infuriated ecclesiastics, parasites,
> eunuchs, and slaves.[17]

The myth of the flat Earth is an example of the preposterous caricatures
employed by Draper and his followers. One of the platitudes that "everybody
knows" about the Middle Ages is that medieval people thought the Earth was
flat. But in fact no educated person in the Middle Ages thought so. The myth
would have faded if Draper and his allies had not used it to bludgeon their
opponents by claiming that they were just as stupid as the medieval people
who allegedly thought the Earth was flat.[18] The alleged war between science
and religion is real only insofar as people construct it as such.

Biological evolution became the focus of the "war." No story in science,
even the Galileo affair, is more fixed in the contemporary public consciousness—at least in America—than the Scopes trial. In the late eighteenth and
early nineteenth century the idea that the geological and biological features of
Earth today are the products of change through vast eons of time had gained
strength. This geological and biological succession of life through time is compatible with traditional Christian theology, and it was so accepted by most

theologians. However, some theologians created a problem. Assuming first that the Bible is without error and second that it must be read in an overt way whenever possible, they maintained that the account of creation in Genesis was supposed to be a scientific and historical account of the beginning of the world over a short period of time.

Such a position provokes not only scientists and historians but also most theologians, who know that there is no such thing as reading the Bible or any other text without preformed conceptions. A number of evolutionists created a problem too. By assuming that lengthy development through time indicated that the universe was without purpose or intelligent direction, they essentially declared cosmos impossible. When religion and science are each taken overtly and without a sense of the limitations of human understanding, the two exclude one another by definition.

But there is no need for such either/or positions. One of the greatest obstacles to the formation of a coherent new worldview in the twenty-first century is physicalism, materialist reductionism. The origins of the idea are as old as the Greek atomists, but the first English instance of the word "materialism" in the sense of the belief that all actions, thoughts, and feelings can be reduced to physical explanation, first appeared in 1748. "Materialist reductionism" does not mean the "reducing" of scientific questions to their fundamentals, but rather a philosophical assertion that we live in a universe where all phenomena can be reduced to the merely physical. It is reasonable to say that the study of natural phenomena may be reduced to the construction of physical regularities, but it is not reasonable to assume that all truth can be reduced to physical regularities. Physicalism is identifiable by certain key words and phrases such as "just," "merely," "only," and "nothing but." Consciousness is nothing but neural reactions in the brain that will someday be entirely predictable and controllable.

From E. O. Wilson's *Consilience:*

> Everything can be reduced to simple universal laws of physics. Ideas and feelings are merely linkage among the neural networks. It can all eventually be explained as brain circuitry. Everything that is knowable but not yet known to science is open to being explained by science.[19]

Richard Lewontin wrote:

> We take the side of science . . . because we have a prior commitment, a commitment to materialism. It is not that the methods and institutions of science somehow compel us to accept a material explanation of the phenomenal world, but, on the contrary, that we are forced by our *a priori* adherence to materialist causes to create an apparatus of investigation and a set of concepts that produce mate-

rial explanations, no matter how counter-intuitive, no matter how mystifying to the uninitiated. Moreover, that materialism is absolute, for we cannot allow a Divine Foot in the door.[20]

Since there are no scientific means by which materialist reductionists can possibly know that there is no direction or plan, such statements violate a fundamental principle of science itself: science is based upon testable hypotheses; a good hypothesis is one that can be disproved or proved. No a priori assumptions qualify as arguments "Materialism itself is an idea, just as immaterial as any other."[21] If no idea is better than any other idea because they all proceed from purposeless neural interactions, then the idea of reductionism itself is no better than that of astrology.

Reduction of all ideas to neural impulses means that no moral or ethical concept is better than any other. If no behavior is better than another, why bother about whales and rainforests? What is wrong with raping children or genocide? What is wrong with faking scientific evidence? Appeals to "good sense," "right-mindedness," and "you can't think *that*" are simply evasions of the basic principles of reductionist thought. According to E. O. Wilson, we need the "illusion of free will" as biologically adaptive; we need the "self-deception" of altruism.[22] But what possible good—moral, intellectual, or evolutionary— can come from belief in free will and cosmos if they are illusions and lies?

The Marquis de Sade (1740–1814) is admirable for his refusal to flinch from the implications of relativism.[23] He recognized that flinching was either political evasion or an indication that relativists did not believe their own proclamations. In an intrinsically relative, valueless world, Sade argued, the only sensible thing is to seek personal pleasure. If you enjoy torture, fine. If others do not enjoy it, fine, but they have no business imposing their views on you. Why should not a child molester be free to rape and torture his victims? The response that one person should not impose his desires on an unwilling victim, Sade pointed out, is itself a relative assumption without basis.

Metaphor and Healing

The history of concepts recounts how cosmos has been rent. Metaphor is an important instrument in the healing of cosmos. The importance of metaphor is that it expands and extends worldviews. The Greek root *metaphorein* has the sense of transfer of qualities by an identification of two unlike things, but there is no universally agreed meaning to the word "metaphor."[24] I define metaphor as the transfer of meaning from one statement or image to another. Metaphors can point to realities that elude literal, overt vocabulary. Metaphor should not be denied cognitive status: in fact, cognition itself is expanded by metaphor; as metaphor is multidimensional, metaphor adds meaning. Metaphor "is a cognitive act of originality, by which we alter our way of structuring reality."[25] Thus metaphor is as important to human thought as mathematics. Metaphors serve a purpose that "standard discursive language will not and cannot serve."[26] Metaphorical thinking is often rejected merely because the hearer cannot fit it into his or her personal provisional cognitive framework.

A metaphor is the use of a word or phrase or depiction to give a fuller understanding of what is referred to; it operates through the tension between identity and difference. "Man is a wolf" shows both the identity (humans are ferocious) and the difference (humans are not quadrupeds).[27] A metaphor cannot be True or False, but it can be trite or shallow.[28] It has been said that all natural language is metaphorical.[29] Scientific diagrams, creeds, architectural drawings, paintings, maps, poetry, are all metaphorical. Even the most abstract artwork is a metaphor for the culture that has expressed it. Any nontautological statement—any statement with an intended external referent—is metaphorical.

But in a deeper sense, to say that all language is metaphor completely dissipates the meaning of the word "metaphor." Physicalism assumes that meaningful language is restricted to the analytical and descriptive; but expressive, suggestive, figurative language can be even more meaningful. Whereas analytical language narrows down toward an answer, or at least an analytically definable question, figurative language opens up to a rich multitude of meanings. The greater the variety of meanings, the greater the intellectual stimulation, the greater the emotional depth, the more original, the more cultural resonance, the more senses it draws upon,[30] the more archetypal of human experience, the more the richness of the history of the words or phrases, the less worn out: the better metaphors are "depth-metaphors." Depth-metaphors engender meaning that goes beyond the things being compared. Depth-metaphors are "signs," "symbols" (Greek *symbola*) suggesting qualities not immediately evident and implying things beyond. Depth-metaphors convey true meaning, cognitive content.

Some metaphors are so simple that we commonly refer to them as facts, such as "a star is a ball of fire." A vast spectrum exists from such simple metaphors to "see how the heavens are covered with patines of bright gold" (*Merchant of Venice*, 4.1). The more complex the concept is, the greater the range of metaphors it can open up. Metaphors are more authentic as they indicate broader and deeper realities, less valid as they confuse or restrict meaning. A metaphor is most authentic when it is intentional to the ultimate meaning of the cosmos. It is a current academic assumption that there is no such thing as the ultimate meaning of the universe and that therefore it is impossible to consider one metaphor stronger than another. That this is a popular view among clever people setting limits to their own imagination is undeniable; that it is either true or helpful is dubious.

Strong metaphors bring us closer to reality, not by narrowing down but by opening things up. Varieties of language ("dictions") are necessary to express the limitless multiplicity of reality. If properly used, the languages ("dictions") need not contradict one another. Those who view the world only on a purely overt cognitive level deprive themselves of a rich hoard of understanding. Metaphors serve a purpose that "standard discursive language will not and cannot serve."[31]

Metaphor is proper to understanding the history of religion. Metaphors that are intentional to ultimate truth are "depth-metaphors." There are a vast number of types of metaphor. For one example, a metaphor can be humorous: "the stars in the sky are dandruff on God's black shirt." By a depth-metaphor I mean one that is intended by the author (or can be helpfully understood by the reader) as referring to a deeper reality than that of the words or phrases used. ("Deeper reality" is not a term understood by modern physicalists.) A metaphor can be brilliant even though trivial, and a metaphor can be stupid even though aimed at depth: it is not the quality of the metaphor that is in question here but rather its aim. Metaphors can aim at deeper understanding of humanity, the cosmos, and God, and these are the metaphors that I characterize as "depth-metaphors."

Traditional use of language differs from general modern usage. Moderns think in terms of dichotomies between true and false, fact and fiction; we are baffled by terms such as "more real" and "more perfect"; we assume that a so-called "fact" relates "to outside reality" while a metaphor is subjective and unrelated "to outside reality." Such modern assumptions impose a barrier to understanding, particularly in the use of the term "literal." Consider a common statement such as "that's the literal truth," usually intending something like "that's what actually happened." In its root, "literal" means "letter for letter." The word leads to a simple and common problem in understanding the word, particularly as it relates to the Bible.[32] In Christian tradition, the term "literal meaning" in regard to the Bible does not imply modern scientific or historical meaning but rather both what the writer of the text intends and what God intends—which can be historical or metaphorical. For example, Augustine's book *The Literal Interpretation of Genesis*, written in 401, will surprise anyone thinking of Bryant and the Scopes trial: Augustine does not pin down the text to simplistic meanings but rather opens it up (as much as he is able) to what God intends by Genesis, and that, he knew, is largely metaphorical. The traditional mode does not so much analyze, reduce, and narrow down toward definition as it uses metaphor to expand and open out meaning. But that's not what God said? Or is it? "God, like the writers of the texts themselves, is perfectly capable of metaphor and irony."[33] The program put forward by deconstructionists that the intent of the author of a text is irrelevant is, to say the least, an obstruction to understanding concepts.

I use the term "metaphorical ontology" to refer to a truth statement couched in metaphor rather than in scientific terms.[34] Metaphorical ontology is the use of words denoting one kind of object, action, or idea in place of another in order to suggest a deeper meaning beneath both. When the Psalmist says that the Lord will cover you with his feathers and that you shall trust under his wings (Ps. 91.4), he was not suggesting that you will be a fledgling in a nest. When Jesus called himself a shepherd, he did not mean that he planned sermons for ovine creatures. Metaphorical ontology is the use of figures of speech to go beyond science, and history, to indicate the divine reality deep down things. Metaphorical ontology, with its sense of contemplation and wonder, can heal either/or wounds. And restore us to wholeness and cosmos.

The proper language of religion is metaphor, because religious truths are both more nebulous than scientific ones and also more embracing and textured, and the Bible is usually best opened out metaphorically. Take the passage where King David brings the Ark into Jerusalem. What is Jerusalem? It is a city having geographical coordinates and political boundaries. It has a history; before David made it his capital, it was a small Jebusite fort; afterwards it was part of a succession of kingdoms and empires; today it is a source of animosity between Jews and Muslims. But it is also Zion, the land promised eternally to the Jews. And it is the place of resurrection for the Jews. And the place where Jesus died and rose from the dead. And where Muhammad ascended into heaven. It is seen as the moral center of the earth. It represents heaven, the soul, the end of the world, and an untellable number of other things. The meaning of Jerusalem is best not narrowed down to any one thing but rather opened up and expanded.

The theory of metaphorical ontology is not intended to placate physicalists by reducing religion to "mere metaphor"; and it is certainly not intended to yield any ground to deconstructionists, for it takes depth-metaphor as a sign of reality beyond language. Metaphorical truth is at least as real as scientific and historical truth. When properly understood through metaphor, religion and science do not cancel one another out. It is best not to play a zero-sum game where "We are right and deserve to win" and "They are wrong and deserve to lose." There is more than either they or we know. Metaphorical ontology opens up rather than closing down. Only in this way can cosmos be healed.

Former Cosmoses cannot be restored: no matter how much we admire and understand Dante's cosmos, we cannot ignore the context of all the thought since Dante. But cosmos can be healed by a whole, and hopeful, construction of a new cosmos. At present the problem of utopias is not that they are unrealized but that there is none we consider worth striving for. The primary task of this century—even beyond all concerns about environment, terrorism, starvation, war, and disease—is the creation of a new cosmos. Primary, because without cosmos there is no coherent goal for humanity, and consequently every step in what seems at the moment to be a "better" direction will fail, since the direction of the steps will be unknown. Without an idea of where we wish to go, we will end up—not probably but inevitably—reaching no goals other than those of our momentary, changeable wishes. The practical need for healing cosmos is to forestall a century that may be even more lethal than the last. The more important, essential need for healing cosmos is that a purpose for the human race is needed that transcends the diverse, incoherent, and often pointless purposes of individuals, social groups, economic interests, and professional technicians; a purpose that aims toward, and is consistent with, the meaning of the universe and of its Great Poet and Maker.

The ultimate shape of this new cosmos is not yet known. But if it is both to be true, and to work, it will not lack these components: it will be consistent with truth; it will embrace both the rational and the imaginative; it will recognize both the limitations and the expansions of its metaphors; it will give proper due to both the spiritual and the physical; it will embrace the painfully won wisdom of the past along with new ways of seeing; it will incorporate all manifestations of truth in science, religion, history, and every other mode of understanding; it will open up vistas beyond those of science and religion; it will be open to entirely new insights that promote understanding while exercising critical judgment as to their purpose and particulars; it will tend to unite rather than to divide humanity and will not be based on the interests of any one part of society against any other part; it will face the problem of evil squarely; it will recognize justice as an absolute rather than as an engine to promote limited interests; it will recognize human limitations as well as human potentiality in both intelligence and will; it will be neither forced or coercive; by recognizing human limitations it will be practicable; it will help fulfill everyone's human potential for understanding and joy; it will increase the good of each by increasing the good of all; it will increase the love of each by the love of all.

Although reconstruction of cosmos requires a generosity and openness so far uncommon in humanity, we cannot assume failure, and we can hope. *Dum spiramus speremus*: while we breathe, let us hope.

NOTES

1. John Polkinghorne, *Belief in God in an Age of Science* (New Haven: Yale University Press, 1998), 10–11.

2. Arthur O. Lovejoy, *The Great Chain of Being* (Cambridge: Harvard University Press, 1936), 3–23; Arthur C. Danto, *Analytical Philosophy of History* (Cambridge: Cambridge University Press, 1968).

3. Jeffrey Burton Russell, *Witchcraft in the Middle Ages* (Ithaca: Cornell University Press, 1972); *The Devil* (Ithaca, N.Y.: Cornell University Press, 1977).

4. Stephen Toulmin, *Human Understanding* (Princeton: Princeton University

Press, 1972), 8; Hilary Putnam, *Representation and Reality* (Cambridge, Mass.: MIT Press, 1988), 19–20.

5. For widely varied views of witchcraft, for example, see my article in the *Encyclopaedia Britannica*, 2002.

6. Putnam, *Representation*, 21–24. My own examples.

7. Ibid., 11.

8. Isaiah Berlin, *Vico and Herder: Two Studies in the History of Ideas* (New York: Vintage, 1977).

9. Jeffrey Burton Russell, *Satan* (Ithaca, N.Y.: Cornell University Press, 1981), 186–218.

10. Mary Hesse, in *The Construction of Reality*, ed. Michael Arbib and Mary B. Hesse (Cambridge: Cambridge University Press, 1986), 351.

11. Jeffrey Burton Russell, *A History of Heaven: The Singing Silence* (Princeton: Princeton University Press, 1997), 84.

12. Jeffrey Burton Russell, *Lucifer: The Devil in the Middle Ages* (Ithaca, N.Y.: Cornell University Press, 1984), 160–161.

13. Dante, *Paradiso*, cantos 27–33; Russell, *A History*, 155–181.

14. William Barrett, *The Illusion of Technique: A Search for Meaning in a Technological Civilization* (Garden City, N.J.: Anchor Press, 1978).

15. David C. Lindberg, *The Beginnings of Western Science* (Chicago: University of Chicago Press, 1992), 362.

16. Ibid.; see also Edward Grant, *The Foundations of Modern Science in the Middle Ages* (Cambridge: Cambridge University Press, 1996).

17. John W. Draper, *History of the Conflict between Religion and Science* (New York: Appleton, 1874), vi–vii.

18. Russell, *Inventing the Flat Earth: Columbus and Modern Historians* (Westport, Conn.: Praeger, 1991).

19. Edward O. Wilson, *Consilience* (New York: Knopf, 1998), 261.

20. Richard Lewontin, Review of Carl Sagan's *The Demonized World*, *New York Review of Books*, January 9, 1997.

21. Wendell Berry, *Life Is a Miracle* (Washington, D.C.: Counterpoint, 2000), 50.

22. Wilson, *Consilience*, 97, 119–120.

23. Susan Neiman, *Evil in Modern Thought* (Princeton: Princeton University Press, 2002); Jeffrey Burton Russell, *Mephistopheles* (Ithaca, N.Y.: Cornell University Press, 1986), 146–149.

24. Norman Kreitman, *The Roots of Metaphor* (Brookfield, Vt.: Ashgate, 1999), 140.

25. Ibid., 154.

26. Ibid., 155.

27. Ibid., 120–121.

28. Philip Wheelwright, *The Burning Fountain* (Bloomington, Ind.: Indiana University Press, 1968), 201.

29. Hesse, *Reality*, 352.

30. For example, Dante's "where the sun is silent."

31. Kreitman, *Roots*, 169.

32. Muslims believe that God's angel dictated the Qur'an word for word in Ara-

bic. Some Christians believe that the Bible was dictated (in Hebrew? Greek? Aramaic? seventeenth-century English?) word for word to the various authors of the Bible, but that has always been a minority view in Christian thought.

33. Hesse, *Reality*, 233.

34. Russell, *Heaven*, 6–9. (Ontology is the philosophical understanding of "being.")

BIBLIOGRAPHY

Arbib, Michael A., and Mary B. Hesse. *The Construction of Reality*. Cambridge: Cambridge University Press, 1986.

Barfield, Owen. *Saving the Appearances: A Study of Idolatry*. New York: Harcourt, Brace, and World, 1965.

Barr, Stephen. *Modern Physics and Ancient Faith*. Notre Dame, Ind.: University of Notre Dame Press, 2003.

Barrett, William. *Irrational Man: A Study in Existential Philosophy*. Garden City, N.Y.: Doubleday Anchor, 1958.

———. *The Illusion of Technique: A Search for Meaning in a Technological Civilization*. Garden City, N.Y.: Anchor Press, 1978.

Berry, Wendell. *Life Is a Miracle: An Essay Against Modern Superstition*. Washington, D.C.: Counterpoint, 2000.

Brooke, John, and Geoffrey Cantor. *Reconstructing Nature: The Engagement of Science and Religion*. Oxford: Oxford University Press, 1998.

Danto, Arthur C. *Analytical Philosophy of History*. Cambridge: Cambridge University Press, 1968.

Denham, A. E. *Metaphor and Moral Experience*. Oxford: Clarendon Press, 1992.

Gould, Stephen J. *Rocks of Ages: Science and Religion in the Fullness of Life*. New York: Ballantine, 1999.

Grant, Edward. *The Foundations of Modern Science in the Middle Ages: Their Religious, Institutional, and Intellectual Contexts*. Cambridge: Cambridge University Press, 1996.

———. *God and Reason in the Middle Ages*. Cambridge: Cambridge University Press, 2001.

Kreitman, Norman. *The Roots of Metaphor: A Multidisciplinary Study in Aesthetics*. Brookfield, Vt.: Ashgate, 1999.

Lindberg, David C. *The Beginnings of Western Science: The European Scientific Tradition in Philosophical, Religious, and Institutional Context, 600 B.C. to A.D. 1450*. Chicago: University of Chicago Press, 1992.

Lindberg, David C., and Ronald L. Numbers, eds. *God and Nature: Historical Essays on the Encounter between Christianity and Science*. Berkeley: University of California Press, 1986.

Lovejoy, Arthur O. *The Great Chain of Being: A Study of the History of an Idea*. Cambridge: Harvard University Press, 1936.

Olson, Richard. *Science Deified and Science Defied: The Historical Significance of Science in Western Culture*. Berkeley: University of California Press, 1982.

Polkinghorne, John C. *Belief in God in an Age of Science*. New Haven: Yale University Press, 1998.

———. *Faith, Science, and Understanding*. New Haven: Yale University Press, 2000.

Putnam, Hilary. *Representation and Reality*. Cambridge, Mass.: MIT Press, 1988.

Radman, Zdravko, ed. *From a Metaphorical Point of View: A Multidisciplinary Approach to the Cognitive Content of Metaphor*. Berlin: W. de Gruyter, 1995.

Russell, Jeffrey Burton. *The Devil: Perceptions of Evil from Antiquity to Primitive Christianity*. Ithaca, N.Y.: Cornell University Press, 1977.

———. *Inventing the Flat Earth: Columbus and Modern Historians*. Westport, Conn.: Praeger, 1991.

———. *A History of Heaven: The Singing Silence*. Princeton, N.J.: Princeton University Press, 1997.

Stark, Rodney. *For the Glory of God: How Monotheism Led to Reformations, Science, Witch-Hunts, and the End of Slavery*. Princeton: Princeton University Press, 2003.

Swinburne, Richard. *Revelation: From Metaphor to Analogy*. Oxford: Clarendon Press, 1992.

Toulmin, Stephen. *Human Understanding*. Princeton: Princeton University Press, 1972.

Wheelwright, Philip. *The Burning Fountain: A Study in the Language of Symbolism*. Bloomington: Indiana University Press, 1968.

7

Kabbalah and Contemporary Cosmology: Discovering the Resonances

Daniel C. Matt

Relating Religion and Science

How can one interpret a religious text in the light of contemporary cosmology?[1] Many would object to any attempt to integrate the realms of science and religion, either because only one of them is valid or because, though each is valid, the two should remain separate. To a skeptical cosmologist, the biblical account of creation may seem like a primitive folktale. To a fundamentalist who believes that God created the world in six days in approximately 3761 B.C.E., the scientific debate over whether the big bang took place 15 or 13.7 billion years ago is irrelevant. More open-minded scientists and religious thinkers acknowledge the validity of the other realm of discourse but insist that the boundary between the two should not be blurred: science deals with empirical facts and falsifiable theory, while religion focuses on the meaning of life and moral values.

My approach is different. I assume that science and religion each offer different pieces of the puzzle of existence and human experience. Their approaches and language differ, but an intelligent, undogmatic person can learn from both. There is no need to rule out one or the other, nor to insist that the two systems remain hermetically sealed. Science and religion can enrich one another. For example, scientists can learn from religion how to cultivate a sense of wonder. Believers can learn from science that dogma can become stifling, that theories are provisional and meant to be questioned and tested.

Look, for example, at how Jewish thinkers interpret the central belief in the revelation of Torah at Mount Sinai. Traditionally, this is sometimes taken to mean that God actually dictated the entire Five Books of Moses—all 304,805 Hebrew letters from Genesis through Deuteronomy! But problems immediately arise: for example, how could God have dictated to Moses the final verses of Deuteronomy, which describe Moses's own death? For that matter, how could God have dictated at Sinai the accounts of Israel's wandering in the desert over the next forty years. Well, according to one authority, Moses received the revelation "scroll by scroll," that is, section by section, as the Children of Israel wandered through the desert. Further, he wrote the account of his own death with tears in his eyes.

Fine, but what words did God actually speak at Mount Sinai? How much of the Torah was heard directly by the people assembled at the foot of the mountain? Was it the Ten Commandments? If we look closely, we see that only the first two are written in the first person: "I am *YHVH* your God. . . . Do not have any other gods before Me." The remaining eight commands are in the second person: You shall do this; You shall not do that. Perhaps only these first two were spoken directly by God, while Moses conveyed the rest.

Or did God speak just the first command, or just the first word? A later, mystical view goes even further: God spoke only the first letter of the Ten Commandments: the *alef* of *Anokhi*, "I am." Now, an *alef* without a vowel has no sound; it simply represents a glottal stop—the position taken by the larynx in preparation for speech. So, according to this view, revelation consists of pure potential, with no specific content spelled out. The written text of the Torah is already a commentary on the *alef*, a human interpretation. It would be difficult to imagine a more radical transformation of the dogma of revelation.

Let's look at one other example of how a traditional notion is expanded, or exploded. I am thinking of the image of God as "Father in Heaven." This image pervades traditional religious texts and the liturgy—so much so that it is difficult for most people to even picture God otherwise. Yet, over four hundred years ago, a learned rabbinic scholar and mystic named Moses Cordovero challenged this notion, contrasting such naïve belief with one that is more sophisticated and boundless. Here is what he writes:

> An impoverished person thinks that God is an old man with white hair, sitting on a wondrous throne of fire that glitters with countless sparks, as the Bible states (Daniel 7:9): "The Ancient-of-Days sits, the hair on his head like clean fleece, his throne—flames of fire." Imagining this and similar fantasies, the fool corporealizes God. He falls into one of the traps that destroy faith. His awe of God is limited by his imagination.

> But if you are enlightened, you know God's oneness; you know that the divine is devoid of bodily categories—these can never be applied

to God. Then you wonder, astonished: Who am I? I am a mustard seed in the middle of the sphere of the moon, which itself is a mustard seed within the next sphere. So it is with that sphere and all it contains in relation to the next sphere. So it is with all the spheres—one inside the other—and all of them are a mustard seed within further expanses. And all of these are a mustard seed within further expanses.

Your awe is invigorated; the love in your soul expands.[2]

This Jewish thinker certainly prayed three times a day to "*YHVH* our God, King of the world." But he was thoroughly and intensely dissatisfied with the limited traditional view of God as a royal Father in Heaven. God must not be confined to familiar, human categories. First, says Cordovero, ask yourself: "Who am I, in the vastness of the cosmos?" As I gaze out from my puny, human self, the appropriate description of transcendent being is not a ruler on a throne but what the Jewish mystics call *Ein Sof,* literally: "there is no end," the Infinite. God as Infinity is a theological formulation that corresponds with reality.

The Big Bang

In the beginning was the big bang, 14 billion years ago. The primordial vacuum was devoid of matter, but not really empty—rather, in a state of minimum energy, pregnant with potential, teeming with virtual particles. Through a quantum fluctuation, a sort of bubble, in this vacuum, there emerged a hot, dense seed, smaller than a proton, yet containing all the mass and energy of our universe. In less than a trillionth of a second, this seed cooled and expanded wildly, faster than the speed of light, inflating into the size of a grapefruit. The expansion then slowed down, but it has never stopped.

In its first few seconds, the universe was an undifferentiated soup of matter and radiation. It took a few minutes for things to cool down enough for nuclei to form, and at least 300,000 years for atoms to form. For eons, clouds of gas expanded. Huge glimmering balls of hot gas formed into stars. Deep within these stars, nuclear reactions gave birth to elements such as carbon and iron. When the stars grew old, they exploded, spewing these elements into the universe. Eventually this matter was recycled into new solar systems. Our solar system is one example of this recycling, a mix of matter produced by cycles of stars—stars forming and exploding. We, along with everything else, are literally made of stardust.

The Earth took shape and began cooling down about 4.5 billion years ago. By about a billion years later, various microorganisms had developed. Exactly how, no one knows. We do know that Earth's early atmosphere was composed of hydrogen, water vapor, carbon dioxide, and simple gases such as ammonia and methane. In such a climate, organic compounds may have synthesized spontaneously.

Or perhaps life drifted to Earth in the form of spores from Mars or from another solar system in our galaxy or another galaxy in the universe. However life began, all its forms share similar genetic codes and can be traced back to a common ancestor. All living beings are cousins.

We humans like to think of ourselves as the pinnacle of creation, and it is true that we are the most complicated things in the universe. Our brain contains 100 billion cells, linked by 100 trillion synaptic connections. Yet we are part of the evolutionary process, descended from bacteria who lived 3.5 billion years ago. In our mother's womb each of us retraces the entire developmental span from amoeba to human being.[3] Our species—*Homo sapiens*—is a primate that developed in Africa, splitting away from the chimpanzee line about 7 million years ago. We still share with the chimps 99.4 percent of our active genes. If you'll pardon the expression, we are an improved ape.

The big bang is a theory, not a fact. To cosmologists, it offers the most convincing explanation of the evolution of the universe, "the best approximation to truth that we currently possess."[4] It may be proven wrong. More likely, it will eventually be enfolded within a larger theory. The scientific consensus is that the big bang theory is correct within its specific domain: the evolution of our universe from perhaps one-billionth of a second after its origins up to the present. Whatever happened before that first fraction of a second lies beyond the limits of the theory.[5] The term "big bang" suggests a definite beginning a finite time ago, but the theory does not extend that far. The ultimate origin of the universe is still unfathomed.

One version of the theory, known as "eternal inflation," was developed by Andrei Linde. This version portrays a universe that, by continually reproducing itself, attains immortality. Our universe is just one of countless baby universes, one of countless inflating, self-reproducing balls or "bubbles."[6] In each of these bubbles, the initial conditions differ and diverse kinds of elementary particles interact in unimagined ways. Perhaps, different laws of physics apply in each.[7]

Not all the domains inflate into large bubbles, but those that do, like ours, dominate the volume of the universe and sprout other bubbles in a perpetual chain reaction. The entire universe is a tree of life, a cluster of bubbles attached to each other, growing exponentially in time. Each baby universe is born in what can be considered a big bang—or should we say a little bang?—a fluctuation of the vacuum followed by inflation.

If Linde's speculations are correct, perhaps we should translate the opening words of Genesis not as "In *the* beginning," but "In *a* beginning, God created heaven and earth."[8] In fact, this represents a more literal rendering of the original Hebrew: *Be-Reshit,* "In a beginning."

The Universe: Myth and Meaning

Let us return to contemporary cosmology. Science has no consensus on the ultimate origin. Some theories espouse a well-defined beginning; others, like Stephen Hawking's, do not. But both suggest a radically new reading of Genesis. If God spoke the world into being, the divine language is energy; the alphabet, elementary particles; God's grammar, the laws of nature.[9] Many scientists have sensed a spiritual dimension in the search for these laws. For Einstein, discerning the laws of nature was a way to discover how God thinks.[10]

But does the universe have a purpose? Is there meaning to our existence? Why should we live ethically? Here, cosmology cannot help us very much. Darwin intensifies our problem. Are we different from other animals? Can we transcend violence and savagery? As the wife of an Anglican bishop remarked upon hearing of Darwin's theory: "Descended from apes! My dear, let us hope that it is not true; but if it is, let us pray that it will not become generally known."[11] Her comment echoes the fear that knowing the true nature of our ancestors threatens to unravel the social fabric.

We have lost our myth. A myth is a story, imagined or true, that helps us make our experience comprehensible by offering a construction of reality. It is a narrative that wrests order from chaos. We are not content to see events as unconnected, as inexplicable. We crave to understand the underlying order in the world. A myth tells us why things are the way they are and where they came from. Such an account is not only comfortable, assuring, and socially useful, it is essential. Without a myth, there is no meaning or purpose to life. There is just vast emptiness.

Myths do more than explain. They guide mental processes, conditioning how we think, even how we perceive. Myths come to life by serving as models for human behavior. On Friday evening, as my family begins *Shabbat* (the Sabbath), I sometimes imagine God, having created the world in one very packed week, finally taking a break. According to the Bible, *Shavat va-yinnafash*, "God rested and was refreshed."[12] This mythical image enables me to pause, to slow down, and appreciate creation. By observing *Shabbat*, I am imitating the divine. Order reemerges out of the impending chaos of life.

What do we do when the myths of tradition have been undone, when the God of the Bible seems so unbelievable? Is there really someone "up there" in control, charting the course of history, reaching down to rescue those in need, tallying up our good and bad deeds for reward and punishment? Many people have shed the security of traditional belief; they are more likely to experience a gaping, aching void than the satisfying fullness of God's presence. If they believe in anything, perhaps it's science and technology. And what does science provide in exchange for this belief? Progress in every field except for one: the ultimate meaning of life. Some scientists insist that there is no meaning. As one leading physicist has written, "The more we know about the universe, the more it is evident that it is pointless and meaningless."[13]

The Big Bang as Creation Myth

The big bang is a contemporary creation story. Energy turns into matter, which turns back into energy. There is no precise plan for creation, worked out in advance. By an intricate and unrepeatable combination of chance and necessity, humanity has evolved from and alongside countless other forms of life over billions of years. Ultimately, our evolutionary history is uplifting: It enables us to see that we are part of a wholeness, a oneness.

To be "religious" means, in the words of a contemporary physicist, to have an intuitive feeling of the unity of the cosmos.[14] This oneness is grounded in scientific fact: we are made of the same stuff as all of creation. Everything that is, was, or will be started off together as one infinitesimal point: the cosmic seed.

Life has since branched out, but this should not blind us to its underlying unity. The deepest marvel is the unity *in* diversity, the vast array of material manifestations of energy. Becoming aware of the multifaceted unity can help us learn how to live in harmony with other human beings and with all beings, with all our fellow transformations of energy and matter.

If the big bang is our new creation myth, the story that explains how the universe began, then who is God? "God" is a name we give to the oneness of it all.

How can you name oneness? How can you name the unnamable? The Jewish mystical tradition, the Kabbalah, offers a number of possibilities. One is *Ein Sof,* the Infinite, or, to borrow a phrase from the Christian mystic Meister Eckhart, the God beyond God.

Sometimes the kabbalists use a more radical name than *Ein Sof.* This is the name *ayin*—nothingness. We encounter this bizarre term among Christian mystics as well: John Scotus Erigena calls God *nihil;* Eckhart, *nihts;* St. John of the Cross, *nada.*[15] To call God "Nothingness" does not mean that God does not exist. Rather, it conveys the idea that God is no thing. God animates all things and cannot be contained by any of them. God is the oneness that is no particular thing, no thingness.

This mystical nothingness is neither empty nor barren; it is fertile and overflowing, engendering the myriad forms of life. The mystics teach that the universe emanated from divine nothingness. Similarly, as we have seen, cosmologists speak of the quantum vacuum, teeming with potential, engendering the cosmic seed. This vacuum is anything but empty—a seething froth of virtual particles, constantly appearing and disappearing.

How did the universe emerge out of prolific nothingness? According to

Kabbalah and classical big bang theory, this transition was marked by a single point. Physicists call this point a singularity: an infinitely dense point in spacetime. A singularity is both destructive and creative. Anything falling into a singularity merges with it, losing its identity, while energy emerging from a singularity can become anything. The laws of physics do not apply to the split second in which energy or mass emerges.[16]

According to the thirteenth-century kabbalist, Moses de León, "The beginning of existence is the secret concealed point. This is the beginning of all the hidden things, which spread out from there and emanate, according to their species. From a single point you can extend the dimensions of all things."[17]

As emanation proceeds, as God begins to unfold, the point expands into a circle. Similarly, ever since the big bang, our universe has been expanding. We know this thanks to the astronomer Edwin Hubble, who measured the speed at which other galaxies are moving away from us. In 1929, Hubble determined that the farther a galaxy is from us, the faster it is moving away. The universe is expanding in all directions. It's not that the universe is expanding *within* space. Space itself is expanding.[18]

The most dramatic consequence of Hubble's discovery is what it tells us about the origin of our universe. Just play the Hubble tape in reverse: if the universe is now expanding, that means it was once much smaller. How small? According to classical big bang theory, if we go back far enough in spacetime and retrace the paths of the galaxies and their formation, the entire mass-energy of the universe contracts into the size of a singularity—the infinitesimal point from which the cosmos flashed into existence.

One kabbalist, Shim'on Lavi, understands expansion as part of the rhythm of creation:

> With the appearance of the light, the universe expanded.
> With the concealment of the light, the things that exist were created
> in all their variety.
> This is the mystery of the act of creation.
> One who understands will understand.[19]

When light flashed forth, time and space began. But the early universe was an undifferentiated soup of energy and matter. How did matter emerge from the stew? The mystic writes that the light was concealed. A scientist would say that energy congealed. Matter is frozen energy. No nucleus or atom could form until some energy cooled down enough that it could be bound and bundled into stable particles of matter.

Einstein discovered the equivalence of mass and energy. Ultimately, matter is not distinct from energy, but simply energy that has temporarily assumed a particular pattern. Matter is energy in a tangible form; both are different states of a single continuum, different names for two forms of the same thing.

Like the physicist, the mystic, too, is fascinated by the intimate relation of matter and energy, though the mystical description is composed in a different key. Material existence emerges out of *ayin,* the pool of divine energy. Ultimately, the world is not other than God, for this divine energy is concealed within all forms of being. Were it not concealed, there could be no individual existence; everything would dissolve back into oneness, or nothingness.

Breaking of the Vessels and Broken Symmetry

Around the middle of the sixteenth century in the mountaintop city of Safed in Galilee, the most famous kabbalist who ever lived—Isaac Luria—pondered creation and asked himself, "What came before?" He believed there was only *Ein Sof,* God as infinity. But if *Ein Sof* pervaded all space, how could there be room for anything other than God? Luria concluded that the first act of creation was not emanation, but withdrawal: "Before the creation of the universe, *Ein Sof* withdrew itself into its essence, from itself to itself within itself. Within its essence, it left an empty space, in which it could emanate and create."[20]

This is *tsimtsum,* which literally means "contraction,"[21] but here suggests withdrawal, a withdrawal by which God made room for something other than God. The primordial void carved out by *tsimtsum* became the site of creation: no larger than an infinitesimal point in relation to *Ein Sof,* yet spacious enough to house the cosmos. But the void was not really empty: it retained a trace, a residue of the light of *Ein Sof,* just as the vacuum preceding the big bang was not completely empty, but rather in a state of minimum energy, pregnant with creative potential and virtual particles.

As *Ein Sof* began to unfold, a ray of light was channeled into the void through vessels. Everything went smoothly at first, but some of the vessels, less translucent, could not withstand the power of the light. They shattered. Most of the light returned to its infinite source, "to the mother's womb." But the rest, falling as sparks along with shards of the shattered vessels, was eventually trapped in material existence. Our task, according to Kabbalah, is to liberate these sparks of light and restore them to divinity. By living ethically and spiritually, we raise the sparks and thereby bring about *tikkun,* the "repair" or mending of the cosmos.

The breaking of the vessels may seem to be a catastrophe; yet if the vessels had not broken, our world of multiplicity would not exist. In a profound sense, we exist because we have lost oneness.

Modern cosmology has a theory that parallels the breaking of the vessels: the theory of broken symmetry. As we know from experience, symmetry can be unstable. Picture yourself at an elegant wedding dinner, sitting with a dozen other guests around a circular table. Champagne glasses have been placed precisely between each dinner plate and the next: perfect right-left symmetry. A waiter fills the glasses with champagne and everyone sits, waiting for someone else to lift a glass. You're a little thirsty and, realizing that the pink bubbles will not last forever, you decide to take a sip. But which champagne glass should you pick? Not fully versed in the rules of etiquette, you could as easily choose the glass to your left as the one to your right. Either way, as soon as you reach for one or the other, the symmetry is broken. Unless everyone else does what you do, someone will have to reach across the table to get a glass.

Let's take a more mundane example. Imagine that you're holding a handful of sharpened pencils, just snug enough that they stand on their points. Now let go. For a moment, the pencils remain balanced and rotationally symmetrical. Looking down from above, you see a perfect circle of pencil erasers. But the symmetry is quickly broken, as the pencils fall into a tangle of thick pickup sticks.[22]

The pencils are a metaphor for the universe. The jumble of fallen pencils is the universe today, while the symmetrical bundle is the universe in its original state. One of the challenges of science is to discover the symmetry hidden within the tangle of ordinary life.

The universe began in an extremely hot state of utmost simplicity and symmetry. As it expands and cools, this perfect symmetry is broken, giving rise to the world of diversity and structure we inhabit.[23] To us today, the fundamental forces of nature appear distinct: gravity, electromagnetism, and two other forces known as the strong and weak nuclear forces. The balance between these forces determines the existence and behavior of everything in the visible universe. Originally all four forces were linked, and today scientists dream of finding a single set of equations describing all four. By colliding subatomic particles, physicists have discovered that at extremely high temperatures the differences between the forces begin to disappear.

One more act of imagination. Imagine yourself journeying back in time, closer and closer to the moment of the big bang. The further you go, the hotter and denser the universe becomes, and broken symmetries are restored. You go back millions and billions of years. Finally you reach the tiniest fraction of time a physicist can imagine: 10^{-43} second after the big bang, a ten-millionth of a millionth of a trillionth of a trillionth of a second after the beginning. Earlier than this is hard to probe, because the density of matter becomes so great that the structure, and perhaps the meaning, of space and time break down. At this point, all interactions between the fundamental forces are indistinguishable. Perfect symmetry.

How did the symmetry of the beginning become so disguised over the course of time? As the universe expands and starts to cool, its radiation and particles lose energy. The various forces become distinct. Meanwhile, matter is also losing its oneness. By the time the universe is just one billionth of a second old, there are four forces and two dozen kinds of elementary particles. This fracturing of symmetry creates the particles of matter and energy found today around us—and within us.

Perfect symmetry sounds alluring, but it is sterile. If the primal force had not broken into four forces, the universe would be a very different place, if it existed at all. Tiny deviations from complete uniformity now give rise to nuclei, atoms, and molecules; then galaxies, stars, planets, and people. We exist today in our present condition, with all our flaws and imperfections, because of broken symmetry, just as Kabbalah teaches that our jumbled, blemished reality derives from the breaking of the vessels.

Broken symmetry and the breaking of the vessels are distinct theories, each generated by a different approach to the question of the origin of the universe; yet, their resonance is intriguing. The human mind has devised alternative strategies—scientific and spiritual—to search for our origin. The two are distinct, but complementary. Science enables us to probe infinitesimal particles of matter and unimaginable depths of outer space, understanding each in light of the other, as we grope our way back toward the beginning. Spirituality guides us through inner space, challenging us to retrace our path to oneness and to live in the light of what we discover.

Both science and spirituality are valid and vital components of human experience. Each can shed light on the ultimate questions that we sometimes ask and often avoid. Naturally, the vast majority of people feel more comfortable in one of these two realms of discourse—either the scientific or the spiritual—but we should challenge ourselves to cultivate an appreciation of both perspectives and thereby gain stereoscopic vision. We become more fully human when we embrace both of these modes.

As we have noted, the Jewish mystics picture divine sparks in every thing that exists. A scientist would say there is energy latent in subatomic particles. The spiritual task is to raise the sparks, to restore the world to God, to become aware that every single thing we do or see or touch or imagine is part of the oneness, a pattern of energy. Raising the sparks is a powerful metaphor; it transforms religion from a list of dos and don'ts, or a list of dogmas, into spiritual adventure.

God is not some separate being up there. She is right here, in the bark of a tree, in a friend's voice, in a stranger's eye. The world is teeming with God. Since God is *in* everything, you can serve God *through* everything. In looking for the divine spark, we discover that what is ordinary is spectacular. The holy deed is doing what needs to be done now.

The world is fractured, and God needs us to mend it. By mending the world—socially, economically, politically—we mend God, whose sparks lie scattered everywhere. But we shouldn't fool ourselves: there will never be a complete *tikkun,* a complete mending of the world. Things will never be perfect; society will never be completely just. How will it all end? Is there a Messiah coming to redeem us? Messiahs captivate our imagination because the world is so unfair, history is so fickle. When the Messiah comes, we are told, everything will be set right: good will finally triumph and evil will be eliminated. That would be nice, but is it the way things work?

What is the long-range future of our planet, according to science? Here's the forecast: our Sun is about 5 billion years old—middle aged and reliable. But 5 billion years from now, the hydrogen fuel in the Sun's core will run out. The core will sag while the atmosphere of the Sun will mushroom, engulfing several of its closest planets, probably including Earth. Gradually, most of this atmosphere will fall away, leaving a hot, dense ball of inert matter.[24]

Life will not necessarily come to an end. By then, human beings, or whatever type of intelligent life evolves from us, will have developed the technology to move to another, safer solar system. Meanwhile, here we are. We still have quite a while until the year 5 billion. There will be no final perfection. No one has arranged the future ahead of time; nothing is preordained. Chance will play a leading role in the way things unfold, as it always has. We should learn to negotiate with chance. We should work on mending our own brokenness, our social fabric, our planet as best we can.

What kind of God can we believe in? The Hebrew word *emunah*, "belief," originally meant trust and faithfulness, both human and divine. Without trusting another person, we cannot love; without trusting others, we cannot build and sustain community. But how can we trust the cosmos, or this God of oneness?

We can trust that we are part of something greater: a vast web of existence constantly expanding and evolving. When we gaze at the nighttime sky, we can ponder that we are made of elements forged within stars, out of particles born in the big bang. We can sense that we are looking back home. The further we gaze into space, the further we see back into time. If we see a galaxy 10 million light years away, we are seeing that galaxy as it was 10 million years ago: it has taken that long for its ancient light to arrive here. Beyond any star we will ever identify, beyond any quasar, lies the horizon of spacetime, 14 billion light years away. But neither God nor the big bang is that far away. The big bang didn't happen somewhere out there, outside of us.[25] Rather, we began *inside* the big bang; we now embody its primordial energy. The big bang has never stopped.

And what about God? God is not an object or a fixed destination. There is no definite way to reach God. But then again, you don't need to reach something that's everywhere. God is not somewhere else, hidden from us. God is right here, hidden from us. We are enslaved by routines. Rushing from event to event, from one chore to another, we rarely let ourselves pause and notice the splendor right in front of us. Our sense of wonder has shriveled, victimized by our pace of life.

How, then, can we find God? A clue is provided by one of the many names of *Shekhinah*, the feminine aspect of God, the divine presence. In Kabbalah, She is called ocean, well, garden, apple orchard. She is also called *zot*, which means simply "this." God is right here, in this very moment, fresh and un-expected, taking you by surprise. God is *this*.

NOTES

1. I want to thank Professors Walter Kohn and Barbara Holdrege, whose thoughtful responses to my essay stimulated my thinking about this problem.

2. Moses Cordovero, *Or Ne'erav*, ed. Yehuda Z. Brandwein (Jerusalem: Yeshivat Qol Yehudah, 1965), 2:2, 18b–19a.

3. J. B. S. Haldane, cited in Richard Dawkins, *The Blind Watchmaker* (New York: W. W. Norton, 1986), 249.

4. John D. Barrow and Joseph Silk, *The Left Hand of Creation: The Origin and Evolution of the Expanding Universe*, 2nd ed. (New York: Oxford University Press, 1993), 21.

5. See Willem B. Drees, *Beyond the Big Bang: Quantum Cosmologies and God* (La Salle, Ill.: Open Court, 1990); Hubert Reeves, "Birth of the Myth of the Birth of the Universe," in *New Windows to the Universe*, ed. F. Sanchez and M. Vasquez (Cambridge: Cambridge University Press, 1990), 2: 141–149.

6. Andrei Linde, "The Self-Reproducing Inflationary Universe," *Scientific American*, November 1994, 48–55. See also Alan H. Guth, *The Inflationary Universe: The Quest for a New Theory of Cosmic Origins* (Boston: Addison-Wesley, 1997).

7. Andrei Linde, "Particle Physics and Inflationary Cosmology," *Physics Today* 40.9 (1987): 68.

8. Joel R. Primack and Nancy Ellen Abrams, " 'In a Beginning . . . ': Quantum Cosmology and Kabbalah," *Tikkun* 10.1 (January–February 1995): 71.

9. See Don Page, cited in Alan Lightman and Roberta Brawer, *Origins: The Lives and Worlds of Modern Cosmologists* (Cambridge: Harvard University Press, 1990), 409.

10. See Norbert M. Samuelson, *Judaism and the Doctrine of Creation* (Cambridge: Cambridge University Press, 1994), 237.

11. Carl Sagan and Ann Druyan, *Shadows of Forgotten Ancestors: A Search for Who We Are* (New York: Random House, 1992), 276.

12. Exodus 31:17.

13. Steven Weinberg, cited in Heinz Pagels, *Perfect Symmetry: The Search for the Beginning of Time* (New York: Simon and Schuster, 1985), 363–364. Weinberg makes a similar statement at the end of *The First Three Minutes: A Modern View of the Origin of the Universe* (New York: Basic Books, 1988), 154; see his discussion of the reactions to this statement in *Dreams of a Final Theory: The Scientist's Search for the Ultimate Laws of Nature* (New York: Vintage Books, 1994), 255–256. For a wide range of responses to Weinberg from some two dozen leading cosmologists (including Weinberg himself), see Lightman and Brawer, *Origins*, passim.

14. Harald Fritzsch, *The Creation of Matter: The Universe from Beginning to End* (New York: Basic Books, 1984), 276.

15. The Taoist *wu* and the Buddhist *sunyata* and *mu* are similar to Western mystical nothingness but not identical. See Daniel C. Matt, "Varieties of Mystical Nothingness: Jewish, Christian and Buddhist," *Studia Philonica Annual* 9 (1997): 316–331. For a history of *ayin*, see Matt, "*Ayin:* The Concept of Nothingness in Jewish Mysticism,"

in *Essential Papers on Kabbalah*, ed. Lawrence Fine (New York: New York University Press, 1995), 67–108.

16. John Gribbin, *In the Beginning: The Birth of the Living Universe* (Boston: Little, Brown and Company, 1993), 165.

17. Moses de León, *Sheqel ha-Qodesh*, ed. A. W. Greenup (London, 1911), 26; see Daniel C. Matt, *The Essential Kabbalah: The Heart of Jewish Mysticism* (San Francisco: HarperSanFrancisco, 1995), 70.

18. Stephen W. Hawking, *A Brief History of Time: From the Big Bang to Black Holes* (New York: Bantam Books, 1988), 45.

19. Shim'on Lavi, *Ketem Paz* (Jerusalem: Ahavat Shalom, 1981), 1:124c; see Matt, *Essential Kabbalah*, 91.

20. Shabbetai Sheftel Horowitz, *Shefa Tal* (Lemberg: M. P. Paremba, 1859): 3:5, 57b; Hayyim Vital, "On the World of Emanation," in *Liqqutim Hadashim* (Jerusalem: Mevaqqeshei ha-Shem, 1985), 17–18; see Matt, *Essential Kabbalah*, 93–94.

21. On *tsimtsum*, see Gershom Scholem, *Sabbatai Sevi: The Mystical Messiah* (Princeton: Princeton University Press, 1973), 28–31. On the various interpretations of *tsimtsum*, see Matt, *Essential Kabbalah*, 91–95; Rachel Elior, *The Paradoxical Ascent to God: The Kabbalistic Theosophy of Habad Hasidism*, trans. Jeffrey M. Green (Albany: State University of New York Press, 1993), 79–91; Michael Wyschogrod, *The Body of Faith: Judaism as Corporeal Election* (New York: Seabury Press, 1983), 98; and from a Christian perspective, Jürgen Moltmann, *God in Creation: A New Theology of Creation and the Spirit of God* (San Francisco: Harper and Row, 1985), 86–89, 152–57. Here I build on the Hasidic conception.

22. See Timothy Ferris, *Coming of Age in the Milky Way* (New York: Doubleday, 1989) 313.

23. Pagels, *Perfect Symmetry*, 18, 246.

24. Kip S. Thorne, *Black Holes and Time Warps: Einstein's Outrageous Legacy* (New York: W. W. Norton, 1994), 159; David Darling, *Deep Time* (New York: Dell, 1991), 139–141.

25. See Edwin Turner, cited in Lightman and Brawer, *Origins*, 320.

BIBLIOGRAPHY

Barrow, John D., and Joseph Silk. *The Left Hand of Creation: The Origin and Evolution of the Expanding Universe*. 2nd ed. New York: Oxford University Press, 1993.

Drees, Willem B. *Beyond the Big Bang: Quantum Cosmologies and God*. La Salle, Ill.: Open Court, 1990.

Ferris, Timothy. *Coming of Age in the Milky Way*. New York: Doubleday, 1989.

Guth, Alan H. *The Inflationary Universe: The Quest for a New Theory of Cosmic Origins*. Boston: Addison-Wesley, 1997.

Hawking, Stephen W. *A Brief History of Time: From the Big Bang to Black Holes*. New York: Bantam Books, 1988.

Linde, Andrei. "Particle Physics and Inflationary Cosmology," *Physics Today* 40.9 (1987): 68.

———. "The Self-Reproducing Inflationary Universe." *Scientific American* 271.5 (November 1994): 48–55.

Matt, Daniel C. "*Ayin*: The Concept of Nothingness in Jewish Mysticism." In *Essential Papers on Kabbalah,* edited by Lawrence Fine. New York: New York University Press, 1995.

———. *The Essential Kabbalah: The Heart of Jewish Mysticism.* San Francisco: HarperSanFrancisco, 1995.

———. *God and the Big Bang: Discovering Harmony between Science and Spirituality.* Woodstock, Vt.: Jewish Lights, 1996.

Primack, Joel R., and Nancy Ellen Abrams. " 'In a Beginning . . . ': Quantum Cosmology and Kabbalah." *Tikkun* 10.1 (January–February 1995): 66–73.

Weinberg, Steven. *The First Three Minutes: A Modern View of the Origin of the Universe.* New York: Basic Books, 1988.

8

The Complementarity of Science and Religion

Harold H. Oliver

Gérard de Vaucoleurs published a popular account of astronomy in which he stated that man was an infinitesimal speck on an insignificant planet revolving around a garden variety star in a spiral arm of a galaxy in a small corner of the universe. When the Basel theologian, Fritz Buri, became aware of these words, he replied: "Man is the astronomer," thus reminding us that science always has a human face. All cosmological theories are human creations. Some philosophers would say the same about religious symbols. It is about the nature and scope of science and religion that I wish to write, specifically, about the complementarity of science and religion.

The late Alfred North Whitehead, pioneer in the philosophy of science, will be long remembered for his twofold claim that "science and religion are the two strongest general forces which influence [humanity]" and that "it is no exaggeration to say that the future course of history depends upon the decision of this generation as to the relations between them."[1] While he did not offer a scheme of their relationship through time, as others have done, he insisted that we must distinguish genuine science from pseudoscience and informed religion from superstition. Several published schemata of the relationship between science and religion have appeared since his time, one of which I first suggested in an article in 1978.[2] So far as I can tell, this was this first time anyone made the notion of "domain" essential to the schema. According to the "domain" theory, science and religion are either about the same or different domains. These claims further subdivide as follows: science and religion say the same things about the same domain, or they say different, possibly conflicting or complementary things about the same domain. The claim that science and religion are about different domains may lead to the conclusion that either or both may be valid or nonvalid, but not contradictory.

Complementarity: The Thesis

In that article I defended the thesis of the complementarity of science and religion, arguing in favor of the position of Donald MacKay against that of Hugo Bedau, the latter of whom insisted that the term "complementarity" should be limited to its original use, namely, that which characterized Bohr's solution to the quantum dilemma.[3] Later, in 1992, Sir John Templeton introduced a new kind of publication, entitled *Who's Who in Theology and Science*, with the words:[4]

> It is hoped that [this] publication will provide a stimulus to communication between individuals and organizations and between scientific and theological communities generally. Most (but not all) of those included see science and theology as related, complementary avenues of truth, and seek in some sense an integration of the ideas and concepts of these two spheres of research, often recognizing that the God of Creation is the source of both the natural and the spiritual.

In words that are resonant with the definition of complementarity presented earlier, Templeton stated what he believes to be the contemporary consensus:[5]

> For some scientists and theologians, the two [spheres] are seen as complementary. Yet they are talking about the same things, with complementary accounts, presenting different aspects of the same event which in its full nature cannot be described adequately by either alone.

In October 1999, a conference was held at the Harvard-Smithsonian Center for Astrophysics by the new Templeton Commission on the Future of Planetary Cosmology. What was new in such a gathering of scientists was "the emphasis on extrasolar astronomy, with an eye to its ultimate significance as a spiritual quest."[6] It is of special interest that one of the persons attending the session pointed out[7]

> that the prestigious British science institutions are beginning to open up to the deeper significance of scientific discovery, inviting lectures of "God and Science" at formerly closed institutions such as

the British Association for the Advancement of Science and the 300-year-old Royal Society.

There is even an Oxford Institute of Science and Spirit that awards a certificate in conjunction with the American, Union Institute.

Upon close inspection it would appear that there are two versions of the complementarity principle as it relates to the relationship of science and religion: a weak version, according to which nonconflictual cooperation between scientists and religionists prevails, but the level of cooperation is not specified, and a strong version according to which, for all complementary statements, the alteration or absence of one of the statements would necessitate a change in the other, as MacKay held.[8] Here the relationship between science and religion must be closely monitored by each to insure integrity. This latter definition is implied in Templeton's description: "they are talking about the same things, with complementary accounts, presenting different aspects of the same event which in its full nature cannot be described by either alone."[9] Whatever version one chooses, the result is that science and religion are allies that cooperate at a fundamental level. MacKay used a model proposed by C. A. Coulson to explain this version of complementarity.[10] He said that science and religion are like the front and side projections of a the plan of a building. One would need both to reconstruct the building, though the projections are orthogonal, and hence "blind," to each other.

Another form of the one domain thesis is the conflict theory, according to which science and religion say different, contradictory things about the same domain. This is the view of certain conservative Christians for whom the biblical view of creation differs from scientific theories of cosmology and for whom evolution is considered both bad religion and bad science, while religion is thought to be good science. On this basis, many of these groups have sponsored efforts to have evolution taught concurrently with what they dubiously call creation science. Even though it is called "science," it conducts no independent research.

When it is held that science and religion do not conflict, this is often based on the supposition that they are about two domains, the natural and supernatural. I have labeled this the "compartment theory," and the strategic advantage of this theory is that science and religion cannot be in conflict, since they are about different things. The ground is open in this claim for scientists to deny the reality of the supernatural, but when this happens, scientific naturalism simply prevails. I will try to make a reasonable case for the belief that there is but one domain, and it is human experience.

A recent advocate of the compartment theory is Stephen Jay Gould who calls it the "separationist" claim.[11] He seems to have been swayed into a pronouncement about this claim by his reaction to two developments. The first is the theories of the discoverer and curator of the Burgess Shale fauna, C. D.

Walcott, who was influenced in his practice of science by (a) assuming, under the spell of the prevailing scheme of the social theory of progress, the cogency of "a view of life as a single progressive chain"[12] and (b) his belief that science should serve "the altruistic, or, as some would call it, the spiritual nature of man," a claim that Gould connects with Walcott's attempt to deal positively with the Scopes trial of 1925.[13] The second provocation for Gould's pronouncement concerns the antievolutionists trials in 1925 and 1987. His statement warrants quoting.[14]

> The canonical attitude of scientists then and now—and the argu-
> ment that finally secured our [!] legal victory before the Supreme
> Court in 1987—holds that science and religion operate in equally le-
> gitimate but separate areas. This "separationist" claim allots the
> mechanisms and phenomena of nature to scientists and the basis
> for ethical decisions to theologians and humanists in general—the
> age of rocks versus the rock of ages, or "how heaven goes" versus
> "how to go to heaven" in the old one-liners. In exchange for free-
> dom to follow nature down all her pathways, scientists relinquish
> the temptation to base moral inferences and pronouncements upon
> the physical state of the world—an excellent and proper arrange-
> ment, since the facts of nature embody no moral claims in any case.

While Gould's legally driven "separationist" position protects both science and religion from improper encroachments on one another, his reduction of the realm of the religious to the "ethical" and "moral" will appall theologians, who view religion as a rich symbolic world.[15]

The Grounds for the Complementarity Thesis

No one can speak for the whole of science and religion, but I shall argue that science, especially modern physics, and religion are converging on a relational paradigm. My reason for highlighting "modern physics" is that relativity theory and quantum theory, both of which emerged in the first years of the twentieth century, displaced Newtonian physics and set physics on a course which is decidedly "relational." Relativity theory replaced the "substantives" of Newtonian physics—space, time, and matter—with spacetime events and merged space and time into spacetime. The classical Newtonian theory of matter as composed of substantial particles was displaced by the theory of matter as matter-energy. Though the issues are more controversial, quantum physics raised questions about what seems to be the paradox of particles and waves, apparent in the fact that if one sets up an experiment to test for waves, one finds waves, and conversely, if one sets up an experiment to test for particles, one finds particles. This prompted Bohr to introduce the term "complementarity" to resolve the paradox. The classical theory of particles collapsed. They can only with reservations be called "substantives." Bohm wrote the following to elucidate the Copenhagen position:[16]

> the properties of matter are incompletely defined and opposing potentialities that can be fully realized only in interactions with other systems. . . . Thus, at the quantum level of accuracy, an object does not have any "intrinsic" properties (for instance, wave or particle) belonging to itself alone; instead it shares its properties mutually and indivisibly with the systems with which it interacts.

He had already written:[17]

> The existence of reciprocal relationships of things implies that each "thing" existing in nature makes some contribution to what the universe as a whole is, a contribution that cannot be reduced completely, perfectly and unconditionally, to the effects of any specific set or sets of other things with which it is in reciprocal interconnection. And, vice versa, this also means evidently that no given thing can have a complete autonomy in its mode of being, since its basic characteristics must depend on its relationship with other things. The notion of a thing is thus seen to be an abstraction, in which it is conceptually separated from its infinite background and substructure.

In this same spirit, the physicist Richard Schlegel argued that[18]

> Physics is the most abstract of the physical sciences, since it does not take any particular set of entities as its subject matter. . . . Physicists attempt to describe and explain the properties of space, time, matter and energy everywhere in the universe. Their science is expected to be valid for discussion of all material things: of stars, of man-made machines, or of living cells, without, however, taking as its domain the particular properties of any of those entities.

Modern physicists are still working within this paradigm of "relationality," according to which the physical realities are not things with their properties, but the properties themselves. In a recent *New York Times* review by Michael Riordan of a new book by Lee Smolin, entitled *Three Roads to Quantum Gravity*, the reviewer notes the following viewpoint of Smolin:[19]

> This is a deeply philosophical work that makes us rethink the epistemological roots of the mental pictures we make about nature. Smolin maintains that we must adopt a "relational" viewpoint in which space and time are nothing but networks of relationships.

Smolin's bold stand on relationality is made throughout his book. The essence of his claim appears early on:[20]

> The lesson that the world is at root a network of evolving relationships tells us that this is true to a lesser or greater extent of all things. There is no fixed, eternal frame to the universe to define what may or may not exist. There is nothing beyond the world except what we see, no background to it except its particular history.

Smolin, who teaches at Penn State and on occasion conducted his research with Ted Jacobson at the Institute for Theoretical Physics at Santa Barbara, even identifies himself as one of the founders of "relational quantum theory."[21] On the same page he asserts: "The universe of events is a relational universe. That is, all its properties are described in terms of relationships between the events." His work on loop quantum gravity has led him to maintain, over against string theory, that on the Planck scale the theory must be background independent. This means that space to him is not continuous, but discrete; this further reinforces the idea that fundamental entities are not located in space; rather, space—and time—are aspects of relations. It follows, further, that the fundamental entities, to use his term, are processes "by which information is conveyed from one part of the world to another."[22] Smolin then surmises that finally, perhaps, "the history of the universe is nothing but the flow of information."[23] I have presented these ideas, not to suggest that his theories are to be preferred to others, but that relational models are still being championed on the frontiers of physics.

To return to our thesis of complementarity: for some it is sufficient for the thesis of complementarity to promote a spirit of cooperation among scientists and theologians, as desirable as that may be. For others, there must be some basis for this thesis in the nature of the two disciplines. Since they are historically different modes, some other discipline must mediate between these two modes. Traditionally, metaphysics has played this role, because it is the most generalized form of thinking.

One of the lessons we learn from modern metaphysics is that, in contrast to the East, Western thought has become substantialistic and egoistic. Beings are considered substances and their relations are accidents, and reality belongs to substances. This Western bias can be traced to the influence of Aristotle who based his philosophy on the subject-object structure of the Greek language. Aristotelian substantialism did much to shape science and religion in the West. In the modern world Descartes institutionalized substantialism and through his Methodic Doubt developed the notion of the Modern Subject, ensuring the egoistic tendency of Western philosophy, theology, and physics.

We have seen how modern physics moved toward a relational paradigm; now we must turn to the philosophical situation in the twentieth century, and especially to the metaphysical thesis of universal internality, to determine the nature of the emerging relational paradigm in physics and metaphysics. To do this, we turn to the modern debate among philosophers about the nature of relations.

It was in the closing years of the nineteenth century that a British philosopher, F. H. Bradley, first proposed that all relations are internal. This case was made in the appendix to the second edition of his magnum opus, *Appearance and Reality*, published in 1893, where he argued, among other things, that "Nothing in the whole or in the end can be external, and everything in the Universe is an abstraction from the whole."[24] Bradley's compatriot, A. C. Ewing, stated that position as follows:[25]

> The world known to us constitutes a system in which every particular is linked to the rest of the system by a relation of logical entailment. . . . It implies that the nature of any one thing taken by itself is incomplete and incoherent without the whole system on which it depends. Things by their very essence belong together.

While many responsible philosophers opposed this doctrine of universal relatedness, as did Charles Hartshorne, who properly labeled it, it claimed the allegiance of Brand Blanshard of Yale who argued in connection with the doctrine, that scientific method is reductionist because it intentionally dissociates things that belong together. He continues:[26]

> Everyone of the experimental canons . . . does its work by elimination, that is, by showing that all but certain factors are unconnected with a given result, either because they are present when it is absent, or absent when it is present, or independently variable.

It was Blanshard who gives us this definition of internal relatedness:[27]

> A relation is internal to a term when in its absence the term would be different; it is external, when its addition or withdrawal would make no difference to a term.

Bradley had his opponents, mainly Bertrand Russell in his early years, who argued that all relations are external, while William James and G. E. Moore made the more cautious case that some relations are internal, some external. Both men were opponents of Bradley's neo-Hegelian monism and sought to dethrone it by defending the thesis that at least some relations are external. The American philosopher, Charles Hartshorne, devoted his whole career to articulating and defending the doctrine that some relations are internal to the terms, and some are external. Yet, it is the case that Hartshorne could not break completely free of monism, as we see in the following quotation:[28]

> The interaction between two molecules is slightly peculiar to those molecules, yet it is one thing even though they are two, or rather, it

is one thing with various aspects. In this oneness is expressed the unity of the world. All relations, internal and external, involve a substantial unity embracing the relata.

For over thirty years I have defended the thesis of universal internality as a metaphysical position of greatest cogency. Metaphysics is the study of reality and proceeds by locating the irreducible component, or components, of experience. Relational metaphysics claims that the most economical thing that can be said about experience is that it consists of relatedness. It further argues that experience consists of what is fundamental and what is derivative, and that what is fundamental is relatedness. All the other so-called fundamentals, such as subjects and objects, mind and brain, are derivatives. These derivatives are harmless enough in everyday discourse unless they are treated as fundamental.

One might say that the quest in metaphysics is for the answer to Heidegger's question, "What is a thing?" It is feasible to argue now that the usual things that were thought of as fundamental are best considered derivatives. Continuing to treat them as fundamentals unduly complicates metaphysics. What Whitehead had to say about what we have usually thought of as "enduring things" I should like to apply to all pseudofundamentals:[29]

> The simple notion of an enduring substance sustaining persistent qualities, either essentially or accidentally, expresses a useful abstract for many purposes of life. But whenever we try to use it as a fundamental statement of the nature of things, it proves itself mistaken. It arose from a mistake and has never succeeded in any of its applications. But it has had one success: it has entrenched itself in language, in Aristotelean logic, and in metaphysics. For its employment in language and logic there is . . . a sound pragmatic defence. But in metaphysics the concept is sheer error.

Having established reasons for believing that physics and metaphysics both present relational features, it now remains to be shown how all this pertains to religion. My thesis is that relational metaphysics provides a hermeneutical paradigm which comes closest to respecting the original intentionality of the religious traditions. Religion has been plagued by reification, whereby derivatives have been treated as fundamental.

"Saying Different Things": The Language of Religion and the Language of Science

The thesis of complementarity holds that religion and science "are saying different things about the same domain." What is the nature of this "difference"? First, we shall consider the language of religion.

Religion comes to us as mythical discourse and the language derived from it. The aboriginal sources of religion are dramatic mythical narratives. They image reality as relatedness. They are symbolic discourse about the symbolic world. They achieve this as dramatic narratives that "character-ize" experience, that is, set it forth in characters. The stories are staged, that is to say, they intend an audience. What they portray is what Urs von Balthasar called the drama of existence. He had this to say about drama:[30]

> Nowhere is the drama of existence demonstrated more clearly than in stage drama; we are drawn to watch it, and initially it is immaterial whether in doing so we are searching for or fleeing from ourselves, immaterial whether the performance is showing us the serious- or play-dimension, the destructive or the transfiguring aspect, the absurdity or the hidden profundity of our life. Probably nowhere else but in this interplay of relationships (which is the essence of theater) can we see so clearly the questionable nature not only of the theater but also of existence itself, which the theater illuminates.

The myths do not intend to make declarations outside of the parameters of the stories about the "reality" of the characters. This means that all the characters of mythical drama have dramatic reality. To say more about their reality transcends the limits of the story. We may be tempted to do this nevertheless, but we thereby approach myths with an alien intentionality. This happens when we reify the characters into realities transcendent of their dramatic home, whether human or divine.

The reification of religious characters is the result of taking these stories literally rather than symbolically. This claim applies equally to the divine and the human characters in the stories. When we lose sight of the dramatic context of these characters, whether of gods or humans, we are tempted to portray them as realities outside of the stories. We then say things like, God is transcendent or immanent, or both, or neither, and engage in debates about the divine nature as we transgress the boundaries of myth. "God created the world" is mythical discourse, not wholly unlike that of Israel's neighbors in the ancient Near East. If we take these words literally we approach them with an alien intentionality. We are then tempted to say theological things like "God gives us faith," when it more germane to say, with the Japanese philosopher, Daisetz Suzuki, that it is "faith that gives us God."[31]

I would argue that it is more appropriate to speak of God as the eminent other of the myth, but here, from a relational perspective, "other" means mutuality, not nonmutuality. God is the divine presence in the stories. To take the stories literally leads us into problematical assertions, such as "God is super agent," or "God is the Absolute Subject" (Barth). This problematic underlies many of the statements of philosophers, such as "God has a primordial and a consequent nature" (Whitehead) or "God is finite" (Brightman). We can never speak univocally about such matters; we must honor the symbolic nature of all religious discourse.

It follows from these claims that all the biblical narratives, including the Gospels, are dramatic narrative. If we try to treat them as historical biographies we immediately run into difficulties that are insurmountable. All the so-called quests for the historical Jesus have failed. David Friedrich Strauss was the first postenlightenment scholar to respect the mythical limits of the Gospels and he soon lost sight of this fact. Kierkegaard said that if we had only the story, that would be enough. And that is what we have. To use the Gospels to try to discover what lies hidden behind them, misses the intention of myth. It instrumentalizes the myth by putting it to an impossible task. Suddenly, what the texts meant to say or failed to say becomes more important than what they do say.

As dramatic narratives, the texts are iconic. They image experience as relatedness. They are not referential; they do not refer to entities, but present characters. It is relatedness that is presented in the stories. They depict that divinity and humanity are both relevant dimensions of life, that we are the sum of our relationships, nothing less or more.

It is true that prior to the Enlightenment, according to the Yale professor, Hans Frei, the narratives were regarded as "realistic or story-like," though he adds: "not necessarily historical."[32] It was with the coming of the Enlightenment and one of its by-products, the supernaturalists, that the earlier viewpoint was displaced. Frei describes this change in perspective as follows:[33]

> They [the Supernaturalists] argued the historical factuality of the biblical reports of miracles and the fulfillment of prophecy. . . . [These] Conservative commentators increasingly treated the narrative portions of the Bible as a factually reliable repository of divine revelation.

In the ancient world and more or less through the Middle Ages, mythic consciousness was still in place. To the question, What are the stories about? the answer would be: About the gods. With the Enlightenment the question was extended to: What are the stories of the gods about? With this question, mythic consciousness was broken and gave way to the primacy of reason alone. Those who continued to live within the faith community did so on a different basis. The rationalists had argued that the statement, God exists, is false; the believers countered, not that God exists, but that the statement that God exists is false, is false. Supernaturalism continued the earlier traditions, as it does in some places today, not as something positive, but as something doubly negative. This is the seedbed of the some of the conflicts between religion and science. It is not in the true spirit of religion to seek to undermine any genuine human endeavor, especially one so significant as science, for religion, too, seeks to elevate the human spirit.

Turning to science, the difference of language becomes obvious. Rather than myth, we find that science is characterized as the most economical way of speaking of the natural world. Economy of hypothesis is to be preferred. Science is an idiom of the subjunctive mode. It is an idiom of "if, then." Unfortunately, in media presentations the "if" is omitted. Then things are stated as fact without regard to what a fact may be. An article might begin by saying that "if the red shift is cosmological, the universe is expanding," only then continue, "The universe is expanding." Science depends upon methods which are time-tested but not necessarily without flaws. Since the time of Bacon it has been assumed that the law of induction is trustworthy. But as late as the twentieth century, logicians have challenged the adequacy of inductive reasoning.

One of the advantages of science is that it is public and universal. The community of scientists is not bound to a specific culture and seeks to escape the idiosyncracies of local cultures. Science does not depend upon individual sleight-of-hand, nor does it make room for revelation in the religious sense. Nor is it dogmatic in a negative sense; it is ever revising its more trusted conclusions. I am always a bit suspicious when I see the word "really" in scientific papers. In 1971, I was in Cambridge where tensions ran high between "steady state" and big bang cosmologies. At that time, I ran across an article by Geoffrey Burbidge, who is now at the University of California at San Diego, entitled, "Was there really a Big Bang?" My first thought was that the article would reach a new level of profundity, but discovered, upon inspection, that it was simply a routine defense of steady state theory.[34] When scientists use the word "real," it is often for apologetic reasons.

"The Same Domain": Human Experience

It has often been said that religion is about the supernatural and science is about the natural. Scientists do not like this division because it plays into the hands of the religionist. The scientist who denies the existence of the supernatural is accused of espousing naturalism. It is more economical to say that religion and science are about the same domain, namely, human experience. This is because, as I like to say, experience is all there is. Experience is very tolerant; it answers the questions we put to it. If we ask spiritual questions, we get spiritual answers; and conversely, if we ask physical questions, we get physical answers. If I ask, why the planets move, I don't expect to get the answer, "because they are put in motion by angels," even though Newton thought so. If I ask if there is a heaven, I do not expect a scientific confirmation. It was simple ignorance when the early Russian astronaut said God was not to be found in space. It was a remark clearly out of touch with the true nature of science and religion.

The domain of experience is difficult to agree upon. If we draw on a relational metaphysics of experience, we come to the conclusion that experience is relating. It is not the experience of an experiencer. The experiencer qua experience does not precede the experiencing. Nor does what-is-experienced precede the experiencing. The reality is the action, the acting, relating. The terms of the relationship are derivatives, useful abstractions, but we must not make them fundamental.

It is this metaphysical perspective that makes some aspects of quantum theory so interesting. When Heisenberg maintained that the reality of the particle comes into existence when we observe it, some realists thought that he had introduced the "ghost of the observer" into quantum mechanics. I should argue that it is a metaphysically responsible position, in that in the words of David Bohm, the observer and the world represent an indivisible system. Under this rubric he elaborates upon the nature of the world:[35]

> the world cannot be analyzed correctly into distinct parts; instead it must be regarded as an indivisible unit in which separate parts appear as valid approximations only in the classical limit.

One thing I have insisted upon in my relational position is that we need only one metaphysics for the whole of experience. In the previous state of affairs people had several: one metaphysics for science at the macroscopic level, another for the quantum level, another for the social level, and still another for religious matters. The relational schema I am proposing has in its favor extreme economy. We may say that the observer—the observing—and the observed reduce to the observing. The observer and the observed are co-derivative abstractions. In the social world, the self—the relating—and other reduce fundamentally to the relating. The self and the other are co-derivatives. In religious discourse, the worshiper—the worshiping—and the Worshiped reduce to the worshiping. The Worshiped is not demeaned by this formulation, for it is worship that gives us God, as I shall argue later. In this connection Whitehead's words are worth remembering: "The power of God is the worship He inspires."[36]

In the West where there is almost an idolizing of the "subject"—as witness the long entrenchment of the philosophy of idealism—some may feel that this relational system demeans the subject, namely the individual. This objection I should counter with the insight of the Kyōto philosopher, Nishida Kitarō— somewhat influenced by William James—who argued: "It is not that there is experience because there is an individual, but that there is an individual because there is experience."[37] It is only along this line of reasoning that we can say that experiencing is all there is. One of his colleagues, Keiji Nishitani, elaborated upon this notion which Nishida associated with what he called "pure experience" in memorable words:[38]

> There is a single life that vitalizes the universe as a whole. In reality no separate, individual things exist on their own. The only such self is the one that we have thought up; nothing in reality is so patterned. This view of the world may seem to leave us out of the picture altogether, but it only means that in our looking and listening the activities of looking and listening have emerged somewhere from the depths of the universe. Our looking and listening and all the other things we do issue from a point where things form a single living bond. This is why these activities are united with all sorts of other things and why we cannot think in terms of things existing on the outside and a mind existing on the inside. This is a later standpoint; the prior standpoint is that of pure experience where subject and object are one and undifferentiated. It is here that all experience takes place.

Science, Religion, and Truth

The question naturally arises when speaking of complementarity, whether science or religion, or both, or neither, gives us truth. In the quotation above Sir John Templeton cautiously speaks of science and religion as "complementary avenues of truth." This is a fairly optimistic assessment of science and religion; a more pessimistic view holds that either science or religion speaks truth, but not both. Perhaps we should approach this weighty question by first considering science and religion seriatim, then together.

Science and Truth

We have been taught to think that scientists are laboring in the service of truth. In the steady growth of science, many supposed truths have given way to what are thought to be more certain truths. Some of these supposed truths were earlier scientific theories, while others were prevailing notions associated with religion. Cosmologies came and went, all in the interest of a better understanding of the physical world.

Scientists have been vigorous in their pursuit of better understanding. But not all have agreed upon the nature of their conclusions. Some use the word "truth" more confidently of their theories than others. There are endless anecdotes about this, but I shall call attention to an interview between Richard Feynman and Fred Hoyle which was aired on the BBC in 1972. Feynman was questioning the propriety of saying that the laws of physics evolved over time, but realized that this was a point on which he and Hoyle differed. He said to Hoyle: "I think of the possibilities; you are the one who speculates." Whereupon Hoyle replied: "I do not set as a requirement that the answers be right." This reminds us of the famous words of Whitehead: "[It] is more important that a proposition be interesting than that it be true."[39] Here the remark of J. D. North is relevant: "The individual theory of cosmology is neither true nor false; like any other scientific theory, it is merely an instrument of what passes for our understanding."[40]

We should be reluctant today to say of any scientific theory that it is true. In the eighteenth century this is precisely what was said of Newton's theory. D'Alembert wrote in 1757: "The true system of the world has been recognized, developed and perfected."[41] In the nineteenth century, confidence in Newton's theories began to wane, and in 1900, quantum theory, and in 1905–16, special and general relativity brought a new era in physics. When Einstein predicted that starlight is bent when it moves past a massive body in space, Arthur Eddington led an expedition designed to test the prediction. After much checking of the data, he went on record as saying that his findings "prove" general relativity. When this was announced to Einstein, his response was: "The truth of a theory is in your mind, not in your eyes." But when it was brought to the attention of the Royal Society, its president, J. J. Thomson, remarked: "It [general relativity] is the greatest discovery since Newton enunciated his principles."[42] Eddington's expedition had set out to "confirm" or "verify" Einstein's theory. Now that it was "confirmed," what was to said of the new physical theories, that they are right and the older theories wrong? The philosophy of science arose in this century to respond to this question.

Michael Ovenden, an astronomer friend, expressed a belief about the older physics that shows how far some physicists have come on the truth question in light of the new situation in physics:[43]

> The [laws of motion] could in no sense be proven wrong; they are
> wholly tautologous, in that, if you measure a force by the rate of
> change of momentum, then whenever there is a change of momen-
> tum you will automatically say a force is acting. Of course, when
> you go from this to applying it to our experience, then the question
> you have to ask is, does that particular way of looking at things
> make the world look simple? If so, it is a good theory. If not, then it
> is not a good theory. And of course, eminently so does Newton's
> theory do this.

Karl Popper, the eminent philosopher of science, was more of a realist, though expressing caution in what we say about prevailing theories. He proposed that we say that a prevailing scientific theory is one that is "corroborated" rather than "verified," but then threw caution to the wind by claiming that there is a growth of scientific knowledge in that the successive development of theories brings us "closer and closer to the truth." This optimism is not shared by all, for how can one say that we are moving closer to the truth without knowing what the truth is? I prefer to say that scientific theories add new features to our experience. Einstein's general theory made us look at the universe in a different way, and there is no going back. This is not to say that general relativity is true. The theory is rather, with all of its shortcomings, what passes for our understanding. It has come to be what Thomas Kuhn calls "normal science," and will continue to function in that way until some more comprehensive theory of gravity prevails.

Religion and Truth

So far, some of our discussion of scientific "truth" has assumed that truth is the right term for the actual state of affairs. We were cautioned by Heisenberg that the observer and the observed are not to be conceived as "subject and object," that there is a more unified way of conceiving of physical reality. It is in quantum theory that physicists have become quite philosophical in speaking of relationality. Some philosophers of science have yet to conceive of the question of truth in the physical sciences taking this fully into account. Whitehead is a notable exception to this indictment.

When we turn to a consideration of religion and truth, we must make every effort to avoid the subject-object model. When this has not been done, religious conceptions are conceived as "external" to the believer. The time has come to think of religious truth in a relational way, because this way is most compatible with religion itself. The believing self is not a subject-self over and against an object-God. A quotation from Whitehead's *Process and Reality* is worth noting in this regard:[44]

> Consider a Christian meditating on the sayings in the Gospels. He is not judging 'true or false'; he is eliciting their value as elements in feeling. In fact, he may ground his judgment of truth upon his realization of value.

All of the world's great religions equate believing and knowing, but the knowing is not of the subject-object kind. Religion is an iconic way of manifesting the relationality that lies at the root of all experience, as I have argued throughout this essay. Relational metaphysics is the notional form of the same insight. As an iconic manifestation of relatedness, religion emphasizes community over individualism, altruism over self-interest. It is, as Whitehead said, "the vision of something which stands beyond, behind and within, the passing flux of immediate things; something which is real, and yet waiting to be realised."[45]

Religion is a primal knowing which is easier to illustrate than to define. The finest contemporary example of which I am aware appeared in an interview of the octogenarian Carl Gustav Jung by John Freeman of the BBC. The dialogue between them is instructive:[46]

FREEMAN   When you were young did you go to church?

JUNG   Oh yes! We all went to church.

FREEMAN   And did you believe in God?

JUNG   Oh yes! We all believed.

And then as if to ensnare Jung, Freeman asked: "Now, do you believe?" Jung replied: "Now? Difficult to answer. Now . . . I know."

Jung, who claimed to be scientific in his work, did not think of his knowledge of God as objective. In his unusual life, the world of science and the symbolic world were conjoined.

As regards religion and truth we must make a difference between rationality and relativism if we want to avoid the appearance of the superiority of one religion over another. In this regard the following words of Raimundo Pannikar are instructive:[47]

Truth is constituted by the total relationship of things, because things are insofar as they are in relation to one another. But this relation is not a private relation between a subject and an object. It is a universal relationship so that it is not for any private individual or group to exhaust any relationship. Truth is relational, thus relational to me. But never private.

Conclusion

I have held up the ideal of the complementarity of science and religion. Now I want to suggest that the highest ideal is reached when scientific understanding and religious truth are found in the same person. While the example we think of most readily is Einstein, there is a story about Robert Oppenheimer that well illustrates what I have in mind. It tells how at the test site of the first atomic bomb he saw the spiritual significance of this triumph of physics. At the experimental area called "Death Tract" (Jornado del Muerto) the observers of the first blast did not know what to expect. Robert Jungk tells us that "Oppenheimer oscillated between fears that the experiment might fail and fears that it would succeed."[48] Jungk then proceeds to describe the actual moment:[49]

People were transformed with fright at the power of the explosion. Oppenheimer was clinging to one of the uprights in the control room. A passage from the Bhagavad-Gita, the sacred epic of the Hindus, flashed into his mind:

If the radiance of a thousand suns
were to burst into the sky,
that would be like
the splendor of the Mighty One.

Yet, when the sinister and gigantic cloud rose up in the far distance over Point Zero, he was reminded of another line from the same source:

I am become Death, the shatterer of worlds.

Finally, I cannot stress strongly enough the unity that is the basis of the complementarity thesis. It was perhaps best expressed in 1911 by Nishida in *An Inquiry into the Good*:[50]

[N]ature and spirit are not two completely different kinds of reality. The distinction between them results from different ways of looking at one and the same reality. Anyone who deeply comprehends nature discerns a spiritual unity at its base. Moreover, complete, true spirit is united with nature; only one reality exists in the universe.

Perhaps we could say that this insight is the ultimate justification for the use of the term "cosmology" by both scientists and metaphysicians alike. What I have said in this essay is offered in the spirit of this insight.

NOTES

1. *Science and the Modern World*, Lowell Lectures 1925 (New York: The Free Press, [1925] 1967), 181.

2. Harold H. Oliver, "The Complementarity of Theology and Cosmology," *Zygon* 13 (1978): 19–33. Reprinted in Oliver, *Relatedness: Essays in Metaphysics and Theology* (Macon, Ga.: Mercer University Press, 1984), 1–20.

3. Hugo Adam Bedau, "Complementarity and the Relation between Science and Religion," *Zygon* 9 (1974): 202–224.

4. *Who's Who in Theology and Science*, compiled and edited by the John Templeton Foundation (Notre Dame: University of Notre Dame Press, 1992), 7.

5. Ibid.

6. *Progress in Theology: The Newsletter of the John Templeton Foundation* 8 (March–April, 2000): 1.

7. Ibid.

8. Oliver, *Relatedness*, 12.

9. *Progress in Theology*, 9.

10. D. M. MacKay, " 'Complementarity' in Scientific and Religious Thinking," *Zygon* 9 (1974), 229.

11. Stephen Jay Gould, *Wonderful Life: The Burgess Shale and the Nature of History* (New York: W. W. Norton, 1989), 261.

12. Ibid., 260.

13. Ibid., 261. Gould here quotes Walcott's letter, dated January 7, 1926, to R. B. Fosdick.

14. Ibid.

15. Advocates of the right and/or duty of scientists to critique religion will not respond positively to Gould's theory. Cf. Thomas W. Clark, "Faith, Science and the Soul: On the Pragmatic Virtues of Naturalism," *Humanist* 53 (May–June 1993): 7–12.

16. David Bohm, *Quantum Theory* (London: Constable and Company, 1951), 161.

17. Ibid., 147.

18. Richard Schlegel, "Quantum Physics and Human Purpose," *Zygon* 8 (1973): 200–220.

19. Michael Riordan, "Three Roads to Quantum Gravity: Space-Time Is of the Essence," *The New York Times*, August 19, 2001. I wish to thank my former student, John Thatamanil, now professor at Vanderbilt Divinity School, for bringing this review to my attention.

20. Lee Smolin, *Three Roads to Quantum Gravity* (New York: Basic Books, 2001), 20.

21. Ibid., 53.

22. Ibid., 176.

23. Ibid., 178.

24. F. H. Bradley, *Appearance and Reality A Metaphysical Essay*, 2nd ed. (Oxford: Clarendon Press, 1893), 521.

25. A. C. Ewing, *Idealism: A Critical Survey* (New York: The Humanities Press, 1934), 187.

26. Brand Blanshard, *The Nature of Thought*, The Muirhead Library of Philosophy (New York: Macmillan, 1940), 2: 454.

27. Ibid., 431.

28. Charles Hartshorne, *Man's Vision of God and the Logic of Theism* (New York: Harper and Row, [1941] 1984), 238.

29. Alfred North Whitehead, *Process and Reality: An Essay in Cosmology*, eds. David Ray Griffin and Donald W. Sherburne (New York: The Free Press, 1978), 79.

30. Hans Urs von Balthasar, *Theo-drama: Theological Dramatic Theory*, trans. Graham Harrison (San Francisco: Ignatius Press, 1988), 1: 17ff.

31. Daisetz Suzuki, "The Awakening of a New Consciousness in Zen," *Eranos-Jahrbuch* (Zurich: Rhein-Verlag, 1955), 285.

32. Hans Frei, *The Eclipse of Biblical Narrative: A Study in Eighteenth and Nineteenth Century Hermeneutics* (New Haven: Yale University Press, 1974), 10.

33. Ibid., 87.

34. Burbidge is still using the idea of "reality" in his recent book, coauthored with Fred Hoyle and J. V. Narlikar, entitled, *A Different Approach to Cosmology: From a Static Universe through the Big Bang towards Reality* (Cambridge: Cambridge University Press, 2000).

35. Bohm, *Quantum*, 49.

36. Alfred North Whitehead, *Science and the Modern World*, Lowell Lectures 1925 (New York: The Free Press, [1925] 1967), 192.

37. Kitaro Nishida, *An Inquiry into the Good*, trans. Masao Abe and Christopher Ives, intro. Masao Abe (New Haven: Yale University Press, 1990), 19.

38. Nishitani Keiji, *Nishida Kitarō*, trans. Yamamoto Seisaku and James Heisig, intro. D. S. Clarke Jr. (Berkeley: University of California Press, 1991), 54f.

39. Whitehead, *Process and Reality*, 259.

40. J. D. North, *The Measure of the Universe: A History of Modern Cosmology* (Oxford: Clarendon Press), 407.

41. From D'Alembert's *Elements of Philosophy*, cited from Gerd Buchdahl, *The Image of Newton and Locke in the Age of Reason* (London: Sheed and Ward, 1961), 7.

42. Ronald W. Clark, *Einstein: The Life and Times* (New York: World Publishing, 1971), 232.

43. Private interview, December 1971.

44. Whitehead, *Process and Reality*, 185.

45. Whitehead, *Science and the Modern World*, 191f.

46. John Freeman interview with Carl Gustav Jung, *Face to Face*, BBC, October 1959.

47. Raimundo Panikkar, "Religious Pluralism: The Metaphysical Challenge," in *Religious Pluralism*, ed. Leroy S. Rouner (Notre Dame: University of Notre Dame Press, 1984), 113.

48. Robert Jungk, *Brighter than a Thousand Suns: A Personal History of the Atomic Scientists*, trans. James Cleugh (New York: Harcourt, Brace, 1958), 200.

49. Ibid., 201.

50. Nishida, *Inquiry*, 78.

BIBLIOGRAPHY

Bedau, Hugo Adam. "Complementarity and the Relation between Science and Religion." *Zygon* 9 (1974): 202–224.

Blanshard, Brand. *The Nature of Thought*. Vol. 2 of The Muirhead Library of Philosophy. New York: Macmillan, 1940.

Bradley, F. H. *Appearance and Reality: A Metaphysical Essay*. 2nd ed. Oxford: Clarendon Press, 1893.

Bohm, David. *Quantum Theory*. London: Constable and Company, 1951.

Buchdahl, Gerd. *The Image of Newton and Locke in the Age of Reason*. London: Sheed and Ward, 1961.

Burbidge, Geoffrey, Fred Hoyle, and J. V. Narlikar. *A Different Approach to Cosmology: From a Static Universe through the Big Bang towards Reality*. Cambridge: Cambridge University Press, 2000.

Clark, Ronald W. *Einstein: The Life and Times*. New York: World Publishing, 1971.

Clark, Thomas W. "Faith, Science and the Soul: On the Pragmatic Virtues of Naturalism." *Humanist* 53 (May–June 1993): 7–12.

Ewing, A. C. *Idealism: A Critical Survey*. New York: The Humanities Press, 1934.

Freeman, John. Interview with Carl Gustav Jung. *Face to Face*. BBC, October 1959.

Frei, Hans. *The Eclipse of Biblical Narrative: A Study in Eighteenth and Nineteenth Century Hermeneutics*. New Haven: Yale University Press, 1974.

Gould, Stephen Jay. *Wonderful Life: The Burgess Shale and the Nature of History*. New York: W. W. Norton, 1989.

Hartshorne, Charles. *Man's Vision of God and the Logic of Theism*. New York: Harper & Row, [1941] 1984.

Jungk, Robert. *Brighter than a Thousand Suns: A Personal History of the Atomic Scientists*. Translated by James Cleugh. New York: Harcourt, Brace, 1958.

MacKay, D. M. " 'Complementarity' in Scientific and Religious Thinking." *Zygon* 9 (1974).

Nishida, Kitarō. *An Inquiry into the Good*. Translated by Masao Abe and Christopher Ives. New Haven: Yale University Press, 1990.

Nishitani, Keiji. *Nishida Kitarō*. Translated by Yamamoto Seisuki and James Heisig. Berkeley: University of California Press, 1991.

North, J. D. *The Measure of the Universe: A History of Modern Cosmology*. Oxford: Clarendon Press, 1965.

Oliver, Harold H. "The Complementarity of Theology and Cosmology." *Zygon* 13 (1978): 19–33. (Reprinted in Harold H. Oliver. *Relatedness: Essays in Metaphysics and Theology*. Macon, Ga.: Mercer University Press, 1984).

Panikkar, Raimundo. "Religious Pluralism: The Metaphysical Challenge." In *Religious Pluralism*, edited by Leroy S. Rouner. Notre Dame: University of Notre Dame Press, 1984.

Progress in Theology: The Newsletter of the John Templeton Foundation, 8 (March–April 2000).

Riordan, Michael. "Three Roads to Quantum Gravity: Space-Time Is of the Essence." *The New York Times*, August 19, 2001.

Schlegel, Richard. "Quantum Physics and Human Purpose." *Zygon* 8 (1973):200–220.

Smolin, Lee. *Three Roads to Quantum Gravity*. New York: Basic Books, 2001.

Suzuki, Daisetz. "The Awakening of a New Consciousness in Zen." *Eranos-Jahrbuch* 1954, 23. Zurich: Rheim-Verlag, 1955.

Von Balthasar, Hans Urs. *Theo-drama: Theological Dramatic Theory*. Vol. 1. Translated by Graham Harrison. San Francisco: Ignatius Press, 1988.

Whitehead, Alfred North. *Process and Reality: An Essay in Cosmology*. Edition by David Ray Griffin and Donald W. Sherburne. New York: The Free Press, 1978.

———. *Science and the Modern World*. Lowell Lectures, 1925. New York: The Free Press, [1925] 1967.

Who's Who in Theology and Science. Compiled and edited by the John Templeton Foundation. Notre Dame: University of Notre Dame Press, 1992.

PART III

Life

9

Darwin, Design, and the Unification of Nature

John Hedley Brooke

Despite obvious differences between the practices of science and the practicing of a religion, there is at least one important resemblance. While they are both rooted in human experience and culture, they also seek to transcend the particularities of time and place to yield truths that claim a more universal significance.

Science, as with religion, has been rooted in local cultures; and the shaping of Darwin's theory of evolution would be a good example. Darwin claimed that it was after he had read a work of political economy, the *Essay on Population* of the Reverend Thomas Malthus, that he had at last developed a theory to work by.[1] The Malthusian image of disproportion between an expanding population and limited resources, featured in debates about charity to the poor, helped to crystallize the idea of natural selection in Darwin's mind. When recalling the impact of Malthus's *Essay*, Darwin also said that he had been "well prepared to appreciate the struggle for existence."[2] On the voyage of the *Beagle*, he had had the opportunity to see nature in the raw, to see the giant condors in South America preying on young cattle. From the study of fossil forms he had come to appreciate the extent of extinction. But such experiences were only possible for him because Britain was an expanding imperial and naval power. The main purpose of the voyage was to improve the accuracy of earlier surveys of the coastline of South America.

Prior to the voyage, Darwin had been studying at Cambridge to become a priest in the Anglican Church. Here was another influence that was culturally specific.[3] Among his mentors were clergyman naturalists who interpreted the natural world as a work of creation in which the structures of living organisms had been beautifully adapted for their functions. Darwin's lifelong preoccupation with adaptation and how it had been achieved was inspired at least in part by his reading of theologians, such as William Paley, who saw evidence of design in impressive organs like the human eye.[4] An old Darwin reminisced that in Cambridge he had preferred beetles to books, but he had nevertheless absorbed the customary references to a Creator. In his early transmutation notebooks he suggested that "the Creator creates through laws."[5] When he wrote his *Descent of Man* (1871), he was explicit in saying that ideas drawn from a prevailing Christian culture had shaped his theory: it was from works of natural theology that he had uncritically accepted the view that every detail of structure must have had some use for the creature that possessed it.[6]

Despite the shaping of Darwin's science by these historical and cultural contingencies, evolutionary biologists would also want to say that the final mature theory transcended them and has a universal application. It would not be difficult to find comparable examples from the history of religious thought.

In this essay I focus on an idea that illustrates the quest for truths that are rooted in human experience, but that also purport to transcend it. This is the idea of the "unity of nature," which has featured in both scientific and religious discourse. My argument is that both science and the monotheistic religions have had an investment in the unity of nature, and consequently that, because Darwin achieved an unprecedented unification of biology, his science actually provided a new resource for theologians, even if it was not always welcomed. I also intend to show how ideas about the unity of nature have mediated between scientific and religious discourse. References to the unity of nature provide a window through which many different connections between scientific and religious concerns can be observed. We should not imagine that the relations between them are always best understood in terms of conflict. Popular anecdotes certainly encourage the dualities and the dichotomies. Alluding to the Darwinian theory, the British politician Benjamin Disraeli declared that it seemed one had to be on the side of the apes or of the angels, and he was for the latter, sprouting angel wings when depicted in the popular press. Good jokes, however, are not always the best guide to good history. It was not that difficult, in principle, to interpret evolution as a method of creation.

I begin with historical examples that predate Darwin and show that monotheistic concepts could do real work in the sciences. I shall then examine reasons why Darwin inclined to an agnostic position on matters of faith and consequently shed some of the metaphysics that had previously driven the quest for unity. To associate Darwinism with divisiveness rather than unity may seem to make sense on other grounds too. But my conclusion will be that Darwin unified nature as never before. Therefore, intentionally or not, paradoxically or not, he lent support to modified theologies of nature.

Historical Perspectives on the Unification of Nature

The subject of nature's unity is absorbing because it gives another twist to an ironic thread running through the literature on science and religion—that forms of scientific inquiry once legitimated by theological discourse have subsequently bitten the hand that fed them.[7] Concepts of the unity of nature, once derived from theological considerations, have been appropriated by popular science writers who wish to laud the sciences at the expense of religion.[8]

A first question might be whether ideas about the unity of nature might not have had several origins *including* the theological. It is of course necessary to distinguish between the unity of nature and the unity of science, though arguments for the former have often drawn on arguments for the latter. The very intelligibility of nature has been seen as a mark of its unity. To admit the relevance of theological categories was no embarrassment to Whitehead, who in *Science and the Modern World* (1925) spoke of an intelligible order antecedently guaranteed:

> I am not arguing that the European trust in the scrutability of nature was logically justified even by its own theology. My only point is to understand how it arose. My explanation is that the faith in the possibility of science, generated antecedently to the development of modern scientific theory, is an unconscious derivative from medieval theology.[9]

To focus on the unity of nature can be instructive here, because it was one of the metaphysical underpinnings of much of seventeenth-century natural philosophy. When Descartes likened his activity as a natural philosopher to an architect or lawmaker, he insisted there was not as much perfection in works made by many masters "as in those on which one man alone has worked".[10] Buildings designed by a single architect, he added, usually have more beauty and are better planned than those that many have tried to design. From Descartes, we can see some of the many different levels on which unity might be affirmed. In his cosmology, the concept of vortices of subtle matter, driving and constraining planetary motion, constituted a unifying concept, embracing all solar systems. At a deeper level he insisted on a unique set of laws of impact pertaining to this world. And despite his dislocation of the human soul from the world machine, he did envisage a reunification of the human with the physical world: "If we love God and for his sake unite ourselves in will to all that he has created, then the more grandeur, nobility and perfection we conceive things to have, the more highly we esteem ourselves, as parts of a whole that is a greater work."[11]

We should note the confluence of the philosophical with the theological to produce that last sense of unification—a union of the knower with the known.

In characterizing what might be meant by the unity of nature, Ian Hacking considers the formula: "one world, one reality, one truth."[12] But he dismisses that formula because it misses a crucial feature of the scientific life that he observes in James Clerk Maxwell, and which is certainly discernible in earlier scientists. It leaves out a feeling of awe, wonder, and respect. Maxwell spoke of a duty to impress on our minds "the extent, the order and the unity of the universe." And this included the appreciation of a harmony that was worthy of praise. The aesthetic graduated into the reverential, as it had done for Kepler two-hundred-and-fifty years before.[13]

In seventeenth-century natural philosophy we find well known metaphors for nature that were attractive because they did convey a sense of awe, as well as granting a degree of autonomy to empirical investigation. These were metaphors that, in their circulation, reinforced nature's unity. In many cases, the metaphors mediated directly between empirical and religious concerns. They could also be read in many different ways. The metaphor of nature as a book is perhaps the perfect example. In Kepler, the language of each of God's two books is said to be accommodated to the human intellect by their divine author.[14] For Francis Bacon, an appeal to the two books underscored a sense of obligation to study the book of God's works just as there was a duty to study the book of God's words.[15] For Galileo, the book of God's words had meanings accessible to the vulgar, but also deeper meanings to which only the study of the book of nature gave access.[16] For Isaac Newton, how one book was read had implications for the reading of the other: a single definitive meaning for each biblical text was the equivalent of a definitive account of each natural phenomenon.[17] And the attraction, in every case, was that one could always argue that since the two books *did* have the same author there could never be a real contradiction between them when both were properly understood.

Or take the metaphor of the clock. If the universe is like the cathedral clock in Strasbourg (to which it was often compared in the seventeenth century), it has a unity. But it also has workings that the natural philosopher may investigate, without prejudice to the fact that its various parts have been designed with intent. On the subject of design, Robert Boyle could be overawed by a mite. To describe it as curious "engine" emphasized the work of a designer in that captivating underworld revealed through the microscope. The microscope itself mediated between empirical enquiry and a revitalised natural theology in which the sense of awe was often explicit, magnified by new contrasts between the natural and the artificial.[18] Human artifacts, such as a finely drawn needle, looked crude and defective when magnified, whereas the most mundane of natural objects, such as the scales on a fish, would reveal an unsuspected beauty.

My point is that a presupposition of the unity of nature allowed both sci-

entific activity and religious sensibility to coexist even if the theology was sometimes bent in heterodox directions. Newton provides perhaps the best example
for testing a claim that unity principles might do real work in the sciences. In
exploring what the unity of *science* might mean, Ian Hacking has identified
three metaphysical theses that might find expression in scientific practice. One
is a thesis of interconnectedness, which he notes in some minds "is rooted in
a religious conception of the world and how God must have made it"—religious in the sense of the major monotheistic religions.[19] Newton would be an
exemplar through his connecting lunar and planetary orbits with terrestrial
gravitation. A second metaphysical thesis, which Hacking calls the structural,
refers to the unification achieved by subsuming laws of nature under those of
higher generality, which Newton would again illustrate through his explanation
of Kepler's laws. Hacking's third metaphysical thesis he describes as taxonomic
since it refers to the belief that there is "one fundamental, ultimate, right
system of classifying everything".[20] Nature contains natural kinds. One of the
clearest examples of this principle in Newton would be his taxonomy of natural
forces. When in Query 31 of his *Opticks* he referred to the attractions of gravity,
electricity, and magnetism, Newton added that "these Instances shew the Tenor
and Course of Nature, and make it not improbable but that there may be more
attractive powers than these. For Nature is very consonant and conformable to
herself."[21] As has long been recognized, there was a dream here of quantifying
all of nature's forces including the uncooperative one of chemical affinity.
There were times, too, when Newton would construct analogues between the
intervals of the musical scale, the optical spectrum and planetary distances,
seeking an overarching unity.[22]

The consonance of Nature and the analogy of nature did do work for Newton. It would be difficult to deny that one of his arguments for the universality
of the laws of motion derived from his understanding of divine omnipresence:
"If there be an universal life and all space be the sensorium of a thinking being
who by immediate presence perceives all things in it . . . the laws of motion
arising from life or will may be of universal extent."[23] The God who perceived
everything was the God to whom Newton in his youth confessed such sins as
telling lies about a louse, eating an apple in the house of God, making a mouse-
trap on the Sabbath, and dreaming of burning down his mother's house with
his stepfather in it![24]

The inverse move from the unity of nature to the unity of the godhead,
despite its circularity, was to prove extremely resilient in standard works of
natural theology. Devoting an entire chapter to the unity of the deity, William
Paley began it by declaring that there was proof in the uniformity of plan
observable in the universe. One principle of gravitation caused a stone to drop
toward the Earth and the moon to wheel around it. One law of attraction carried
all the planets about the Sun.[25] Paley was a bit worried by lobsters despite the
fact that the taste of good food was evidence of divine goodness. Their exterior

skeleton perhaps made them anomalous? But no; this was merely a structural inversion adding to the wonderful variety of adaptations in which a deeper unity could be discerned. In the work of the Creator had been an "imitation, a remembrance, a carrying on of the same plan."[26] We smile at the naïvety especially when we read that the human epiglottis is so wonderfully designed that no alderman had ever choked at a feast. But, as recent scholarship has shown, Paley's text and the later *Bridgewater Treatises*, however naïve their theology, played an important role in popularizing the sciences in a politically safe form.[27]

At a deeper level we can ask more critical questions about the drive for unification. Surely the consonance between belief in a unified nature and the espousal of a monotheistic religion was no guarantee that experimental programs to consolidate a unification would be successful? Geoffrey Cantor has suggested that Michael Faraday's convictions about interconvertible forces, their conservation and their role in the economy of Creation were reinforced by his Sandemanian religious beliefs. They certainly generated a research program. There is a diary entry for March 19, 1849, that reads: "*Gravity*. Surely this force must be capable of an experimental relation to Electricity, Magnetism and the other forces, so as to bind it up with them in reciprocal action and equivalent effect. Consider for a moment how to set about touching this matter by facts and trial."[28] Ingenious trials did ensue. A helix of wire connected to a galvanometer was dropped a full 36 feet in the Royal Institution lecture theater; but, as Cantor nicely puts it, the galvanometer remained unmoved. The gravitational force retained its peculiarity. Faraday did not preempt Steven Weinberg's title, *Dreams of a Final Theory*, but he did write in block capitals "ALL THIS IS A DREAM."[29]

The presence of diversity as a precondition of unification manifests itself in the natural theology of the early nineteenth century; and I might perhaps be forgiven for choosing an Oxford example: William Buckland, who fought valiantly to secure a place for geology in the university.[30] Buckland was the eccentric who took a blue bag to dinner parties in order to take home fish bones for further investigation, who so littered his rooms in Christ Church with dusty fossils that they became impenetrable, and whose culinary empiricism resulted in guests dining on hedgehog and crocodile. But how was he to vindicate geology from a suspicion of irreligion in a university dominated by its religious traditions? It was a pertinent question given the increasing evidence for extinction and concerns about what this might mean for belief in a caring Providence. Did fossil finds not destroy that most pleasing of taxonomies, the great chain of being—pleasing in part because diversity was so elegantly incorporated within an overarching unity? If one followed Georges Cuvier, the chain had to be fractured into different sections. In Buckland's rhetoric, however, a theological drive for unity comes across loud and clear. The fact of extinction need not compromise a principle of plenitude—that the

Creator had created every living form that could possibly exist. It was simply that they had not all coexisted. Fossil forms were the missing links not in an evolutionary sequence, but links in what Nicolaas Rupke has called the great chain of history. This is Buckland himself: "[The] discovery, amid the relics of past creations, of links that seemed wanting in the present system of organic nature, affords to natural Theology an important argument, in proving the unity and universal agency of a common great first cause; since every individual in such an uniform and closely connected series, is thus shown to be an integral part of one grand original design."[31] Creatures were wanted dead or alive, but they were assuredly still creatures. After Robert Chambers and then Charles Darwin, perhaps they were not? Perhaps, as they had earlier been for Lamarck, they were merely products of nature?[32]

Darwin's Naturalism and Agnosticism

Here I turn to Darwin's loss of faith in the Creator, who might have guaranteed the unity of nature. Late in life, Darwin did his best to answer an earnest inquirer:

> I am very busy, and am now an old man, in delicate health, and have not time to answer your questions fully, even assuming that they are capable of being answered at all—Science and Christ having nothing to do with each other, except in so far as the habit of scientific investigations makes a man cautious about accepting any proofs: as far as I am concerned, I do not believe that any revelation has been made: with regard to a future life, every one must draw his own conclusion, from vague and contradictory probabilities.[33]

This is agnosticism of a kind: it is more than hinted that some questions are unanswerable and that scientific practice breeds caution, perhaps even scepticism. I also see pathos in this letter because more than forty years earlier, when Charles had just become engaged to Emma Wedgwood, she had worried about that very point—that the mind-set associated with the *practice* of science might distance him from the biblical verses she most cherished. To understand Darwin's agnosticism, a few distinctions may help. A popular understanding might be that theism affirms the existence of God, atheism denies it, and agnosticism declares the question unanswerable. But we know there are many kinds of theism, in some of which a deity is supposed not merely to exist, but also to be active in the world. We also know that there can be many kinds of atheist. Charles Bradlaugh put the point well: "I am an Atheist, but I do not say that there is no God; and until you tell me what you mean by God I am not mad enough to say anything of the kind."[34] Similarly for the agnostic who might not doubt the existence of a first cause but who, like David Hume, might deny that anything could be known about it. These are elementary distinctions, but they have to feature in any story told of Darwin's trajectory from belief in a personal God to his self-description as increasingly agnostic. There is, for example, a distinction he makes in the *Descent of Man*. He is discussing whether races have existed that had no idea of one or more gods. His answer from his experiences on the *Beagle* voyage is a resounding yes. Some races have had no words in their language to express the idea of deity. But this question, he immediately adds, is "wholly distinct from that higher one, whether there exists a Creator and Ruler of the universe".[35] *That* question he continued, "has been answered in the affirmative by some of the highest intellects that have ever existed." If Darwin intends to count himself among those affirmers, then a possible source of agnosticism—the lack of a universal sense of God—is overridden by an appeal to superior intellects. But this very passage introduces yet another problem: the ambiguity of Darwin's *public* statements. He does not actually *say* that he agrees with these high intellects.

Darwin's distinctions are important. It has been said that Darwin's inexorable exposure of the process of natural selection removed the need to posit a first cause as the origin of life on Earth. It is not clear that Darwin would have agreed with that. The adjective "inexorable" is inappropriate since even in his agnostic days Darwin admitted that, while the fact of evolution was widely accepted, there was no consensus on the mechanism. Importantly, Darwin had not solved the riddle of those first few living forms. It worried Huxley's contemporary John Tyndall that Darwin had not given a naturalistic account of the origin of life.[36] The option to believe in a god-of-the-gaps, if one was so inclined, was clearly still open.

A further complication concerns the nature of religious belief. It has been tempting for historians to streamline Darwin's progression from Christianity to deism to agnosticism, as if there must be a linear and irreversible attenuation of belief. Darwin himself preferred to say that his beliefs often fluctuated. When he spoke of an increasing agnosticism as he grew older, he included the three words "but not always."[37] What one sees is an oscillation between evolutionary theism and an outright agnosticism. To complicate matters further, a thoughtful agnosticism could itself become, accompany, or nurture a religious position. As Bernard Lightman has insisted, there were many shades of agnosticism, some reverent and devout, some expressly Christian.[38]

The temptation to ascribe Darwin's loss of faith to his science has been irresistible. At work was not only that cautious mind-set we have already seen, but also the success of what is sometimes called a methodological naturalism. The more we know of the fixed laws of nature, he famously wrote, the more incredible do miracles become.[39] His process of natural selection could counterfeit design: Paley's argument from contrivance to contriver was denatured. The ramifications were serious if one wished to see the world as Paley had seen it: happy and contented with its buzzing insects on a summer night.

Darwin emphatically did replace that image: once one had been staggered, as he claimed to be, by the extent of nature's extinctions, it was those insects that cruelly and horribly buried their eggs in the bodies of caterpillars that buried themselves in his mind. Darwin did not destroy the argument from laws of nature to their lawgiver. This is an important, often neglected, qualification. But if his belief in a personal God had ever rested on the adaptive minutia of living organisms, it would certainly have been shaken by his theory. As he protested to Asa Gray in October 1861, "when I think of my beloved orchids, with rudiments of five anthers, with one pistil converted into a rostellum, with all the cohesion of parts, it really seems to me incredibly monstrous to look at an orchid as created as we now see it."[40] Earlier, he had tried to clarify his position when Gray had suggested that the variations on which natural selection worked might have been designed. Darwin objected. It was not that "designed variation" made his "deity 'Natural Selection' superfluous"; but rather from studying domestic variations he had come to see what an enormous field of undesigned variability there was for natural selection to appropriate.[41] In Darwin's reference there to natural selection as his "deity," we catch a glimpse of what Susan Cannon observed long ago—that Darwin did not so much destroy the universe of the natural theologians as *steal* it from them.[42] But was this enough to induce agnosticism with reference to the being of a God—the kind of God who might be described as the ground of the possibility of there being a mechanism of natural selection at all? Darwin's use of language suggests that perhaps it was not. Certainly, in the letters to Gray, he pleads a lack of clarity on the matter. He would say he was in a hopeless muddle or that he did not feel sure of his ground. In the early drafts of his theory he had even used the device of a "Being with forethought" to explicate what he meant by natural selection: "Let us now suppose a Being with penetration sufficient to perceive differences in the outer and innermost organization quite imperceptible to man, and with forethought extending over future centuries to watch with unerring care and select for any object the offspring of an organism produced under the foregoing circumstances; I can see no conceivable reason why he could not form a new race . . . adapted to new ends."[43] Darwin's "Being" was a heuristic device, to be sure, but in the light of such remarks it would surely be odd to say that the being of such a Being was excluded by his science?

Were there, then, other sources of unbelief to which we might point? Here are a few that we find in recent literature. The river of dissent that ran through his family from his radical grandfather through his skeptical father to his atheist brother, Erasmus, has to be considered. If Christian preachers put unbelievers beyond the pale, then members of his own family were destined for perdition. The doctrine of eternal damnation he would describe as a "damnable doctrine."[44] The issue took on an existential dimension when his father died in the late 1840s. As many commentators have observed, Darwin shared in that moral revolt against Christian orthodoxies that was to exact its toll in so many minds. Add to this Darwin's realization that one could lead an exemplary moral life as a freethinker or an atheist and foundations might crumble. As Fiona Erskine has argued, this realization came to him vividly during his London years through contact with Harriet Martineau and her circle.[45]

Darwin would even authenticate his dissent through the family lineage. James Moore has noted the hereditary linkage he saw between his grandfather's attitudes and his own. The grandson put it this way: "a man who has no assured and ever present belief in the existence of a personal God or of a future existence with retribution and reward" can find a basis for morality apart from religion in the cultivation of hereditary "social instincts."[46]

Moore's answer to the question of why Darwin gave up Christianity is the most sensitive yet because it highlights not merely the physical pain and suffering that Charles found so difficult to square with a beneficent God, but the mental pain and anguish that accompanied the cruel loss of his daughter, Annie, at the tender age of 10. That was early 1851, later than the dates routinely given for his renunciation of a Christian faith. Annie's death, with its crucifixion of hope, looks like the last straw.[47] This was an event that tore him apart, but it was also part of a wider pattern of events that I have always felt disposed him against a caring Providence. That pattern was the absence of a pattern. It was the sheer contingency, the fortuitousness of the accidental in human lives and in the rest of nature. He once asked Asa Gray to consider the case of an "innocent and good man" who, standing under a tree, is killed by lightning. "Do you believe," he asked Gray, pointing up the question by adding that he really would like to hear, "Do you believe that God *designedly* killed this man? Many or most persons do believe this; I can't and don't."[48] The case was surely no different from that of the luckless gnat swallowed by a swallow. Random events that refused to be part of a coherent story undoubtedly weighed upon him.

In what sense then was Darwin's agnosticism scientific? There was an ulterior respect in which his theory did bear on his own convictions. Curiously, he often spoke of one conviction, an "inward conviction" that this wonderful universe could not be the product of chance. The details of an orchid or even the human eye, he could not believe were designed. But what of the wonderful whole? Might there be designed laws, with the details left to chance? He was never satisfied, even with that formulation. And this was the reason he repeatedly gave in his agnostic years: if the human mind is itself the product of evolution, if it is only that little more refined than the mind of a dog, what grounds have we for supposing it capable of solving the metaphysical riddles? Darwin was not above holding convictions. For some that did make him distinctive among the agnostics. But he was distinctive, too, because it was he above all, who had supplied the scientific reasons for mistrusting his own convictions: "The horrid doubt always arises whether the convictions of man's mind, which has been developed from the mind of the lower animals, are of any value or at all trustworthy. Would anyone trust in the convictions of a monkey's mind?"[49]

Darwinism and the Unity of Nature

Was it possible to be a Darwinian and still believe in the unity of nature? In many respects the theory of natural selection proved so divisive that it may be difficult to think in terms of unities. It emphatically did not unite those elements of nature we call human beings. As Gillian Beer has pointed out in her delightful book *Darwin's Plots*, many of the metaphors Darwin used to articulate his theory, including that of selection, could be read in different ways.[50] The metaphor of a branching tree, which Darwin used to illustrate divergence from common ancestors, was ambiguous in that it both denied and affirmed progress. There was no linear progression to the human race as top dog; and yet the overall growth of a tree was upwards. The theory was ambiguous on what was to become the sensitive question of race. All humans were ultimately from a single origin and yet the subtitle of Darwin's *Origin* was The Preservation of Favoured Races in the Struggle for Life.

Within Christendom, the theory was deeply divisive. The Bishop of Oxford, Samuel Wilberforce, fell out with one of his own ordinands, Frederick Temple, over the correct response to Darwin and other liberalizing trends. The pervasive legend that Wilberforce baited Darwin's disciple, Thomas Henry Huxley, by asking whether he would prefer to think of himself descended from an ape on his grandmother's or grandfather's side, only to be humiliated by a scathing reply in which Huxley implied that he would prefer to have an ape for an ancestor than a certain bishop, misses the seriousness with which Wilberforce reviewed Darwin's *Origin of Species* and the fact that the story was largely a retrospective invention, one of the foundation myths of scientific professionalism.[51] Unlike Temple, who was to become both an evolutionist and Archbishop of Canterbury, Wilberforce was, however, a resolute critic of Darwin. In America, there were similar divisions. At Princeton, Charles Hodge found the mechanism of natural selection atheistic, while James McCosh simply concluded that the prevalence of accident could not be accidental.

We may associate Darwinism with divisiveness for another reason. As a scientific theory it has been exploited to support every political creed from socialism to an unrestrained capitalism to a vehement nationalism. Nor, surely, does Darwin give us a picture of nature at one with itself? Images of gladiatorial struggle and of nature "red in tooth and claw" were a long way from Paley's happy world. The contented face of nature, Darwin once wrote, is but a mask.

And yet in such statements nature was still in the singular. Were there not respects in which Darwin achieved one of the most remarkable unifications in the entire history of science? Scientists themselves almost invariably believe so. The manner in which data from biogeography, paleontology, embryology, variation under domestication, and taxonomy were coordinated in a single conceptual framework has often been seen as a perfect fulfillment of William Whewell's demand for consilience in a theory worth defending.[52] Darwin could explain why there had been so much extinction, why (given divergence from a common ancestor) the more ancient a fossil was the more intermediate a form it had between existing species. He could explain why island species resembled those of neighboring continents. He could incorporate the Malthusian struggle for limited resources, which in September 1838 had given him the key to his mechanism. He could even embrace fancy pigeons to show what human selectors could do and thereby give substance to his metaphor of natural selection. If breeders could achieve such diversity from the common rock pigeon, what might not nature have done with other species and with so much more time on its hands?

A subtle unification was achieved at a metaphysical level. The birth and death of species were presented as quintessentially no different in their explicability from the birth and death of individuals. This was an important move in rebutting naïve religious objections that supposed a Christian doctrine of creation to require separate divine intervention for the origin of each and every species. There is, however, one other aspect of Darwin's unification that deserves special comment. This is his preference for locating the ultimate origin of all species in a single life form. A predilection for unity might simply translate into a thesis about a singularity of origin. In the closing lines of his *Origin of Species,* Darwin had been careful to refer to one or a *few* primordial forms into which life had been breathed; but even he could not resist the lure of the most economical solution. He was often tempted to take the further step, to the belief that all animals and plants have descended from just one prototype. This means that during the 1860s at least four explanations predicated on a unity of origin were on the table for a world occupied by human beings.

At one extreme was the simple theism in which all was resolved into the will of a single deity—an explanation that for Darwin explained nothing. At the other extreme was the complete naturalism of a Darwinian such as John Tyndall.[53] Competing intermediates were Darwin's ambiguous position on whether the first material form of life could be said to be the work of a Creator, who created by laws; and the theism of Richard Owen, in which creation was continuous as new instantiations of a divine archetype (a single archetype) came into being.[54] In that competition, different models for the unity of nature were in serious contention, and it almost goes without saying that deeply held religious or metaphysical convictions helped to shape each of them.

And so to my concluding observation. Some commentators saw theological advantages in a unified process of evolution in which, as Darwin had put it in one of his early notebooks, we are all "netted together." Darwin's correspondent and advocate in America, Asa Gray, certainly found theological advantages. He even detected the possibility of a new theodicy:

> Darwinian teleology has the special advantage of accounting for the imperfections and failures as well as for successes. It not only accounts for them, but turns them to practical account. It explains the seeming waste as being part and parcel of a great economical process. Without the competing multitude, no struggle for life; and without this, no natural selection and survival of the fittest, no continuous adaptation to changing surroundings, no diversification and improvement, leading from lower up to higher and nobler forms. So the most puzzling things of all to the old-school teleologists are the *principia* of the Darwinian.[55]

Gray may not have carried the world with him; but in that passage a unified nature survived in the form of a unified process. As he put it elsewhere, evolutionary relationships showed how biological species are "all part of one system, realizations in nature . . . of the conception of One Mind."[56]

I conclude with Gray because he identified a further respect in which a unification effected through Darwin's science might have deep religious significance. An ultimately single origin of all living things meant that claims for *primordially* different races could surely be silenced? The polygenetic theories of the nineteenth century, which proposed multiple origins for humankind, were not surprisingly perceived as subversive of an orthodox Christianity. Gray was not alone in seeing in Darwinian evolution support for the monogenetic case. To defend the unity of humankind required the different races to have diverged from a common ancestor. This was precisely the kind of process that Darwin had expounded. It was the polygenists who were now up against it. As Gray put it: those who "recognize several or numerous human species, will hardly be able to maintain that such species were primordial and supernatural in the ordinary sense of the word."[57] The use of natural selection to account for racial differentiation while simultaneously reinforcing a monogenism was a feature of early responses to Darwin's theory, as in that of the Ulster Presbyterian George Macloskie.[58]

Conclusion

I conclude not with the past, but with the present. In the summer of 1999, one of the best known British newspapers, *The Daily Telegraph*, carried an editorial headed "Faith in Darwin." Wherever you go, it stated, "whatever animal, plant or bug you look at, if it is alive, it will use the same genetic code." It follows that "there was only one creation." The editor's conclusion, if not entirely accurate, is certainly arresting: "For centuries scientists have been picking holes in the unified world view of the great monotheistic religions. Yet, through the DNA code, one branch of their learning, genetics, has uncovered an astonishing unity in all created things. Its findings point to a common ground on which both sides of the debate could fruitfully meet."[59]

The historical observation in that first sentence is surely misleading because, as I have argued in this paper, from the seventeenth century onwards, there have been many facets of scientific activity that have contributed to a further articulation, rather than a critique, of a unified world view. The possibility of a fruitful meeting of minds, seemingly engendered anew by the DNA code, is a possibility that has been actualized around the theme of unity many times in the past. But it is also true that we should not overlook the existence of a rich diversity in the world of nature with which attempts to unify stand in dialectical relation. There assuredly have been advances in science associated with shifts away from simplistic and premature schemata. In the life sciences there is the well-known example of Georges Cuvier's splitting the single great chain of being into independent chains in order to achieve a more refined taxonomy. The interplay between unity and diversity has, nevertheless, surfaced in so many contexts that it surely takes us beyond particularities of time and place. We do not have to accept the Kantian principle that the imposition of unity is one of the preconditions of the possibility of attaining a knowledge of nature to recognize that ideals of unification have exercised a regulative role in both scientific and religious thought.

NOTES

1. David Kohn, "Theories to Work By: Rejected Theories, Reproduction and Darwin's Path to Natural Selection," *Studies in the History of Biology* 4 (1980): 67–170; Dov Ospovat, "Darwin after Malthus," *Journal of the History of Biology* 12 (1979): 211–230; Antonello La Vergata, "Images of Darwin," in *The Darwinian Heritage*, ed. David Kohn (Princeton: Princeton University Press, 1985), 901–972, especially 953–958.

2. Charles Darwin, *The Autobiography of Charles Darwin*, ed. Nora Barlow (London: Collins, 1958), 120.

3. Walter (Susan) Cannon, "The Bases of Darwin's Achievement: A Revaluation," *Victorian Studies* 5 (1961): 109–134; David Kohn, "Darwin's Ambiguity: The Secularization of Biological Meaning," *British Journal for the History of Science* 22 (1989): 215–239.

4. David Burbridge, "William Paley Confronts Erasmus Darwin: Natural Theology and Evolutionism in the Eighteenth Century," *Science and Christian Belief* 10 (1998): 49–71.

5. John Brooke, "The Relations between Darwin's Science and His Religion," in *Darwinism and Divinity*, ed. John Durant (Oxford: Blackwell, 1985), 40–75.

6. Charles Darwin, *The Descent of Man*, 2nd ed. (London: Murray, 1906), 92.

7. John Brooke, *Science and Religion: Some Historical Perspectives* (Cambridge: Cambridge University Press, 1991), 117–151.

8. For example, Steven Weinberg, *Dreams of a Final Theory: The Search for the Fundamental Laws of Nature* (New York: Pantheon, 1992). For a recent critique of the drive for unification, see Nancy Cartwright, *The Dappled World: A Study of the Boundaries of Science* (Cambridge: Cambridge University Press, 1999).

9. Alfred Whitehead, *Science and the Modern World* (New York: Mentor Books, 1964), 19. For a much fuller account of the interpenetration of scientific and theological discourse in the formative processes of Western science, see Amos Funkenstein, *Theology and the Scientific Imagination from the Middle Ages to the Seventeenth Century* (Princeton: Princeton University Press, 1986).

10. Keith Hutchison, "Idiosyncrasy, Achromatic Lenses, and Early Romanticism," *Centaurus* 34 (1991): 125–171.

11. René Descartes, *Philosophical Writings: A Selection*, ed. Elizabeth Anscombe and Peter Geach (London: Nelson, 1954), 296.

12. Ian Hacking, "The Disunities of the Sciences," in *The Disunity of Science*, ed. Peter Galison and David Stump (Stanford: Stanford University Press, 1996), 37–74.

13. Richard Westfall, "The Rise of Science and the Decline of Orthodox Christianity: A Study of Kepler, Descartes and Newton," in *God and Nature: Historical Essays on the Encounter between Christianity and Science*, ed. David Lindberg and Ronald Numbers (Berkeley and Los Angeles: University of California Press, 1986), 218–237.

14. Kenneth Howell, *God's Two Books: Copernican Cosmology and Biblical Interpretation in Early Modern Science* (Notre Dame: University of Notre Dame Press, 2002), 109–135.

15. Peter Hess, " 'God's Two Books': Revelation, Theology and Natural Science in the Christian West," in *Interdisciplinary Perspectives on Cosmology and Biological Evolution*, ed. Hilary Reagan and Mark Worthing (Adelaide: Australian Theological Forum, 2002), 19–49, especially 32–33; James Moore, "Geologists and Interpreters of Genesis in the Nineteenth Century," in Lindberg and Numbers, *God and Nature*, 322–350.

16. Galileo, "Letter to the Grand Duchess Christina" (1615), in *The Galileo Affair: A Documentary History*, ed. Maurice Finocchiaro (Berkeley: University of California Press, 1989), 87–118.

17. For the contextualizing of this particular analogy, see Peter Harrison, *The Bible, Protestantism and the Rise of Natural Science* (Cambridge: Cambridge University Press, 1998).

18. John Brooke and Geoffrey Cantor, *Reconstructing Nature: The Engagement of Science and Religion* (Edinburgh: T and T Clark, 1998), 144–145.

19. Hacking, "The Disunities of the Sciences," 46.

20. Ibid., 47.

21. Isaac Newton, *Opticks* (New York: Dover, 1952), 376.

22. Penelope Gouk, *Music, Science and Natural Magic in Seventeenth-Century England* (New Haven: Yale University Press, 1999), 224–257.

23. Cited by Richard Westfall, *Force in Newton's Physics* (London: Macdonald, 1971), 397.

24. Isaac Newton, "Accounts Book" (1662), Fitzwilliam Museum, Cambridge.

25. William Paley, *Natural Theology* (1802), in *Selections*, ed. Frederick Ferré (Indianapolis: Bobbs-Merrill, 1963), 50.

26. Ibid., 52.

27. Jonathan Topham, "Science and Popular Education in the 1830s: The Role of the *Bridgewater Treatises*," *British Journal for the History of Science* 25 (1992): 397–430; and "Beyond the 'Common Context': The Production and Reading of the *Bridgewater Treatises*," *Isis* 89 (1998): 233–262.

28. Geoffrey Cantor, *Michael Faraday: Sandemanian and Scientist* (London: Macmillan, 1991), 247.

29. Ibid., 248.

30. Nicolaas Rupke, *The Great Chain of History: William Buckland and the English School of Geology, 1814–1849* (Oxford: Oxford University Press, 1983).

31. Ibid., 173.

32. For Chambers, see James Secord, *Victorian Sensation: The Extraordinary Publication, Reception, and Secret Authorship of "Vestiges of the Natural History of Creation"* (Chicago: University of Chicago Press, 2000); for Lamarck: Ludmilla Jordanova, "Nature's Powers: A Reading of Lamarck's Distinction between Creation and Production," in *History, Humanity and Evolution*, ed. James Moore (Cambridge: Cambridge University Press, 1989), 71–98.

33. From a letter dated June 5, 1879, for a copy of which I am grateful to Dr. Basil Hetzel, Adelaide.

34. Michael Buckley, *At the Origins of Modern Atheism* (New Haven: Yale University Press, 1987), 15.

35. Darwin, *Descent of Man*, 143.

36. Brooke, *Science and Religion*, 303.

37. Francis Darwin, *The Life and Letters of Charles Darwin* (London: Murray, 1887), 1: 304.

38. Bernard Lightman, "Ideology, Evolution and Late-Victorian Agnostic Popularizers," in Moore, *History, Humanity and Evolution*, 285–309.

39. Darwin, *Autobiography*, 86.

40. Frederick Burkhardt, ed., *The Correspondence of Charles Darwin* (Cambridge: Cambridge University Press, 1994), 9:302.

41. Ibid., 162.

42. Cannon, "Bases of Darwin's Achievement."

43. Charles Darwin, *Essay* (1844), in *Evolution by Natural Selection*, ed. Gavin de Beer (Cambridge: Cambridge University Press, 1958), 114.

44. Darwin, *Autobiography*, 87.

45. Fiona Erskine, "Darwin in Context: The London Years, 1837–1842," Ph.D. dissertation, Open University, 1987.

46. Cited by James Moore, "Of Love and Death: Why Darwin 'Gave Up Christianity,'" in Moore, *History, Humanity and Evolution*, 195–229, 205.

47. Adrian Desmond and James Moore, *Darwin* (London: Michael Joseph, 1991), 375–387.

48. Darwin to Asa Gray, July 1860, in Francis Darwin, *Life and Letters*, 1: 315.

49. Darwin in Francis Darwin, *Life and Letters*, 1: 316.

50. Gillian Beer, *Darwin's Plots: Evolutionary Narrative in Darwin, George Eliot and Nineteenth-Century Fiction* (London: Routledge and Kegan Paul, 1983).

51. John Brooke, "The Wilberforce-Huxley Debate: Why Did It Happen?" *Science and Christian Belief* 13 (2000): 127–141.

52. David Wilson, "Convergence: Metaphysical Pleasure versus Physical Constraint," in *William Whewell: A Composite Portrait*, ed. Menachem Fisch and Simon Schaffer (Oxford: Oxford University Press, 1991), 233–254, especially 239–240.

53. John Tyndall, "Presidential Address to the British Association for the Advancement of Science," in *Victorian Science*, ed. George Basalla, William Coleman, and Robert Kargon (New York: Anchor Books, [1874] 1970), 441–478.

54. Richard Owen, *On the Nature of Limbs* (London: Van Voorst, 1849); Adrian Desmond, *Archetypes and Ancestors* (London: Blond and Briggs, 1982), 19–55; Nicolaas Rupke, *Richard Owen: Victorian Naturalist* (New Haven: Yale University Press, 1994), 196–197.

55. Asa Gray, *Darwiniana*, ed. A. Hunter Dupree (Cambridge: Harvard University Press, 1963), 310–311.

56. Asa Gray, *The Elements of Botany for Beginners and Schools* (New York: Ivison, 1887), 177.

57. Gray, *Darwiniana*, 144.

58. George Macloskie, "The Natural History of Man," *The Ulster Magazine* 3 (1862): 217–237. I am grateful to Professor David Livingstone for this reference.

59. *The Daily Telegraph*, August 16, 1999.

BIBLIOGRAPHY

Beer, Gillian. *Darwin's Plots: Evolutionary Narrative in Darwin, George Eliot and Nineteenth-Century Fiction.* London: Routledge and Kegan Paul, 1983.

Brooke, John. "The Relations Between Darwin's Science and His Religion." In *Darwinism and Divinity*, edited by John Durant. Oxford: Blackwell, 1985.

———. *Science and Religion: Some Historical Perspectives.* Cambridge: Cambridge University Press, 1991.

———. "The Wilberforce-Huxley Debate: Why Did It Happen?" *Science and Christian Belief* 13 (2000): 127–141.

Brooke, John, and Geoffrey Cantor. *Reconstructing Nature: The Engagement of Science and Religion.* Edinburgh: T and T Clark, 1998.

Buckley, Michael. *At the Origins of Modern Atheism.* New Haven: Yale University Press, 1987.

Burbridge, David. "William Paley Confronts Erasmus Darwin: Natural Theology and Evolutionism in the Eighteenth Century." *Science and Christian Belief* 10 (1998): 49–71.

Burkhardt, Frederick, ed. *The Correspondence of Charles Darwin.* Vol. 9. Cambridge: Cambridge University Press, 1994.

Cannon, Walter (Susan). "The Bases of Darwin's Achievement: A Revaluation." *Victorian Studies* 5 (1961): 109–134.

Cantor, Geoffrey. *Michael Faraday: Sandemanian and Scientist.* London: Macmillan, 1991.

Cartwright, Nancy. *The Dappled World: A Study of the Boundaries of Science.* Cambridge: Cambridge University Press, 1999.

Darwin, Charles. *Essay* (1844). In *Evolution by Natural Selection,* edited by Gavin de Beer. Cambridge: Cambridge University Press, 1958.

———. *The Descent of Man.* 2nd ed. London: Murray, 1906.

———. *The Autobiography of Charles Darwin.* Edited by Nora Barlow. London: Collins, 1958.

Darwin, Francis. *The Life and Letters of Charles Darwin.* London: Murray, 1887.

Descartes, René. *Philosophical Writings: A Selection.* Edited by Elizabeth Anscombe and Peter Geach. London: Nelson, 1954.

Desmond, Adrian. *Archetypes and Ancestors.* London: Blond and Briggs, 1982.

Desmond, Adrian, and James Moore, *Darwin.* London: Michael Joseph, 1991.

Erskine, Fiona. "Darwin in Context: The London Years, 1837–1842." Ph.D. dissertation. Open University, 1987.

Funkenstein, Amos. *Theology and the Scientific Imagination from the Middle Ages to the Seventeenth Century.* Princeton: Princeton University Press, 1986.

Galileo, "Letter to the Grand Duchess Christina." In *The Galileo Affair: A Documentary History,* edited by Maurice Finocchiaro. Berkeley and Los Angeles: University of California Press, 1989.

Gouk, Penelope. *Music, Science and Natural Magic in Seventeenth-Century England.* New Haven: Yale University Press, 1999.

Gray, Asa. *The Elements of Botany for Beginners and Schools.* New York: Ivison, 1887.

———. *Darwiniana.* Edited by A. Hunter Dupree. Cambridge: Harvard University Press, 1963.

Hacking, Ian. "The Disunities of the Sciences." In *The Disunity of Science,* edited by Peter Galison and David Stump. Stanford: Stanford University Press, 1996.

Harrison, Peter. *The Bible, Protestantism and the Rise of Natural Science.* Cambridge: Cambridge University Press, 1998.

Hess, Peter. "'God's Two Books': Revelation, Theology and Natural Science in the Christian West." In *Interdisciplinary Perspectives on Cosmology and Biological Evolution,* edited by Hilary Reagan and Mark Worthing. Adelaide: Australian Theological Forum, 2002.

Howell, Kenneth. *God's Two Books: Copernican Cosmology and Biblical Interpretation in Early Modern Science.* Notre Dame: University of Notre Dame Press, 2002.

Hutchison, Keith. "Idiosyncrasy, Achromatic Lenses, and Early Romanticism." *Centaurus* 34 (1991): 125–171.

Jordanova, Ludmilla. "Nature's Powers: A Reading of Lamarck's Distinction between Creation and Production.'" In *History, Humanity and Evolution,* edited by James Moore. Cambridge: Cambridge University Press, 1989.

Kohn, David. "Theories to Work by: Rejected Theories, Reproduction and Darwin's Path to Natural Selection." *Studies in the History of Biology* 4 (1980): 67–170.

———. "Darwin's Ambiguity: The Secularization of Biological Meaning." *British Journal for the History of Science* 22 (1989): 215–239.

La Vergata, Antonello. "Images of Darwin." In *The Darwinian Heritage,* edited by David Kohn, 901–972. Princeton: Princeton University Press, 1985.

Lightman, Bernard. "Ideology, Evolution and Late-Victorian Agnostic Popularizers."

In *History, Humanity and Evolution*, edited by James Moore. Cambridge: Cambridge University Press, 1989.

Macloskie, George. "The Natural History of Man." *The Ulster Magazine* 3 (1862): 217–237.

Moore, James. "Geologists and Interpreters of Genesis in the Nineteenth Century." In *God and Nature: Historical Essays on the Encounter between Christianity and Science*, edited by David Lindberg and Ronald Numbers. Berkeley and Los Angeles: University of California Press, 1986.

———. "Of Love and Death: Why Darwin 'Gave Up Christianity.' " In *History, Humanity and Evolution*, ed. James Moore. Cambridge: Cambridge University Press, 1989.

Newton, Isaac. *Opticks*. New York: Dover, 1952.

Ospovat, Dov. "Darwin after Malthus." *Journal of the History of Biology* 12 (1979): 211–230.

Owen, Richard. *On the Nature of Limbs*. London: Van Voorst, 1849.

Paley, William. *Natural Theology, Selections*. Edited by Frederick Ferré. Indianapolis: Bobbs-Merrill, [1802] 1963.

Rupke, Nicolaas. *The Great Chain of History: William Buckland and the English School of Geology, 1814–1849*. Oxford: Oxford University Press, 1983.

———. *Richard Owen: Victorian Naturalist*. New Haven: Yale University Press, 1994.

Secord, James. *Victorian Sensation: The Extraordinary Publication, Reception, and Secret Authorship of "Vestiges of the Natural History of Creation."* Chicago: University of Chicago Press, 2000.

Topham, Jonathan. "Science and Popular Education in the 1830s: The Role of the Bridgewater Treatises." *British Journal for the History of Science* 25 (1992). 397–430.

———. "Beyond the 'Common Context': The Production and Reading of the *Bridgewater Treatises*." *Isis* 89 (1998): 233–262.

Tyndall, John. "Presidential Address to the British Association for the Advancement of Science." In *Victorian Science*, edited by George Basalla, William Coleman, and Robert Kargon. New York: Anchor Books, [1874] 1970.

Weinberg, Steven. *Dreams of a Final Theory: The Search for the Fundamental Laws of Nature*. New York: Pantheon, 1992.

Westfall, Richard. *Force in Newton's Physics*. London: Macdonald, 1971.

———. "The Rise of Science and the Decline of Orthodox Christianity: A Study of Kepler, Descartes and Newton." In *God and Nature: Historical Essays on the Encounter between Christianity and Science*, edited by David Lindberg and Ronald Numbers. Berkeley and Los Angeles: University of California Press, 1986.

Whitehead, Alfred North. *Science and the Modern World*. New York: Mentor Books, 1964.

Wilson, David. "Convergence: Metaphysical Pleasure versus Physical Constraint." In *William Whewell: A Composite Portrait*, edited by Menachem Fisch and Simon Schaffer. Oxford: Oxford University Press, 1991.

IO

Darwinism and Christianity: Must They Remain at War or Is Peace Possible?

Michael Ruse

Since the time of the Greeks, science and religion have been two of the chief contenders for the role of human-produced systems or activities that yet in some sense and for some reason transcend the human experience. For much of the Christian era, it was religion particularly that was taken as the enterprise above all that tells of something over and above the lives of us mere mortals. But since the Enlightenment in the eighteenth century, increasingly, it has been science that has taken the front role and made the strongest claims as something that goes beyond the daily existence of humankind and tells of the deeper truths about reality. So long as religion was firmly in the driver's seat, it was happy to take science along as a passenger—less metaphorically, science was seen to fill out certain areas of knowledge and understanding within the overall picture provided by religion—by the Christian religion in particular. But as science grew and made its move to power and supremacy, increasingly science and religion have been seen as rivals. If one succeeds, the other cannot. Let me agree, at least for the purposes of argument, that as we enter the twenty-first century, science has won. It is seen—rightly fully seen—as the enterprise above all that tells us about the world as it truly is, the world that is not infected by the desires and activities of us humans. The question I now want to address is what this means for religion. Some would argue that this is the end of the matter. Religion is dead, and good riddance. Others, including nonbelievers like myself, are not so sure. Perhaps the success of science does not necessarily spell the failure of religion? The essay that follows is an attempt to explore some aspect of this question. I doubt it will be the final word, but for me at least it is a first word. And every journey starts with a single step.

Prologue

We all know that the Christian fundamentalists—the biblical literalists or so-called creationists—have argued that Darwinism and Christianity are incompatible.[1] For these Christians, every word of the Bible must be taken at immediate face value. Understanding by "Darwinism," the belief that all organisms living and dead have arrived by a slow process of evolution from forms very different and probably much simpler, and that the process of change was natural selection—the survival of the fittest—the incompatibility follows at once. What one also finds today, and this perhaps one might not expect, is that a number of articulate, prominent Darwinians agree entirely with the creationists. They, too, see science and religion in open contradiction.

> It is completely unrealistic to claim . . . that religion keeps itself
> away from science's turf, restricting itself to morals and values. A
> universe with a supernatural presence would be a fundamentally
> and qualitatively different kind of universe from one without. The
> difference is, inescapably, a scientific difference. Religions make ex-
> istence claims, and this means scientific claims.[2]

Those who think in this way want to argue—with the creationists—that Darwinism is atheism with a scientific face. They too want to argue that, if one is a Darwinian, then logically one should deny the existence of God. To deny this is a sad reflection of the fact that a "cowardly flabbiness of the intellect afflicts otherwise rational people confronted with long-established religions."[3]

In this essay, I shall look at this claim that Darwinism and atheism are different sides of the same coin. I shall consider what connection exists between the two. Although my interests are conceptual, as an evolutionist I like to set discussions in historical frameworks.[4] Hence, I shall begin with a brief history showing why it is that Darwinism and Christianity have fallen out. Then, ignoring the fundamentalists, for nothing will change their minds—and in any case, their theology is in worse shape than their science or their philosophy—I shall consider the arguments of three people (Darwinians) who claim that there are tensions between Darwinism and Christianity. I shall argue that their arguments are less powerful than they might suppose and that perhaps the time has come to bury the hatchet. Peace between Darwinism and Christianity may be more constructive all around.

A Very Quick History of Evolution

Evolution, the idea that all organisms are the end product of a long, slow, natural process from simple forms (perhaps ultimately from inorganic materials), is very much a child of the Enlightenment, that secular flowering of thought in the eighteenth century. In particular, evolution was an epiphenomenon of hopes and ideas of progress: the social and cultural belief that, through human effort and intelligence, it is possible to improve knowledge, to use more efficiently our machines and technology, and overall to drive out superstition and prejudice and to increase the happiness of the peoples of the world. Believing strongly in the rule of law, enthusiasts for progress increasingly read their philosophy into the world of nature and saw there the same process of development and improvement. Then, they promptly read this developmentalism back into the social world, as confirmation of their beliefs![5]

In many respects, obviously, these transmutationists were breaking with traditional religious forms and beliefs. Less upsetting than their contradiction of Genesis was their challenge to the belief that human destiny lies entirely at the mercy of God's unwarranted grace and that Divine Providence makes hopes of progress unnecessary and impossible. But, they were far from atheistic or agnostic. To a person, the evolutionists tended to think of God as Unmoved Mover—a being whose actions come through law and not miracle. In other words, they subscribed (as did many intellectuals of the day) to the philosophy of deism, as opposed to the faith of the theist, the belief in interventionist god of Christianity. And this in a sense set the tone for evolution, for its first hundred years, right up to the publication of the *Origin* in 1859. It was—and was seen as—a kind of extension of religious commitment and progressivist philosophy. It had the status of an unjustified and unjustifiable belief system. Judged as an empirical doctrine, it was a pseudoscience, akin to astrology or (and people drew this analogy) phrenology, the study of character through brain bumps. It was certainly not a respectable science—in many respects as all (except the evolutionists themselves) could see, it was not a science at all but a background commitment on which one could hang all sorts of social and religious beliefs.

Charles Darwin set out to alter all of this. He was not just a serious thinker, he was (as much as it was possible for someone in the England of his day) a professional scientist. He had had training, he worked hard at science (first geology and then biology) all of his life, he mixed with the right people, he knew the rules of scientific method. His theory of evolution was intended to jack up the subject from the pseudo level to the professional level. He wanted, with his theory of natural selection as expounded in the *Origin*, to put forward what Thomas Kuhn[6] has described as a paradigm—not merely a system that tears people's allegiances from earlier thought patterns, but something that would provide work for future generations of scientists. He wanted to make a science on a par with physics and chemistry.

One should understand that although Darwin's thinking and work was revolutionary, he was not the Christian God. He did not make things out of nothing. He came from a rich and settled background.[7] He drew on this and on the ideas to which he was exposed as he grew up into a very comfortable position in middle-class Britain. In particular, not only did Darwin draw on the philosophical and social ideals of his class—progress, laissez-faire economics, the virtues of industrialism, revulsion at such institutions as slavery, belief in the inherent superiority of the English—he drew also on elements of deism (particularly through his mother's family, which was Unitarian) and also Christian theism (not only through his own Anglican family, but also through his training at Cambridge University). Hence, although there may well have been tensions, for all that Darwin was promoting a view of origins that challenged older thought patterns, in respects one can see ways in which Christianity ought to have been able to reconcile itself with Darwinism. For instance, Darwin (unlike earlier evolutionists) spoke directly and strongly to Christian concerns with the evidence of God's labors in the world, specifically the ways in which organisms seem as if fitted or designed for their struggles. Again, whatever Darwin's own views on progress, as many have noted, natural selection is far from a ready and enthusiastic support for such a philosophy. It may be possible to preserve a role for Providence on the Darwinian scheme.

Nothing worked out as expected. It is true that people did become evolutionists. But Darwin's hope of a functioning, professional science, based on natural selection, simply did not come to be. Selection was ignored or brushed aside, evolution was pushed from the universities to the public lecture halls, and every social and cultural idea—and then some—was justified in the name of evolution. Those who did try to pursue some version of evolutionism in a systematic and professional way turned their backs on Darwin, preferring rather to embrace methods based on German idealism. They pulled back from the cutting edge of biology. They were stuck in the realm of transcendental morphology, forever spinning fantastical histories of their own making, with little regard for facts or method. Evolution as a science was deeply second-rate—evolutionists as scientists were deeply second-rate—and seen to be so. At the same time, from the moment the *Origin* appeared, evolution continued to function—to flourish—as a secular religion, as an inherently anti-Christian manifesto. With reason, many churchmen and scientists alike took it to be the line in the sand, the revealing litmus paper, between those who wanted to revert to the spiritual ways of the past and those who wanted to move forward to the secular ways of the future. The warfare between science and religion raged as though the aged Galileo had never risen from his knees.

Why did this happen? There is a simple and understandable reason. The moment that the *Origin* appeared was the moment when many Victorians—and others elsewhere in Europe and (after the Civil War) in America also—realized that society could no longer function as it had in the past, with the rich and landed controlling everything, and with social issues and problems left simply to amateurs and to hopes of personal beneficence. Paternalism and privilege were out. Democracy and meritocracy were in. Large cities—London, Birmingham, Glasgow, Paris, Berlin, New York, Chicago—needed proper policing, proper local government, sewers, schooling, wholesome entertainment, and much more. The medical profession had got to stop killing people and to start curing. The military had to be properly trained—no more buying of commissions—and had to protect its soldiers from disease and poverty. Earlier in the decade there had been an absolute disaster in the Crimea, followed almost immediately by the trauma of the Indian Mutiny. Civil servants needed training and opportunities to advance on merit rather than simply on connection. Schools had to built and staffed, they had to be places that taught skills for a modern world, breaking from the sterility of religious, rote learning.

Darwin's supporters—Thomas Henry Huxley in particular—were at the head of this movement.[8] They worked hard and successfully to change their society. Huxley himself, first a college professor and then a dean, created and steered science education, at the primary, at the secondary, and at the university level. He found jobs for his graduates—medicine for the physiologists, teaching for the morphologists—and university posts for those who were the very best to come under his influence. And here's the rub! Ardent evolutionist though he became, Huxley could see no practical value in Darwinism. It would not cure a pain in the belly and it was far too speculative for the untrained minds of the young. But there was one role into which it fit naturally. Realizing that the church, the Anglican church particularly, was a bastion of support for the old ways—the vicar and the squire ruled together, often they were brothers—Huxley and his fellows determined to oppose Christianity tooth and nail. Realizing also that simple critique would not be enough, Huxley and friends grasped gratefully at evolution as their own banner, their own ideology, their own secular religion. It would tell us where we came from; it would stress the unique status of humans—the highest end point of the evolutionary process; it would offer hope for the morrow, if only we strive to conquer the beast within and to make for a better world, culturally and biologically; it would do all of these things and more.

Because Darwin himself did not provide such an ideology—although given his status, he certainly gave the movement respectability—the post-*Origin* evolutionists turned to other sources, notably Herbert Spencer in England and Ernst Haeckel in Germany.[9] These men were happy to spin world pictures and to churn out moral dictates. And, before long, the evolutionists—indeed, almost all of those Victorian reformers—had their own true belief. Like the Jesuits of old, they had their standard around which they could all gather and from which they could go forth. It was not for nothing that Huxley was jocularly known as "Pope" Huxley. Moreover, as good churchmen, the evolutionists even built their own cathedrals, where one could go to worship at the new altars. Except these cathedrals were called "museums" and they celebrated, not the crucified Christ, but the inevitable progress of life from blob to human, from savage to white man. Generations of little Londoners and New Yorkers were shipped over to the British Museum (Natural History) in South Kensington and up to the American Museum of Natural History alongside Central Park. Filled (as these institutions still are today) with those fabulous fossil finds pouring forth from the American West, there the citizens of tomorrow gazed and wondered at the marvels of evolution, imbibing the new religion for the new age.

Evolution moved up the social scale. It was no longer mere pseudoscience. But it did not reach the top levels, those of functioning, mature, professional science. Like the Grand Old Duke of York, it was stuck somewhere in the middle, as a kind of pop science, a sort of secular religion. And there it stayed right into the twentieth century, and for several decades of that era also. Finally, around 1930, seventy years after the *Origin* and after the development of the needed theory of heredity, Mendelian genetics, things finally began to change and to improve. A number of highly sophisticated mathematicians devised models to show how Darwin's selection could be combined with the new genetics, thus producing a new theory of evolutionary change. And then the empiricists, especially those based in England and America, worked hard to put factual flesh on the mathematical skeletons of the theoreticians. "Neo-Darwinism" or the "synthetic theory of evolution," a new professional science—that of which Charles Darwin could only dream—had finally arrived.

At least, that is what people hoped and—with a certain bravado—claimed. And, in fact, there is much truth to the claim that, by about the middle of the last century, evolutionary theory was finally a functioning paradigm. It provided a conceptual background for workers and new problems for those who would make careers on and around it. But, even now, all was not well. In America especially, there were still many out there who distrusted evolution and all for which it stood. In the 1920s, spurred by evolutionists' practice of promoting their thinking less as a science and more as an ideology for new social movements, the biblical literalists had brought things to a head with the Scopes Monkey Trial, when a young teacher was prosecuted (and convicted) for teaching human origins. By mid-century these people were quiet, but it was the quiet of slumber, not death. They would be ready to rise again and to strike if evolution showed its social yearnings. And evolutionists themselves were not exactly best qualified to carry through their ends or even fully committed to what they preached—or rather, they were too fully committed to what they preached. For even the most ardent would-be professionals, the mathematics of the theoreticians was quite over their heads, used mainly as propaganda against those who claimed that they had no theory rather than the basis for new and innovative understandings of the evolutionary process. Moreover, almost every one of the new would-be professional evolutionists was deeply committed to the nonscientific side of the subject, and most wrote book after book claiming that evolution may now be a science, but it was, and always will be, a lot more than a science. The extrascientific stain was still there, and most were not particularly keen to rub it out.

It was no wonder that many, including—perhaps, especially including—the aggressive new molecular biologists of the mid-century, regarded Darwinism with suspicion and contempt. There was a feeling that it is truly not top-quality science and that its practitioners have altogether too many extrascientific interests driving their studies. That, whatever might be claimed, it had not truly escaped the legacy of the past. With people like Julian Huxley—biologist grandson of Thomas Henry Huxley—preaching, from the chapel pulpit, the virtues of Darwinian humanism at *Origin* centenary celebrations at the University of Chicago, perhaps the critics had a point.

With Theodosius Dobzhansky, the most important American-based evolutionist of his generation, assuming the presidency of the Teilhard de Chardin Society, the critics almost certainly had a point.

Another half century has now passed. The past four or five decades have seen much effort by evolutionists to move on. Without suppression of personal yearnings and values, the goodies of modern science—grants, posts, students, prizes, fame—are forever barred. And, to be fair, there are now, at most good universities, professional evolutionists plying their trade for the sake of the science—discovery, explanation, prediction—without implicit or explicit motives, ideological, religious, or whatever.[10] But one cannot truly say that modern professional evolutionism is yet the queen of the sciences—or even in the highest league. Apart from the continued dominance of the physical sciences, in biology it is still the molecular world that gains the biggest grants, gets the first crop of the students, has the status and facilities and glamour and prizes. Intellectually, modern evolutionary biology can be very exciting, but—despite proselytizing efforts by enthusiasts for so-called Darwinian medicine—it still has little (or, rather, is perceived to have little) or no practical value. It still suffers fatally from a lack of compelling reasons for funding. Even when it allies itself with such trendy topics as ecology, it tends to be down the scientific totem pole, and this tells. The bright and the ambitious look elsewhere.

This is not all. There is still the fact that—for all of the efforts at professionalization—many evolutionists are in the business, in part if not primarily, for the extrascientific juices to be wrung from the theory. Juices, that critics complain with reason, had first to be injected into the system. There are those who openly devote much or most of their labors to the broader meanings of evolution, and there are many others who, for all that they pretend to full-time scientific studies, are certainly not beyond using their ideas and models to further social and political agendas that they favor. And, as with religion—as with Christianity, especially—one gets sects and denominations, and the differences and fighting between evolutionists gets as sour and personal as it so usually is when close relatives fall out.

Edward O. Wilson

History gives us a reason why people think that Darwinism and Christianity are going to be things apart, at war rather than peace. But is this inevitable? What about the arguments? Is there reason to think that a Darwinian cannot possibly be a Christian, or is the opposition truly a legacy from intentions and aims from the past—intentions and aims that we today do not necessarily share? Let us turn now to some of the arguments used by those who would put Christianity and Darwinism apart. I shall take in turn the arguments of three recent writers: the Harvard entomologist and sociobiologist Edward O Wilson; Richard Dawkins, popularizer and spokesman for atheism; and myself, a historian and philosopher of science.[11]

Edward O. Wilson is an interesting case. Although he is no Christian, in many respects he is significantly more sympathetic to religion in general and perhaps even to Christianity in particular than many Darwinian nonbelievers. Wilson recognizes the importance of religion and its widespread nature: he is very far from convinced that one will ever eliminate religious thinking from the human psyche, at least as we know it. "The predisposition to religious belief is the most complex and powerful force in the human mind and in all probability an ineradicable part of human nature."[12] As far as Wilson is concerned, religion exists purely by the grace of natural selection: those organisms that have religion survive and reproduce better than those that do not. Religion gives ethical commandments, which are important for group living; also, religion confers a kind of group cohesion—a cohesion that is a very important element of Wilson's picture of humankind:

> religions are like other human institutions in that they evolve in directions that enhance the welfare of the practitioners. Because of this demographic benefit must accrue to the group as a whole, it can be gained partly by altruism and partly by exploitation, with certain sectors profiting at the expense of others. Alternatively, the benefit can arise as the sum of the generally increased fitness of all of the members."[13]

Wilson makes it clear that in fact he thinks that religion is ingrained directly into our biology. Thanks to our genes, it is part of our innate nature. "The highest forms of religious practice, when examined more closely, can be seen to confer biological advantage. Above all they congeal identity."[14]

Wilson does believe that giving a Darwinian explanation—Wilson would call it giving a "sociobiological" explanation—does make it possible to deny religion the status of a body of true claims. And indeed, given our religious needs, this means that in some sense Wilson's position requires that the biology itself become an alternative secular religion.

> But make no mistake about the power of scientific materialism. It presents the human mind with an alternative mythology that until now has always, point-for-point in zones of conflict, defeated traditional religion. Its narrative form is the epic: the evolution of the universe from the big bang of fifteen billion years ago through the origin of the elements and celestial bodies to the beginnings of life on earth. The evolutionary epic is mythology in the sense that the laws it adduces here and now are believed but can never be definitively proved to form a cause-and-effect continuum from physics to the social sciences, from this world to all other worlds in the visible universe, and backward through time to the beginning of the universe. Every part of existence is considered to be obedient to physical laws requiring no external control. The scientist's devotion to parsimony in explanation excludes the divine spirit and other extraneous agents. Most importantly, we have come to the crucial stage in the history of biology when religion itself is subject to the explanations of the natural sciences. As I have tried to show, sociobiology can account for the very origin of mythology by the principle of natural selection acting on the genetically evolving material structure of the human brain.
>
> If this interpretation is correct, the final decisive edge enjoyed by scientific naturalism will come from its capacity to explain traditional religion, its chief competition, as a wholly material phenomenon. Theology is not likely to survive as an independent intellectual discipline.[15]

I am not interested here in critiquing Wilson's scientific position. Let us take his position at face value and ask what Wilson's implication has for Christianity, particularly vis-à-vis the whole issue of atheism. I take it that, in Wilson's own mind, what is happening is that Darwinism is explaining religion (including Christianity) as a kind of illusion: an illusion that is necessary for efficient survival and reproduction. Once this explanation has been put in place and exposed, one can see that Christianity has no reflection in reality. In other words, epistemologically one ought to be an atheist. What makes Wilson particularly interesting is that—atheist although he may be—he still sees an emotive and social power in religion. He would, therefore, replace spiritual religion with some kind of secular religion. Which secular religion, as it turns out, happens to be Darwinian evolutionism.

Of course, the kind of argument that Wilson is promoting is hardly new. Both Karl Marx and Sigmund Freud proposed similar sorts of arguments: trying to offer a naturalistic explanation of religion, arguing that once one has this explanation in place, one can see that the belief system is false. So already I doubt the absolutely essential Darwinian component to the general form of the argument. But even if the argument were sometimes well taken, what of the specific case of Darwinism and Christianity? The missing elements in Wilson's case are crucial. The fact that one has an evolutionary explanation of religion is surely not in itself enough to dismiss the belief system as illusory or false. We might offer an evolutionary explanation as to why somebody spots a speeding train, but the fact that it is an evolutionary explanation does not make the existence of the speeding train fictitious.[16] Indeed, if anything, the evolutionary explanation convinces us that we do have a true perception of the speeding train. If evolution led us think that it was turtledove rather than a train it would not be of much survival value. None of this is to deny that people have proposed arguments suggesting that belief in Christianity is unsound, ridiculous even. There are all sorts of paradoxes that the Christian must face. But whether or not one can defend Christianity against such charges, I do not see that the charges themselves have been brought on by Darwinism: which is the nub of this discussion. Hence, although Wilson may be right about the evolutionary basis of a belief in Christianity, he is wrong in thinking that this necessarily destroys the truth-value of Christianity.

Richard Dawkins

Let me start by quoting a couple of paragraphs from an interview that Dawkins gave recently.

> I am considered by some to be a zealot. This comes partly from a passionate revulsion against fatuous religious prejudices, which I think lead to evil. As far as being a scientist is concerned, my zealotry comes from a deep concern for the truth. I'm extremely hostile towards any sort of obscurantism, pretension. If I think somebody's a fake, if somebody isn't genuinely concerned about what actually is true but is instead doing something for some other motive, if somebody is trying to appear like an intellectual, or trying to appear more profound than he is, or more mysterious than he is, I'm very hostile to that. There's a certain amount of that in religion. The universe is a difficult enough place to understand already without introducing additional mystical mysteriousness that's not actually there. Another point is esthetic: the universe is genuinely mysterious, grand, beautiful, awe inspiring. The kinds of views of the universe which reli-

gious people have traditionally embraced have been puny, pathetic, and measly in comparison to the way the universe actually is. The universe presented by organized religions is a poky little medieval universe, and extremely limited.

I'm a Darwinist because I believe the only alternatives are Lamarckism or God, neither of which does the job as an explanatory principle. Life in the universe is either Darwinian or something else not yet thought of.[17]

These paragraphs are very revealing, not the least for showing the emotional hostility that Dawkins feels towards religion, including (obviously) Christianity. I am sure the reader will not be surprised to learn that Dawkins has recently characterized his move to atheism from religious belief as a "road to Damascus" experience.[18] Saint Paul would have recognized a kindred spirit. But my purpose in quoting Dawkins's words here is not so much to pick out the emotion, as to point to the logic of Dawkins's thinking. This comes through particularly in the second paragraph just quoted. It is clear that for Dawkins we have here an exclusive alternation. Either you believe in Darwinism or you believe in God, but *not both*. For Dawkins there is no question for what philosophers call an inclusive alternation, that is to say either A or B or possibly both. (The third way mentioned is Lamarckism, the inheritance of acquired characteristics. But neither Dawkins nor anybody else today thinks that this is a viable evolutionary mechanism.)

Why not simply slough off Christianity and ignore it? Things are not this simple. Dawkins—like any good Darwinian, including Charles Darwin himself—recognizes that the Christian religion poses the important question, namely that of the design-like nature of the world.[19] Moreover, Dawkins believes that until Charles Darwin no one had shown that the God hypothesis, that is to say the God-as-designer hypothesis, is untenable: more particularly, Dawkins argues that until Darwin no one could avoid using the God hypotheses. He makes reference to William Paley, Archdeacon of Carlyle, whose *Natural Theology* of 1802 contained the definitive statement of the argument from design—the eye is like a telescope, telescopes have telescope makers, hence the eye has an eye maker, the Great Optician in the Sky.

I feel more in common with the Reverend William Paley than I do with the distinguished modern philosopher, a well-known atheist, with whom I once discussed the time before 1859, when Darwin's *Origin of Species* was published. "What about Hume?" replied the philosopher. "How did Hume explain the organized complexity of the living world?" I asked. "He didn't," said the philosopher. "Why does it need any special explanation?"[20]

Why should we not say, with earlier Darwinians who were also Christians, that the alternation is inclusive? Why should we not say that Dawkins is certainly right in stressing the design-like nature of the organic world, but he is wrong in thinking that it is either Darwinism or God, but not both? At least, even if he is not wrong, he has failed to offer an argument for this? There have been many evolutionists in the past who quite happily argued that the design-like nature of the world testifies to God's existence? It is simply that God created through unbroken law. Indeed, people in the past would argue that the very fact that God creates through unbroken law attests to his magnificence. Such a God is much superior to a God who had to act as Paley's watchmaker would have acted, that is through miracle.

But is this an acceptable position to take? Let us go back to Darwin and to an argument he had with his great American supporter Asa Gray. The American feared that pure Darwinism insists that natural selection works on random variation and the very fact of randomness in some sense weakens any kind of Christian design. "So long as gradatory, orderly, and adapted forms in Nature argue design, and at least while the physical cause of variation is utterly unknown and mysterious, we should advise Mr. Darwin to assume, in the philosophy of his hypothesis, that variation has been led along certain beneficial lines."[21] Against this Darwin responded that this was really most improbable. "I come to differ more from you. It is not that designed variation makes, as it seems to me, my deity "Natural Selection" superfluous, but rather from studying, lately, domestic variation, and seeing what an enormous field of undesigned variability there is there ready for natural selection to appropriate for any purpose useful to each creature."[22] Darwin's point seems to be that, although the world is indeed design-like, the mechanism of natural selection somehow precludes any kind of God except at a very distant sort of way: eighteenth-century deism rather than nineteenth-century Anglo-Catholicism. Darwin's argument bears on the unlikelihood that the Christian God would have been quite as indifferent to organic need as selection supposes at this point.

However, interestingly, with respect to this line of argument, Dawkins himself downplays the significance of the randomness of variation—the point of worry for Asa Gray. In a brilliant chapter of *The Blind Watchmaker*, Dawkins shows how computer programs can, very rapidly indeed, generate order from randomness.

> We have seen that living things are too improbable and too beauti-
> fully designed to have come into existence by chance. How, then,
> did they come into existence? The answer, Darwin's answer, is by
> gradual, step-by-step transformations from simple beginnings, from
> primordial entities sufficiently simple to have come into existence by
> chance. Each successive change in the gradual evolutionary process
> was simple enough, *relative to its predecessor*, to have arisen by
> chance. But the whole sequence of cumulative steps constitutes any-
> thing but a chance process, when you consider the complexity of the

final end-product relative to the original starting point. The cumulative process is directed by nonrandom survival. The purpose of this
chapter is to demonstrate the power of this *cumulative selection* as a
fundamentally nonrandom process.[23]

Precisely! The randomness of mutation is reduced to a mere technical
detail. It is not something with profound implications, and certainly not something with profound theological implications. It is simply the raw material on
which evolution builds: the fact that it is random is really quite irrelevant given
the swamping nature of the selective process. The possibility that God creates
through Darwinian law is still a live option.

Dawkins has other arguments for his case that Darwinism is incompatible
with Christianity. Let me look at just one, an argument penned in response to
the "Message to the Pontifical Academy of Sciences" sent by Pope John Paul
II on October 22, 1996, in which the pontiff states that new discoveries have
made the theory of evolution more than a mere hypothesis. To say that Dawkins
is less than overwhelmed or grateful is to understate matters considerably.
"Given a choice between honest to goodness fundamentalism on the one hand,
and the obscurantist, disingenuous doublethink of the Roman Catholic Church
on the other, I know which I prefer."[24] Dawkins main argument against the
Pope, one which does see explicit conflict between Darwinism and Christianity,
comes over the evolution of humankind. The Pope says:

> Revelation teaches us that [man] was created in the image and like-
> ness of God. . . . if the human body takes its origin from pre-existent
> living matter, the spiritual soul is immediately created by God. . . .
> Consequently, theories of evolution which, in accordance with the
> philosophies inspiring them, consider the mind as emerging from
> the forces of living matter, or as a mere epiphenomenon of this mat-
> ter, are incompatible with the truth about man. . . . With man, then,
> we find ourselves in the presence of an ontological difference, and
> ontological leap, one could say.[25]

To which, Dawkins sneers: "Catholic morality demands the presence of a
great gulf between Homo sapiens and the rest of the animal kingdom. Such a
gulf is fundamentally antievolutionary. The sudden injection of an immortal
soul in the time-line is an antievolutionary intrusion into the domain of science."[26] In Dawkins's thinking, the coming of the soul not only infringes on
the domain of science, it is profoundly antievolutionary. It makes for the arrival
of a new entity in a way incompatible with a Darwinian perspective. But is this
so? The answer obviously depends on what precisely one is supposing to have
arrived. If one simply identifies mind with soul, then one is indeed in trouble.
Qua Darwinian, one is indeed going to think that the mind is a product of
evolution and came about naturally and gradually. There is no such ontological

gap between humans and animals. Hence, there does here seem to be a clash between Darwinism and Christianity. But in fact—for all the influence of Greek thought (which as against Jewish thought did identify the mind as the distinguishing and separable characteristic of humankind) on early Christianity—it is not part of Christian theology that it is the mind which separates us from the beasts. Rather it is our souls. Newborn babies have no minds, but they have souls. In fact, speaking of minds, the biblical term is less that of "mind" and more that of "spirit"; although, even with this clarification, there is no clear guidance on the exact relationship between spirit and soul—trichotomists separating them (with body as the third element) and dichotomists putting them together. (The Fourth Council of Constantinople, 869–879 AD, condemned the trichotomous view, but there is biblical support for it.)

One helpful student of "Christian anthropology" writes on this whole matter as follows:

> What is distinctive about human beings is not that they have a 'soul' which animals do not possess, nor that they have a 'spirit' which other creatures do not possess, but that, as 'ensouled body' and 'embodied soul', the 'spirit' of that existence is opened towards God in a unique way as the source of life. The whole of human life, body and soul, is thus oriented towards a destiny beyond mortal or natural life. This endowment of life is experienced as the image and likeness of God. While the physical body itself is not held to be in the image of God, human beings as 'embodied souls' are in the image of God.
>
> The consensus of modern theologians seems to be that the human spirit should not be viewed as a third aspect of the self, as distinguished from body and soul. Rather, the human spirit is the existence of the self as ensouled body and embodied soul as the particular moral and spiritual agent responsible for loving God with all one's heart, mind and soul, and one's neighbor as oneself (Matt. 22: 37–9). The 'life' which is constitutive of human being is at the same time a bodily life, a life of the soul, and a spiritual life. It would not be the life of the spirit if it were not for the fact that body and soul in their interconnection constitute a living person. Because there is a precedence which the soul exercises with respect to the body, the soul becomes the primary orientation of the spirit in this life. This allows for a duality of human being without creating a dualism and opposition between body and soul. In the resurrection, there will be a 'spiritual body,' suggesting that the concept of a disembodied soul is alien to a biblical anthropology even through the experience of death and resurrection (1 Cor. 15: 44; 2 Cor. 5: 1–10).[27]

What is clear from this discussion is that the Christian notion of soul and/ or spirit is not simply that of mind—which latter is the natural entity (whether or not material) which is the subject of evolution. You may not think that the notion of soul is coherent or makes much sense—I am not sure that I do. But that is another matter. The point is that the Christian notion is very clearly not something which is a natural entity and as such is not subject to scientific understanding. I agree that the Christian now has problems about when exactly humans got souls and whether it was a one-shot event for a limited number of humans or whether (contrary to the Pope) souls evolved in some way. Do dogs have souls? Did the Neanderthals have souls? But these are surely theological questions which, although they may be influenced or constrained by science (if full intelligence is needed for souls, then one doubts that four million years ago there were beings—beings such as Lucy, *Australopithecus afarensis*—which had souls), are not themselves scientific questions. In other words, I do not see that Dawkins's critique is well taken.

Michael Ruse

I want now to consider a Darwinism-based argument that I have myself put forward against Christian belief. This is an argument which centers in on the moral aspects of Christian belief: in particular, the claims by the Christian, based on the sayings of Jesus and his followers, that one has a moral obligation to love one's neighbor as oneself. It was a claim that worried me when I was a Christian, and worries me still, now that I have lost my faith. My concern is that there are good biological reasons for thinking that morality will be a differential affair. That we will (and do) have a moral sense which leads us to think that we have special obligations to our closest relatives. Then we will feel lesser obligations to those further from our central bloodline. Next, to our own particular group of acquaintances. Finally, we reach out morally to strangers in other lands. I am not saying that Darwinian biology suggests that we have no obligations whatsoever to total strangers. What I am suggesting is that we will feel that we have stronger obligations to close relatives and that this is the way that morality functions. And my worry is that this belief or conclusion clashes with the love commandment. There is a clash here: Jesus intends us to love everyone, friend and stranger indifferently, not just our children and siblings.[28]

How does one set about countering this worry? Obviously, I am not the best of all possible people to do this; but let me at least try to probe weaknesses in my own position. There are two tacks that one can take. One is simply to agree that the love commandment has a somewhat restricted differential import. One suggests that when Jesus told us to love our neighbours as ourselves, he was not telling us to go off and seek out absolute strangers, willy-nilly.

Certainly, Jesus intended us to care for strangers when they come into our orbit: remember the parable of the good Samaritan. But, basically, what Jesus expected of us was good behaviour toward those in our immediate group. The centurion did not get a dressing-down because it was his own daughter that caused him concern. Jesus obviously intended that we should look after our children and our aged parents and the like, and then our friends in distress and so on and so forth, as the circle widens out. This kind of interpretation of the love commandment fits in absolutely with the biological interpretation and seems to cause no tensions whatsoever.

The other way in which one could set about to try to solve this problem would be by agreeing that the love commandment does reach to all people indifferently: I have as much of an obligation to the unknown starving child in central Africa as I have to my own children. Here, one has to recognize that the biology does not fit well with the Christian imperatives. But surely it is open for someone to say that that is precisely the point! When Jesus was preaching the binding nature of the love commandment, he was not preaching to the converted. He was rather addressing people who fell badly short of this. The relevance of biology at this point lies in the way that it points to our limited nature: in some sense, one might say that it picks up on the Christian notion of original sin.[29] Not that biology supports the idea of a literal Adam and Eve eating the apple that God had forbidden, but rather that Darwinism picks up on the essential truth behind the doctrine of the original sin, namely that we humans fail abysmally against the moral standards that God has set. Here, then, one could argue that far from Darwinism undermining the Christian position, in a way it could be seen to support it.

I rather like this second argument. It takes the offensive, making Darwinism a positive part of the solution, not merely something to be excused and explained away. But is it adequate? One might argue that the whole point about original sin is that this is something that we humans freely choose. Of course, there are questions about why those of us who are descended from Adam continue to be tainted with original sin, even though we did not ourselves originally taste the apple. But, the point about original sin is that it was a free and conscious choice at some level, whereas the whole point about the Darwinian explanation is that this is something laid on us by our evolution, which the Christian must ultimately put down to God's responsibility. So in a way, the original sin is not our fault but God's!

I expect that there is some way around this problem, but I draw attention to it to show there is going to be some tensions at this point. I am afraid, however, I am going to have to leave the discussion as an exercise for the reader, reminding you that I went into this discussion acknowledging that I of all people was not the best suited for the argument and its counters! I certainly do not claim that the Darwinian position necessarily leads to atheism. I have never claimed this. Although, I do confess that my arguments were intended to throw some doubt on the existence and workings of the Christian God.

Conclusion

My conclusion is simple. Darwinism and Christianity were put in opposition, primarily by the Darwinians, for social and political reasons of the mid-nineteenth century. Although many today think that there still is this opposition—and socially it certainly exists—I am not at all sure that intellectually there need be such a gap. If Wilson, Dawkins, and Ruse are representative of the opposition, then intellectually there need be no such gap. I am not saying that bringing Darwinism and Christianity together is an easy job. But, as I have said elsewhere,[30] whoever said that the worthwhile things in life are easy?

NOTES

1. P. Johnson, *Darwin on Trial* (Washington, D.C.: Regnery Gateway, 1991); *Reason in the Balance* (Downer's Grove: Intervarsity Press, 1995).

2. R. Dawkins, "Obscurantism to the Rescue," *Quarterly Review of Biology* 72 (1997): 397–399.

3. Ibid., 397

4. Michael Ruse, *The Darwinian Revolution* (Chicago: University of Chicago Press, 1979); *Monad to Man: The Concept of Progress in Evolutionary Biology* (Cambridge: Harvard University Press, 1996); *The Evolution Wars* (Santa Barbara: ABC-CLIO, 2000).

5. Ruse, *Monad: Mystery of Mysteries* (Cambridge: Harvard University Press, 1999).

6. *The Structure of Scientific Revolutions* (Chicago: University of Chicago Press, 1962).

7. J. Browne, *Charles Darwin: Voyaging* (New York: Knopf, 1995).

8. A. Desmond, *Huxley: The Devil's Disciple* (London: Michael Joseph, 1994); *Huxley. Evolution's High Priest*, 1997.

9. R. J. Richards, *Darwin and the Emergence of Evolutionary Theories of Mind and Behavior* (Chicago: University of Chicago Press, 1987).

10. Ruse, *Monad: Mystery of Mysteries*.

11. See also Ruse, *Can a Darwinian Be a Christian?* (Cambridge: Cambridge University Press, 2001).

12. E. O. Wilson, *On Human Nature* (Cambridge: Harvard University Press, 1978), 169.

13. Ibid., 174–175.

14. Ibid., 188.

15. Ibid., 192.

16. R. Nozick, *Philosophical Explanations* (Cambridge: Harvard University Press, 1981).

17. R. Dawkins, "Richard Dawkins: A Survival Machine," in *The Third Culture*, ed. J. Brockman (New York: Simon and Schuster, 1995), 85–86.

18. Richard Dawkins, "Religion Is a virus," *Mother Jones*, November–December 1997.

19. Richard Dawkins, *The Blind Watchmaker* (New York: W. W. Norton, 1986).

20. Ibid., 5.

21. Asa Gray, *Darwiniana* (Cambridge: Harvard University Press, [1876] 1963), 121–122.

22. J. Moore, *The Post-Darwinian Controversies* (Cambridge: Cambridge University Press, 1979), 274.

23. Dawkins, *Watchmaker*, 43.

24. Dawkins, "Obscurantism," 399.

25. John Paul II, "The Pope's Message on Evolution," *Quarterly Review of Biology* 72 (1997): 377–383.

26. Dawkins, "Obscurantism," 398.

27. R. S. Anderson, "Christian Anthropology," in *Blackwell Encyclopedia of Modern Christian Thought* (Oxford: Blackwell, 1993), 5–9.

28. See Ruse, *Taking Darwin Seriously* (Oxford: Blackwell, 1986); "Evolutionary Ethics," *Zygon* 21 (1986): 95–112; *The Darwinian Paradigm* (London: Routledge, 1989); and *Evolutionary Naturalism* (London: Routledge, 1995). Also E. Wallwork, "Thou Shalt Love Thy Neighbor as Thyself," *Journal of Religious Ethics* 10 (1982): 264–319.

29. Ruse, *Can a Darwinian Be a Christian?*

30. Ibid.

BIBLIOGRAPHY

Anderson, R. S. "Christian Anthropology." *Blackwell Encyclopedia of Modern Christian Thought*, edited by A. McGrath. Oxford: Blackwell, 1993.

Browne, J. *Charles Darwin: Voyaging*. Vol. 1. New York: Knopf, 1995.

Dawkins, R. "Richard Dawkins: A Survival Machine." In *The Third Culture*, edited by J. Brockman. New York: Simon and Schuster, 1995.

———. *The Blind Watchmaker*. New York: W. W. Norton, 1986.

———. "Religion Is a Virus." *Mother Jones* (November/December 1997).

———. "Obscurantism to the Rescue." *Quarterly Review of Biology* 72 (1997): 397–399.

Desmond, A. *Huxley: The Devil's Disciple*. London: Michael Joseph, 1994.

———. *Huxley: Evolution's High Priest*. London: Michael Joseph, 1997.

Gray, A. *Darwiniana*. Cambridge: Harvard University Press, 1963.

John Paul II. "The Pope's Message on Evolution." *Quarterly Review of Biology* 72 (1997): 377–383.

Johnson, P. E. *Darwin on Trial*. Washington, D.C.: Regnery Gateway, 1991.

———. *Reason in the Balance: The Case Against Naturalism in Science, Law and Education*. Downers Grove, Ill.: InterVarsity Press, 1995.

Kuhn, T. *The Structure of Scientific Revolutions.* Chicago: University of Chicago Press, 1962.

Moore, J. *The Post-Darwinian Controversies: A Study of the Protestant Struggle to Come to Terms with Darwin in Great Britain and America, 1870–1900.* Cambridge: Cambridge University Press, 1979.

Nozick, R. *Philosophical Explanations.* Cambridge: Harvard University Press, 1981.

Paley, W. *Natural Theology: Collected Works.* Vol. 4. London: Rivington, [1802] 1819.

Richards, R. J. *Darwin and the Emergence of Evolutionary Theories of Mind and Behavior.* Chicago: University of Chicago Press, 1987.

Ruse, M. *The Darwinian Revolution: Science Red in Tooth and Claw.* Chicago: University of Chicago Press, 1979.

———. "Evolutionary Ethics: A Phoenix Arisen." *Zygon* 21 (1986): 95–112.

———. *Taking Darwin Seriously: A Naturalistic Approach to Philosophy.* Oxford: Blackwell, 1986.

———. *The Darwinian Paradigm: Essays on Its History, Philosophy and Religious Implications.* London: Routledge, 1989.

———. *Evolutionary Naturalism: Selected Essays.* London: Routledge, 1995.

———. *Monad to Man: The Concept of Progress in Evolutionary Biology.* Cambridge: Harvard University Press, 1996.

———. *Mystery of Mysteries: Is Evolution a Social Construction?* Cambridge: Harvard University Press, 1999.

———. *The Evolution Wars: A Guide to the Controversies.* Santa Barbara: ABC-CLIO, 2000.

———. *Can a Darwinian Be a Christian? The Relationship Between Science and Religion.* Cambridge: Cambridge University Press, 2001.

Wallwork, E. "Thou Shalt Love Thy Neighbour as Thyself: The Freudian Critique." *Journal of Religious Ethics* 10 (1982): 264–319.

Wilson, E. O. *On Human Nature.* Cambridge: Cambridge University Press, 1978.

II

Experiencing Evolution: Varieties of Psychological Responses to the Claims of Science and Religion

Ronald L. Numbers

In the early twentieth century the psychologist Sigmund Freud noted that science had already inflicted on humanity "two great outrages upon its naïve self-love": the first, associated with the sixteenth-century astronomer Nicolaus Copernicus, "when it realized that our earth was not the centre of the universe, but only a tiny speck in a world-system of a magnitude hardly conceivable"; the second, associated with Charles Darwin, "when biological research robbed man of his peculiar privilege of having been specially created, and relegated him to a descent from the animal world." Conceitedly, Freud went on to observe that "man's craving for grandiosity is now suffering the third and most bitter blow," this time at the hands of psychoanalysts, such as himself, who were showing that humans behavior was influenced by unconscious urges.[1]

Freud need not have worried so much about the mental sufferings inflicted by modern science. Copernicanism had indeed dislodged humans from the center of the cosmos, but in the Aristotelian world the center was the lowliest place in the universe; there is little evidence that humans felt diminished by being hurled into space.[2] Psychoanalysis never achieved the prominence its founder dreamed of, and so never caused the trauma he anticipated. But what of Darwinism? How much emotional distress did the revelation of ape ancestry cause humans? How often did their encounters with evolution produce spiritual crises? And what was the nature of the crises that occurred?

Two of these queries can be dealt with quickly. Darwin's indelicate announcement in *The Descent of Man* (1871), that humans had "descended from a hairy quadruped, furnished with a tail and pointed ears," indeed attracted considerable attention. And some conservative Christians did express abhorrence at the prospect of relinquishing an honored position at the head of created beings only to be herded together "with four-footed beasts and creeping things," over which man had formerly held dominion. Darwinism, complained one contemptuous critic, "tears the crown from our heads; it treats us as bastards and not sons, and reveals the degrading fact that man in his best estate—even Mr. Darwin—is but a civilized, dressed up, educated monkey, who has lost his tail." There is no reason to believe, however, that such die-hard creationists ever took human evolution seriously enough to be more than rhetorically distressed.[3]

More revealing of genuine concern was the fundamentalist A. C. Dixon's confession to feeling "a repugnance to the idea that an ape or an orang outang was my ancestor." But even he promised not to let the "humiliating fact" stand in the way of accepting human evolution, "if proved." The Southern Baptist New Testament scholar A. T. Robertson put the choice somewhat more colorfully in stating his openness to theistic evolution: "I can stand it if the monkeys can." Despite lots of humor about routing "the biological baboon boosters" and shaking "the monkey out of the cocoanut tree," I have found no evidence that the prospect of having monkeys for uncles caused emotional distress anywhere near the level of that created by biblical and philosophical concerns.[4]

Somewhat more surprising, given the widespread assumption that evolution played a major role in the secularization of Western thought, is the relative infrequency with which evolution seems to have been implicated in the loss of religious faith. Fairly typical of intellectuals who rejected Christianity was the experience of Charles Darwin himself. By the time he returned to England from the voyage of the *Beagle*, he was entertaining doubts about the reliability of the Bible. He tried to staunch these doubts, but, despite persistent effort, he reported in his autobiography that "disbelief crept over me at a very slow rate," causing "no distress." Instead, he came to find Christianity revolting:

> I can indeed hardly see how anyone ought to wish Christianity to be true; for if so the plain language of the text seems to show that the men who do not believe, and this would include my Father, Brother and almost all my best friends, will be everlastingly punished. And this is a damnable doctrine.

As these words suggest, and as the historian James R. Moore has shown, Darwin finally abandoned Christianity not primarily because of his developing views on evolution but for moral concerns awakened by the death of his kind but unbelieving father in 1848 and the passing of his favorite child, lovable, delightful 10-year-old Annie, two and a half years later. How, reasoned the distraught father, could an omnipotent, benevolent God let such a perfect child suffer so much and die so young? Too broken even to attend Annie's funeral, Darwin turned his back on God.[5]

A number of years ago the sociologist Susan Budd studied the biographies of 150 British secularists or freethinkers who lived between 1850 and 1950, hoping to test the prevailing view that "The effects of developing scientific knowledge, especially Darwinism, and of the higher criticism have been . . . mainly responsible for weakening belief in the literal truth of scriptural religion for some, and for forcing others to abandon belief in God altogether." She discovered that only two of her subjects "mentioned having read Darwin or Huxley *before* their loss of faith." A few years back, I examined the reactions of eighty prominent nineteenth-century American scientists to Darwinism and found no evidence to suggest that a single one of them severed his religious ties as a direct result of his encounter with evolution.[6] It is no wonder that in writing the sensational Victorian novel *Robert Elsmere* (1888), in which the clerical hero experiences a crisis of faith and abandons Christianity, Mrs. Humphry Ward said nothing about Darwin or evolution. Although she had initially intended to invoke the "converging pressure of science & history," she decided in the end that it would be truer to the times to feature only the latter.[7]

Even personal testimonies about the corrosive effects of evolution on religious beliefs cannot always be taken at face value. The Victorian writer Samuel Butler supposedly told a friend "that the *Origin of Species* had completely destroyed his belief in a personal God." But, as one of his biographers points out, "He had . . . already quarreled with his father [a cleric], refused to be ordained, thrown up his Cambridge prospects, and emigrated to New Zealand as a sheep-farmer before Darwin's book came out." He quit praying the night before he left for the Antipodes.[8]

In this essay I want to explore the emotional experiences of some of the people who *did* suffer spiritual crises associated with Darwinism. Most historians of evolution and Christianity—indeed of science and religion generally— have focused on intellectual issues and have largely ignored or downplayed experiential factors; they have treated spiritual and emotional crises as mere "decorative episodes" in the lives of their subjects. But, as Robert J. Richards has argued in one of the few historical studies to highlight the importance of psychological crises in the lives of scientists, emotions have often been as significant as ideas.[9] To identify as clearly as possible some of the actual roles that evolution played in creating and resolving spiritual crises, I examine how four scientific Americans, who together nearly span the spectrum of reactions to evolution, wrestled with the teachings of Christ and Darwin: Joseph LeConte, George Frederick Wright, J. Peter Lesley, and George McCready Price.[10]

Joseph LeConte (1823–1901)

Joseph LeConte was arguably the most influential—and certainly one of the most interesting—American harmonizers of evolution and religion in late-nineteenth-century America. His widely quoted definition of evolution as "(1) continuous *progressive change*, (2) *according to certain laws*, (3) and by means of *resident forces*" served for years as a standard. More of a popularizer than an original investigator, he took great pride in showing that "evolution is entirely consistent with a rational theism." But this achievement did not come without a struggle; for decades, he repeatedly "wrestled in agony . . . with [the] demon of materialism."[11]

Young LeConte grew up in an "intensely religious" community in rural Georgia. His pious Presbyterian mother died when he was a toddler; his father, a medically trained plantation owner and unbeliever, passed away when Joseph was 14. The death of his father "outside the pale of the church" distressed him greatly and precipitated "a very great crisis," followed by a classic conversion to orthodox Christianity. For a time, while attending the University of Georgia, he considered becoming a Presbyterian minister. Instead, he studied medicine, then apprenticed himself to Louis Agassiz at Harvard's Lawrence Scientific School. Early in his career, he taught at both the universities of Georgia and South Carolina.[12]

About the mid-1850s LeConte encountered the "dragon of materialism," in the form of August Comte's positivism, which held that only physical phenomena were knowable, that God-talk was meaningless. As an ardent believer in the reliability of human reason, LeConte stood briefly on the "brink of the edge of materialism," only to pull back in horror when he recognized the full implications of this "degrading" philosophy, "which destroys [man's] spirituality, his immortality, every noble upward striving of his nature." For the rest of his life, he shunned materialism, a term he used synonymously with atheism and agnosticism.[13]

In 1861, LeConte experienced a life-altering loss: the death of his 2-year-old daughter, Josie, from whooping cough. During her last hours, he cuddled her small body, wracked by spasms. So traumatic was her passing, it left him "prostrated" for several days. Decades later he still felt the raw pain:

> Little Josie, dear little Josie! I can not even mention her name without the tenderest emotions. She was the most beautiful child we ever had, with that rare combination of flaxen hair and dark eyes. Alas! We lost her just two years later. The light, the sunlight, the spiritual light seemed to have gone out of my house.

As we have seen, Darwin's loss of his unbelieving but Christlike physician father and of his favorite daughter had destroyed his faith in Christianity. Virtually identical events produced in LeConte a lifelong obsession with immortality. Late in life he was still reassuring himself of the impossibility "that the object of such love [Josie] can be other than immortal?"[14]

By the early 1870s, LeConte had passed through the trauma of the Civil War and relocated at the new University of California. In 1873, in a series of published lectures on religion and science, he announced that he had become a "reluctant evolutionist" of the theistic kind. Adopting the age-old argument that God had revealed himself in *"two divine books,"* Nature and Scripture, LeConte repeatedly alluded to the "distress and doubt" he had suffered as "one who has all his life sought with passionate ardor the truth revealed in the one book, but who clings no less passionately to the hopes revealed in the other":

> During my whole active life, I have stood just where the current
> runs swiftest. I confess to you, that, in my earlier life, I have strug-
> gled almost in despair with this swift current. I confess I have some-
> times wrestled in an agony with this fearful doubt, with this demon
> of materialism, with this cold philosophy whose icy breath withers
> all the beautiful flowers and blasts all the growing fruit of humanity.
> This dreadful doubt has haunted me like a spectre, which would not
> always down at my bidding.

He had come to reject the idea of "the creation of species *directly* and without secondary agencies and processes," but he believed that "the real cause of evolution" remained unknown.[15]

By the end of the decade he had evolved into a "thorough and enthusiastic," if somewhat unorthodox, evolutionist. In what he regarded as "one of the most important" of his scientific contributions, he proposed in 1877 a theory of "paroxysmal" evolution, which correlated "rapid changes of physical conditions and correspondingly rapid movement in evolution." That same year he gave the first of many talks sharing his insights into the relationship between evolution and religion. Harmonizing religion and evolution, including the evolution of the human body, quickly became his great mission, his divine calling: "It is, indeed, glad tidings of great joy which shall be to all peoples. Woe is me, if I preach not the Gospel." His efforts along this line culminated in the publication of his oft-reprinted *Evolution and Its Relation to Religious Thought* (1888).[16]

To mitigate the "difficulty and distress" of coming to terms with evolution, LeConte insisted on two conditions: that it not promote godless materialism and that it not endanger his faith in immortality, "the most dearly cherished and most universal of all human beliefs." Thus, he claimed not only that evolution and materialism were entirely distinct but that there was "not a single philosophical question connected with our highest and dearest religious and spiritual interests that is fundamentally affected, or even put in any new light, by the theory of evolution." On this point LeConte may have protested too much. Although it is difficult at this late date to sort out what orthodox doctrines he ditched because of evolution and which ones he abandoned for other reasons, we do know that by the last decade of his life he had come to reject the idea of a transcendent God, the notion of the Bible as "a direct revelation," the divinity of Christ, the existence of heaven and of the devil, the efficacy of intercessory prayer, the special creation and fall of humans, and the plan of salvation. Only the existence of an imminent, pantheistic God and personal immortality survived. Yet, despite toying at times with leaving organized religion, LeConte remained a nominal Presbyterian and an ecumenical Christian till the end.[17]

In his early years as a harmonizer LeConte insisted that because science could "say absolutely nothing" about the soul and immortality, the field remained "open for evidence from any quarter, and of any degree." By the 1890s, however, he had concluded that science, particularly the doctrine of evolution, could indeed say something—and something positive—about immortality. "Do you not see," he asked fervently, *without immortality, the whole purpose is balked—the whole process of cosmic evolution is futile.* Shall God be so long and at so great pains to achieve a *spirit*, capable of communing with Him, and then allow it to lapse again into nothingness?" Besides, there was always Josie to think about. Even after Joseph's death, his wife, Bessie, would write him letters on their birthdays and wedding anniversary. "How happy you must be dear to be with so many loved ones," she wrote tearfully on one of these occasions; among those she mentioned was "our little Josie."[18]

LeConte's crises—especially those brought on by the loss of his daughter and his encounter with materialism—made it psychologically impossible for him to accept any nontheistic version of evolution, including Darwin's own. At the same time these traumatic experiences facilitated his identification with the emotional and theological needs of other liberal Christians struggling with evolution and thus helped in his becoming the reconciler of evolution and religion par excellence.

J. Peter Lesley (1819–1903)

During the last quarter of the nineteenth century, the distinguished geologist and sometime minister J. Peter Lesley ranked among the most prominent scientists in America who rejected Darwinism; yet his experience, which included spiritual crises and mental breakdowns, remains little known. This is especially surprising since, unlike most antievolutionists, Lesley disliked orthodox Christianity even more than Darwinism and was among the first Americans to make the case for human evolution.

As a religiously devout youth, who memorized most of the Bible, he studied at the University of Pennsylvania in anticipation of entering the Presbyterian ministry. But the first of numerous bouts of ill health, physical and mental, led to a postponement of his seminary studies, while he spent a few years as a subassistant on the Geological Survey of Pennsylvania, headed by Henry Darwin Rogers. Hoping to become a missionary to rural Pennsylvania, he attended Princeton Theological Seminary for three years, then spent some time in Europe, exposing himself to German rationalism and higher criticism of the Bible. He returned with his faith pretty much intact and began working as a colporteur among the poor German settlers in the hills of Pennsylvania.[19]

The strenuous labor undermined his health, and after two years he rejoined the geological survey. By 1848, having received a ministerial license from the Presbytery of Philadelphia, he was pastoring a Congregational church in Milton, Massachusetts, near Boston, where he came under the influence of Unitarians, including his wife-to-be, Susan Lyman. Under circumstances that remain vague, the Presbytery charged him with harboring "infidel" sentiments and "denying the Inspiration of the Scriptures." He adamantly denied being an infidel, but confessed to putting the truths of science above the teaching of the church. In May 1849, the Presbytery withdrew his license to preach. His "theological troubles" literally split the church and exacerbated his poor health. In 1851, he left the ministry yet again and returned to the geological survey. However, his behavior was so erratic and his temper so terrible that Rogers fired him, fearing that "insanity is evidently growing upon him."[20] For years thereafter Lesley struggled to earn a living, working variously as a coal expert for the Pennsylvania Railroad, as secretary of the American Iron Association, and as librarian of the American Philosophical Society.[21]

Shortly after the end of the Civil War, Lesley returned to Boston to deliver the prestigious Lowell Lectures, on "Man's Origin and Destiny, Sketched from the Platform of the Sciences." His liberal wife, perhaps sensing the manic mood of her husband, urged him not to offend his audience by unduly criticizing religion. Though he prided himself on always speaking the truth, he assured her that he had trimmed his language and made his "statements of the oppositions of Science and Religion as mild as possible." Despite his promise, he began his lectures sounding like an American Huxley or Tyndall, arguing that "Jewish Theology and Modern Science . . . are irreconcilable enemies" and that Genesis is "a poem, not a text-book." He dismissed theology as "science falsely so called" and blamed the "unchristian state of the theological and social sciences" for retarding the progress of science.[22]

Hearing such rhetoric, his auditors might have anticipated an early endorsement of Darwin's new theory. But no. Lesley professed to accept organic evolution only "if kept within the regions of variety." Before admitting more extensive evolution—of genus, family, or class—he wanted to observe "nature in the very act of exchanging one species for another." Even then he was confident that the evidence would show not one but four lines of evolutionary development, each corresponding to one of Georges Cuvier's divisions of the animal kingdom: *Radiata, Articulata, Mollusca, and Vertebrata.* Addressing Darwin, Lesley pointed out the resulting difficulties:

> My dear sir, you have four times as much to do as you thought you
> had. You must not only explain how a man came from a monkey,
> and a monkey from a squirrel, and a squirrel from a bat, and a bat
> from a bird, and a bird from a lizard, and a lizard from a fish; but
> you must suggest some possible means of transforming a vertebrate
> fish out of a shell fish, or out of a jelly fish, or out of a lobworm or
> trilobite; then you must go on to show us how the first trilobite, or
> the first coral animal, or the first shizopod was obtained by your
> process of natural selection out of still earlier *vegetable* species. Nay,
> you cannot even stop there. You must explain the very first appear-
> ance of living tissue out of the inorganic elements of dead matter.

Darwinism, he concluded, remained "an open question . . . that ought to be no
bugbear in the path of generous and truthful minds."[23]

Many early Darwinists, such as the Harvard botanist Asa Gray, accepted
organic evolution in general but made a special exception for humans. Lesley—
uniquely, as far as I can tell—rejected what has come to be called macroevo-
lution, but argued that humans had descended from apes. With Darwin, Lesley
believed "that man is a developed monkey," but instead of one evolutionary
track for humans he argued for three: each descending from a different type
of "manlike ape, viz. the orang, the chimpanzee, and the gorilla, the three
principal divisions of the family of apes." The only barrier to accepting such a
human history, he maintained, was the "tissue of absurdity, called the biblical
history of the origin of mankind." No wonder he reported to his wife following
this lecture: "You can't imagine what amusement my flat-footed advocacy of
the monkey origin of man occasioned. There was no end to the jokes."[24]

Despite "threatening symptoms and occasional illness," Lesley had maintained a heavy work load. But shortly after completing his Lowell lectures, he
suffered from what a nephew described as a "completely broken down" ner-
vous system, or what we would call severe depression. According to an intimate
friend, a "black cloud of cerebral exhaustion" came over him, and his "brain-
battery" ceased to function. A couple of years recuperating in Europe helped,
but more years passed before he could put in a full day of work.[25] In 1872, the
University of Pennsylvania appointed him professor of geology and mining
and dean of the "Scientific Department." Two years later he replaced Rogers
as the state geologist of Pennsylvania. In the early 1890s, his incapacitating
depression returned, and this time he never recovered. It is unlikely that we
will ever know what role religious and scientific doubts played in his repeated
breakdowns, though indirect evidence suggests that they were not insignificant.[26]

Although Lesley occasionally attended a Unitarian church with his family, he, like LeConte, had become a pantheist, believing that "God is Nature, and Nature is God." He remained deeply spiritual, but skeptical of, if not hostile to, virtually all theology and organized religion. For him, the ideal religion was "simply Morality and Philanthropy." Again like LeConte, he clung to the prospect of immortality.[27]

Late in life Lesley described evolution as "the prevalent epidemic scientific superstition of the day" and insisted in a letter to the editor of *Science* that he was "not a Darwinist, and [had] never accepted the Darwinian hypothesis so called." Yet his early advocacy of the evolution of humans from apes—to say nothing of his scorn for traditional religion—left even those close to him confused about his true views. His nephew found it ironic that during the 1860s and early 1870s, before the scientific community had reached a consensus, Lesley had seemed inclined toward Darwinism but never fully embraced it. "Twenty years later, when the theory had gained almost universal acceptance even among theologians, he was fully decided, and would at times express complete disapproval of it." Some friends attributed his late-life denunciations of evolution to "senile decay." But Lesley had never found the evidence for Darwinism sufficiently convincing to join the evolutionist camp.[28]

Lesley's precarious mental health and his idiosyncratic response to evolution make it hazardous to venture any generalization based on his experience. Because he lost his faith in traditional Christianity long before his encounter with evolution, it seems unlikely that his religious beliefs had much influence on his negative attitude toward Darwinism. And because his bouts of depression antedated the *Origin of Species*, his mental illness can hardly be blamed on the disturbing effects of evolution. The most that can be claimed in his case is that Darwinism sometimes irritated his sensitive psyche.

George Frederick Wright (1838–1921)

George Frederick Wright, a seminary-trained Congregational minister and amateur geologist, emerged in the 1870s as a leader of the so-called Christian Darwinists and a recognized expert on the ice age in North America. As a young minister he read Darwin's *Origin of Species* and Charles Lyell's *Geological Evidences of the Antiquity of Man* (1863), which clashed with the views he had been taught as a youth, but his autobiographical writings do not reveal the extent to which these books may have precipitated a crisis of faith. They do indicate, however, that he found in Asa Gray's theistic interpretation of Darwinism a compromise that allowed him simultaneously to embrace organic evolution and to retain his belief in a divinely designed and controlled universe.[29]

Wright especially appreciated a passage in which Gray described "the popular conception" of efficient cause: "Events and operations in general go on in virtue simply of forces communicated at the first, but that now and then, and only now and then, the Deity puts his hand directly to the work." This view of God's relationship to the natural world appealed to Wright as an ideal solution to the problem of reconciling the respective demands of science and Scripture. As he later wrote, it "allows us to retain our conceptions of reality in the forces of nature, makes room for miracles, and leaves us free whenever necessary, as in the case of the special endowments of man's moral nature, to supplement natural selection with the direct interference of the Creator."[30]

In making the case for the natural origin of species, Wright blunted the possible psychological shock of Darwin's theory by retaining such familiar concepts as God, miracles, and the special creation of humans. He also repeatedly used language that seemed to restrict natural selection to the lower end of the taxonomic scale while attributing kingdoms and the broader taxonomic groupings to special creation. According to Wright's paraphrase of Darwin's views, "The Creator first breathed life into one, or more probably, four or five, distinct forms," after which a process combining miraculous variations and natural selection split each "order" into families, genera, and species. Wright thought the appearance of humans might legitimately remain outside the evolutionary process, writing that "the miraculous creation of man might no more disprove the general theory of natural selection than an ordinary miracle of Christ would disprove the general reign of natural law." Like Gray, Wright derived great comfort from Darwin's inability to explain the origin of the variations preserved by natural selection, because this limitation seemed to open the door for divine intervention. It "rob[bed] Darwinism of its sting," "left God's hands as free as could be desired for contrivances of whatever sort he pleased," and preserved a "reverent interpretation of the Bible."[31]

Because he believed that the inspired writers intended only to state the *"fact of creation by divine agency"*—not to provide a historically or scientifically accurate account of creation—Wright professed to see "no difficulty at all in adjusting the language of the first chapter of Genesis to that expressing the derivative origin of species." But he remained too much of a biblical literalist simply to dismiss the story of Eve's creation from one of Adam's ribs. And, though he readily accepted the natural evolution of the human body, he insisted on a supernatural infusion of the soul. "No! man is not merely a developed animal; but the inventive genius displayed in the rudest flint implement stamps him as a new creation," he declared. "The new creation, however, is spiritual rather than material or physical."[32]

As far as I can tell, Wright experienced little, if any, psychological trauma in absorbing this watered-down version of Darwinism. A serious crisis of faith did not erupt till the early 1890s, and then from higher criticism, not evolution. Wright's long-festering fears about the implications of higher criticism for an orthodox view of the Bible reached a critical level when he fell under the "spell" of the eloquent and controversial Charles A. Briggs (1841–1913), a Presbyterian theologian who rejected the inerrancy of the original scriptural autographs and questioned the Mosaic authorship of the first five books of the Bible. "So violent has been the shock," Wright candidly reported, "that out of self-respect I have found it necessary to turn a little aside from my main studies to examine anew the foundations of my faith." Wright emerged from this soul-searching convinced more firmly than ever in the Mosaic authorship of the Pentateuch and in a supernatural view of history.[33]

In the wake of this episode, Wright turned sharply rightward. He repudiated his earlier belief that Genesis was merely a protest against polytheism and embraced Arnold Guyot's widely held interpretation of the days of Genesis as cosmic ages. Wright confessed that "in writing upon this subject at previous times I have dwelt, I now believe, somewhat too exclusively upon the adaptation of the document to the immediate purpose of counteracting the polytheistic tendencies of the Israelites and, through them, of the world." The story of a six-day creation might not be literally true, but at least it was scientifically accurate.[34]

By this time Wright was also denouncing the evolutionists, such as Herbert Spencer and John Fiske, who rashly pushed beyond Darwin's "limited conclusions" to construct a system of cosmic evolution. Wright frequently contrasted the modest, cautious Darwin, who had allegedly sought to explain only the origin of species and who had limited his theory of descent to no more than "all the members of the same great class or kingdom," with the impetuous—and often impious—souls who tried to explain the evolution of the entire world and who described development from "the first jelly speck of protoplasm to the brain of a Newton or a Gladstone" without any direct reference to the Creator. This, he declared, was "Darwinism gone to seed in barren soil."[35]

Even as a spokesman for Christian Darwinism in the 1870s and 1880s Wright had excluded the origin of matter, life, and the human soul from the rule of natural law; by the late 1890s he was sounding more and more like a special creationist. In discussing the origin of humans, Wright emphasized the great gap between "the highest animal and the lowest man," though he allowed that a divine miracle might have bridged the gap, thereby joining humans and animals. The opening years of the twentieth century found him damning "the antiquated Uniformitarian geology of Lyell and Darwin" and arguing for "the traditional view that man originated, through supernatural interference, at a comparatively recent time, somewhere in Central Asia."[36]

If Wright's identity as an evolutionist was in doubt at the turn of the century, it practically disappeared during the next two decades, when he joined forces with the leaders of the emerging fundamentalist movement. Writing on "The Passing of Evolution" for *The Fundamentals*, the founding documents of the movement, Wright stressed the special creation of the earliest forms of plants, animals, and, most important, humans. Man, he wrote, differed so greatly from the higher animals, it was "necessary to suppose the he came into existence as the Bible represents, *by the special creation of a single pair*, from

whom all the varieties of the race have sprung." Exactly how this "special creation" happened remained a mystery.[37]

Wright found his early encounter with Darwinism more exhilarating than
spiritually threatening. His modification of Darwin's theory, especially the limitations on the extent of natural selection, allowed Wright to preserve his belief
in an active Creator God—and temporarily to escape a spiritual crisis. But
when theological danger appeared in the form of higher criticism, Wright
found it theologically and psychologically soothing to abandon Christian Darwinism for fundamentalism.

George McCready Price (1870–1963)

George McCready Price, the founder of what in the 1970s came to be called
"scientific creationism," was born in eastern Canada in 1870. When his wid-
owed mother joined the Seventh-day Adventist Church, he, too, at the age of
14, embraced that faith. Seventh-day Adventists not only commemorated a
literal six-day creation by celebrating sabbath on the seventh day; they accepted
as authoritative the "visions" and "testimonies" of the founder of the sect, Ellen
G. White. On one occasion she claimed to be "carried back to the creation and
was shown that the first week, in which God performed the work of creation
in six days and rested on the seventh day, was just like every other week."
White also endorsed the largely discarded view of Noah's flood as a worldwide
catastrophe that had buried the fossils and reshaped the earth's surface.[38]

During the early 1890s, young Price attended Battle Creek College for two
years and subsequently completed a teacher-training course at the provincial
normal school in New Brunswick, Canada. While serving as principal of a small
high school in an isolated part of the province, he read for the first time about
the paleontological evidence for evolution. To Price, the theory of evolution
seemingly *all turned on its view of geology, and that if its geology were true, the
rest would seem more or less reasonable.*" On at least three occasions, he later
recalled, he nearly succumbed to the lure of evolution, or at least to what he
always considered its basic tenet: the progressive nature of the fossil record.
Each time he was saved by sessions of intense prayer—and by reading Mrs.
White's "revealing word pictures" of earth history. As a result of this experience, he decided on a career championing what he call the "new catastrophism," in contrast to the old catastrophism of the French naturalist Georges
Cuvier.[39]

Still, he puzzled over ways to interpret the evidence that apparently indicated the Earth's antiquity, which at first glance seemed "so strong and plausible." Only after poring over the standard geology texts and "almost tons of
geological documents, government reports, memoirs, and monographs on special geological topics" did he discover "how the actual facts of the rocks and

fossils, *stripped of mere theories*, splendidly refute this evolutionary theory of the invariable order of the fossils, *which is the very backbone of the evolution doctrine.*" This discovery not only resolved his intellectual crisis but determined his future course. Believing that he had found a fatal flaw in the logic of evolutionary geology, he grew increasingly convinced that God wanted him "to enter this unworked field; accordingly I threw myself into it with all the energy I possessed, constantly asking and receiving special help from the guiding and enlightening Spirit of God." Responding to this call not only satisfied his spiritual needs, but also allowed him to fulfill his dream of becoming a writer.[40]

Price completed his first antievolution book, *Outlines of Modern Christianity and Modern Science*, in 1902, but instead of elation came desperation, as a sense of failure engulfed him. In the spring of that year he abandoned teaching in New Brunswick to become an Adventist evangelist on Prince Edward Island. His experiment in the pulpit proved disastrous, as did as brief stint as the administrator of small boarding academy. Thoroughly discouraged and driven by guilt to earn a living for his wife and three children, he returned in the summer of 1904 to the one job that had brought him a measure of success: selling religious books. But as he pedaled his bicycle over the rough roads of eastern Canada, he continued to dream of a literary career, "the thing for which I am best fitted and which I thoroughly enjoy above everything else." He had tried various lines of church work only to find "black, dismal Failure" mocking him at every turn. By late summer he had grown so depressed by his situation that he was contemplating suicide. However, out of consideration for his family he decided instead to leave church employment and head for New York City to try his hand at writing "hack stuff for the Metropolitan newspapers and magazines." If life did not improve in the city, he planned to sell his watch, buy a revolver, and rid the world "of another useless, good-for-nothing man."[41]

In the city his circumstances only worsened. Unable to find steady work, he suffered unspeakable privations—and the torment of knowing that his family was "destitute and almost starving" back in Canada. Since his conversion to Adventism he had derived strength from his religious faith, but now in his neediest hour he quit even attending church. His wife, fearing the worst, wrote to church headquarters in Takoma Park, Maryland, begging for help for her husband. Moved by the family's plight, the president of the church personally offered the estranged worker a temporary construction job. Price gratefully accepted the offer, noting that he was willing to go anywhere and do anything, "even if it means hard manual labor."[42]

By 1906, Price, still "heartbroken" over his failure in life, was living in southern California and working as a handyman at the Adventists' Loma Linda Sanitarium. That year he published a slim volume entitled *Illogical Geology: The Weakest Point in the Evolution Theory*, in which he confidently offered a $1,000 reward "to any who will, in the face of the facts here presented, show me how to prove that one kind of fossil is older than another." In brief, he argued that Darwinism rested "logically and historically on the succession of life idea as taught by geology" and that "if this succession of life is not an actual scientific fact, then Darwinism . . . is a most gigantic hoax."[43]

During the next fifteen years, Price taught in several Adventist schools and authored six more books attacking evolution, particularly its geological foundation. Although not unknown in fundamentalist circles before the early 1920s, he did not begin attracting widespread national attention until then. Shortly after the fundamentalist controversy entered its antievolution phase, Price published *The New Geology*, the most systematic and comprehensive of his two dozen or so books. In it, he restated his "great 'law of conformable stratigraphic sequences' . . . by all odds the most important law ever formulated with reference to the order in which the strata occur." According to this law, "Any kind of fossiliferous beds whatever, 'young' or 'old,' may be found occurring conformably on any other fossiliferous beds, 'older' or 'younger.'" To Price, so-called deceptive conformatives (where strata seem to be missing) and thrust faults (where the strata are apparently in the wrong order) proved that there was no natural order to the fossil-bearing rocks, all of which he attributed to Noah's flood.[44] Despite repeated attacks from the scientific establishment, Price's influence among non-Adventist fundamentalists grew rapidly. By the mid-1920s, the editor of *Science* could accurately describe Price as "the principal scientific authority of the Fundamentalists," and Price's byline was appearing with increasing frequency in a broad spectrum of religious periodicals.[45]

Price's success as an internationally known spokesman for creationism unquestionably fulfilled a craving for public recognition, though for the rest of his life he chafed at the failure of fellow fundamentalists to abandon their old-earth creationism for his "flood geology." His uncompromising creationism remained on the fringes of fundamentalism until 1961, when John C. Whitcomb Jr. and Henry M. Morris brought out their landmark book, *The Genesis Flood*, which launched the revival of young-earth creationism in the late twentieth century. Designed as a defense of Price against his critics, it was, as one perceptive reader described it, "a reissue of G. M. Price's views brought up to date." Flattered by the attention he was finally receiving, Price, then in his early nineties, uncharacteristically ignored the near absence of his name in the book.[46]

Among the four individuals we have been examining, Price seems to have suffered the most intensely as a result of entertaining evolution, largely because, as an Adventist, he had so little room for theological compromise. For him, unlike for LeConte, Lesley, or Wright, the acceptance of evolution would have meant a virtually complete rejection of his religious faith, or so it seemed. Yet his deepest psychological crisis, which prompted thoughts of suicide, apparently resulted more from his failure to find a satisfying job than from fear of succumbing to Darwinism. In the end, his thoroughgoing rejection of evolution gave direction to his life and served as the foundation of a rewarding career.

Fleeing Fundamentalism

Over a quarter-century ago, the well-known science writer and skeptic Martin Gardner published a wonderfully evocative, quasi-autobiographical novel called *The Flight of Peter Fromm* (1973). It tells the story of a young creationist from Oklahoma who fell hard for Price's flood geology. In the late 1930s, he packed up his copy of *The New Geology* and went to Chicago to attend divinity school. As a dyed-in-the-wool fundamentalist, he joined the Moody Memorial Church and hung out with friends in the Chicago Christian Fellowship. During his second year at the University of Chicago "his fundamentalism was dealt a mighty death blow"—not from any of his seminars in the divinity school, but from a course he had decided to audit on historical geology. When Fromm asked the professor, named Blitz, if all of the sedimentary rock could have been deposited during Noah's flood, the geologist was "dumbfounded." He "didn't want to embarrass the kid by arguing with him in front of the class," but, nevertheless, he devoted "the rest of the hour going over all the evidence [he] could think of that proves sedimentation has been going on for hundreds of millions of years." In so doing, he

> had driven the point of a geological hammer into the rock of Peter's fundamentalism. He had opened the first tiny fissure through which the waters of modern science could begin their slow erosion. Now the metaphor breaks down. It may take a million years for a boulder to crumble. A religion can crumble in a few centuries. A man's faith can crumble in less than a year. . . . Peter threw away his copy of *The New Geology*.

Despite his growing distrust of biblical science and history, Peter continued to believe in the Bible as God's inspired word. But he began sliding down the path of unbelief: from fundamentalism to Roman Catholicism and eventually to a vague theism. Finally, after the war, while preaching an Easter sermon at the liberal Midway Community Church in Hyde Park, he suffered a psychotic break and had to be taken from the pulpit to a nearby hospital—which is where the novel begins.[47]

My own experience (minus the mental breakdown) closely paralleled Fromm's. Growing up as the son and grandson of Seventh-day Adventist ministers, I attended church schools from first grade through college and unquestioningly accepted the authority of both the biblical prophets and the Adventist prophetess, Ellen G. White. Although I majored in physics and mathematics at Southern Missionary College, an Adventist institution, I do not recall ever doubting that God had created the world within the past six or seven thousand years or that virtually all of the fossil-bearing rocks had been deposited during the year of Noah's flood. The first serious book I remember buying with my own money was *Studies in Creationism*, a defense of young-earth creationism by one of Price's disciples, Frank Lewis Marsh. For years I felt nothing but sorrow for evolutionists, theistic and otherwise, who failed to recognize the "truth" about the history of life on earth.

Then, in the mid-1960s, I found myself at Berkeley studying for a doctorate in the history of science. No godless professors challenged my beliefs, which I kept pretty much to myself. But learning to read and think critically proved my spiritual undoing. One night a friend of mine, Joe Willey, an Adventist graduate student in neurophysiology, and I attended a slide presentation on the famous fossil forests of Yellowstone National Park, where some two dozen layers are stacked one on top of the other. The speaker argued that even using the most rapid rates of volcanic decomposition and tree-growing, the sequence of forests could not be explained in under thirty thousand years. It seems like a miniscule number today, but then it was huge. For me, it challenged the divine authority of both Moses and Mrs. White. My friend, Joe, and I wrestled with the implications of this knowledge for hours that night following the talk. By early in the morning, we had decided to trade in the teachings of inspired writers for the authority of science. We knew we were making a momentous decision, but we had no idea where it would lead, intellectually or otherwise. Despite repeated prayers for divine guidance, I quickly moved from young-earth creationism to old-earth creationism and then on to theistic evolutionism and finally to agnosticism. The journey proved to be mostly liberating, but punctuated at times by episodes of fear, pain, and isolation. Hopes of eternal life faded, and relationships with many Adventist friends and family members became frayed.[48]

I soon learned that I was not alone. I discovered that a number of other conservative Christians had passed through equally trying circumstances. One was J. Frank Cassel, a leader in the evangelical American Scientific Affiliation (ASA), who had graduated from a conservative Christian college, earned a Ph.D. in biology, and gone on to a successful academic career. His autobiographical testimony poignantly captured some of the emotional turmoil he and his friends in the ASA experienced coming to grips with the evidence for evolution in the 1950s:

> First to be overcome was the onus of dealing with a "verboten" term and in a "non-existent" area. Then, as each made an honest and objective consideration of the data, he was struck with the validity and undeniability of datum after datum. As he strove to incorporate each of these facts into his Biblico-scientific frame of reference, he found that—while the frame became more complete and satisfying—he

began to question first the feasibility and then the desirability of an effort to refute the total evolutionary concept, and finally he became impressed by its impossibility on the basis of existing data. This has been a heart-rending, soul-searching experience for the committed Christian as he has seen what he had long considered the *raison d'être* of God's call for his life endeavor fade away, and he has struggled to release strongly held convictions as to the close limitations of Creationism.

The distress suffered by Cassel and his liberal friends elicited little sympathy from conservatives within the ASA, who thought the affiliation had, in the colorful phrase of one member, "gone to the apes." In the opinion of the latter, the drift toward evolution was motivated not by intellectual honesty but by "the malignant influence of 'that old serpent, called the Devil, and Satan, which deceiveth the whole world' (Revelation 12:9)."[49]

On occasion, Darwinism resolved, as well as induced, spiritual crises. A good example of this is the experience of the psychologist William James, who suffered through a protracted crisis, accompanied by such debilitating depression that it pushed him to "the continual verge of suicide" and briefly through the doors of an insane asylum. Then he discovered in Darwinism what he interpreted as evidence that "mind acted irrespectively of material coercion." This realization, the historian Robert Richards has suggested, "helped heal his emotional sickness."[50]

The life stories I have presented, whether representative or not, show the historical poverty and incompleteness of a purely intellectual account of science and religion. Feelings count—often more than facts. That is why even today we have so many varieties of evolutionists and why the majority of Americans still prefer to consider themselves "creationists" rather than "evolutionists" (with nearly half of them believing that "God created human beings pretty much in their present form at one time within the last 10,000 years or so)."[51]

NOTES

I wish to thank Stephen Wald for his research assistance and his insightful observations and Jon H. Roberts and Lester D. Stephens for their critical reading of the manuscript.

1. Sigmund Freud, *Introductory Lectures on Psycho-Analysis: A Course of Twenty-Eight Lectures Delivered at the University of Vienna*, trans. Joan Riviere (London: George Allen and Unwin, 1922), 240–241.

2. Edward Grant, *Planets, Stars, and Orbs: The Medieval Cosmos, 1200–1687* (Cambridge: Cambridge University Press, 1994), 239–243. *See also* Dennis R. Danielson, "The Great Copernican Cliché," *American Journal of Physics* 69 (2001): 1029–1035.

3. Charles Darwin, *The Descent of Man, and Selection in Relation to Sex* (London: John Murray, 1871), 2: 389; P. R. Russel, "Darwinism Examined," *Advent Review and Sabbath Herald*, May 18, 1876, 153. For similar rhetoric, see H. L. Hastings, *Was Moses*

Mistaken? or, Creation and Evolution, no. 36 of the Anti-Infidel Library (Boston: H. L. Hastings, 1896), 25–26.

4. A. C. Dixon, *Reconstruction: The Facts against Evolution* (N.p., n.d.), 18, from a copy in the Dixon Collection, Dargan-Carver Library of the Historical Commission of the Southern Baptist Convention, Nashville, Tennessee; A. T. Robertson, quoted in James Moore, *The Darwin Legend* (Grand Rapids, Mich.: Baker Books, 1994), 119; Andrew Johnson, "The Evolution Articles," *Pentecostal Herald* 38 (September 29, 1926): 6 (baboon boosters). See also the statement of Charles Kingsley quoted in Adrian Desmond, *Huxley: From Devil's Disciple to Evolution's High Priest* (Reading, Mass.: Addison-Wesley, 1997), 288.

5. James R. Moore, "Of Love and Death: Why Darwin 'Gave Up Christianity,'" in *History, Humanity and Evolution: Essays for John C. Greene,* ed. James R. Moore (Cambridge: Cambridge University Press, 1989), 195–230. See also Adrian Desmond and James Moore, *Darwin* (London: Michael Joseph, 1991), 314 (murder), 375–387 (Annie).

6. Susan Budd, *Varieties of Unbelief: Atheists and Agnostics in English Society, 1850–1960* (London: Heinemann, 1977), 104–107; Ronald L. Numbers, *Darwinism Comes to America* (Cambridge: Harvard University Press, 1998), 40–43. Bernard Lightman, *The Origins of Agnosticism: Victorian Unbelief and the Limits of Knowledge* (Baltimore: Johns Hopkins University Press, 1987), 31, also plays down the role of science in the creation of agnosticism. Frank Miller Turner, in a superb examination of six late Victorians who lost their faith in orthodox Christianity, describes George Romanes as "one of the very few men whose loss of faith in the truth of religion can be directly ascribed to the influence of scientific naturalism"; see Turner, *Between Science and Religion: The Reaction to Scientific Naturalism in Late Victorian England* (New Haven: Yale University Press, 1974), 143–144. See also Turner, "The Victorian Crisis of Faith and the Faith that Was Lost," in *Victorian Faith in Crisis: Essays on Continuity and Change in Nineteenth-Century Religious Belief,* ed. Richard J. Helmstadter and Bernard Lightman (Stanford: Stanford University Press, 1990), 9–38. In his pioneering scientific study of the loss of belief among college students and scientists, *The Belief in God and Immortality* (Boston: Sherman, French, 1916), 282–288, James H. Leuba devotes a chapter to the causes of the rejection of traditional beliefs, but evolution does not appear among them. Peter Bowler, however, has claimed that Darwinism "established a complete break between science and religion"; see his *The Eclipse of Darwinism: Anti-Darwinian Evolution Theories in the Decades around 1900* (Baltimore: Johns Hopkins University Press, 1983), 27.

In an influential analysis of the Darwinian controversies James R. Moore has drawn attention to the frequency with which evolution precipitated spiritual crises in the lives of those forced to contend with it. In partial confirmation of his thesis, Moore cites the alleged experiences of two Americans, James Dwight Dana and Jeffries Wyman, whom earlier scholars had described, respectively, as experiencing "a long soul-searching struggle" over evolution and as suffering from "deep distress, emotional as well as rational," over the prospect of apelike ancestors. Moore neglects, however, to mention that his authority for Dana pointedly stated that, despite his expectations, he had found "no evidence" to support the supposition that "an inner conflict involving his religious beliefs" lay behind Dana's struggle. And a recent study of Wyman, based on new evidence, has concluded that Wyman experienced "very little difficulty in embracing evolution." Moore, *The Post-Darwinian Controversies: A Study of the Protestant Struggle to Come to Terms with Darwin in Great Britain and America, 1870–1900* (Cambridge: Cambridge University Press, 1979), 109; William F. Sanford Jr., "Dana and Darwinism," *Journal of the History of Ideas* 26 (1965): 531–546, quotations on 531, 543; A. Hunter Dupree, "Jeffries Wyman's Views on Evolution," *Isis* 44 (1953): 243–246, quotation on 245 (distress); Toby A. Appel, "Jeffries Wyman, Philosophical Anatomy, and the Scientific Reception of Darwin in America," *Journal of the History of Biology* 21 (1988): 69–94, quotation on 71 (little difficulty). Dana's friend Arnold Guyot did on one occasion express concern that the public debate over Dana's views on evolution was causing him emotional distress; see Arnold Guyot to Mrs. J. D. Dana, January 17, 1880, and Arnold Guyot to J. D. Dana, February 16, 1880, James Dwight Dana Correspondence, Yale University Library.

7. Mrs. Humphry Ward, *Robert Elsmere* (New York: J. S. Ogilvie, n.d.), 398; William S. Peterson, *Victorian Heretic: Mrs Humphry Ward's "Robert Elsmere"* (Leicester, U.K.: Leicester University Press, 1976), 148.

8. Basil Willey, *Darwin and Butler: Two Versions of Evolution* (New York: Harcourt, Brace, 1960), 63. On Butler in New Zealand, see John Stenhouse, "Darwinism in New Zealand, 1859–1900," in *Disseminating Darwinism: The Role of Place, Race, Religion, and Gender,* ed. Ronald L. Numbers and John Stenhouse (Cambridge: Cambridge University Press, 1999), 61–90.

9. Robert J. Richards, *Darwin and the Emergence of Evolutionary Theories of Mind and Behavior* (Chicago: University of Chicago Press, 1987), 409–410. In *The Post-Darwinian Controversies,* Moore invokes Leon Festinger's "theory of cognitive dissonance" to help explain various responses to Darwinism; but in treating individual writers, he focuses more on intellectual than on emotional matters. The best intellectual history of Darwinism and Christianity is Jon H. Roberts, *Darwinism and the Divine in America: Protestant Intellectuals and Organic Evolution, 1859–1900* (Madison: University of Wisconsin Press, 1988), but see also Moore, *The Post-Darwinian Controversies;* Ronald L. Numbers, *The Creationists* (New York: Knopf, 1992); and David N. Livingstone, *Darwin's Forgotten Defenders: The Encounter between Evangelical Theology and Evolutionary Thought* (Grand Rapids, Mich.: William B. Eerdmans, 1987). On the history of science and Christianity generally, see David C. Lindberg and Ronald L. Numbers, eds., *God and Nature: Historical Essays on the Encounter between Christianity and Science* (Berkeley and Los Angeles: University of California Press, 1986); Lindberg and Numbers, eds., *When Science and Christianity Meet* (Chicago: University of Chicago Press, 2003); and John Hedley Brooke, *Science and Religion: Some Historical Perspectives* (Cambridge: Cambridge University Press, 1991).

10. All four of these men were Protestants. For parallels in the Catholic community, see, e.g., Jacob W. Gruber, *A Conscience in Conflict: The Life of St. George Jackson Mivart* (New York: Columbia University Press, 1960); and Ralph E. Weber, *Notre Dame's John Zahm: American Catholic Apologist and Educator* (Notre Dame: University of Notre Dame Press, 1961). Regarding Zahm, see also R. Scott Appleby, "Exposing Darwin's 'Hidden Agenda': Roman Catholic Responses to Evolution, 1875–1925," in *Disseminating Darwinism,* ed. Numbers and Stenhouse, 173–208.

11. Joseph LeConte, *Evolution and Its Relation to Religious Thought* (New York: D. Appleton, 1888), 8 (definition); LeConte, *The Autobiography of Joseph LeConte,* ed. Wil-

liam Dallam Armes (New York: D. Appleton, 1903), 335 (rational theism); LeConte, *Religion and Science: A Series of Sunday Lectures on the Relation of Natural and Revealed Religion, or the Truths Revealed in Nature and Scripture* (New York: D. Appleton, 1873), 276 (demon). For a typical reference to LeConte's definition of evolution, see Andrew Johnson, "Evolution Outlawed by Science [No. 3]," *Pentecostal Herald* 37 (December 9, 1925): 9.

12. LeConte, *Autobiography*, 16–17, 41–44. See also Lester D. Stephens, *Joseph LeConte: Gentle Prophet of Evolution* (Baton Rouge: Louisiana State University Press, 1982); and Timothy Odom Brown, "Joseph LeConte: Prophet of Nature and Child of Religion" (M.A. thesis, University of North Carolina at Chapel Hill, 1977).

13. Joseph LeConte, *Inaugural Address: Delivered in the State House, Dec. 8, 1857, by Order of the Board of Trustees of the South Carolina College* (Columbia, S.C.: R. W. Gibbes, 1858), 27. See also LeConte, "The Relation of Organic Science to Sociology," *Southern Presbyterian Review* 13 (1861): 39–77; LeConte, *Autobiography*, 290; and Brown, "Joseph LeConte," 72. On positivism, see Charles D. Cashdollar, *The Transformation of Theology, 1830–1890: Positivism and Protestant Thought in Britain and America* (Princeton: Princeton University Press, 1989).

14. LeConte, *Autobiography*, 177; Stephens, *Joseph LeConte*, 77–78.

15. LeConte, *Religion and Science*, 3, 9–10, 22–24, 28–29, 230–233, 276–277. LeConte recycled the comment about standing "where the current runs swiftest" in "Evolution in Relation to Materialism," *Princeton Review*, 4th ser., 7 (1881): 149–174. The reference to being "a reluctant evolutionist" at the time appeared in LeConte, *Autobiography*, 336. See also Ronald L. Numbers, "Reading the Book of Nature through American Lenses," in *The Book of Nature: Continuity and Change in European and American Attitudes towards the Natural World*, ed. Klaas van Berkel et al. (Leuven, Belgium: Peeters, in press).

16. Joseph LeConte, "On Critical Periods in the History of the Earth and Their Relation to Evolution," *American Journal of Science* 114 (1877): 99–114, quotation on 101; LeConte, *Autobiography*, 266 (most important), 336 (thorough and enthusiastic; woe is me): LeConte, "Evolution in Relation to Religion," *Proceedings at the Annual Dinner of the Chit-Chat Club*, San Francisco, 1877, 1–12, quoted in Stephens, *Joseph LeConte*, 165; LeConte, *Evolution and Its Relation to Religious Thought*, a second edition of which appeared under the title *Evolution: Its Nature, Evidences, and Relation to Religious Thought* (New York: D. Appleton, 1896). See also LeConte's pamphlet, *The Relation of Evolution to Religious Thought* (San Francisco: Pacific Coast Conference of Unitarian and other Christian Churches, 1887).

17. LeConte, *Religion and Science*, 233 (difficulty and distress); LeConte, "Man's Place in Nature," *Princeton Review*, 4th ser., 2 (1878): 789 (dearly cherished); LeConte, "Evolution in Relation to Materialism," 159–160 (distinct); LeConte, "A Brief Confession of Faith, Written in 1890, Slightly Revised and Added to in 1897," LeConte Family Papers, Box 1, Bancroft Library, University of California, Berkeley. In "Man's Place in Nature," 794, LeConte insisted that "Christian pantheism is the only true philosophic view." On the innocuous effects of evolution on religion, see also LeConte, *Relation of Evolution to Religious Thought*, 2. For LeConte's later views on the harmony of Genesis and geology, see [LeConte], Review of *Creation; or, The Biblical Cosmogony in the Light of Modern Science*, by Arnold Guyot, *Science* 3 (1884): 599–601.

18. Joseph LeConte, "Immortality in Modern Thought," *Science* 6 (1885): 126–127 (science says nothing); Josiah Royce, *The Conception of God*, with comments by Sidney Edward Mezes, Joseph LeConte, and G. H. Howison (Berkeley: Philosophical Union of the University of California, 1895), 49–50 (whole purpose balked); Bessie LeConte to Joseph LeConte, March [?], 1903, LeConte Family Papers, Box 1. On LeConte's preoccupation with immortality, see Brown, "Joseph LeConte," 130, 168. On immortality, see also LeConte, "The Natural Grounds of Belief in a Personal Immortality," *Andover Review* 14 (1890): 1–13; and Stephen E. Wald, "Revelations of Consciousness: Joseph LeConte, the Soul, and the Challenge of Scientific Naturalism," unpublished MS, Duke University, 1998. I am especially indebted to Timothy Odom Brown, "Joseph LeConte," for his insights into LeConte's changing views on immortality.

19. Mary Lesley Ames, ed., *Life and Letters of Peter and Susan Lesley* (New York: G. P. Putnam's Sons, 1909), 1: 22–23, 39, 114–116, 134; Benjamin Smith Lyman, "Biographical Notice of J. Peter Lesley," reprinted ibid., 2: 452–483; see esp. 2: 455–458. Ames was Lesley's daughter; Lyman, his nephew. There is no scholarly biography of Lesley, but on his career as a consulting geologist, see Paul Lucier, "Commercial Interests and Scientific Disinterestedness: Consulting Geologists in Antebellum America," *Isis* 86 (1995): 245–267.

20. Ames, *Life and Letters*, 1: 162–166; Lyman, "Biographical Notice," 2: 458–461; Patsy Gerstner, *Henry Darwin Rogers, 1808–1866: American Geologist* (Tuscaloosa. University of Alabama Press, 1994), 184; W. M. Davis, "Biographical Memoir of Peter Lesley, 1819–1903," National Academy of Sciences, *Biographical Memoirs* 8 (1919): 174, 192–193. The British geologist Charles Lyell, who had recently visited the United States, reported in his published memoir, that an unnamed young ministerial candidate in America had failed to receive ordination because he believed that the first book of Genesis was "inconsistent with discoveries now universally admitted, respecting the high antiquity of the earth and the existence of living beings on the globe long anterior to man." Charles Lyell, *A Second Visit to the United States* (London, 1849), 1: 218, quoted in Lyman, "Biographical Notice," 2: 461–462. Lesley insisted that "Lyell was quite wrong," but something of the sort seems to have happened; see Davis, "Biographical Memoir," 174–175.

21. Davis, "Biographical Memoir," 176–197.

22. Ames, *Life and Letters*, 1: 504–515; J. P. Lesley, *Man's Origin and Destiny* (Philadelphia: J. B. Lippincott, 1868), 19, 43, 45, 50.

23. Lesley, *Man's Origin and Destiny*, 76–82. On the response of American scientists to evolution, see Numbers, *Darwinism Comes to America*, 24–48.

24. Lesley, *Man's Origin and Destiny*, 18, 117, 119; Lesley to Susan Lesley, January 11, 1866, quoted in Ames, *Life and Letters*, 1: 512. Regarding Gray, see Numbers, *Darwinism Comes to America*, 27. On the history of polygenism in America, see William Stanton, *The Leopard's Spots: Scientific Attitudes toward Race in America, 1815–59* (Chicago: University of Chicago Press, 1960); and David N. Livingstone, *The Preadamite Theory and the Marriage of Science and Religion* (Philadelphia: American Philosophical Society, 1992). In the early 1880s, Lesley returned briefly to the subject of evolution, adding six new chapters to *Man's Origin and Destiny* (Boston: Geo. H. Ellis, 1881).

25. Lyman, "Biographical Notice," 2: 471–475, 482; Charles Gordon Ames, "A Memorial Discourse, Preached in the Church of the Disciples, Boston, January 24,

1904," in Ames, *Life and Letters*, 2: 530–531. Ames, a Unitarian minister, was not only a close friend of the Lesleys but the father-in-law of their daughter.

26. Lyman, "Biographical Notice," 2: 473–475, 482. Since 1859 he had held a nominal position as professor of mining at the University of Pennsylvania.

27. J. P. Lesley to Allen Lesley, February 15, 1867, in Ames, *Life and Letters*, 2: 17 (pantheist); Lesley to his son-in-law Charles, March 11, 1888, ibid., 2: 350–351 (God is Nature). On Lesley's connection to Unitarianism, see Ames, "A Memorial Discourse," 2: 524; and Davis, "Biographical Memoir," 166. On his belief in immortality, see Lesley to Susan Lesley, June 18, 1888, and June 24, 1890, Ames, *Life and Letters*, 2: 359, 393; and Lesley, "The Idea of Life after Death," *The Forum* 10 (1890–91): 207–215,

28. J. P. Lesley to Susan Lesley, July 8 and 9, 1880, quoted in Ames, *Life and Letters*, 2: 253–255; Lesley, Letter to the Editor, *Science* 10 (1887): 308–309; Lyman, "Biographical Notice," 2:472–473. Davis paraphrased Lyman in his "Biographical Memoir," 215. Regarding Darwinism, see also Lesley's essay in the *United States Railroad and Mining Register*, December 13, 1873, quoted in Lyman, "Biographical Notice," 472.

29. G. Frederick Wright, *Story of My Life and Work* (Oberlin, Ohio: Bibliotheca Sacra, 1916), 116, 123, 132. See also Wright, "Recent Works on Prehistoric Archaeology," *Bibliotheca Sacra* 30 (1873): 381–384; and Wright, *Studies in Science and Religion* (Andover, Mass.: Warren F. Draper, 1882), 352–354. For Asa Gray's views, see his *Darwiniana: Essays and Reviews Pertaining to Darwinism*, ed. A. Hunter Dupree (Cambridge: Harvard University Press, 1963); and [G. F. Wright], Review of *Letters of Asa Gray*, ed. Jane Loring Gray, *Bibliotheca Sacra* 51 (1894): 182. For Gray's influence on Wright, see G. F. Wright to Asa Gray, June 26, 1875, Archives, Gray Herbarium, Harvard University. This discussion of Wright is taken from Ronald L. Numbers, "George Frederick Wright: From Christian Darwinist to Fundamentalist," *Isis* 79 (1988): 624–645, and Numbers, *The Creationists*, 20–36.

30. Gray, *Darwiniana*, 130; G. Frederick Wright, "The Debt of the Church to Asa Gray," *Bibliotheca Sacra* 45 (1888): 527.

31. George F. Wright, "Recent Works Bearing on the Relation of Science to Religion: No. II—The Divine Method of Producing Living Species," *Bibliotheca Sacra* 33 (1876): 455, 466, 474, 487, 492–494. Wright stopped short of identifying himself as "a disciple of Mr. Darwin or as a champion of his theory."

32. Wright, *Studies in Science and Religion*, 347–350, 368–370.

33. G. Frederick Wright, "Some Will-o'-the-Wisps of Higher Criticism," *Congregationalist*, March 12, 1891, 84. See also [Wright], "Professor Wright and Some of His Critics," *Bibliotheca Sacra* 42 (1885): 352. About this time Green turned to B. B. Warfield and W. H. Green for help in accommodating estimates of human life on earth that exceeded the six thousand years commonly attributed to the Old Testament genealogies. See G. Frederick Wright, "How Old Is Mankind?" *Sunday School Times* 55 (January 25, 1913): 52; Wright, "Recent Discoveries Bearing on the Antiquity of Man," *Bibliotheca Sacra* 48 (1891): 309. On Warfield, see Livingstone and Mark A. Noll, "B. B. Warfield (1851–1921): A Biblical Inerrantist as Evolutionist," *Isis* 91 (2000): 283–304. On Green, see Ronald L. Numbers, " 'The Most Important Biblical Discovery of Our Time': William Henry Green and the Demise of Ussher's Chronology," *Church History* 69 (2000): 257–276.

34. G. Frederick Wright, "The First Chapter of Genesis and Modern Science,"

Homiletic Review 35 (1898): 392–393. See also Wright, "Editorial Note on Genesis and Geology," *Bibliotheca Sacra* 54 (1897): 570–572; and Wright, *Scientific Confirmations of Old Testament History* (Oberlin, Ohio: Bibliotheca Sacra, 1906), 368–386. On Guyot, see Ronald L. Numbers, *Creation by Natural Law: Laplace's Nebular Hypothesis in American Thought* (Seattle: University of Washington Press, 1977), 91–100. The Princeton theologian Charles Hodge also endorsed Guyot's interpretation; see Ronald L. Numbers, "Charles Hodge and the Beauties and Deformities of Science," in *Charles Hodge Revisited: A Critical Appraisal of His Life and Work*, ed. John W. Stewart and James H. Moorhead (Grand Rapids, Mich.: William B. Eerdmans, 2002), 77–102.

35. [G. F. Wright], Review of *Darwinism and Other Essays*, by John Fiske, *Bibliotheca Sacra* 36 (1879), 784; [Wright], "Transcendental Science," *Independent* 41 (October 3, 1889): 10. See also Wright, "Darwin on Herbert Spencer," *Bibliotheca Sacra* 46 (1889): 181–184.

36. G. Frederick Wright, "Present Aspects of the Questions Concerning the Origin and Antiquity of the Human Race," *Protestant Episcopal Review* 11 (1898): 319–323; Wright, "The Revision of Geological Time," *Bibliotheca Sacra* 60 (1903): 580; Wright, "The Uncertainties of Science," *Advance* 43 (1902): 624–625.

37. George Frederick Wright, "The Passing of Evolution," *The Fundamentals* (Chicago: Testimony Publishing Co., n.d.), 7: 5–20, emphasis added. For a fuller discussion of Wright's somewhat ambiguous views on the origin of humans, see Numbers, *The Creationists*, 32–36.

38. Ellen G. White, *Spiritual Gifts: Important Facts of Faith, in Connection with the History of Holy Men of Old* (Battle Creek, Mich.: Seventh-day Adventist Publishing Association, 1864), 77–79, 90–91. On White and Adventism, see Ronald L. Numbers, *Prophetess of Health: A Study of Ellen G. White* (New York: Harper and Row, 1976).

39. G. M. Price to H. W. Clark, June 15, 1941, Price Papers, Adventist Heritage Center, Andrews University Library; Price, *Genesis Vindicated* (Washington: Review and Herald Publishing Association, 1941), 300. See also Price, "Some Early Experiences with Evolutionary Geology," *Bulletin of Deluge Geology* 1 (November 1941): 77–92. This discussion of Price is taken from Numbers, *The Creationists*, 72–101.

40. Price, "Some Early Experiences," 79–80; Price, "If I Were Twenty-One Again," *These Times* 69 (September 1, 1960): 22.

41. George E. McCready Price, *Outlines of Modern Christianity and Modern Science* (Oakland, Calif.: Pacific Press, 1902); Price to William Guthrie, August 26, 1904; Price to W. H. Thurston, August 28, 1904; Thurston to A. G. Daniells, January 19, 1905; Guthrie to Daniells, January 23, 2905; all in RG 11 of the Archives of the General Conference of Seventh-day Adventists, Silver Spring, Maryland, hereinafter cited as SDA Archives. I am indebted to Bert Haloviak for bringing these and related documents to my attention.

42. George E. Price to William Guthrie, December 28, 1904; A. G. Daniells to Mrs. G. E. Price, January 16, 1905; Daniells to C. H. Edwards, January 16, 1905; Daniells to Price, January 17 and 31, 1905; Price to Daniells, January 25 and March 19, 1905; all in RG 11, SDA Archives.

43. George McCready Price, "I'd Have an Aim," *Advent Review and Sabbath Herald* 138 (February 16, 1961): 14–15; Price, *Illogical Geology: The Weakest Point in the*

Evolution Theory (Los Angeles: Modern Heretic, 1906), 9; Price to Martin Gardner, May 13, 1952, courtesy of Martin Gardner.

44. George McCready Price, *The New Geology* (Mountain View, Calif.: Pacific Press, 1923), 637–638.

45. *Science*, March 5, 1926, 259; Price to Molleurus Couperus, November, 1946, courtesy of the late Molleurus Couperus. On Price's reputation, see also Martin Gardner, *Fads and Fallacies in the Name of Science* (New York: Dover Publications, 1957), 127. For a typically negative review by a prominent geologist, see Charles Schuchert, Review of *The New Geology*, by George McCready Price, *Science*, May 30, 1924, 486–487.

46. G. M. Price to E. T. Brewster, May 2, 1930, Price Papers; Price, "A Brief History of the Flood Theory," *Signs of the Times* 61 (October 30, 1934): 15; J. C. Whitcomb to D. J. Whitney, August 31, 1957, Whitcomb Papers, courtesy of John C. Whitcomb Jr.; Roy M. Allen, Letter to the Editor, *Journal of the American Scientific Affiliation* 17 (June 1965): 62. Price's reaction to *The Genesis Flood* appeared in an undated brochure advertising the book, Price Papers. On Price's seminal influence on the creationist revival of the late twentieth century, see Numbers, *The Creationists*.

47. Martin Gardner, *The Flight of Peter Fromm* (Los Altos, Calif.: William Kaufmann, 1973), esp. 48–51. On Gardner's own brand of theism, see *The Whys of a Philosophical Scrivener* (New York: Quill, 1983). The Quaker animal ecologist Warder Clyde Allee found his faith challenged in a course on evolution at the University of Chicago; see Gregg Mitman, *The State of Nature: Ecology, Community, and American Social Thought, 1900–1950* (Chicago: University of Chicago Press, 1992), 52–53.

48. Accepting the geological timescale, or a piece of it, was only the beginning of my loss of faith; for the rest of the story, see Jonathan M. Butler, "The Historian as Heretic," in *Prophetess of Health: Ellen G. White and the Origins of Seventh-day Adventist Health Reform*, by Ronald L. Numbers (Knoxville: University of Tennessee Press, 1992), xxv–lxviii.

49. J. Frank Cassel, "Evolution of Evangelical Thinking on Evolution," *Journal of the American Scientific Affiliation* 11 (December 1959): 27; Philip B. Marquart, Letter to the Editor, ibid. 14 (September 1963): 100; Henry M. Morris, *The Twilight of Evolution* (Grand Rapids, Mich.: Baker Book House, 1963), 93. One of the most poignant cases of conflict with evolution was that of the Missouri Lutheran Alfred H. Meyer; see Numbers, *The Creationists*, 274–275.

50. Richards, *Darwin and the Emergence of Evolutionary Theories*, 409–450. Richard Dawkins, *The Blind Watchmaker* (New York: W. W. Norton, 1986), 6, has famously thanked Darwin for making "it possible to be an intellectually fulfilled atheist."

51. Deborah Jordan Brooks, "Substantial Numbers of Americans Continue to Doubt Evolution as Explanation for Origin of Humans," Gallup Poll Releases, March 5, 2001.

BIBLIOGRAPHY

Allen, Roy M. Letter to the Editor. *Journal of the American Scientific Affiliation* 17 (June 1965): 62.

Ames, Mary Lesley, ed. *Life and Letters of Peter and Susan Lesley*. 2 vols. New York: G. P. Putnam's Sons, 1909.

Appel, Toby A. "Jeffries Wyman, Philosophical Anatomy, and the Scientific Reception of Darwin in America." *Journal of the History of Biology* 21 (1988): 69–94.

Appleby, R. Scott. "Exposing Darwin's 'Hidden Agenda': Roman Catholic Responses to Evolution, 1875–1925." In *Disseminating Darwinism: The Role of Place, Race, Religion, and Gender*, ed. Ronald L. Numbers and John Stenhouse. Cambridge: Cambridge University Press, 1999.

Bowler, Peter. *The Eclipse of Darwinism: Anti-Darwinian Evolution Theories in the Decades around 1900*. Baltimore: Johns Hopkins University Press, 1983.

Brooke, John Hedley. *Science and Religion: Some Historical Perspectives*. Cambridge: Cambridge University Press, 1991.

Brown, Timothy Odom. "Joseph Le Conte: Prophet of Nature and Child of Religion." M.A. thesis, University of North Carolina at Chapel Hill, 1977.

Budd, Susan. *Varieties of Unbelief: Atheists and Agnostics in English Society, 1850–1960*. London: Heinemann, 1977.

Butler, Jonathan M. "The Historian as Heretic." In *Prophetess of Health: Ellen G. White and the Origins of Seventh-day Adventist Health Reform*, by Ronald L. Numbers. Knoxville: University of Tennessee Press, 1992.

Cashdollar, Charles D. *The Transformation of Theology, 1830–1890: Positivism and Protestant Thought in Britain and America*. Princeton, N.J.: Princeton University Press, 1989.

Cassel, J. Frank. "Evolution of Evangelical Thinking on Evolution." *Journal of the American Scientific Affiliation* 11 (December 1959): 27.

Danielson, Dennis R. "The Great Copernican Cliché." *American Journal of Physics* 69 (2001). 1029–1035.

Darwin, Charles. *The Descent of Man, and Selection in Relation to Sex*. 2 vols. London: John Murray, 1871.

Davis, W. M. "Biographical Memoir of Peter Lesley, 1819–1903." National Academy of Sciences, *Biographical Memoirs* 8 (1919): 174–193.

Dawkins, Richard. *The Blind Watchmaker*. New York: W. W. Norton, 1986.

Desmond, Adrian. *Huxley: From Devil's Disciple to Evolution's High Priest*. Reading, Mass.: Addison-Wesley, 1997.

Desmond, Adrian, and James R. Moore. *Darwin*. London: Michael Joseph, 1991.

Dixon, A. C. *Reconstruction: The Facts against Evolution*. N.p., n.d.

Dupree, A. Hunter. "Jeffries Wyman's Views on Evolution." *Isis* 44 (1953): 243–246.

Freud, Sigmund. *Introductory Lectures on Psycho-Analysis: A Course of Twenty-Eight Lectures Delivered at the University of Vienna*. Translated by Joan Riviere. London: George Allen and Unwin, 1922.

Gardner, Martin. *Fads and Fallacies in the Name of Science*. New York: Dover Publications, 1957.

———. *The Flight of Peter Fromm*. Los Altos, Calif.: William Kaufmann, 1973.

———. *The Whys of a Philosophical Scrivener*. New York: Quill, 1983.

Gerstner, Patsy. *Henry Darwin Rogers, 1808–1866: American Geologist*. Tuscaloosa: University of Alabama Press, 1994.

Grant, Edward. *Planets, Stars, and Orbs: The Medieval Cosmos, 1200–1687*. Cambridge: Cambridge University Press, 1994.

Gray, Asa. *Darwiniana: Essays and Reviews Pertaining to Darwinism*. Edited by A. Hunter Dupree. Cambridge: Harvard University Press, 1963.

Gruber, Jacob W. *A Conscience in Conflict: The Life of St. George Jackson Mivart*. New York: Columbia University Press, 1960.

Hastings, H. L. *Was Moses Mistaken? or, Creation and Evolution*. No. 36 of the Anti-Infidel Library. Boston: H. L. Hastings, 1896.

Johnson, Andrew. "Evolution Outlawed by Science [No. 3]." *Pentecostal Herald* 37 (December 9, 1925): 9.

———. "The Evolution Articles." *Pentecostal Herald* 38 (September 29, 1926): 6.

LeConte, Joseph. *Inaugural Address: Delivered in the State House, Dec. 8, 1857, by Order of the Board of Trustees of the South Carolina College*. Columbia, S.C.: R. W. Gibbes, 1858.

———. "The Relation of Organic Science to Sociology." *Southern Presbyterian Review* 13 (1861): 39–77.

———. *Religion and Science: A Series of Sunday Lectures on the Relation of Natural and Revealed Religion, or the Truths Revealed in Nature and Scripture*. New York: D. Appleton, 1873.

———. "On Critical Periods in the History of the Earth and Their Relation to Evolution." *American Journal of Science* 114 (1877): 99–114.

———. "Man's Place in Nature." *Princeton Review*, 4th ser., 2 (1878): 789.

———. "Evolution in Relation to Materialism." *Princeton Review*, 4th ser., 7 (1881): 149–174.

———. Review of *Creation; or, The Biblical Cosmogony in the Light of Modern Science*, by Arnold Guyot. *Science* 3 (1884): 599–601.

———. "Immortality in Modern Thought." *Science* 6 (1885): 126–127.

———. *The Relation of Evolution to Religious Thought*. San Francisco: Pacific Coast Conference of Unitarian and Other Christian Churches, [1887].

———. *Evolution and Its Relation to Religious Thought*. New York: D. Appleton, 1888.

———. "The Natural Grounds of Belief in a Personal Immortality." *Andover Review* 14 (1890): 1–13.

———. *Evolution: Its Nature, Evidences, and Relation to Religious Thought*. New York: D. Appleton, 1896.

———. *The Autobiography of Joseph Le Conte*. Edited by William Dallam Armes. New York: D. Appleton, 1903.

Lesley, J. P. *Man's Origin and Destiny*. Enlarged edition. Boston: Geo. H. Ellis, [1868] 1881.

———. Letter to the Editor. *Science* 10 (1887): 308–309.

———. "The Idea of Life after Death." *The Forum* 10 (1890–91): 207–215.

Leuba, James H. *The Belief in God and Immortality*. Boston: Sherman, French, 1916.

Lightman, Bernard. *The Origins of Agnosticism: Victorian Unbelief and the Limits of Knowledge*. Baltimore: Johns Hopkins University Press, 1987.

Lindberg, David C., and Ronald L. Numbers, eds. *God and Nature: Historical Essays on the Encounter between Christianity and Science*. Berkeley and Los Angeles: University of California Press, 1986.

————, eds. *When Science and Christianity Meet*. Chicago: University of Chicago Press, 2003.

Livingstone, David N. *Darwin's Forgotten Defenders: The Encounter between Evangelical Theology and Evolutionary Thought*. Grand Rapids, Mich.: William B. Eerdmans, 1987.

————. *The Preadamite Theory and the Marriage of Science and Religion*. Philadelphia: American Philosophical Society, 1992.

Livingstone, David N., and Mark A. Noll. "B. B. Warfield (1851–1921): A Biblical Inerrantist as Evolutionist." *Isis* 91 (2000): 283–304.

Lucier, Paul. "Commercial Interests and Scientific Disinterestedness: Consulting Geologists in Antebellum America." *Isis* 86 (1995): 245–267.

Lyell, Charles. *A Second Visit to the United States*. London, 1849.

Marquart, Philip B. Letter to the Editor. *Journal of the American Scientific Affiliation* 14 (September 1963): 100.

Mitman, Gregg. *The State of Nature: Ecology, Community, and American Social Thought, 1900–1950*. Chicago: University of Chicago Press, 1992.

Moore, James R. *The Post-Darwinian Controversies: A Study of the Protestant Struggle to Come to Terms with Darwin in Great Britain and America, 1870–1900*. Cambridge: Cambridge University Press, 1979.

————. "Of Love and Death: Why Darwin 'Gave Up Christianity.' " In *History, Humanity and Evolution: Essays for John C. Greene*, edited by James R. Moore. Cambridge: Cambridge University Press, 1989.

————. *The Darwin Legend*. Grand Rapids, Mich.: Baker Books, 1994.

Morris, Henry M. *The Twilight of Evolution*. Grand Rapids, Mich.: Baker Book House, 1963.

Numbers, Ronald L. *Prophetess of Health: A Study of Ellen G. White*. New York: Harper and Row, 1976.

————. *Creation by Natural Law: Laplace's Nebular Hypothesis in American Thought*. Seattle: University of Washington Press, 1977.

————. "George Frederick Wright: From Christian Darwinist to Fundamentalist." *Isis* 79 (1988): 624–65.

————. *The Creationists*. New York: Knopf, 1992.

————. *Darwinism Comes to America*. Cambridge: Harvard University Press, 1998.

————. " 'The Most Important Biblical Discovery of Our Time': William Henry Green and the Demise of Ussher's Chronology." *Church History* 69 (2000): 257–276.

————. "Charles Hodge and the Beauties and Deformities of Science." In *Charles Hodge Revisited: A Critical Appraisal of His Life and Work*, edited by John W. Stewart and James H. Moorhead. Grand Rapids, Mich.: William B. Eerdmans, 2002.

————. "Reading the Book of Nature through American Lenses." In *The Book of Nature: Continuity and Change in European and American Attitudes towards the Natural World*, edited by Klaas van Berkel et al. Leuven, Belgium: Peeters, in press.

Peterson, William S. *Victorian Heretic: Mrs Humphry Ward's "Robert Elsmere."* Leicester, U.K.: Leicester University Press, 1976.

Price, George McCready. *Outlines of Modern Christianity and Modern Science*. Oakland, Calif.: Pacific Press, 1902.

———. *Illogical Geology: The Weakest Point in the Evolution Theory.* Los Angeles: Modern Heretic Co., 1906.

———. *The New Geology.* Mountain View, Calif.: Pacific Press, 1923.

———. "A Brief History of the Flood Theory." *Signs of the Times* 61 (October 30, 1934): 15.

———. *Genesis Vindicated.* Washington, D.C.: Review and Herald Publishing Association, 1941.

———. "Some Early Experiences with Evolutionary Geology." *Bulletin of Deluge Geology* 1 (November, 1941): 77–92.

———. "If I Were Twenty-One Again." *These Times* 69 (September 1, 1960): 22.

———. "I'd Have an Aim." *Advent Review and Sabbath Herald* 138 (February 16, 1961): 14–15.

Richards, Robert J. *Darwin and the Emergence of Evolutionary Theories of Mind and Behavior.* Chicago: University of Chicago Press, 1987.

Roberts, Jon H. *Darwinism and the Divine in America: Protestant Intellectuals and Organic Evolution, 1859–1900.* Madison: University of Wisconsin Press, 1988.

Royce, Josiah. *The Conception of God,* with comments by Sidney Edward Mezes, Joseph LeConte, and G. H. Howison. Berkeley: Philosophical Union of the University of California, 1895.

Russel, P. R. "Darwinism Examined." *Advent Review and Sabbath Herald,* May 18, 1876, 153.

Sanford, William F., Jr. "Dana and Darwinism." *Journal of the History of Ideas* 26 (1965): 531–556.

Schuchert, Charles. Review of *The New Geology,* by George McCready Price. *Science,* May 30, 1924, 486–487.

Stanton, William. *The Leopard's Spots: Scientific Attitudes toward Race in America, 1815–59.* Chicago: University of Chicago Press, 1960.

Stenhouse, John. "Darwinism in New Zealand, 1859–1900." In *Disseminating Darwinism: The Role of Place, Race, Religion, and Gender,* edited by Ronald L. Numbers and John Stenhouse. Cambridge: Cambridge University Press, 1999.

Stephens, Lester D. *Joseph LeConte: Gentle Prophet of Evolution.* Baton Rouge: Louisiana State University Press, 1982.

Turner, Frank Miller. *Between Science and Religion: The Reaction to Scientific Naturalism in Late Victorian England.* New Haven: Yale University Press, 1974.

———. "The Victorian Crisis of Faith and the Faith that Was Lost." In *Victorian Faith in Crisis: Essays on Continuity and Change in Nineteenth-Century Religious Belief,* edited by Richard J. Helmstadter and Bernard Lightman. Stanford: Stanford University Press, 1990.

Wald, Stephen. "Revelations of Consciousness: Joseph LeConte, the Soul, and the Challenge of Scientific Naturalism." Unpublished MS, Duke University, 1998.

Ward, Mrs. Humphry. *Robert Elsmere.* New York: J. S. Ogilvie, n.d.

Weber, Ralph. E. *Notre Dame's John Zahm: American Catholic Apologist and Educator.* Notre Dame, Ind.: University of Notre Dame Press, 1961.

White, Ellen G. *Spiritual Gifts: Important Facts of Faith, in Connection with the History of Holy Men of Old.* Battle Creek, Mich.: Seventh-day Adventist Publishing Association, 1864.

Willey, Basil. *Darwin and Butler: Two Versions of Evolution*. New York: Harcourt, Brace, 1960.

Wright, G. Frederick. "Recent Works on Prehistoric Archaeology." *Bibliotheca Sacra* 30 (1873): 381–384.

———. "Recent Works Bearing on the Relation of Science to Religion: No. II—The Divine Method of Producing Living Species." *Bibliotheca Sacra* 33 (1876): 455–494.

———. Review of *Darwinism and Other Essays*, by John Fiske. *Bibliotheca Sacra* 36 (1879): 784.

———. *Studies in Science and Religion*. Andover, Mass.: Warren F. Draper, 1882.

———. "Professor Wright and Some of His Critics." *Bibliotheca Sacra* 42 (1885): 352.

———. "The Debt of the Church to Asa Gray." *Bibliotheca Sacra* 45 (1888): 527.

———. "Transcendental Science." *Independent* 41 (October 3, 1889): 10.

———. "Darwin on Herbert Spencer." *Bibliotheca Sacra* 46 (1889): 181–184.

———. "Some Will-o'-the-Wisps of Higher Criticism." *Congregationalist*, March 12, 1891: 84.

———. "Recent Discoveries Bearing on the Antiquity of Man." *Bibliotheca Sacra* 48 (1891): 309.

———. Review of *Letters of Asa Gray*, edited by Jane Loring Gray. *Bibliotheca Sacra* 51 (1894): 182.

———. "Editorial Note on Genesis and Geology." *Bibliotheca Sacra* 54 (1897): 570–572.

———. "The First Chapter of Genesis and Modern Science." *Homiletic Review* 35 (1898): 392–393.

———. "Present Aspects of the Questions Concerning the Origin and Antiquity of the Human Race." *Protestant Episcopal Review* 11 (1898): 319–323.

———. "The Uncertainties of Science." *Advance* 43 (1902): 624–625.

———. "The Revision of Geological Time." *Bibliotheca Sacra* 60 (1903): 580.

———. *Scientific Confirmations of Old Testament History*. Oberlin, Ohio: Bibliotheca Sacra, 1906.

———. "The Passing of Evolution." In *The Fundamentals*. Chicago: Testimony Publishing Co., 1910–1915.

———. "How Old Is Mankind?" *Sunday School Times* 55 (January 25, 1913): 52.

———. *Story of My Life and Work*. Oberlin, Ohio: Bibliotheca Sacra, 1916.

PART IV

Mind

12

Gods and the Mental Instincts That Create Them

Pascal Boyer

The science-religion debate is generally focused on a comparison of the distinct (and, some hope, complementary) contributions of these two types of cultural traditions to our understanding of human experience. In these pages I wish to start from a rather different angle, asking to what extent science can actually explain religion itself, explain the appearance and spread of religious ideas and behaviors in human beings, and explain its specific contribution to human experience.

How would one *explain* religion? We know that most past attempts were unsatisfactory, but I think we can now do better. This is not (or not just) *hubris* on my part; at any rate it is (emphatically) not a self-aggrandizing claim, for I am not saying that *I* can explain it better, but that scientific developments for which I cannot claim any credit can help us finally understand, or understand much better, why there is religion and why it is the way it is. Scientific progress means we have a much better grasp of why people have religious notions and norms, than we would have had fifty years ago, and we are only at the beginning of this voyage of discovery. This is mainly because scientific explanations of how *minds* work have got incredibly better in the last few decades.

We can better understand why there is religion and why it is the way it is. I must emphasize this last point, for it is a major flaw in many theories about religion, from anthropology or philosophy (*und leider auch Theologie*, of course) that they try to explain some ideal religion, or some local religion, or some reasonable reconstruction of religion, but do not take the full measure of religious concepts and norms as a culturally variable phenomenon. Here are a few facts we all know but should keep at the forefront of our attention when we discuss religion:

1. Most religious systems in the world are not about an eternal Creator.
2. In fact, the creation of the universe is of limited interest to most people in the world.
3. People can have many gods, or a few gods, or a combination of several gods and many spirits, or a few spirits and many gods, or many ancestors and no spirits, and so on.
4. Gods are said to die in many traditions.
5. They are remarkably stupid in many others.
6. The "salvation of the soul" is alien to most people's ideas about death.

The point of this is to emphasize how parochial, as it were, many accounts of religion can be. Religion probably does not stem from a desire to explain the origin of the universe, since most people get by perfectly well without any creation account; there is no instinct for transcendence in human beings, since the most frequent religious beings are ancestors who are assumed to be as real as the living, only more elusive; you cannot explain religion as moral coercion combined with promised rewards, since in many places the soul needs no salvation and will in due time become an ancestor.

Paying attention to the true diversity of religious concepts and norms is certainly necessary, but it is far from sufficient. We can compile lists of different religious concepts and measure the relative frequency of particular notions. This is what anthropologists have done and this is a necessary starting point. But is it enough? To take a distant example, philologists have for a long time documented the variety of languages, the relative distance between them, their plausible historical connections, as well as established a catalog of extant grammatical systems. But at some point linguists decided to *explain* linguistic structure, which in effect meant this: underneath the luxuriant variety of systems, there are a few underlying rules. These rules do not come from nowhere: they are the consequence of how human brains function.

A similar scenario is conceivable for the diversity and underlying common features of religious ideas. As in the case of language, it implies that we should consider, beyond the actual concepts and norms that we call religion, the mental systems that support them. This I think is now possible, in a way that is quite different from what it would have been thirty years ago, because of our constantly increasing knowledge of the mind-brain.

In the following pages I use various kinds of evidence to suggest how different mental systems are involved in the selection of religious concepts. The human mind is not a single system designed to produce an accurate representation of the world. Rather, it consists of multiple systems geared to representing and predicting various parts of the environment, or guiding action in different domains according to different principles. None of these systems is about religion. But some of them may be activated, in the context of representing religious agents, in such a way that concepts of such agents have a high probability of transmission. So examining which systems are activated in this way, and how they fashion different aspects of viable cultural concepts, should explain not only just why we have these religious notions, but also why we do not have others, in other words explain the recurrent features of such concepts.

This requires that we go beyond what people know and believe, to the underlying systems that support such knowledge and belief. The main strategy in the study of religion so far was to just *ask* people about their religious concepts. This is of course an indispensable first step, but we cannot stop there. It is not just that people's explanations may be vague and idiosyncratic (though they are). It is also that we have no good reason to assume that people have much access to the cognitive machinery that produces those concepts. People after all have no access to the way their brains turn two-dimensional retinal images into three-dimensional visual representations, or to how they produce syntactic sentences. People can feel the difference between two sentences ("who did you see me with?" and "who did you see me and?," respectively) without being able to explain why one is ungrammatical. The same point applies to concepts. Some notions are easier to acquire than others, some conceptual associations are better recalled, and some create stronger emotional effects. All this depends on processes largely beyond conscious access, in the same way as the workings of the visual cortex.

What I am offering here is a multiple-system explanation of religion. I do not believe in magic bullet, single-cause explanations of religion, not just because religion is complex, but also because religion is a cultural phenomenon. It is something you get from other people and something you will contribute to transmit to others. What we call "religion" are *successful* religious concepts and norms. That is, they are the ones that survived many cycles of individual acquisition and transmission. The rest, these possible variants that were entertained but then forgotten, or adopted by a few but distorted by others, these unsuccessful variants just do not register. That religion is successful religion, in this sense, suggests that it activates many different mental systems in ways that favor retention and transmission. The emphasis should be on *multiple* mental systems. A durably successful cultural institution is like a durably successful economy, which probably owes its perennial success not to one single factor (good natural resources, just enough people, the right kind of culture, a lucky history, etc.) but to the fortunate combination of most of these. The same goes for cultural transmission, so that religion is successful for many reasons instead of one. It may be frustrating for those who hoped that a single-shot account would do most of the explanatory work. As we will see, the brain-based explanation is not only more complex, but also much more interesting than that.

Religious Notions Are Supernatural Notions

The world over, people's supernatural repertoire includes a variety of concepts of imagined artifacts, animals, persons, and plants: concepts of floating islands, of mountains that digest food or have blood circulation, of trees that listen, of animals that change species, or of people who can disappear at will. These are found in folktales, anecdotes, myths, dreams and religious ritual and correspond to a small "catalog" of templates for supernatural concepts.[1] We also find that a particular subset of these concepts is associated with more serious commitment, strong emotions, important rituals, and/or moral understandings. An association between a supernatural concept and one or several of these social effects is our main intuitive criterion for what is "religious."[2]

There are, to simplify matters a great deal, two major levels of conceptual information in semantic memory. One is that of "kind-concepts," notions like "table" and "tiger" and "tarmac" and "tree." The other consists of "domain-concepts," such as "intentional agent," "manmade object," "living thing." Most of the information associated with these broader concepts comes in the format, not of declared statements (e.g., "living things grow with age") but of intuitive expectations and inferences. Without being aware of it, one expects living things to grow, intentional agents to have goals, and their behavior to be caused by those goals, the structure of artifacts to be explained by a function, and the latter by a designer's intention.

Now supernatural concepts describe minimal violations of such expectations: a tree is said to listen to people's conversations, a statue is said to bleed on particular occasions, a person is described as being in several places at once, another one as going through walls, and so on. Note that such concepts violate domain-level and not kind-level expectations. A talking ebony tree goes against expectations not because ebony trees in particular are usually silent but because all plants are assumed to be nonintentional. Also, note that the violations are minimal, keeping in place all the (nonviolated) default assumptions that usually accompany a given domain concept. A talking tree is still assumed to grow like all plants, ghosts that go though walls still perceive and represent their environment like other intentional agents. Indeed, these nonviolated assumptions provide an indispensable grounding for people's inferences about supernatural entities and agents.[3]

This twofold condition: (a) include a violation of domain-level intuitions and (b) allow inferences from relevant nonviolated assumptions, is sufficient to account for the recurrent features of supernatural concepts the world over. That is, the subject matter of fantastic imagination, dreams, folktales, and religion generally revolves around a small catalog of concepts built in that way.[4] The *concepts* may be very different from one pace to another, but the *templates* are few, consisting of a combination of one particular domain-concept and one particular violation (e.g., "intentional agent" and "physical solidity" for the "ghost" concept). Also, experimental work in different cultures suggests that concepts built in this way are more likely to be recalled than either predictable conceptual associations, or oddities constructed by violating kind-level associations. A table made of sausages (violation of kind-level expectations) may be quite striking, but in the end is not quite as easily acquired and recalled as a table that understands conversations (violation of domain-level expectations). This effect seems to work in fairly similar ways in different cultural environments.[5]

Religious concepts are a subset of supernatural notions, with special additional features. But it is worth insisting on the fact that they belong to this broader domain, as this explains their mode of acquisition. In supernatural concepts, most of the relevant information associated with a particular notion is given by domain-level intuitions. In other words, it is spontaneously assumed to be true in the absence of contrary information. This is why no one in the world needs to be told that ghosts see what happens when it happens, or that gods who want some result will try to do what it takes to achieve it: such inferences are given for free by our specialized mental systems (intuitive psychology in this case). In religion, as in other supernatural domains, the violations are made clear to people, but the rest is inferred. Concepts that are both salient (because of the violation) and very cheaply transmitted (because of spontaneous inferences) are optimal from the viewpoint of cultural transmission.

Now some supernatural concepts matter much more than others. Whether Puss-in-boots did run faster than the wind or not is of no great moment, but whether the ancestors noticed that we offered them a sacrifice certainly is. The question is, why do some concepts of imagined entities and agents rather than others, matter to people? Because, I will argue, other specialized mental systems are involved in their representation. In the following pages, I will outline the ways in which this occurs, that is, how religious concepts are associated with intuitions about agency, about social interaction, about moral understandings, and about dead bodies.

Religious Concepts Are about Agents

Although there are many templates for supernatural concepts, the ones that really matter to people are invariably personlike. There is certainly a tendency in the human imagination to project humanlike and personlike features onto nonhuman or nonpersonlike aspects of the environment; such representations are attention-grabbing or enjoyable; they are certainly found in many aspects of religious agency, as Stewart Guthrie has demonstrated.[6] Guthrie also explains such projections do not stem from an urge to make various situations or occurrences more familiar or more reassuring (which is seldom the result anyway), but to afford richer inferences about them. Projections of humanlike features add complexity to the world, which is why they are easily created and transmitted by human minds.[7]

This constant search for relevant inferences may well be the reason why the anthropomorphism of religious concepts is in fact rather selective. That is, the domain of intuitions and inferences that is projected is *intentional agency*, more frequently and more consistently than any other domain of human characteristics. Besides, intuitions concerning intentional agency are activated not just when interacting with humans, but also in our dealings with animals.[8] This is why one can postulate an intentional agent around, and run various inferences about what it can perceive, what its next reactions might be, and so on, without making it a human person in other respects.[9]

This is consistent with developmental and other cognitive evidence concerning the complex intentional psychology or "theory of mind" present in all normal human minds. This "mind-reading" system is geared to interpreting other agents' (or one's own) behavior, as well as figuring out what their goals, beliefs, intentions, memories, and inferences are. Rudimentary forms of such mind-reading capacities appear very early in development,[10] they develop in fairly similar forms in normal children. Their working is out of reach for conscious inspection; only the outcome of their computations is conscious.

A widely accepted evolutionary scenario is that we (higher primates) evolved more and more complex intentional psychology systems to deal with social interaction. Having larger groups, more stable interaction, and more efficient coordination with other agents brings out significant adaptive benefits for the individual. But these conditions require finer and finer grained descriptions of others' mental states and behavior. This is why we find, early developed in most humans, a hypertrophied "theory of mind" that tracks the objects of other people's attention, computes their states of minds, predicts their behavior.[11] Another possible account is that at least some aspects of our "theory of mind" capacities evolved in the context of predator-prey interaction.[12] A heightened capacity to remain undetected by either predator or prey, as well as a better sense of how these other animals detect us, are of obvious adaptive significance. In the archaeological record, changes toward more flexible hunting patterns in modern humans suggest a richer, more intentional representation of the hunted animal.[13]

Different subsystems are involved in the representation of agency. A disorder like autism stems from an inability to represent other people's thoughts, but it does not seem to impair primitive animacy-detection (realizing that some objects in the environment are goal-directed) or gaze-following.[14] Children with Williams syndrome are very good at detecting, following, and displaying emotional cues relevant to social interaction, although they often have a very poor understanding of the beliefs and intentions that motivate behavior.[15] In a similar way, chimpanzees may pay attention to gaze-direction without associating it with specific intentions, which shows that these two capacities are separable.[16]

Now, if there are several distinct theory of mind components, there may be different ways in which human minds can postulate agents without much evidence. Indeed, I would argue that supernatural agents are made salient and relevant to human minds by two distinct routes, each of which contributes a particular aspects of these imagined agent. The first route is through those systems we developed in predator-prey interaction; the second one is though those systems that are especially dedicated to social interaction.

As Guthrie emphasized, detecting agents around, often on the basis of scant or unreliable evidence, is a hallmark of human minds. When we see branches moving in a tree or when we hear an unexpected sound behind us, we immediately infer that some *agent* (animal or human) is the cause of this perceptually salient event and that some goal of that agent explains its behavior. Note that the systems that detect agency do not need much solid evidence. On the contrary, they "jump to conclusions," that is, give us the intuition that an agent is around, in many contexts where other interpretations (the wind pushed the foliage, a branch just fell off a tree) are equally plausible. There are many everyday situations where we detect agency and then abandon this interpretation, once we realize there was no agent around. But, that is the important point, we spontaneously create these interpretations anyway. For Justin Barrett, there are important evolutionary reasons why we (as well as other animals) should have "hyperactive agent detection." In a species evolved to deal with both predators and prey, the expense of false positives (seeing agents where there are none) is minimal, if we can abandon these misguided intuitions quickly. By contrast, the cost of not detecting agents when they are actually around (either predator or prey) could be very high. So our cognitive systems work on a better-safe-than-sorry principle that leads to hypersensitive agent detection.[17]

According to this evolutionary interpretation, predation-related capacities not only makes it easy to detect agents when there is little or no evidence for their presence, but also informs some of their features. For one thing, our agent-detection systems trigger emotional arousal in a way that is quite automatic. That is, these systems lead us intuitively to assume, not just that there are agents around but that this presence may have rather dramatic consequences for us. This is a feature that directly translates in supernatural imagination. People may well imagine all sorts of supernatural agents that are irrelevant to their well-being (like elves, goblins, and suchlike); but the ones whose traces people think they *saw* are generally of greater emotional import. Second, agents are postulated, not on the basis of direct perception of their presence, but of indirect cues. As Barrett points out, what people claim to perceive are more often "traces in the grass" than "faces in the clouds." A sudden noise, an unexplained shadow, a broken twig or someone's sudden death are explained as indices of the spirits' presence; this is far more frequent than a direct encounter with those agents. This feature makes much more sense once we understand the contribution of predation-related mental systems, which after all are by design concerned with the interpretation of indirect cues and fragmentary signals as evidence for some agent's presence.

An association with predation-related intuitions is probably only part of what makes religious concepts salient. We need additional factors to explain what makes people's notions of supernatural agents so stable and plausible, and why they are so strongly informed by what other people say. To take the first aspect, religious concepts are much less transient than experiences of hyperactive agent detection, that is, of interpreting some noise or movement as the presence of an agent. The latter are often discarded as mistakes. As I said above, it makes sense to "over-detect" agents only if you can quickly discard false positives, otherwise you would spend all your time recoiled in fear, which is certainly not adaptive. But thoughts about gods and spirits are not like that. These are *stable* concepts, in the sense that people have them stored in memory, reactivate them periodically and assume that these agents are a permanent fixture in their environment. Now consider the sources of information that shape people's religious concepts. True, having experiences of elusive shadows and sounds probably strengthens the general notion that there may be unseen agents around. However, it is also striking that the details of such representations are generally derived, not from what one has experienced (hyperactive detection), but rather of what others have said. People take their information about the features of ghosts and spirits and gods, to an overwhelming extent, from socially transmitted information, not direct experience. Conversely, intrinsically vague experiences are seen through the conceptual lenses provided by what others said about the gods and spirits. To sum up, people know vastly more about gods and spirits by listening to other people than by encountering these mysterious agents.

I insist on this seemingly obvious point because it introduces yet another way in which religious concepts activate mental systems. Information about gods and spirits mainly comes from other people. It is also connected to our representations of what other people believe and want in a crucial way. That is, the way people construe religious agents is informed by mental systems geared to describing and managing interaction with other human agents.

Religious Concepts Are about Social Interaction

A good part of the information concerning social interaction is processed by specialized *social mind systems*. An important part of our mental architecture consists of inference systems that deal with social interaction. For instance, human beings are very good at:

- monitoring social exchange, that is, finding out who is cooperating with whom, and under what circumstances, as well as punishing cheaters and avoiding people who fail to punish cheaters;[18]
- Keeping track of other people's personality, especially in terms of reliability, on the basis of indirect but emotionally charged cues;[19]
- building and maintaining social hierarchies, based either directly on resources or on indirect, seemingly arbitrary criteria for dominance;[20]
- building coalitions, that is, stable cooperation networks where benefits are shared, the cost of others defecting is high, and measures are taken to preempt it;[21]
- gossiping, that is, taking pleasure at receiving or imparting information on adaptively significant domains (sex, resources, hierarchy), about and with other members of one's social network;[22]

and many other such social interaction skills. It is quite likely that such capacities are supported by a variety of functional systems, so that one does not so much have a "social mind" as distinct social mind capacities.

In another paper,[23] I emphasized a crucial difference between representations of other people and representations of possible supernatural agents. All standard social interaction, from a young age, is based on a principle of "imperfect access:" that is, the assumption that other people (and we ourselves) only have partial access to the strategic information pertinent to a particular situation. By contrast, supernatural agents seem to be implicitly construed as "perfect access" agents. A tacit assumption is that, given a situation x, and given some information about it that would be strategic, the supernatural agent has access to it.

I must emphasize a few points that may be ambiguous in the above formulation. This assumption often remains tacit. You do not need to represent an explicit principle like "the ancestors have access to what matters to our social mind systems" anymore than we need to represent a principle of the form "objects that are bounced against a wall will bounce at an angle equal to the collision angle."

The assumption does not require that people represent what the strategic information in question amounts to. You can represent that "if there is strategic information about this situation, the ancestors know it" without having any description of the strategic information in question. (In the same way, your inferences work on the assumption that there is something in giraffes that makes them grow differently from horses, and that it is innate in giraffes, without knowing or indeed having any representation of what this "something" is.)

To illustrate this and some further arguments about concepts of gods and spirits, let me make use of anthropologist Roger Keesing's vivid description of Kwaio religion.[24] The Kwaio concept of spirit-ancestor (*adalo*) illustrates my contrast between contemplative, theological understandings and the more mundane business of representing religious agents in practical contexts. The Kwaio live in the Solomon Islands; most of their religious activities, as described by Keesing, involve interacting with ancestors, especially the spirits of deceased members of their own clans, as well as more dangerous wild spirits. Interaction with these *adalo* (the term denotes both wild spirits and ancestors) is a constant feature of Kwaio life. People frequently pray to the dead or give them sacrifices of pigs or simply talk to them. Also, people "meet" the ancestors in dreams. Most people are particularly familiar with and fond of one particular *adalo*, generally the spirit of a close relative, and maintain frequent contact with that spirit.

Now Kwaio people need not be told that spirits can perceive what happens, or that they can make a difference between their wishes and reality. People are just told that, for instance, "the spirits are unhappy because we failed to sacrifice a pig for them." To make sense of that utterance one must activate one's intuitive psychology inference systems. In the same way, no one is ever told that "gods (or spirits or ancestors) have access to whatever is strategic in any particular situation." What is made explicit is most often a vague assumption that the spirits or the gods simply know more than we do. But it seems that people in fact assume something much more specific, namely that the gods and spirits have access to *strategic* information (as defined here) rather than information in general.

Kwaio people's statements about their ancestors highlight this. At first sight, what they say would seem to confirm that ancestors simply know more:

> "The *adalo* see the slightest small things. Nothing is hidden from
> the *adalo*. It would be hidden from us [living people, but not from
> them]" or again "an *adalo* has unlimited vision." But when people
> illustrate these statements, notice how they immediately move from
> "agents who know more" to the much more specific "agents who
> know more about what is strategic": "An *adalo* has unlimited vision
> . . . something happens in secret and [the *adalo*] will see it; [if] some-
> one urinates, someone menstruates [in improper places: doing this
> is an insult to the ancestors] and tries to hide it . . . the *adalo* will see
> it."[25]

In other words, although you can say that the *adalo* in general see what humans cannot see, what first comes to mind is that they can detect behaviors that would have consequences for social interaction: someone who has polluted a particular place puts others in danger and should perform appropriate purification rites. Whether someone did violate these rules or not is clearly strategic information. When people represent possible violations, this activates their inference systems for social interaction. For them, it also goes without saying that it is *that* particular kind of information that the *adalo* have access to. It may be hidden to people (this is the "imperfect access principle": people's access to strategic information is not guaranteed), but not to supernatural agents (they have full access). People are told that "Someone urinates in a house; we humans cannot see it; but that makes the *adalo* very angry," or some other statement of that kind. Interpreting such statements requires that the *adalo* (or whatever supernatural agent people in your group talk about) have access to strategic information.

The same remark would apply to agents (like the Christian god) described by theologians and other religious specialists as omniscient. Most believers would readily assent to statements such as "God knows everything" or "God sees everything." This, however, does not mean that the religious agent is literally assumed to represent every aspect of every situation in the world. In people's conversations and trains of thought concerning God, it would seem that such statements as "I bought broccoli *and God knows about it*" are somehow less frequent and salient than thoughts like "He lied to her *and God knows it*" or "I did my best *and God knows it.*" In other words, if something counts as strategic information, in the precise sense used here, it is more easily and naturally included in thoughts about God's thoughts.

In detailed experimental work, Justin Barrett has shown that people's explicit notions of an omniscient God are combined with an intuitive understanding of God as having a humanlike mind.[26] A person may (explicitly) declare that the gods see and hear everything yet show them an offering or say a prayer out loud. The assumption of full access to strategic information is just another aspect of this discrepancy between official, and explicitly entertained, descriptions of supernatural agents, and the intuitive assumptions activated when thinking about them. Now why is the full-access expectation so important to interaction? I would claim that it changes the way one considers a situation, and this has effects in several domains. One of them is the construal of *moral understandings*, and the other one is the possible link between religious agents and *misfortune*.

Religious Concepts Are Parasitic upon Moral Intuitions

A consideration of cognitive process involved in representing religious agents can help us discard a widespread but misleading account of religious morality. In this account, people are for some reason convinced of the reality of some supernatural agents; these are described as particularly anxious that people should follow particular moral rules; so people follow these precepts, often against their inclination. Against this, it seems that moral intuitions and understandings develop in all human beings because of specialized, early developed mental capacities connected with social interaction. This in turn creates all sorts of intuitions about possible courses of action. The intuitions do not require concepts of supernatural agents, but if there are such concepts around, moral intuitions will be associated with them. In other words, religious concepts are in part parasitic upon moral understandings.

To understand why this is the case, we must first examine the various ways in which people establish a link between their supernatural concepts and their moral understandings. I will call these three connections the "legislator," "exemplar," and "interested party" models.

In the "gods as legislators" model, there are moral principles because the gods or ancestors themselves decided what these norms would be. Several world religions include lists of prohibitions and prescriptions of varying length attributed to some direct communication from the supernatural legislature.

In the "exemplar" model, some supernatural agents provide a model to follow. Saints or holy people are both different enough from common folk that they approach an ideal and close enough so their behavior can serve as a model. This is the way people conceive of individuals with supernatural qualities like Gautama, Muhammad, or the many Christian and Muslim saints, as well as the miraculous rabbis of Judaism.

Supernatural agents are also represented as "interested parties" in moral choices. This means that the gods or the ancestors are not indifferent to what we do, and this is why we must act in particular ways or refrain from certain courses of action. Interaction with the Kwaio ancestors is of this kind. But the interested-party model is much more general than that. We find it in many world religions, whether or not the theologians find it acceptable. Most Christians entertain this notion that every single one of their moral choices is relevant to their personal connection to God. That is, God not only gave laws and principles, but also pays attention to what people do. For obvious reasons, the notion that supernatural agents are interested parties is generally associated with the idea that the gods or spirits are powerful and that it is within their capacities to inflict all sorts of calamities upon people—or help them prosper—depending on their behavior.

In people's reasoning about particular situations, in the practical business of judging people's behavior and choosing a course of action, the interested-party model is largely dominant. As far as anthropologists know, people in most places conceive of some supernatural agents as having some interest in their decisions. This can take all sorts of forms. The Christians, for instance, consider that God expects some particular kinds of behavior and will react to departures from the norm. People who interact with their ancestors, like the Kwaio, have a much less precise description of what the ancestors want, but it is part of their everyday concerns that the *adalo* are watching them. In either case, people do not really represent why the ancestors or gods would want to sanction people's behavior. It is just assumed that they will.

When I say that this way of thinking about morality is dominant I simply mean that it is constantly activated and generally implicit. It is the most natural way people think of the connection between powerful agents and their own behavior. The legislator and exemplar representations both have their limits. Explicit moral codes are often too abstract to provide definite judgments on particular cases (this is why scholars often augment them with a tradition of commentary and exegesis); conversely, exemplars provide examples that are too specific to be easily applied to different circumstances.

More important, however, is the fact that there is something intuitive and natural in the notion of agents that are attentive and responsive to the way people behave. Indeed, this notion may be rooted in the way moral intuitions are developed from an early age. A conventional view would be that children acquire moral concepts by generalizing and gradually abstracting from social conventions. In this view, children start by noticing correlations between specific courses of action (e.g., beating up one's sibling or being noisy during class) and sanctions. They then abstract general principles of right and wrong from these specific cases. Also, children are described as building moral feelings by internalizing people's emotional reactions to their actions.[27] Both models may have underestimated the child's intuitive access to specifically moral dimensions of actions. Indeed, psychologist Eliot Turiel showed that even preschoolers have a good intuitive understanding of the difference between social conventions and moral prescriptions (so that beating up people is wrong even if no one told you so, while being noisy is wrong only if there was an injunction to keep quiet).[28] Also, children found it much easier to imagine a revision of *major* social conventions (e.g., a situation where boys wore skirts) than a revision of *minor* moral principles (e.g., a situation where it would be all right to steal an eraser). Finally, children make a difference between moral principles and prudential rules (do not leave your notebook near the fireplace). They justify both in terms of their consequences, but assume that social consequences are specific to moral violations.[29]

So experimental studies show that there is an early developed specific inference system, a specialized moral sense underlying moral intuitions. Notions of morality are distinct from those used to evaluate other aspects of social interaction (this is why social conventions and moral imperatives are so easily distinguished). They provide an initial basis on which children can understand adult moral views. This capacity for entertaining abstract intuitions about the moral nature of courses of action (without, of course, being able to explicate them) was found also in children with various amounts of experience with other children,[30] in different cultures,[31] and even in children with exceptional experiences of abuse or neglect.[32]

That children have early moral concepts does not mean that they have the same moral understandings as adults, far from it. First, young children have more difficulty in figuring out other agents' intentions and feelings; second, they do not have a rich repertoire of past episodes to draw from when representing the key features of a situation; third, they may not be aware of local parameters of social interaction (they may resist sharing their toys with a cousin, noticing that their parents are not giving their car to the cousin's parents). But what is important here is that, from an early age, (a) children's moral understandings are founded on the *intuition* that some courses of action are right and others are not, (b) this intuition stems from feelings that cannot be further explicated, and (c) it is assumed that a course of action is right or wrong in itself, regardless of who is considering it. All three assumptions are found in adults too, and form an intuitive basis for moral inferences. Obviously, they are also supplemented by explicit understandings of moral principles, as well as (in some places) their connections with religious concepts.

The main conclusion to draw from this research is that moral understandings, far from being dependent upon socially transmitted (e.g., religious) explications, appear before such concepts are intelligible, indeed, they develop regardless of whether there are *any* religious or other concepts in the child's cultural environment. But another aspect of these cognitive findings is also important. Early developed moral understandings may well provide a context in which concepts of supernatural agents become more salient.

To the extent that people represent a situation in a way that triggers particular moral intuitions and feelings, they generally assume that these intuitions and feelings are true regardless of who is considering the situation. They also assume that the only way to disguise the true moral nature of an action is to mislead people about the action itself. If you want to exculpate yourself, you cannot argue that beating up one's sibling is right, but you can claim that what *seemed* to be beating up one's sibling was something entirely different. You assume that, to the extent that people share your information (or information you hold true) about what happened, they probably share the same moral intuition about it, and therefore will be led to react to it in similar ways.

In other words, the way our moral intuitions allows for an empty placeholder, for the position of "some agent who has access to my information about the situation at hand." The moral system itself does not provide any description of that agent, although we try and make other people become such agents by explaining situations to them. Now, as I said above, some supernatural agents are represented by default as having full access to strategic information. That is, people represent a given situation, and represent some information about it that is relevant to social interaction, and they assume that the supernatural agent also has that information. (Again, all this consists in tacit assumptions.) This means that, in morally relevant situations, a concept of god or spirit or ancestor is very likely to be activated as the most relevant way to fill in the empty placeholder. After representing a particular behavior as wrong, and feeling guilty, it seems quite natural to assume that some other agent with full access also feels the behavior was wrong.

Indeed, this connection may gain additional salience from the fact that the moral intuition system, like other inference systems in our minds, is not really open to conscious inspection. That is, we have moral intuitions without having much access to the computational operations whereby the system produced such intuitions. Associating concepts of full-access supernatural agents to moral intuitions may well provide a post hoc rationalization of the intuitions. So, in a sense, concepts of gods and spirits are made more *relevant* by the organization of our moral thoughts, which themselves do not especially require any gods or spirits. What I mean by "relevant" is that the concepts, once put in this moral context, are both easy to represent and generate many new inferences. For instance, most people feel some guilt when acting in a way which they suspect is immoral. That is, whatever their self-serving justifications, they may have the intuition that an agent with a full description of the situation would still classify it as wrong. Now, thinking of this intuition as "what the ancestors think of what I did" or "how God feels about what I did" provides an easy way of representing what is otherwise extremely vague. That is, most of our moral intuitions are clear but their origin escapes us, because it lies in mental processing that we cannot consciously access. Seeing these intuitions as someone's viewpoint is a simpler way of understanding why we have these intuitions. But this requires the concept of an agent with full access to strategic information. These associations are not the origin of the moral feelings, but a convenient way of commenting upon them. In this sense, moral intuitions and feelings contribute to the relevance of some supernatural concepts. The latter, again, can be seen as parasitic upon intuitions that would be there, spirits and gods or not.

Religious Concepts Exploit Our Intuitions about Misfortune

It may seem that gods and spirits matter to people mainly because these supernatural agents are described as having special powers. The ancestors can make you sick, or ruin your plantations, God sends people various plagues. On the positive side, gods and spirits are also represented as protectors, guarantors of good crops, social harmony, and so on. But why are supernatural agents construed as having such causal powers? The notion that gods and spirits matter because of their powers does not just beg the question of why they are represented as having such powers. It also creates difficult puzzles. For instance, in many places the most powerful supernatural agents are not the ones that matter most. The Fang of Cameroon and Gabon, among whom I conducted anthropological fieldwork, have all these rituals and complex emotions associated with the possible presence of the ghosts-ancestors. Now the Fang also say that the world (meaning earth and sky and all living things) was created by a god called *Mebeghe*, vastly more powerful than either the living or the dead. His work was completed by another god, *Nzame*, who invented all cultural objects: tools, houses, and so on, and taught people how to hunt, domesticate animals, and raise crops. Neither of these gods seems to matter that much. That is, there are no cults or rituals specifically directed at *Mebeghe* or *Nzame*, although they are assumed to be around, and they are in fact very rarely mentioned. For a long time, this puzzled many travelers, anthropologists, and, of course, missionaries. Many African people seemed to recognize a Creator in the same sense as the biblical one, yet were remarkably indifferent to Him. We will see below the explanation for this apparent paradox.

What matters is not so much the "powers" of supernatural beings considered in the abstract as those powers that are relevant to *practical* concerns. In particular, ancestors, gods, and spirits are readily mentioned when people represent or try to explain salient situations of misfortune. Indeed, this connection is so frequent that, for many nonspecialists, it seems to provide an easy explanation for the origin and persistence of religious concepts. People are afflicted with various calamities, they cannot explain the amoral nature of their destiny, so they imagine gods and spirits that pull the strings. This, like many other popular origin-of-religion scenarios, points to a real association, but in my view fails to appreciate the complexity of the mental operations involved.

We often assume that people want to understand what happens to them. This is where gods and spirits, however feeble as explanations, at least provide some measure of intelligibility. A weak explanation is better than no explanation. But why would people want to understand their own misfortune? What drives their minds to seek an explanation? Again, this seems to have an obvious explanation. Minds are designed that way, because a mind that produces a richer understanding of what happens (especially bad things that happen) is certainly better equipped for survival.

Accepting this, it remains that some aspects of the association between religious agents and misfortune may seem paradoxical. To see this, let me return to the Kwaio example. The ancestors are generally responsible for whatever happens in a village: "Spirits, a child learns early, are beings that help and punish: the source of success, gratification, and security, and the cause of illness, death, and misfortune; makers and enforcers of rules that must at first seem arbitrary."[33] Good taro crops and prolific sows indicate that the ancestors are happy with the way the living behave. Illness and misfortune are generally an effect of the ancestors' anger. True, the Kwaio like most people in the world, accept that some events just happen and have no particular cause. Some illnesses may be interpreted as a straightforward weakening of the body with no special implications; the fact that some ailments are cured by Western medicine shows that they are in that category of mere mishaps. But in general any salient event, particularly any remarkable misfortune, is seen as the action of the *adalo*. As a Kwaio diviner tells Keesing: "If we see that a child is sick . . . we divine and then we sacrifice a pig [to the *adalo*]." Divination is required to understand which spirit is angry and why. A diviner will take a set of knotted leaves and pull them to see which side breaks first, indicating either a positive answer or no answer to a particular question. In most cases, ancestors are unhappy either because people have broken rules about what is proper and what is *abu* (forbidden or dangerous—from the Oceanian root *tapu* that gave us our "taboo"). Ancestors, like humans, crave pork and demand frequent sacrifices of pigs.[34] Interaction with the ancestors can be quite complex, because it is not always clear which ancestor is causing trouble: "If it is not really that adalo [discovered in divination] that asked for a pig, in order that our pigs or taro grow well, then even though we sacrifice it, nothing will happen." So people may go through several cycles of divination followed by sacrifice to reach a satisfactory arrangement with the ancestors.

This case highlights some very common features of the association between misfortune and religious agents. Although people assume that the ancestors are involved in many occurrences (like bad crops, illnesses, death, etc.) they do not bother to represent *in what way* they bring about all these states of affairs. That is, people's reasoning, when thinking about such situations, is entirely centered on the *reasons* why an ancestor would want them to fall ill or have many children, certainly not on the *causal process* whereby they make it happen.

This is also true of other kinds of supernatural notions that people commonly associate with misfortune. One of the most widespread explanations of mishaps and disorders, the world over, is in terms of witchcraft, the suspicion that some people (generally in the community) perform magical tricks to steal other people's health, good fortune, or material goods. Concepts of witches are among the most widespread supernatural ones. In some places, there are explicit accusations and the alleged witches must either prove their innocence or perform some special rituals to pay for their transgression. In most places, the suspicion is a matter of gossip and rarely comes out in the open. You do not really need to have actual witches around to have very firm beliefs about the existence and powers of witches. Witchcraft is important because it seems to provide an explanation for all sorts of events: many cases of illness or other misfortune are spontaneously interpreted as evidence for the witches' actions.

Witchcraft beliefs are only one manifestation of a phenomenon that is found in many human groups, the interpretation of misfortune as a consequence of envy. For another such situation, consider the widespread beliefs in an "evil eye," a spell cast by envious people against whoever enjoys some good fortune or natural advantage.[35] Witchcraft and evil-eye notions do not really belong to the domain of religion, but they show that, religious agents or not, there is a tendency to focus on the possible *reasons* for some agents to cause misfortune, rather than on the *processes* whereby they could do it.

People focus on an agent's reasons for causing them harm, but note that these reasons always have to do with people's *interaction* with the agents in question. The way these reasons are expressed is, in a great majority of cases, supported by our social-exchange intuitions. People refused to follow God's orders; they polluted a house against the ancestors' prescriptions; they had more wealth or good fortune than their God-decreed fate allocated them, and so on. All this supports what anthropologists have been saying for a long time on the basis of evidence gathered in the most various cultural environments: misfortune is generally interpreted in *social* terms. But this familiar conclusion implies that the evolved cognitive resources people bring to the understanding of interaction should be crucial to their construal of misfortune.

To return to our examples: the Kwaio ancestors afflict people with some disease because they want some sacrifice. In some of these cases, people admit that they should have performed the sacrifice to start with. They are guilty of neglecting a particular ancestor. They failed to maintain proper relations with him. These are clearly construed as exchange relations. Ancestors provide some form of protection, and people provide roasted pigs. In some cases, people tend to think that the ancestors are "pushing it" a little and feel justifiably resentful. This is the kind of emotion that we find in situations where one party in a social exchange seems to be increasing their benefits without paying an increased cost. In other words, relations with ancestors are framed by understandings and associated emotions that are intuitively applied to social exchange. Witchcraft, too, seems to be clearly construed as unfair exchange. The witches are trying to reap some benefit without paying any cost: witches are quite clearly "cheaters" in the technical sense. Indeed, that is precisely what people like the Fang and many others who have witchcraft concepts say about witches: they are the ones who take but never give, who steal other people's health or happiness, who thrive only if others are deprived. Finally, as the evil eye shows, people someone represent misfortune as caused by someone else who takes *them* for cheaters. People interpret your benefits as having cost you nothing. In their view, your benefit should be compensated by a cost. You think they do not perceive any cost in your good fortune, therefore they are jealous of you and this creates calamities.

These examples show that some prior mental process describes misfortune in such a way that it makes sense to include gods and spirits in an explanation of what caused it. That is, people's thoughts about such salient events are organized by the mental templates of social exchange. These do not necessarily require gods and spirits. But if you have concepts of gods and spirits, it is not too surprizing that they should sometimes be included in explanations of salient events. If your representation of misfortune generally treats it as an effect of social exchange violations, it will potentially include any agent with whom you interact. But spirits and gods are precisely represented as engaging in social interaction with people, especially in social exchange. So they are among the potential candidates for originators of misfortune, just like neighbors, relatives, and envious partners.

Religion, Interpretation, and Explanation

This account of religious concepts and behaviors stands in contrast to other traditions in the study of religion in several different ways. First, the kind of evolutionary-cognitive framework outlined here is quite clearly reductionistic. That is, it aims to show that the appearance and spread of religious concepts are adequately explained in terms of underlying mental processes and events. In this sense it stands in sharp contrast to interpretative or hermeneutic frameworks. The point here is not to describe what it is like to entertain religious thoughts, or in what way these thoughts could make sense, but to account for their occurrence and their features.

Second, this accounts suggests that religious processes are not sui generis. They do not require that we assume a specific religious organ or religious mode of function in the mind. Most of the processes described here as constituting religious thought are present in all human minds. In the same way as music is made possible by features of the auditory cortex that would be present, music or no music, our basic cognitive equipment would be the same, religion or not.

Third, this evolutionary account is not dramatic or epic. Our views on religion are generally skewed by an intuitive assumption that dramatic phenomena should have dramatic explanations. Because religion is central to many people's experience, has salient social effects, and has often triggered historical tragedies, we think the explanation should be equally momentous. It may be difficult to think that a slight tweaking of ordinary intuitions, together with small but real effects on memory and inference, are enough to produce all the drama of religion in history. Yet I think that is a common situation in science, that dramatic phenomena have rather prosaic explanations.

Is there a religious instinct? I think the evidence presented here does not quite support the notion of an evolved propensity to religious concepts and norms, with its own brain implementation and its own evolutionary history. People who think there is a religious instinct often choose to focus on one specific feature of religion as being crucial. But religion, being a cultural success story, certainly does not rely on the activation of a single neural system. Religious concepts are a very likely, but not inevitable, outcome of the proper functioning of many different mental systems, which did appear because of natural selection and deserve the label of "mental instincts." Notions of gods, spirits, and ancestors are parasites of our mental instincts.

NOTES

1. P. Boyer, "Cognitive Constraints on Cultural Representations: Natural Ontologies and Religious Ideas," in *Mapping the Mind: Domain-Specificity in Culture and Cognition*, ed. L. A. Hirschfeld and S. Gelman (New York: Cambridge University Press, 1994), 391–411.

2. B. Saler, *Conceptualizing Religion: Immanent Anthropologists, Transcendent Natives and Unbounded Categories* (Leiden: Brill, 1993).

3. J. L. Barrett and F. C. Keil, "Conceptualizing a Non-Natural Entity: Anthropomorphism in God Concepts," *Cognitive Psychology* 31 (1996): 219–247; Boyer, "Cognitive Constraints."

4. P. Boyer, *The Naturalness of Religious Ideas: A Cognitive Theory of Religion* (Berkeley: University of California Press, 1994).

5. J. L. Barrett, "Cognitive Constraints on Hindu Concepts of the Divine," *Journal for the Scientific Study of Religion* 37 (1998): 608–619; P. Boyer and C. Ramble, "Cognitive Templates for Religious Concepts: Cross-Cultural Evidence for Recall of Counter-Intuitive Representations," *Cognitive Science* 25 (2001): 535–564.

6. S. E. Guthrie, *Faces in the Clouds: A New Theory of Religion* (New York: Oxford University Press, 1993).

7. Ibid.

8. P. Boyer, "What Makes Anthropomorphism Natural: Intuitive Ontology and Cultural Representations," *Journal of the Royal Anthropological Institute* (n.s.) 2 (1996): 1–15.

9. J. L. Barrett, "Exploring the Natural Foundations of Religion," *Trends in Cognitive Science* 4.1 (2000): 29–34.

10. Andrew N. Meltzoff, "Origins of Theory of Mind, Cognition and Communication," *Journal of Communication Disorders* 32.4 (1999): 251–269.

11. Daniel J. Povinelli and Todd M. Preuss, "Theory of Mind: Evolutionary History of a Cognitive Specialization," *Trends in Neurosciences* 18.9 (1995): 418–424; A. Whiten, ed., *Natural Theories of Mind: The Evolution, Development and Simulation of Everyday Mind-Reading* (Oxford: Blackwell, 1991).

12. H. C. Barrett, "Human Cognitive Adaptations to Predators and Prey" (Ph.D. diss., University of California, Santa Barbara, 1999).

13. S. Mithen, *The Prehistory of the Mind* (London: Thames and Hudson, 1996).

14. S. Baron-Cohen, *Mindblindness: An Essay on Autism and Theory of Mind* (Cambridge: MIT Press, 1995).

15. Helen Tager-Flusberg and Kate Sullivan, "A Componential View of Theory of Mind: Evidence from Williams Syndrome," *Cognition* 76.1 (2000): 59–89.

16. Daniel J. Povinelli and Timothy J. Eddy, "Factors Influencing Young Chim-

panzees' (Pan Troglodytes) Recognition of Attention," *Journal of Comparative Psychology* 110.4 (1996): 336–345.

17. Barrett, "Natural Foundations."

18. Robert Boyd and Peter J. Richerson, "Punishment Allows the Evolution of Cooperation (or Anything else) in Sizable Groups," *Ethology and Sociobiology* 13.3 (1992): 171–195.

19. M. Bacharach and D. Gambetta, "Trust in Signs," in *Trust and Social Structure*, ed. K. Cook (New York: Russell Sage Foundation, 1999); R. Frank, *Passions within Reason: The Strategic Role of the Emotions* (New York: W. W. Norton, 1988).

20. J. Sidanius and F. Pratto, *Social Dominance: An Intergroup Theory of Social Oppression and Hierarchy* (Cambridge: Cambridge University Press, 1999).

21. John Tooby and Leda Cosmides, "Friendship and the Banker's Paradox: Other Pathways to the Evolution of Adaptations for Altruism," in *Evolution of Social Behaviour Patterns in Primates and Man*, ed. W. G. Runciman, John Maynard Smith et al. (Oxford: Oxford University Press, 1996), 119–143.

22. Gambetta, "Godfather's Gossip," *Archives Européennes de Sociologie* 35 (1994): 199–223.

23. Boyer, "Functional Origins of Religious Concepts: Conceptual and Strategic Selection in Evolved Minds [Malinowski Lecture 1999]," *Journal of the Royal Anthropological Institute* 6 (2000): 195–214.

24. R. Keesing, *Kwaio Religion: The Living and the Dead in a Solomon Island Society* (New York: Columbia University Press, 1982).

25. Ibid., 115.

26. Barrett and Keil, "Conceptualizing a Non Natural Entity."

27. John C. Gibbs, "Toward an Integration of Kohlberg's and Hoffman's Moral Development Theories; Special Section: Intersecting Conceptions of Morality and Moral Development," *Human Development* 34.2 (1991): 88–104.

28. E. Turiel, "The Development of Morality," in *Handbook of Child Psychology*, 5th ed., ed. W. Damon (New York: Wiley, 1998), 3:863–932; E. Turiel, *The Development of Social Knowledge; Morality and Convention* (Cambridge: Cambridge University Press, 1983).

29. Marie S. Tisak and Elliot Turiel, "Children's Conceptions of Moral and Prudential Rules," *Child Development* 55.3 (1984): 1030–1039.

30. Michael Siegal and Rebecca M. Storey, "Day Care and Children's Conceptions of Moral and Social Rules," *Child Development* 56.4 (1985): 1001–1008.

31. Myung-ja Song, Judith G. Smetana, and Sang Yoon Kim, "Korean Children's Conceptions of Moral and Conventional Transgressions," *Developmental Psychology* 23.4 (1987): 577–582.

32. Jennifer A. Sanderson and Michael Siegal, "Conceptions of Moral and Social Rules in Rejected and Nonrejected Preschoolers," *Journal of Clinical Child Psychology* 17.1 (1988): 66–72; Judith G. Smetana, Mario Kelly, and Craig T. Twentyman, "Abused, Neglected, and Nonmaltreated Children's Conceptions of Moral and Social-Conventional Transgressions," *Child Development* 55.1 (1984): 277–287.

33. Keesing, *Kwaio Religion: The Living and the Dead*, 33.

34. Ibid., 115.

35. D. F. Pocock, *Mind, Body and Wealth* (Oxford: Basil Blackwell, 1973).

BIBLIOGRAPHY

Bacharach, M., and D. Gambetta. "Trust in Signs." In *Trust and Social Structure*, edited by K. Cook. New York: Russell Sage Foundation, 1999.

Baron-Cohen, S. *Mindblindness: An Essay on Autism and Theory of Mind*. Cambridge, Mass.: The MIT Press, 1995.

Barrett, H. C. "Human Cognitive Adaptations to Predators and Prey." Ph.D. diss., University of California, Santa Barbara, 1999.

Barrett, J. L. "Cognitive Constraints on Hindu Concepts of the Divine." *Journal for the Scientific Study of Religion* 37 (1998): 608–619.

———. "Exploring the Natural Foundations of Religion." *Trends in Cognitive Science* 4.1 (2000): 29–34.

Barrett, J. L., and F. C. Keil. "Conceptualizing a Non-Natural Entity: Anthropomorphism in God Concepts." *Cognitive Psychology* 31 (1996): 219–247.

Boyd, Robert, and Peter J. Richerson. "Punishment Allows the Evolution of Cooperation (or Anything else) in Sizable Groups." *Ethology and Sociobiology* 13.3 (1992): 171–195.

Boyer, P. "Cognitive Constraints on Cultural Representations: Natural Ontologies and Religious Ideas." In *Mapping the Mind: Domain-Specificity in Culture and Cognition*, edited by L. A Hirschfeld and S. Gelman. New York: Cambridge University Press, 1994.

———. *The Naturalness of Religious Ideas: A Cognitive Theory of Religion*. Berkeley: University of California Press, 1994.

———. "What Makes Anthropomorphism Natural: Intuitive Ontology and Cultural Representations." *Journal of the Royal Anthropological Institute* (n.s.) 2 (1996): 1–15.

———. "Functional Origins of Religious Concepts: Conceptual and Strategic Selection in Evolved Minds [Malinowski Lecture 1999]." *Journal of the Royal Anthropological Institute* 6 (2000): 195–214.

Boyer, P., and C. Ramble. "Cognitive Templates for Religious Concepts: Cross-Cultural Evidence for Recall of Counter-Intuitive Representations." *Cognitive Science* 25 (2001): 535–564.

Frank, R. *Passions within Reason: The Strategic Role of the Emotions*. New York: W. W. Norton, 1988.

Gambetta, D. "Godfather's Gossip." *Archives Européennes de Sociologie* 35 (1994). 199–223.

Gibbs, John C. "Toward an Integration of Kohlberg's and Hoffman's Moral Development Theories; Special Section: Intersecting Conceptions of Morality and Moral Development." *Human Development* 34.2 (1991): 88–104.

Guthrie, S. E. *Faces in the Clouds: A New Theory of Religion*. New York: Oxford University Press, 1993.

Keesing, R. *Kwaio Religion: The Living and the Dead in a Solomon Island Society*. New York: Columbia University Press, 1982.

Meltzoff, Andrew N. "Origins of Theory of Mind, Cognition and Communication." *Journal of Communication Disorders* 32.4 (1999): 251–269.

Mithen, S. *The Prehistory of the Mind*. London: Thames and Hudson, 1996.

Pocock, D. F. *Mind, Body and Wealth*. Oxford: Basil Blackwell, 1973.

Povinelli, Daniel J., and Timothy J. Eddy. "Factors Influencing Young Chimpanzees' (Pan Troglodytes) Recognition of Attention." *Journal of Comparative Psychology* 110.4 (1996): 336–345.

Povinelli, Daniel J., and Todd M. Preuss. "Theory of Mind: Evolutionary History of a Cognitive Specialization." *Trends in Neurosciences* 18.9 (1995): 418–424.

Saler, B. *Conceptualizing Religion: Immanent Anthropologists, Transcendent Natives and Unbounded Categories*. Leiden: Brill, 1993.

Sanderson, Jennifer A., and Michael Siegal. "Conceptions of Moral and Social Rules in Rejected and Nonrejected Preschoolers." *Journal of Clinical Child Psychology* 17.1 (1988): 66–72.

Sidanius, J., and F. Pratto. *Social Dominance: An Intergroup Theory of Social Oppression and Hierarchy*. Cambridge: Cambridge University Press, 1999.

Siegal, Michael, and Rebecca M. Storey. "Day Care and Children's Conceptions of Moral and Social Rules." *Child Development* 56.4 (1985): 1001–1008.

Smetana, Judith G., Mario Kelly, and Craig T. Twentyman. "Abused, Neglected, and Nonmaltreated Children's Conceptions of Moral and Social-Conventional Transgressions." *Child Development* 55.1 (1984): 277–287.

Song, Myung-ja, Judith G. Smetana, and Sang Yoon Kim. "Korean Children's Conceptions of Moral and Conventional Transgressions." *Developmental Psychology* 23.4 (1987): 577–582.

Tager-Flusberg, Helen, and Kate Sullivan. "A Componential View of Theory of Mind: Evidence from Williams Syndrome." *Cognition* 76.1 (2000): 59–89.

Tisak, Marie S., and Elliot Turiel. "Children's Conceptions of Moral and Prudential Rules." *Child Development* 55.3 (1984): 1030–1039.

Tooby, John, and Leda Cosmides. "Friendship and the Banker's Paradox: Other Pathways to the Evolution of Adaptations for Altruism." In *Evolution of Social Behaviour Patterns in Primates and Man*, edited by W. G. Runciman, John Maynard Smith, et al. Oxford: Oxford University Press, 1996.

———. "The Development of Morality." In Vol. 3 of *Handbook of Child Psychology*, 5th ed., edited by W. Damon. New York: Wiley, 1998.

Turiel, E. *The Development of Social Knowledge: Morality and Convention*. Cambridge: Cambridge University Press, 1983.

Van Schaik, Carel P., and J. A. Van Hooff. "On the Ultimate Causes of Primate Social Systems." *Behaviour* 85.1–2 (1983): 91–117.

Whiten, A., ed. *Natural Theories of Mind: The Evolution, Development and Simulation of Everyday Mind-Reading*. Oxford: Blackwell, 1991.

13

Empathy and Human Experience

Evan Thompson

This volume addresses the question "How may we understand science and religion as arising from, yet somehow transcending, the human experience?" My work bears on this question because I am interested in the relationship between human experience and the scientific investigation of the mind in cognitive science.[1] One of the central questions that has preoccupied me is "What form should a mature science of the human mind have?" By "mature science" I mean one that has developed to the point where its researchers are experienced and knowledgeable with regard to their subject matter. I believe that a mature science of mind would have to include disciplined first-person methods of investigating subjective experience in active partnership with the third-person methods of biobehavioral science. "First-person methods" are practices that increase an individual's sensitivity to his or her own experience through the systematic training of attention and self-regulation of emotion.[2] This ability to attend reflexively to experience itself—to attend not simply to what one experiences (the object) but to how one experiences it (the act)—seems to be a uniquely human ability and mode of experience we do not share with other animals. First-person methods for cultivating this ability are found primarily in the contemplative wisdom traditions of human experience, especially Buddhism. Throughout history religion has provided the main home for contemplative experience and its theoretical articulation in philosophy and psychology. Thus my work in cognitive science and the philosophy of mind intersects with religion not as an object of scientific study (as it is for

Pascal Boyer),[3] but as a repository of first-person methods that can play an active and creative role in scientific investigation itself.[4]

Religion includes many other things besides contemplative experience, and many religions have little or no place for contemplative experience. On the other hand, contemplative experience is found in important nonreligious contexts, such as philosophy.[5] For these reasons, the term "religion" does not accurately designate the kind of cultural tradition or domain of human experience that I and others wish to bring into constructive engagement with cognitive science. Better designations would be "wisdom traditions" and "contemplative experience." Nor does the phrase "science-religion dialogue" convey the nature of our project, for our aim is not to adjudicate between the claims of science and religion, but to gain a deeper understanding of the human mind and consciousness by making contemplative psychology a full partner in the science of mind.

Three main bodies of knowledge are crucial for this endeavor. I have already mentioned two—cognitive science and contemplative psychology. The third is phenomenological philosophy in the tradition inaugurated by Edmund Husserl. The importance of phenomenology is that it provides a third mediating term between cognitive science and contemplative psychology, especially in the case of non-Western contemplative traditions such as Buddhism. Phenomenology is a Western intellectual tradition with strong roots in the Western scientific style of thought, but it is also a tradition that upholds the importance of rigorous attention to mental phenomena as lived experiential events. Thus, instead of the science-religion dialogue as it is standardly presented, the task in which I see myself engaged is one of circulating back and forth among the three spheres of experimental cognitive science, phenomenology, and contemplative psychology. "Mutual circulation" is the term that Francisco Varela, Eleanor Rosch, and I introduced to describe this approach.[6] According to the logic of mutual circulation, each domain of cognitive science, phenomenology, and contemplative psychology is distinct and has its own degree of autonomy— its own proper methods, motivations, and concerns—but they overlap and share common areas. Thus, instead of being juxtaposed, either in opposition or as separate but equal, they flow into and out of each other, and so are all mutually enriched.

In this essay I will illustrate this approach through a discussion of the human experience of empathy. I choose empathy because it is one important aspect (though by no means the only one) of the intersubjectivity of human experience. Intersubjectivity is important in the context of discussing the relationship between cognitive science and contemplative experience because there has been a tendency in this area to focus on consciousness as if it were an intrinsically "interior" phenomenon or "inner reality" invisible to ordinary perception. I think this way of thinking about consciousness is distorted. It operates within the reified categories of "internal" and "external." These categories are inadequate for understanding how human experience is constituted by our lived body and interpersonal social world. We see the experience of shame in the blushing face, perplexed thought in the furrowed brow, joy in the smiling face; we do not infer their existence as "internal" phenomena from "external" facts. Although it is true that not all experiences need be expressed in this bodily way, and that each of us has first-person access only to his or her own experience, these truths do not mean that experience is "interior" in some special (and unclear) metaphysical sense. Focusing on empathy helps to remind us that we need a better framework for thinking about human experience—whether in cognitive science or contemplative psychology—than the framework of "inner" and "outer."

The key idea of the next part of this essay is that human experience depends formatively and constitutively on the dynamic coupling of self and other in empathy. After presenting this idea by interweaving cognitive science and phenomenology, I will then expand the discussion to include a contemplative perspective on the nonduality of self and other, as presented by the Madhyamaka or "middle way" tradition of Indo-Tibetan Buddhism. Finally, I will return to the importance of contemplative phenomenology for cognitive science in light of the theme of this volume.

Empathy Defined

At the outset, it is best to think of empathy broadly, and then to distinguish different kinds of empathy as we go along. Nevertheless, even in broad terms there are different ways of defining empathy—as a basic "intentional capacity," as a unique kind of "intentional act," and as an "intentional process." (I use the term "intentional" here in its Husserlian sense of mental directedness toward an object or openness to what is other.) As an intentional capacity, empathy is the basic ability to comprehend another individual's experience, a capacity that underlies all the particular feelings and emotions one can have for another.[7] To exercise this capacity is to engage empathy as an intentional act and intentional process. As a unique kind of intentional act, empathy is directed toward, and thereby has as its intentional correlate, the experience of another person.[8] Although empathy so understood is founded on sense perception (of the other's bodily presence), and can involve inference in difficult or problematic situations (when one has to work out how another person feels about something), it is not reducible to some additive combination of perception and inference. This view is contrary to any theory according to which we understand others by first perceiving their bodily behavior, and then inferring or hypothesizing that their behaviour is caused by experiences or inner mental states similar to those that cause similar behavior in us. Rather, in empathy we experience the other directly as a person, that is, as an intentional and mental being whose bodily gestures and actions are expressive of his or her experience and states of mind. Finally, as an intentional process, empathy is any process in which the attentive perception of the other's state or situation generates a state or situation in oneself that is more applicable to the other's state or situation than to one's own prior state or situation.[9]

With this broad conception of empathy in place, we can turn to some of the different kinds of empathy. Psychologists have used the term "empathy" to describe at least three different processes: (1) *feeling* what another person is feeling, (2) *knowing* what another person is feeling, and (3) *responding compassionately* to another person's distress.[10] More structurally detailed analyses, however, have been given by phenomenologists, who have distinguished at least four main aspects of the full performance of empathy:[11]

1. The involuntary coupling or pairing of my living body with your living body in perception and action.
2. The imaginary movement or transposition of myself into your place.
3. The interpretation of you as an other to me and of me as an other to you.
4. The ethical and moral perception of you as a person.

Empathy as Coupling

The first kind of empathy—the dynamic coupling or pairing of the living bodies of self and other—belongs to the level of prereflective perception and action (what Husserl calls the "passive synthesis" of experience).[12] It is passive in the sense of not being initiated voluntarily, and it serves as a support for the other types of empathy. "Coupling" or "pairing" means an associative bonding or linking of self and other on the basis of their bodily similarity. This similarity operates not so much at the level of visual appearance, which forms part of the body image as an intentional object present to consciousness, but at the level of gesture, posture, and movement, that is, at the level of the unconscious body schema.[13] Thus, empathy is not simply the comprehension of another person's particular experiences (sadness, joy, and so on), but the experience of another as a living bodily subject of experience like oneself.

This phenomenological conception of the embodied basis of empathy can be linked to cognitive science by going back to the broad notion of empathy as process—as any process in which the attentive perception of the other generates a state in oneself more applicable to the other's state than to one's own prior state. According to the "perception-action model" of empathy,[14] when we perceive another person's behavior, our own motor representations for that kind of behavior are automatically activated and generate associated autonomic and somatic responses (unless inhibited). For instance, it has been shown that when one individual sees another execute actions with different body parts (mouth actions, hand actions, and foot actions), the neural patterns of activation in the observer's brain correspond to those that would be active were the observer performing the same bodily actions.[15]

This kind of self-other coupling can be called sensorimotor coupling. In addition to sensorimotor coupling, there is affective coupling or "affective resonance."[16] In affective resonance, two individuals engaged in direct interaction affect each other's emotional states.

Empathy as Imaginary Transposition

The second kind of empathy—empathy as the imaginary transposition of oneself to the place of the other—is more active and cognitive than the first kind. Instead of simply the involuntary, bodily pairing of self and other, cognitive perspective-taking processes are used to imagine or mentally transpose oneself into the place of the other.

Comparative studies of empathy from cognitive ethology provide an important window on cognitive empathy. The presence and extent of empathy among nonhuman animals, especially primates, is a subject of much debate. According to an all-or-none view, cognitive empathy (the only kind of empathy, according to this view) requires the cognitive ability to attribute mental states to another individual and to understand the other's behavior in light of them. This ability, usually called "mind reading,"[17] is taken by some to require the possession of a "theory of mind," a theoretical body of knowledge about mental states and their role in generating behavior. Advocates of this way of thinking have argued that chimpanzees fail certain mind-reading tests and therefore do not possess a theory of mind, and accordingly are not capable of cognitive empathy. On the other hand, as I have been suggesting here, and as others have proposed, most notably Frans de Waal, empathy should not be seen as an all-or-nothing phenomenon. In de Waal's words: "Many forms of empathy exist intermediate between the extremes of mere agitation and distress of another and full understanding of their predicament. At one end of the spectrum, rhesus infants get upset and seek contact with one another as soon as one of them screams. At the other end, a chimpanzee recalls a wound he has inflicted, and returns to the victim to inspect it."[18]

Other intermediate cases are consolation behavior and tailored-helping behavior. Consolation behavior is friendly contact by an uninvolved and less distressed bystander toward a victim of a previously aggressive encounter. For instance, de Waal, in his book *Good Natured*, presents a photograph of a juvenile chimpanzee comforting a distressed adult. Consolation behavior has been extensively documented in great apes only (and has not been found in monkey species despite great efforts to find it). Tailored helping is coming to the aid of another (either a conspecific or a member of another species) with behaviors tailored to the other's particular needs (as when one ape helps another out of a tree or tries to help an injured bird fly). Such behavior, in de Waal's words, "probably requires a distinction between self and other that allows the other's situation to be divorced from one's own while maintaining the emotional link that motivates behavior."[19] There exists a large number of anecdotal reports of tailored helping in apes.

Cognitive empathy at its fullest, however, is achieved when one individual can mentally adopt the other's perspective by exchanging places with the other in imagination. Described phenomenologically:[20] I am here and I imagine going there and being at the place where you are right now. Conversely, you are here (the "there" where I imagine being) and you imagine you are going there, to the place where I am (my "here"). Through this imagined movement and spatial transposition, we are able to exchange our mental perspectives, our thoughts and feelings. Whether apes possess this kind of mental ability is unclear and a subject of debate.[21]

In human children, the ability to mentally transpose self and other seems to be linked to the emergence, at around nine to twelve months of age, of a whole cluster of cognitive abilities known collectively as "joint attention."[22] "Joint attention" refers to the triadic structure of a child, adult, and an object or event to which they share attention, and includes the activities of gaze following (reliably following where adults are looking), joint engagement with shared objects or events, using adults as social reference points, and imitative learning (acting on objects as adults do). At around the same time, infants also begin to point to things and hold them up for someone to see, gestures that serve to direct adult attention actively and intentionally. Michael Tomasello has argued that "infants begin to engage in joint attentional interactions when they begin to understand other persons as intentional agents like the self."[23] He proposes a "simulation explanation" of this developmental cognitive milestone, according to which the infant uses her primal understanding of others as "like me" (the groundling process of empathy, in phenomenological terms), and her newly emerging understanding of her own intentional agency, as the basis on which to judge analogically and categorically that others are intentional agents "like me" as well.

Empathy as the Understanding of You as an Other to Me and of Me as an Other to You

The third kind of empathy involves not simply imagining myself in your place, but understanding you as an other who accordingly sees me as an other to you. In other words, the imaginary transposition in this kind of empathy involves the possibility of seeing myself from your perspective, that is, as you empathetically experience me. Empathy thus becomes reiterated, so that I empathetically imagine your empathetic experience of me, and you empathetically imagine my empathetic experience of you. We also talk to each other about our experiences, and so linguistic communication and interpretation participate in and structure this exchange. The upshot is that each of us participates in an intersubjective viewpoint that transcends our own first-person singular perspectives.

We can turn again to developmental psychology for insight into the genesis of this third kind of empathy and the role it plays in constituting an intersubjective perspective. Let me quote a passage from Tomasello's book *The Cultural Origins of Human Cognition* that lucidly describes this genesis in the human infant:

> As infants begin to follow into and direct the attention of others to outside entities at nine to twelve months of age, it happens on occasion that the other person whose attention an infant is monitoring focuses on the infant herself. The infant then monitors that person's attention to *her* in a way that was not possible previously, that is, previous to the nine-month social-cognitive revolution. From this point on the infant's face-to-face interactions with others—which appear on the surface to be continuous with her face-to-face interactions from early infancy—are radically transformed. She now knows she is interacting with an intentional agent who perceives her and intends things toward her. When the infant did not understand that others perceive and intend things toward an outside world, there could be no question of how they perceived and intended things toward *me*. After coming to this understanding, the infant can monitor the adult's intentional relation to the world including herself. . . . By something like this same process infants at this age also become able to monitor adults' emotional attitudes toward them as well—a kind of social referencing of others' attitudes to the self. This new understanding of how others *feel* about me opens up the possibility for the development of shyness, self-consciousness, and a sense of self-esteem. . . . Evidence for this is the fact that within a few months after the social-cognitive revolution, at the first birthday, infants begin showing the first signs of shyness and coyness in front of other persons and mirrors.[24]

As Tomasello goes on to discuss, once the infant understands other individuals as intentional beings and herself as one participant among others in a social interaction, then whole new cognitive dimensions arise. The child comes to be able to participate in "joint attentional scenes"—social interactions in which the child and the adult jointly attend to some third thing, and to one another's attention to that third thing, for an extended period of time, and in which the child can conceptualize her own role from the same "outside" perspective as the other person. Joint attentional scenes in turn provide the framework for the acquisition of language and other kinds of communicative conventions.[25]

Although Tomasello does not use the term "empathy" in this context, the cognitive achievement he describes of being able to conceptualize oneself from the perspective of another person corresponds to what phenomenologists call "reiterated empathy." In reiterated empathy, I see myself from the perspective of another and thus grasp myself as an individual in an intersubjective world.

Tomasello's discussion of the child's achievement of this intersubjective perspective emphasizes the developmental progression from the neonate's understanding of the other as an animate being, to the infant's understanding of the other as an intentional agent with attention and goal-directed behavior, to the four-year-old child's understanding of the other as a mental agent with thoughts and beliefs (which need not be expressed in behavior and can fail to match the world).

Phenomenologists, without neglecting the intentional and mental aspects of the self, draw attention to the ambiguity of the lived body in reiterated empathy. The lived body is that which is most intimately me or mine, but it is also an object for the other. Because it is so intimately *me,* my body cannot stand before me as an object the way that other things can. No matter how I turn, my body is always *here,* at the zero-point of my egocentric space, never *there.* It is through empathetically grasping the other's perception of me that I am able to grasp my own lived body as an object belonging to an intersubjective world. In this way, my sense of self-identity in the world, even at the basic level of embodied agency, is inseparable from recognition by another, and from the ability to grasp that recognition empathetically.

Empathy as the Ethical and Moral Perception of You as a Person

The fourth kind of empathy is the recognition of the other as a person who deserves concern and respect. Empathy in this sense is not to be identified with any particular feeling of concern for another, such as sympathy, love, or compassion, but instead as the underlying capacity to have such other-directed and other-regarding feelings of concern.[26]

This kind of empathy can also be introduced from a developmental perspective. As we have seen, there is a progression from the infant's understanding of others as intentional agents (with attention, behavioral strategies, and goals) to the young child's understanding of others as mental agents (with beliefs, desires, and plans). According to Piaget and Tomasello, moral understanding begins to emerge at around the same time as the child comes to understand others as mental agents. It derives not from the rules adults impose on behavior, but from empathizing with other persons as mental agents and being able to see and feel things from their point of view.[27]

Within Western moral philosophy there is a long tradition going back to Immanuel Kant that privileges reason over feeling. To act out of duties legislated by reason is thought to have greater moral worth than acting on the basis of feeling or sentiment. Yet as Frans de Waal observes, echoing David Hume and Adam Smith: "Aid to others in need would never be internalized as a duty without the fellow-feeling that drives people to take an interest in one another. Moral sentiments came first; moral principles second."[28]

Empathy is the basic cognitive and emotional capacity underlying all the moral sentiments and emotions one can have for another. The point here is not that empathy exhausts moral experience, for clearly it does not, but that empathy provides the source of that kind of experience and the entry point into it. Without empathy, concern and respect for others as persons in the moral sense—as ends-in-themselves—would be impossible. As Mark Johnson has argued:

> the Kantian imperative always to treat others (and oneself) as ends-in-themselves has no practical meaning independent of our imaginatively taking up the place of the other. Contrary to Kant's explicit claims, we cannot know what it means to treat someone as an end-in-himself, in any concrete way, unless we can imagine his experience, feelings, plans, goals, and hopes. We cannot know what respect for others demands of us, unless we participate imaginatively in their experience of the world [29]

The four aspects or kinds of empathy I have presented are not separate, but occur together in face-to-face intersubjective experience. They intertwine through the lived body and through language. You imagine yourself in my place on the basis of the expressive similarity and spontaneous coupling of our lived bodies. This experience of yours contributes to the constitution of me for myself, for I experience myself as an intersubjective being by empathetically imagining your empathetic experience of me. Conversely, I imagine myself in your place, and this experience of mine contributes to the constitution of you for yourself. As we communicate in language and gesture, we interpret and understand each other dialogically. This dialogical dynamic is not a linear or additive combination of two preexisting, skull-bound minds. It emerges from and reciprocally shapes the nonlinear coupling of oneself and another in perception and action, emotion and imagination, and gesture and speech. It is this picture that I had in mind earlier when I said that human experience depends on the dynamic coupling of self and other in empathy.

The Nonduality of Self and Other

To appreciate the experiential depth and developmental possibilities of empathy, we need to turn to the perspective of contemplative psychology. Buddhist contemplative psychology is particularly significant for this discussion because of the way it combines first-person contemplative practices of empathy with a philosophical vision of the nonduality of self and other.

For the purposes of this essay, I will take as my reference point the classic text *The Way of the Bodhisattva (Bodhisattvacharyavatara)* by the eighth-century Indian philosopher Shantideva.[30] According to the Buddhist philosophical system Shantideva expounds—the *Prasangika Madhyamaka* or "Middle Way Consequence" school—"self" and "other" have no independent existence and intrinsic identity, but exist only on the basis of conceptual or mental imputation. In the words of a famous Tibetan commentary:

> Although they have no ultimate grounds for doing so, all beings
> think in terms of "I" and "mine." Because of this, they conceive of
> "other," fixing on it as something alien, although this too is un-
> founded. Aside from being merely mental imputations, "I" and
> "other" are totally unreal. They are both illusory. Moreover, when the
> nonexistence of "I" is realized, the notion of "other" also disappears,
> for the simple reason that the two terms are posited only in relation
> to each other. Just as it is impossible to cut the sky in two with a
> knife, likewise, when the spacelike quality of egolessness is realized,
> it is no longer possible to make a separation between "I" and
> "other," and there arises an attitude of wanting to protect others as
> oneself, and to protect all that belongs to them with the same care
> as if it were one's own. As it is said, "Whoever casts aside the ordi-
> nary, trivial view of 'self' will discover the profound meaning of
> great 'selfhood.' "[31]

It is important to understand that no nihilistic point is intended when it is said that self and other are unreal aside from being mental imputations. The Madhyamaka philosophers uphold the middle way between nihilism and absolutism, and accordingly they distinguish between two kinds of truth—conventional truth and ultimate truth. According to conventional truth, individuals like you and me exist, and thus nihilism is repudiated. According to ultimate truth, on the other hand, there is no intrinsically existent and intrinsically identifiable ego or "I" (and hence no intrinsically existent and identifiable "other" or "alter-I"), and thus absolutism is repudiated. The middle way is the ultimate truth of the dependent origination of "self" on the basis of prior contributing causes and conditions, constantly changing mental and physical processes, and conceptual imputations of "I" and "other" upon those mental and physical processes. Nevertheless, as unenlightened beings, we mistakenly believe on a deep emotional level that there does exist a real "I" or ego within our mind and body, and therefore our experience of ourselves and others is profoundly egocentric. According to Madhyamaka, and indeed all Buddhist schools, it is this egocentric attachment to a mentally imputed self that is the true source of all suffering. Enlightenment, it is said, consists in uprooting this egocentrism at its very source so that one's experience is no longer governed by this attachment to self.

There are, to be sure, significant differences between this philosophical viewpoint and phenomenology. What concerns me here, however, are not those important and interesting differences, but rather the parallel role that active empathetic imagination plays in both traditions in decentering the ego and thus opening human experience to an originary intersubjectivity prior to the reified mental imputations of "self" and "other."

In the eighth chapter of his text, Shantideva presents two meditations the meditation on the equality of self and other, and the meditation on the exchange of self and other. In the first meditation on self-other equality, one starts from the egocentric conviction that "This is my self" and then critically reflects that "my self" is simply a name applied to a collection of physical and mental elements. One mentally imposes an intrinsic "I-ness" and an intrinsic "otherness" onto phenomena, but "I" and "other" are simply relative designations imputed onto elements in which there is no inherently existing "I" and "other." Each "I" is an "other," and each "other" is an "I." All beings are in exactly the same situation of imputing "mineness" and "otherness," and all are in exactly the same predicament of wanting to be happy and not wanting to suffer. On the basis of this realization of the equality of self and other, one then visualizes the sufferings of other beings as one's own. In the words of the Tibetan commentary from which I quoted earlier:

> the teachings affirm that by applying the name *I* to the whole collection of suffering beings, and by entertaining and habituating oneself to the thought "*They are myself*," the thought of "I" will in fact arise with regard to them, and one will come to care for them as much as one now cares for oneself. . . . [F]rom the standpoint of suffering *as such*, the distinction between "*others'* suffering" and "*my* suffering" is quite unreal. It follows that, even if the pain of another does not actually afflict me, nevertheless, if that other is identified as "I" or "mine," the suffering of that other becomes unbearable to me also.[32]

Training in this first meditation on self-other equality is the essential prerequisite for the second meditation on the exchange of self and other. In this second meditation, through empathetic and sympathetic imagination, one visualizes oneself in the position of others and how one appears in their eyes.

This meditation also works explicitly with specific negative emotions, or un-wholesome "mental factors" as they are known in Buddhism.[33] These emotions are pride, competitive rivalry, and jealousy. One feels pride toward someone inferior; competitive rivalry toward an equal; and jealousy toward a superior. As an antidote to these emotions, one looks back at oneself through the eyes of someone inferior, equal, and superior, and generates the corresponding emotion toward oneself so that one knows what it is like to be on the receiving end. For instance, empathetically experiencing an inferior's envy toward one-self and the suffering it involves is the antidote to pride. At the same time, one takes on the sufferings of those others as one's own (as prepared for by the meditation on self-other equality).

The meditation on self-other exchange is thus a disciplined contemplative form of reiterated empathy. By "disciplined," I mean not simply that the med-itation is a step-by-step visualization exercise. It is disciplined also because it requires for its performance—as does the first meditation on self-other equal-ity—the fundamental Buddhist contemplative practices of attentional stability (shamatha) and insightful awareness (vipashyana). To accomplish the visuali-zation, one needs to be able to sustain the mind attentively on the image of the other as "I" and on the image of oneself as seen by this "alter-I," and one needs to have insightful awareness of the myriad mental and physical phenom-ena that arise from moment to moment in the field of intersubjective experi-ence.

From a cognitive scientific perspective the meditations on self-other equal-ity and self-other exchange are remarkable because of the disciplined manner in which they intertwine first-person methods of attentional stability, visuali-zation, and mental imagery, and the cognitive modulation of emotion.[34] From a phenomenological perspective, they are remarkable because of the disci-plined manner in which they make use of the key phenomenological technique of "imaginative variation"—varying phenomena freely in imagination so as to discern their invariant forms.

The Madhyamaka philosophy underlying the meditations also readily lends itself to comparison with the phenomenological analysis of intersubjec-tivity in terms of "ipseity" and "alterity," or "I-ness" and "otherness."[35] This level is deeper than the analysis in terms of empathy, and radically dismantles the egocentric perspective in a manner parallel to Madhyamaka.

According to phenomenology, alterity or otherness belongs to the very structure of experience prior to any actual empathetic encounter. Empathy ex-hibits alterity by being a "self-displacing" or "self-othering" experience. In em-pathy, I imagine myself as other—and in reiterated empathy I become other to myself by looking back on myself through the eyes of another. The same dynamic of self-othering displays itself throughout experience. It occurs in bodily experience when one hand touches the other, and the two alternate and intertwine in their roles of feeling and being felt. Self-othering occurs when I recollect my past self, when I reflect on my just-elapsed experiences, and when I imagine myself. What these self-displacing experiences indicate is that "I" and "other" are not simply co-relative and interchangeable, like the spatial perspectives of "here" and "there," but that "I-ness" is already internally constituted by "otherness." Experience is intrinsically intersubjective in the sense that alterity and openness to the other are a priori characteristics of the formal structure of experience. Thus the key presumption of egocentrism—that subjectivity can assert itself as ego and thereby exclude the other—is exploded.[36]

We have now seen how both phenomenology and contemplative psychology transcend egocentric experience by revealing an originary intersubjectivity prior to the reified conceptions of self and other. In Husserl's phenomenology, this transcendence of egocentrism stays mainly within a theoretical and cognitive orbit, but other phenomenologists, such as Max Scheler and Emmanuel Levinas, have shifted the orbit to an affective and ethical one.[37] One main contribution of Buddhist contemplative psychology is to show how the theoretical, cognitive, affective, and ethical can be yoked together using disciplined first-person methods.

Contemplative Cognitive Science and the Science-Religion Dialogue

Let us recall our opening question, "How may we understand science and religion as arising from, yet somehow transcending, the human experience?" To conclude this essay, I would like to address this question in light of the importance of first-person methods and contemplative experience for a renewed mind science.

Central to the guiding question of this volume is the notion of transcendence. Phenomenologists understand transcendence as a dynamic structure of experience—experience aims beyond itself and is always already open to what is other. Phenomenologists also insist that science is itself a form of human experience. Clearly, scientific experience aims to transcend ordinary experience, in the sense of prescientific experience. Similar aims of transcendence are shared by phenomenological and contemplative modes of investigating the mind: both aim to transcend unreflective or mindless experience. Yet how, exactly, is this movement of transcendence to be understood?

To address this question, let me simplify and idealize scientific practice in the form of the following "ABC strategy," in which the aim is to go from A to C by way of B:[38]

From:

A. the level of ordinary (prescientific) cognition of the actual phenomena under study, via

B. the imagination-based cognition of phenomena as "pure possibilities" subject to invariant laws, to:
C. the level of scientific cognition of the actual phenomena by applying the insights gained at level B.

The classical example is Galileo, who in inaugurating the shift from Aristotelean to modern physics, gave a theoretical account (level C) of the actual
phenomena of falling bodies (level A) by seeing them (at level B) as instances
out of a range of law-governed possibilities using the instrument of mathematics.

Suppose we apply this schema to cognitive science and its attempt to understand human conscious experience. The prevailing strategy in cognitive
science has been to endeavor to go from ordinary (prescientific) cognition of
conscious experience to scientific cognition by relying (at level B) mainly on
third-person observation and functional models. In other words, there has been
no sustained effort at level B to seek out the invariant structures of experience
as such, that is, as they are lived in the first-person. Such an effort requires
disciplined first-person methods of investigating experience.[39] Thus, the force
of this analogy is to suggest that cognitive science needs to incorporate first-
person methods into its research.

First-person methods aim to transcend ordinary experience, not by leaving
it behind, but by cultivating a higher or more intensive form of wakefulness
within it. Consider these basic generic features of first-person methods, common to both phenomenology and the contemplative tradition of mindfulness-
awareness meditation (*shamatha-vipashyana*):[40]

1. *Suspension.* Suspending preconceived ideas, beliefs, and prejudices
   about experience. Inducing an attitude of "suspension" with regard to
   these.
2. *Reorientation.* Orientation of attention not simply to the content of experience (the "what"), but to the experiencing process itself and its
   lived, moment-to-moment quality (the "how").
3. *Intimacy.* Gaining intimacy or familiarity with experience on the basis
   of numbers 1 and 2, and through additional techniques such as imaginative variation.
4. *Training.* Long-term training to acquire know-how and proficiency in
   numbers 1–3.

Practices with these features are important for cognitive science for several
reasons. First, they help subjects gain access to aspects of their experience that
would otherwise remain unnoticed, such as transient affective state or quality
of attention. Second, the refined first-person reports subjects thereby produce
can help experimenters to understand physiological processes that would otherwise remain opaque, such as the variability in brain dynamics as seen in

neuroimaging experiments.[41] For instance, first-person methods have been used to reveal important phenomenological differences in the subjective quality of attention during visual perception, and these differences have been correlated with distinct frequency and phase-synchrony patterns in the large-scale dynamics of brain activity on a millisecond timescale.[42] Finally, individuals who can generate specific sorts of mental states and report on those mental states with a high degree of phenomenological precision, such as adept contemplatives, provide a route into studying the causal efficacy of mental processes, considered neurodynamically as global or large-scale processes that can modify local neural and somatic events.[43]

Cognitive science is only now just beginning to be open to first-person methods, so it is too early to envision all that could be accomplished through the mutual circulation of cognitive science, phenomenology, and contemplative psychology. So far, cognitive science has explored only one small corner of the human mind—the one accessible to phenomenologically naïve subjects reporting to phenomenologically naïve cognitive scientists. The encounter among phenomenology, contemplative psychology, and cognitive science raises another prospect—the prospect of individuals with a high degree of phenomenological expertise reporting to phenomenologically informed cognitive scientists. The prospect of such collaboration and mutual illumination among cognitive science, phenomenology, and contemplative psychology signifies another kind of transcedence for both science and religion—a transcendence of the positivistic dismissal of experience on the part of cognitive science, and a transcendence of dogma and prescientific belief on the part of religion. In both cases the key to such transcendence is to make contemplative psychology and phenomenology a full partner in the science of the mind.

To conclude, let me draw out some implications of this conception of mind science for the broader science-religion dialogue represented by this volume. As I stated at the outset of this essay, the mutual circulation of cognitive science and contemplative wisdom traditions does not fit easily within the established frameworks of the science-religion dialogue. We can appreciate this point by distinguishing the mutual-circulation perspective from some of the main representative positions staked out in the science-religion dialogue, particularly as this dialogue touches on the nature of the human mind.

First, exploring the mutual circulation of mind science and contemplative experience is different from viewing science and religion as "nonoverlapping magesteria."[44] This separate-but-equal strategy of insulating science and religion is highly problematic. It divides science and religion along the lines of a subject-object dualism: science addresses the empirical world conceived as a realm of objectivity, whereas religion address the subjective realm of human purposes, meaning, and value. As I have tried to illustrate in this essay, however, this subject-object dualism breaks down in the face of the intersubjectivity of human experience. Intersubjective experience is the common terrain of both science and religion, and it is poorly understood when fractured along the lines of a subject/object (or fact/value) dichotomy.[45]

Second, the mutual circulation approach is different from looking for the physiological correlates of religious experiences.[46] The key difference is that adept contemplatives are not mere experimental subjects, but scientific collaborators and partners.[47] Thus, the mutual circulation approach enables us to envision future cognitive scientists being trained in contemplative phenomenology, as well as brain-imaging techniques, and mathematical modeling, and future contemplative practitioners being knowledgeable in neuroscience and experimental psychology. Science and contemplative wisdom could thus mutually constrain and enrich each other. It was precisely this prospect that William James envisioned over a century ago in his writings on scientific psychology and religious experience.[48]

Third, the mutual circulation approach is different from the view that religion can be entirely explained and accounted for by evolutionary psychology.[49] This view is well represented by Pascal Boyer's essay in this volume. It will therefore be informative to contrast his project with mine.

Contrary to the nonoverlapping magesteria perspective, I think it is illuminating to examine religion as Boyer does from the perspectives of cognitive science and evolutionary theory. Boyer's analyses linking religious concepts to our intuitive understandings of agency, social relations, and misfortune are enlightening. By the same token, however, in focusing on folk-religious belief structures, Boyer does not address an important aspect of religion, namely, religion (or certain religious traditions) as the main cultural repository of contemplative experience and first-person practices of investigating human experience. Boyer's project takes "religious notions and norms" or "religious concepts" as scientific objects, as something "out there" in the world to be investigated and explained according to third-person, evolutionary and functionalist cognitive science. My project, however, looks both to the role contemplative experience can play in a phenomenologically enriched mind science—a mind science including first-person and second-person modes of phenomenological investigation, in addition to third-person biobehavioral ones—and to the role such a renewed mind science can play in facilitating forms of contemplative experience (or "spirituality," more broadly) appropriate to a pluralistic and nonsectarian scientific culture.

It is interesting to consider how Boyer's approach to religion could also be taken toward science. The upshot would be an anthropology of folk-scientific belief structures. One could ask people what they believe about "genes," "black holes," "neural networks," and so on, and then study how these concepts are related to other concepts and belief structures that inform human life in modern Western societies. It seems likely that the folk-scientific concept of "gene," for instance, would be closely linked to human concepts of agency. As a result of writings by theorists such as Richard Dawkins, as well as popular science journalism, many people believe that genes are hidden inner agents with their own agendas that influence our motives and feelings. On the other hand, some scientists have more sophisticated and nuanced conceptions of genes and their relationship to cellular and evolutionary processes. The point of this analogy is that folk-religious belief structures may stand in the same relationship to contemplative knowledge in certain religious communities as folk-scientific belief structures stand to scientific knowledge in modern Western societies.

Although I have drawn attention to the differences between my project and Boyer's, Boyer does make one claim that could be taken as implying a challenge to my approach. He states that there is no "instinct for transcendence" in human beings, and hence religion cannot be understood (at least from an evolutionary psychological perspective) by appeals to transcendence. My objection to this claim is that it presupposes the problematic notion of a "mental instinct." It is impossible, I believe, to invoke the concept of instinct without falling into the conceptual morass of the nature/nurture, innate/acquired, and instinctual/learned dichotomies. I agree with those theorists in biology and psychology who argue that we need to replace this dichotomous framework with a "developmental systems" approach.[50] According to developmental systems theory, "inherited" (or instinctual) and "acquired" do not name two mutually exclusive classes of developmental characteristics. On the one hand, phenotypic traits are as much "acquired" as "inherited," because they must be developmentally constructed, that is, "acquired" in ontogeny. On the other hand, environmental conditions are as much "inherited" as "acquired," because they are passed on inseparably with the genes, and thus enter into the formation of the organism from the very beginning. The point, as Susan Oyama eloquently argues in her book *The Ontogeny of Information,* "is not that genes and environment are necessary for all characteristics, inherited or acquired (the usual enlightened position), but that there is no intelligible distinction between inherited (biological, genetically based) and acquired (environmentally mediated) characteristics."[51] For this reason, I am suspicious of any explanatory framework that tries to single out a class of biological and mental capacities and label them as "instincts."

How does this relate to religion? Boyer thinks that we have certain instincts that get expressed in our intuitive assumptions about agency and social relations, and that these instincts shape religious concepts, such as those of supernatural agency. On the other hand, other religious inclinations, he believes, are not based on instinct. On this basis he states there is no instinct for transcendence in human beings, and hence that religion cannot be understood on the basis of transcendence.

My response is that this notion of "instinct" is unhelpful. There are no instincts, because the term has no clear application. Organismic life cycles propagate from one generation to the next by reconstructing themselves in development, rather than unfolding according to transmitted, genetic blueprints or programs. The processes of developmental reconstruction involve numerous, interdependent causal elements, which relate to each other reciprocally as process and product, rather than belonging to the conceptually dichotomous categories of genetic nature versus environmental nurture. There is therefore no good basis within science for trying to understand religious concepts and norms using the explanatory construct of "instincts." I, therefore, do not accept the statement that there is no human instinct for transcendence—not because I believe there is such an instinct, but because the concept of "instinct" is simply inapplicable to biological and cultural development.

This debate within psychology and biology over the concept of instinct has an important bearing on the concerns of this volume. Once we set the concept of instinct aside, we are free to say that some religious concepts and norms, and certainly some religious experiences—particularly those in well-developed contemplative traditions—may very well have to be explained in relation to a human striving for transcendence, a striving that can be culturally maintained and transmitted from generation to generation. The developmental psychologist Margaret Donaldson, for instance, has mapped this sort of striving in relation to modes of human intellectual and emotional development throughout the life span, as exemplified in particular by what she calls the "value-sensing transcendent modes" of experience cultivated by the world's contemplative traditions.[52] From a developmental systems perspective, which rejects the concept of instinct, there is no theoretical obstacle to recognizing that human striving for transcendent modes of contemplative experience can form part of the developmental resources that shape the human mind in certain societies and traditions.

A common feature of the three approaches to science and religion I have contrasted with my mutual circulation approach is that they take the concepts of "science" and "religion" largely for granted. These concepts, however, are deeply problematic. They are European intellectual categories that have been shaped in recent Western history by the science-religion conflicts of the European enlightenment and modernity. As such, they do not map in any clear way onto the knowledge formations and social practices of certain other cultural traditions, in particular those of Asian contemplative wisdom traditions.[53] As Wallace has recently written in his introduction to a volume on Buddhism and science:

> The assertion that Buddhism includes scientific elements by no means overlooks or dismisses the many explicitly religious elements within this tradition. . . . Buddhism is very much concerned with human purposes, meaning, and value. But, like science, it is also concerned with understanding the realms of sensory and mental experience, and it addresses the questions of what the universe, including both objective and subjective phenomena, is composed of and how

it works. . . . Buddhism does address questions concerning the meaning and purpose of life, our ultimate origins and destiny, and the experiences of our inner life. But the mere fact that Buddhism includes elements of religion is not sufficient for singularly categorizing it as a religion, any more than it can be classified on the whole as a science. To study this discipine objectively requires our loosening the grip on familiar conceptual categories and preparing to confront something radically unfamiliar that may challenge our deepest assumptions. In the process we may review the status of science itself, in relation to the metaphysical axioms on which it is based.[54]

In this essay (and my book *The Embodied Mind*), I have argued that certain contemplative wisdom traditions (Buddhism most notably though not exclusively) and certain approaches in science (the embodied approach in cognitive science and its more recent elaboration in the research program of "neurophenomenology")[55] are not simply compatible, but mutually informative and enlightening. Through back-and-forth circulation, each approach can reshape the other, leading to new conceptual and practical understandings for both.

At stake in this developments is ultimately not simply whether we can have a methodologically mature science of the human mind, but whether we can have an ethically mature and spiritually informed science of the mind. Put another way, giving subjectivity and contemplative experience an active and creative role to play in cognitive science is as much an ethical step as a methodological one. My long-term hope is to see in my lifetime a flourishing contemplative, phenomenological, and experimental science of the mind.

Dedication

This text is dedicated to the memory of Francisco J. Varela (1946–2001), whose presence as an "all joyful bridge" among science, phenomenology, and contemplative wisdom is deeply missed and continues to inspire.

NOTES

1. See Francisco J. Varela, Evan Thompson, and Eleanor Rosch, *The Embodied Mind: Cognitive Science and Human Experience* (Cambridge, Mass.: MIT Press, 1991).

2. See Francisco J. Varela and Jonathan Shear, eds., *The View from Within: First-Person Approaches to the Study of Consciousness* (Thorverton, UK: Imprint Academic, 1999). Natalie Depraz, Pierre Vermersch, and Francisco J. Varela, *On Becoming Aware: A Pragmatics of Experiencing* (Amsterdam and Philadelphia: John Benjamins Press, 2003).

3. See Pascal Boyer, "Gods, Spirits, and the Mental Instincts that Create Them," this volume.

4. See Antoine Lutz and Evan Thompson, "Neurophenomenology: Integrating Subjective Experience and Brain Dynamics in the Neuroscience of Consciousness," *Journal of Consciousness Studies* 10 (2003): 31–52.

5. See Michael McGee, *Transformations of Mind: Philosophy as Spiritual Practice* (Cambridge: Cambridge University Press, 2000).

6. Varela, Thompson, and Rosch, *The Embodied Mind.*

7. See Arne Johan Vetlesen, *Perception, Empathy, and Judgment: An Inquiry into the Preconditions of Moral Performance* (University Park, Penn.: Pennsylvania State University Press, 1994).

8. See Edith Stein, *On the Problem of Empathy,* trans. Waltraut Stein (The Hague: Martinus Nijhoff, 1964).

9. See Stephanie Preston and Frans B. M. de Waal, "Empathy: Its Ultimate and Proximate Bases," *Behavioral and Brain Sciences* 25 (2002): 1–72.

10. Robert W. Levenson and Anna M. Reuf, "Empathy: A Physiological Substrate," *Journal of Personality and Social Psychology* 63 (1992): 234–246.

11. See Natalie Depraz, "The Husserlian Theory of Intersubjectivity as Alterology: Emergent Theories and Wisdom Traditions in the Light of Genetic Phenomenology," *Journal of Consciousness Studies* 8.5–7 (2001): 169–178, also printed in Evan Thompson, ed., *Between Ourselves: Second Person Issues in the Study of Consciousness* (Thorverton, UK: Imprint Academic, 2001), 169–178.

12. Edmund Husserl, *Analyses Concerning Passive and Active Synthesis: Lectures on Transcendental Logic,* trans. Anthony J. Steinbock (Dordrecht: Kluwer Academic Publishers, 2001).

13. For the distinction between body image and body schema, see Shaun Gallagher, "Body Image and Body Schema: A Conceptual Clarification," *The Journal of Mind and Behavior* 7 (1986): 541–554.

14. Preston and de Waal, "Empathy."

15. G. Buccino, F. Binkofski, G. R. Fink, L. Fadiga, L. Fogassi, V. Gallese, R. J. Seitz, K. Zilles, G. Rizzolatti, and H. J. Freund, "Action Observation Activates Premotor and Parietal Areas in a Somatotopic Manner: An fMRI Study," *European Journal of Neuroscience* 13 (2001): 400–404.

16. See Frans B. M. de Waal, "On the Possibility of Animal Empathy," in *Feelings and Emotions: The Amsterdam Symposium,* ed. T. Manstead, N. Fridja, and A. Fischer (Cambridge: Cambridge University Press, 2002).

17. "Mind reading" seems a poor phrase to describe the fundamental nature of our intersubjective cognitive abilities. It suggests that we are mainly spectators of each other, that human social life is based primarily on a spectatorial or observational ability to "read" inner mental states on the basis of outward behavior (as we read the meaning of words on the basis of written marks). For criticism of this view, see Victoria McGeer, "Psycho-Practice, Psycho-Theory and the Contrastive Case of Autism," *Journal of Consciousness Studies* 8.5–7 (2001): 109–132, also in Evan Thompson, *Between Ourselves,* 109–132, and Shaun Gallagher, "The Practice of Mind: Theory, Simulation, or Primary Interaction?" *Journal of Consciousness Studies* 8.5–7 (2001): 83–108, also in Evan Thompson, *Between Ourselves,* 83–108.

18. Frans B. M. de Waal, *Good Natured: The Origins of Right and Wrong in Humans and Other Animals* (Cambridge: Harvard University Press, 1996), 69.

19. De Waal, "Animal Empathy."

20. This description is taken (with modifications) from Depraz, "The Husserlian Theory," 173.

21. See Gordon Gallup Jr., "Can Animals Empathize? Yes," *Scientific American* 9 (1998): 65–75, and Daniel J. Povinelli, "Can Animals Empathize? Maybe Not," *Scientific American* 9 (1998): 65–75.

22. See Michael Tomasello, *The Cultural Origins of Human Cognition* (Cambridge: Harvard University Press, 1999), 62–63.

23. Ibid., 68.

24. Ibid., 89–90.

25. Ibid., chapter 4.

26. See Vetlesen, *Perception, Empathy, and Judgment.*

27. Tomasello, *The Cultural Origins of Human Cognition,* 179–181.

28. De Waal, *Good Natured,* 87.

29. Mark Johnson, *Moral Imagination: Implications of Cognitive Science for Ethics* (Chicago: University of Chicago Press, 1993), 200.

30. Shantideva, *The Way of the Bodhisattva,* trans. The Padmakara Translation Group (Boston: Shambala, 1997).

31. Ibid., 180–181.

32. Ibid., 182.

33. For discussion of the relationship between the Western concept of "emotion" and the Buddhist concept of "mental factors," see George Dreyfus, "Is Compassion an Emotion? A Cross-Cultural Exploration of Mental Typologies," in *Visions of Compassion: Western Scientists and Tibetan Buddhists Examine Human Nature,* ed. Richard J. Davidson and Anne Harrington (New York: Oxford University Press, 2002), 31–45.

34. It is worth noting that attention and cognitive control, mental imagery, and emotion were the three areas of investigation chosen for the conference on "Investigating the Mind: Exchanges between Buddhism and the Biobehavioral Sciences on How the Mind Works," September 13–14, 2003, with His Holiness the Dalai Lama and a group of cognitive scientists and Buddhist scholars. See http://www.InvestigatingTheMind.org.

35. See Dan Zahavi, *Self-Awareness and Alterity: A Phenomenological Investigation* (Evanston, Ill.: Northwestern University Press, 1999), and his "Beyond Empathy: Phenomenological Approaches to Intersubjectivity," *Journal of Consciousness Studies* 8.5–7 (2001): 151–167, also in Evan Thompson, *Between Ourselves,* 151–167.

36. The resonance between the nonduality of self and other, according to Madhyamaka, and the interplay between ipseity and alterity, according to Husserlian phenomenology, deserve to be explored in much greater detail than is possible here. Let me make one observation as a pointer toward future discussions. Although there is a fascinating parallel between the two traditions with regard to the interdependency of "self" and "other," they appear to diverge in the stance they take toward the "I" or ego. Whereas Madhyamaka asserts that the self is a mental imputation upon impermanent mental and physical phenomena, Husserl asserts that there is a "pure ego," which he conceives as an identity-pole that transcends any particular attentive act and that is shared by all experiences belonging to the same stream of consciousness. The point I wish to make now is that even if the Husserlian pure ego amounts in the end

to the kind of notion of self rejected in Madhyamaka philosophy, it should not be seen as an uncritical or precritical version of that notion, because Husserl introduced the pure ego precisely in connection with the self-othering structure of subjectivity. As Zahavi writes (*Self-Awareness and Alterity*, 150), "subjectivity only acquires an explicit I-consciousness in its *self-othering*" and "Husserl's notion of a pure ego cannot simply be taken as a manifestation and confirmation of his adherence to a metaphysics of presence, since Husserl only introduced the pure ego the moment he started taking intentional acts characterized by self-division, self-absence, and self-alienation seriously." It may be that this aspect of Husserl's phenomenology resembles Advaita Vedanta more than Madhyamaka. On this connection, see Bina Gupta, *The Disinterested Witness: A Fragment of Advaita Vedanta Phenomenology* (Evanston, Ill.: Northwestern University Press, 1998).

37. For an important study of the relationship between Levinas and Prasangika Madhyamaka, see Annabella Pitkin, "Scandalous Ethics: Infinite Presence with Suffering," *Journal of Consciousness Studies* 8.5–7 (2001): 232–246, also in Evan Thompson, ed., *Between Ourselves*, 232–246.

38. See Eduard Marbach, "How to Study Consciousness Phenomenologically, or, Quite a Lot Comes to Mind," *Journal of the British Society for Phenomenology* 19.3 (1998): 252–268.

39. See Lutz and Thompson, "Neurophenomenology."

40. See Natalie Depraz, Francisco J. Varela, and Pierre Vermersch, "The Gesture of Awareness: An Account of Its Structural Dynamics," in *Phenomenal Consciousness*, ed. Max Velmans (Amsterdam and Philadelphia: John Benjamins Publishing Company, 1999), 121–136, and Depraz, Vermersch, and Varela, *On Becoming Aware*.

41. See Lutz and Thompson, "Neurophenomenology."

42. See A. Lutz, J. P. Lachaux, J. Martinerie, and F. J. Varela, "Guiding the Study of Brain Dynamics by Using First-Person Data: Synchrony Patterns Correlate with Ongoing Conscious States During a Simple Visual Task," *Proceedings of the National Academy of Sciences USA* 99 (2002): 1586–1591.

43. For this conception of mental states as causally efficacious, global neurodynamical states, see Evan Thompson and Francisco Varela, "Radical Embodiment: Neural Dynamics and Consciousness," *Trends in Cognitive Sciences* 5 (2001): 418–425.

44. See Stephen Jay Gould, *Rocks of Ages: Science and Religion in the Fullness of Life* (New York: Ballantine, 1999).

45. See B. Alan Wallace, "The Intersubjective Worlds of Science and Religion," this volume.

46. See Andrew Newberg, Eugene D'Aquili, and Vince Rause, *Why God Won't Go Away: Brain Science and the Biology of Belief* (New York: Ballantine Books, 2001).

47. See Lutz and Thompson, "Neurophenomenology."

48. See Eugene Taylor, *William James: On Consciousness beyond the Margin* (Princeton: Princeton University Press, 1996).

49. See Pascal Boyer, *Religion Explained: The Evolutionary Origins of Religious Thought* (New York: Basic Books, 2001).

50. See Susan Oyama, *The Ontogeny of Information: Developmental Systems and Evolution,* 2nd ed. (Durham, N.C.: Duke University Press, 2002), and Susan Oyama,

Paul E. Griffiths, and Russell D. Gray, eds., *Cycles of Contingency: Developmental Systems and Evolution* (Cambridge, Mass.: MIT Press, 2001).

51. Oyama, *Ontogeny*, p. 138.

52. Margaret Donaldon, *Human Minds: An Exploration* (London: Penguin Books, 1991).

53. See Piet Hut, "Conclusion: Life as a Laboratory," in *Buddhism and Science: Breaking New Ground*, ed. B. Alan Wallace (New York: Columbia University Press, 2003), 399–416.

54. B. Alan Wallace, "Introduction: Buddhism and Science," in *Buddhism and Science: Breaking New Ground*, ed. Wallace, 9–10.

55. See Lutz and Thompson, "Neurophenomenology."

BIBLIOGRAPHY

Boyer, Pascal. *Religion Explained: The Evolutionary Origins of Religious Thought*. New York: Basic Books, 2001.
———. "Gods, Spirits, and the Mental Instincts that Create Them," this volume.
Buccino, G., F. Binkofski, G. R. Fink, L. Fadiga, L. Fogassi, V. Gallese, R. J. Seitz, K. Zilles, G. Rizzolatti, and H. J. Freund. "Action Observation Activates Premotor and Parietal Areas in a Somatotopic Manner: An fMRI Study." *European Journal of Neuroscience* 13 (2001): 400–404.
Depraz, Natalie. "The Husserlian Theory of Intersubjectivity as Alterology: Emergent Theories and Wisdom Traditions in the Light of Genetic Phenomenology." *Journal of Consciousness Studies* 8.5 7 (2001). 169–178. Also in *Between Ourselves: Second Person Issues in the Study of Consciousness*, edited by Evan Thompson. Thorverton, UK: Imprint Academic, 2001.
Depraz, Natalie, Francisco J. Varela, and Pierre Vermersch. "The Gesture of Awareness: An Account of Its Structural Dynamics." In *Investigating Phenomenal Consciousness*, ed. Max Velmans. Amsterdam and Philadelphia: John Benjamins Publishing Company, 1999.
———. *On Becoming Aware: A Pragmatics of Experiencing*. Amsterdam and Philadelphia: John Benjamins Publishing Company, 2003.
de Waal, Frans B. M. *Good Natured: The Origins of Right and Wrong in Humans and Other Animals*. Cambridge: Harvard University Press, 1996.
———. "On the Possibility of Animal Empathy." In *Feelings and Emotions: The Amsterdam Symposium*, edited by T. Manstead, N. Fridja, and A. Fischer. Cambridge: Cambridge University Press, 2002.
Donaldon, Margaret. *Human Minds: An Exploration*. London: Penguin Books, 1991.
Dreyfus, George. "Is Compassion an Emotion? A Cross-Cultural Exploration of Mental Typologies." In *Visions of Compassion: Western Scientists and Tibetan Buddhists Examine Human Nature*, edited by Richard J. Davidson and Anne Harrington. New York: Oxford University Press, 2002.
Gallagher, Shaun. "Body Image and Body Schema: A Conceptual Clarification." *The Journal of Mind and Behavior* 7 (1986): 541–554.
———. "The Practice of Mind: Theory, Simulation, or Primary Interaction?" *Journal*

of Consciousness Studies 8.5–7. (2001): 83–108. Also in *Between Ourselves: Second Person Issues in the Study of Consciousness,* edited by Evan Thompson. Thorverton, UK: Imprint Academic.

Gallup, Gordon, Jr., "Can Animals Empathize? Yes." *Scientific American* 9 (1998): 65–75.

Gould, Stephen Jay. *Rocks of Ages: Science and Religion in the Fullness of Life.* New York: Ballantine, 1999.

Gupta, Bina. *The Disinterested Witness: A Fragment of Advaita Vedanta Phenomenology.* Evanston, Ill.: Northwestern University Press, 1998.

Husserl, Edmund. *Analyses Concerning Passive and Active Synthesis: Lectures on Transcendental Logic.* Translated by Anthony J. Steinbock. Dordrecht: Kluwer Academic Publishers, 2001.

Hut, Piet. "Conclusion: Life as a Laboratory." In *Buddhism and Science: Breaking New Ground,* ed. B. Alan Wallace. New York: Columbia University Press, 2003.

Johnson, Mark. *Moral Imagination: Implications of Cognitive Science for Ethics.* Chicago: University of Chicago Press, 1993.

Levenson, Robert W., and Anna M. Reuf. "Empathy: A Physiological Substrate." *Journal of Personality and Social Psychology* 63 (1992): 234–246.

Lutz, A., J. P. Lachaux, J. Martinerie, and F. J. Varela. "Guiding the Study of Brain Dynamics by Using First-Person Data: Synchrony Patterns Correlate with Ongoing Conscious States During a Simple Visual Task." *Proceedings of the National Academy of Sciences USA* 99 (2002): 1586–1591.

Lutz, Antoine, and Evan Thompson. "Neurophenomenology: Integrating Subjective Experience and Brain Dynamics in the Neuroscience of Consciousness." *Journal of Consciousness Studies* 10 (2003): 31–52.

Marbach, Eduard. "How to Study Consciousness Phenomenologically, or Quite a Lot Comes to Mind." *Journal of the British Society for Phenomenology* 19.3 (1998): 252–268.

McGee, Michael. *Transformations of Mind: Philosophy as Spiritual Practice.* Cambridge: Cambridge University Press, 2000.

McGeer, Victoria. "Psycho-Practice, Psycho-Theory and the Contrastive Case of Autism." *Journal of Consciousness Studies* 8.5–7 (2001): 109–132, also in *Between Ourselves: Second Person Issues in the Study of Consciousness,* edited by Evan Thompson. Thorverton, UK: Imprint Academic, 2001.

Newberg, Andrew, Eugene D'Aquili, and Vince Rause. *Why God Won't Go Away: Brain Science and the Biology of Belief.* New York: Ballantine Books, 2001.

Oyama, Susan. *The Ontogeny of Information: Developmental Systems and Evolution.* 2nd ed. Durham, N.C.: Duke University Press, 2002.

Oyama, Susan, Paul E. Griffiths, and Russell D. Gray, eds. *Cycles of Contingency: Developmental Systems and Evolution.* Cambridge, Mass.: MIT Press, 2001.

Pitkin, Annabella. "Scandalous Ethics: Infinite Presence with Suffering." *Journal of Consciousness Studies* 8.5–7 (2001): 232–246. Also in *Between Ourselves: Second Person Issues in the Study of Consciousness,* ed. Evan Thompson. Thorverton, UK: Imprint Academic.

Povinelli, Daniel J. "Can Animals Empathize? Maybe Not." *Scientific American* 9 (1998): 65–75.

Preston, Stephanie, and Frans B. M. de Waal. "Empathy: Its Ultimate and Proximate Bases." *Behavioral and Brain Sciences* 25 (2002): 1–72.

Shantideva. *The Way of the Bodhisattva*. Translated by The Padmakara Translation Group. Boston: Shambala, 1997.

Stein, Edith. *On the Problem of Empathy*. Translated by Waltraut Stein. The Hague: Martinus Nijhoff, 1964.

Taylor, Eugene. *William James: On Consciousness beyond the Margin*. Princeton: Princeton University Press, 1996.

Thompson, Evan, ed. *Between Ourselves: Second Person Issues in the Study of Consciousness*. Thorverton, UK: Imprint Academic, 2001.

Thompson, Evan, and Francisco J. Varela. "Radical Embodiment: Neural Dynamics and Consciousness." *Trends in Cognitive Sciences* 5 (2001): 418–425.

Tomasello, Michael. *The Cultural Origins of Human Cognition*. Cambridge: Harvard University Press, 1999.

Varela, Francisco J., and Jonathan Shear, eds. *The View from Within: First-Person Approaches to the Study of Consciousness*. Thorverton, UK: Imprint Academic, 1999.

Varela, Francisco J., Evan Thompson, and Eleanor Rosch. *The Embodied Mind: Cognitive Science and Human Experience*. Cambridge, Mass.: MIT Press, 1991.

Vetlesen, Arne Johan. *Perception, Empathy, and Judgment: An Inquiry into the Preconditions of Moral Performance*. University Park, Penn.: Pennsylvania State University Press, 1994.

Wallace, B. Alan. "Introduction: Buddhism and Science." In *Buddhism and Science: Breaking New Ground*, edited by B. Alan Wallace. New York: Columbia University Press, 2003.

———, ed. *Buddhism and Science: Breaking New Ground*. New York: Columbia University Press, 2003.

———. "The Intersubjective Worlds of Science and Religion." This volume.

Zahavi, Dan. *Self-Awareness and Alterity: A Phenomenological Investigation*. Evanston, Ill.: Northwestern University Press, 1999.

———. "Beyond Empathy: Phenomenological Approaches to Intersubjectivity." *Journal of Consciousness Studies* 8.5–7 (2001): 151–167. Also in *Between Ourselves: Second Person Issues in the Study of Consciousness*, ed. Evan Thompson. Thorverton, UK: Imprint Academic, 2001.

14

Uneasy Alliances: The Faith Factor in Medicine; the Health Factor in Religion

Anne Harrington

What does medicine have to do with religion, and vice versa? In the modern era, we have become accustomed to hearing a number of specific kinds of responses to this question. One of the oldest and most familiar of these points out that, even though medicine as a methodology and technology has functioned over the past century as a highly successful secularizing force in our society, nevertheless illness and healing remain imperfectly secularized experiences in our culture. Ill people continue to be tempted by the promises and consolations of religion, and doctors should be respectful of that fact. Pastoral care workers—the argument concludes—thus need to have a respected, if modest place, in hospital wards. The vision of the relationship between religion and medicine offered is of nonoverlapping spheres of complementary expertise. Pastors have the right to take care of the soul of the sick person; and they should leave physicians to take care of his or her body.[1]

A second, more recent but still familiar argument is more confrontational. It suggests that modern medicine not only ignores religious and spiritual needs; it itself actually functions as a spiritually corrosive force for many patients. The argument here is that, even as it has had many dazzling technological successes, one overall effect of much of modern medicine has been to dehumanize the experience of illness; turn human suffering into something equivalent to the breakdown of an automobile; and transform the doctor-patient relationship into an alienating, objectifying, utilitarian exchange.[2]

In 1990, the *New York Times* essayist and literary critic Anatole Broyard—dying of prostate cancer—wrote a series of moving meditations on his experience with the world of high-tech health care that seemed to many to get to the heart of the matter. "[T]he real narrative of dying now is that you die in a machine," he began—and the irony of course was that none of those machines were going to do Broyard much good, and both he and his doctors knew it. And yet they—and, in a sense, he—persisted in subjecting him to one high-tech test after another because in a medical culture where death means that medicine has "failed" to do its job, then there are no alternatives to the ritual of cure. The result, though, was that Broyard as a person— his experience of illness—was rendered irrelevant and invisible. Musing on this fact, Broyard wrote:

> I wouldn't demand a lot of my doctor's time. I just wish he would
> brood upon my situation for perhaps five minutes, that he would
> give me his whole mind at least once, be bonded with me for a brief
> space, survey my soul as well as my flesh to get at my illness, for
> each man is ill in his own way. . . . Just as he orders blood tests and
> bone scans of my body, I'd like my doctor to scan me, to grope for
> my spirit as well as my prostate. Without such recognition, I am
> nothing but my illness.[3]

Now: usually the argument that medicine needs to find some way to make room for the soul as well as the body is made on ethical and existential grounds. The people who make the argument usually are not part of the medical establishment but engage with it from one or another outside perspective—as patients, or pastors, or bioethicists. They disagree on many of the nuances of their arguments, but by and large all of them tend to agree that a big problem with medicine today is that it has, so to speak, too much science and too little soul.

The past ten years, however, have seen the rise of a very different argument that is beginning to destabilize our accustomed ways of thinking about the needs of the soul as opposed to those of the body. Advocates of this new argument begin by declaring that the critics of modern biomedicine are essentially right: modern medicine does need to make more room in its practices for the life of the soul. But then they make an unfamiliar move. Instead of blaming modern medicine's spiritual crisis on its obsession with laboratory data, they insist that the laboratory actually has vindicated the importance of the soul in clinical practice. More precisely, they point to new data from epidemiology, from clinical trials, and from experimental research that, they say, strongly suggest that an active religious life can bolster one's health and mitigate the effects of disease. Medicine thus needs to more fully embrace the soul, they say, but not just because it would be nice to do so (although it would be), or because patients have a right to their beliefs and it is therefore professionally advisable to offer them that opportunity (although that is also true). It needs to do so, rather, simply because religion turns out to be *good medicine*.

The argument is new, but, in the span of a few short years, it has begun to eclipse the others. With more than a decade of research now to draw on,[4] the claim that religion is good medicine has been prominently trumpeted in the popular press—most recently (November 2003) in a cover story of *Newsweek*, but before then in high-profile journals ranging from the *New York Times* to *The Atlantic Monthly* to *Psychology Today* to *Readers' Digest*. There also exist a growing number of popular paperback digestions of the arguments: *The Faith Factor*, by Dale Matthews; *Timeless Healing*, by Herbert Benson; *The Healing Power of Faith*, by Harold Koenig; *God, Faith, and Health*, by Jeff Levin.[5]

On the academic front, the last several years have seen the establishment of a series of university-based research centers on the topic: the George Washington Center Institute for Spirituality and Health; the Mind-Body Medicine Institute at Harvard University; the Center for Spirituality and Healing at the University of Minnesota; the Interfaith Health Program at Emory University; the Center for the Study of Religion/Spirituality and Health at Duke Medical School. Medical education is also being affected. Today, more than seventy of the United States' 125 medical schools—from Harvard to Stanford—have integrated discussion of the religion-health connection into their curricula; still others offer continuing education courses on that theme.[6]

Energizing many if not all of these various activities is a vision of a new kind of relationship emerging between medicine and religion. No longer, we are told, do we need to confine pastors and doctors to their own distinct spheres of expertise. Nor do we need any longer to see them as motivated by values that are, at bottom, antagonistic to each other. The discovery of religion's therapeutic powers exposes the lie behind tired old Cartesian oppositions between spirit and body that previously had helped fuel such feelings of antagonism. In so doing, it opens the door to a new era of cooperation between clerics and medics, an alliance without historical precedent.

The Anatomy of the Argument

That all duly noted, it is still not at all obvious what all this adds up to. What does it mean to insist that religion is good medicine? What kind of alliance between medicine and religion is this going to be? What kinds of assumptions does it make about both what medicine is and what religion is, and how we should conceptualize their proper relations? Before any kind of answer can be hazarded to these questions, it is necessary to better understand the anatomy of the argument itself: the empirical basis is for the claims, the assumptions within which they function and how they relate to other medical and theological traditions. When we do look more carefully, we quickly discover something important: that we actually have here to do with, not one, but four discrete claims, each with historical roots in a discrete culture of research in the biomedical and behavioral sciences, and each with a more or less intimate or distant relationship to one or another religious culture. While the argument that religion is good for one's health is generally seen as the common conclusion of all four claims, on a deeper level, it is actually not clear that the four arguments, taken together, add up to a fully coherent whole. There is more complexity and ambiguity lurking in and between the spaces of these four arguments than at first meets the eye.

Let us therefore look at the four arguments in turn.

Going to Church Increases Longevity and Enhances Health

The origins of this claim lie in epidemiological work that began in the late 1960s: a time of great medical interest specifically in rising incidence of heart disease in the United States, and what lifestyle and environmental factors might be contributing to it. Out of this work, *social isolation* emerged as one of the new big watchwords. Some research suggested, for example, that living in traditional close-knit communities acted as a protection against heart disease—and, possibly, other common forms of morbidity and mortality. Other research suggested that more isolated people within a community tended to be sicker and to die earlier than those who were more socially embedded.[7] In the context of the time—dominated by all sorts of talk about the alienation of the American worker and the breakdown of traditional community and the family—the interpretation seemed straightforward. Heart disease was on the rise because we were literally a nation of broken, lonely hearts.[8]

From the beginning, epidemiologists had included membership in a religious community as one independent variable among many that might let them assess a person's relative degree of social embeddedness or isolation. This work did not originally see itself as asking whether or not religion was good medicine. After a while, though, it became increasingly clear that one of the variables that seemed particularly highly associated with protection against mortality and morbidity—especially in the elderly—was being a member of a church or other religious community. Then over some twenty years, beginning in the 1970s, more than eighteen different epidemiological studies were published collectively making the case that, when all other variables were controlled for, an active religious life was independently associated with lower blood pressure, less hypertension, fewer health problems generally in old age, and even overall longer life. [9]

What might be the reason for this? Initially, the tendency still was to reduce church going to social support. Churches, people seemed to want to say, are good for one's health because they provide *really good community*: they reduce stress, they look after their members, they tend to frown on unhealthy behaviors like excessive use of alcohol and drugs, and—in being publicly concerned about their members' health—they might even tend to create a culture in which individuals seek medical assistance earlier than they otherwise might have.

Nevertheless, not everyone was satisfied with this essentially reductionist understanding of why church going might be good for one's health. In 1996, an Israeli epidemiologist named Jeremy Kark and his colleagues looked at mortality rates in a cluster of secular and a cluster of religious kibbutzim between 1970 and 1985, and found that mortality in the secular kibbutzim was nearly twice that of mortality on the religious kibbutzim. At the same time, the authors said, "There was no difference in social support or frequency of social contact between religious and secular kibbutzim." The implications were clear: social support alone could not account for the health benefits of a religious over a secular lifestyle.[10]

How else might one make scientific sense of those health benefits? We come now to the next two research traditions concerned with the health benefits of religion. Both of these are explicitly psychobiological in nature—concerned with the ways in which changes in the mind might affect the body in health and disease—but one is focused on the effects of *practice* and the other is focused on the effects of *attitude*. Again, I take each in turn.

Meditation Reduces Stress

Advocates of this claim point out that virtually all religions advocate or facilitate opportunities for adherents to participate regularly in contemplative activities like focused prayer and meditation. These practices, they say, enhance health by reducing stress, which, when chronic, increases one's susceptibility to any number of both common and serious maladies.[11] What is the evidence that meditation and similar contemplative practices reduce stress and thereby enhance health? The roots of the claim lie culturally in the rise of medical interest in the claims for enhanced health and performance being made by adherents of popular mantra-based Hindu meditative practices like transcendental meditation (TM), originally developed for modern Westerners in the late 1950s by the Maharishi Maresh Yogi of India. A turning point in the cultural fortunes of TM came when the cardiologist Herbert Benson at Harvard in the 1970s began to argue that all people who practiced this technique experienced a characteristic set of physiological changes that could fairly be contrasted, point by point, with those associated with the well-characterized stress response.[12]

Benson called the physiological changes produced by meditation the "relaxation response," and went on (to the displeasure of the Maharishi) to insist that there was nothing about TM itself as a unique practice that was health enhancing. All the health benefits seen in people who practice TM could be elicited using any number of meditative techniques practiced by religious traditions around the world. All of them, in different ways, had recognized and cultivated the existence of this endogenous stress-buster each of us has inside ourselves: the relaxation response.

Beginning in the 1980s, Benson found both a comrade and, to a certain extent, a rival in yoga and meditation teacher, Jon Kabat-Zinn (whose credentials included a Ph.D. from MIT). In 1979, Kabat-Zinn began to teach patients a type of meditative practice that was derived, not from Hindu-based mantra practices but from a certain attention-stabilizing technique cultivated in Theravada Buddhism called *vipassana*. More difficult to theorize as a "stress reduction program" than Benson's relaxation response (the practice can be quite taxing),[13] nevertheless, Kabat-Zinn's Stress Reduction Clinic at the University of Massachusetts Medical School in Worcester, Massachusetts, proved highly popular as an alternative vision of the therapeutic power of meditation, particularly after it was featured in the widely viewed 1993 PBS television documentary hosted by Bill Moyers, *Healing and the Mind*. In books and articles, Kabat-Zinn and his colleagues claimed that mindfulness practice not only helped chronic patients cope better with their disorders; it actually improved their health and resistance to disease, perhaps by strengthening the immune system.[14]

With all their differences, Benson and Kabat-Zinn shared a fundamentally secularizing vision of meditative practice: the therapeutic benefits of meditation, they insisted, could be gained without any commitment to, or even real knowledge of, the Asian religious traditions that spawned them. Not only did one not have to be Buddhist to meditate; one did not even have to be religious. At the same time, if one *were* religious, and one's religion happened not to be Buddhist or Hindu, then there was almost certainly a therapeutically satisfactory meditative tradition in one's own faith to which one could turn. In interviews, Benson has talked about how, when he first began spreading the word about meditation—or what he was now calling the "relaxation response"—he was "startled at the excitement among the religious pros" in the Christian community. They told him that, in introducing them to the relaxation response, he had reminded them of the power of such practices in their own tradition. "'This is why I came into church work in the first place,' said one, 'and I'd lost it.'"[15]

Religious Faith Triggers Health-Enhancing Placebo Effects

Meditation is good for one's health, and it does not matter what faith tradition is used as the basis for the practice. The larger argument, however, does not stop there. It goes on to claim that *belief or faith* is good for one's health—and it *does not matter* what you believe. From a medical point of view, all beliefs in a higher power are equal, because—or so it is assumed—they demonstrate equivalent capacities to marshal the body's endogenous healing abilities.

As Benson has put it in his book, *Timeless Healing*:

I describe "God" with a capital "G" in this book but nevertheless hope readers will understand that I am referring to all the deities of the Judeo-Christian, Buddhist, Muslim, and Hindu traditions, to gods and goddesses, as well as to all spirits worshipped and beloved by humans all over the world and throughout history. In my scientific observations, I have observed that no matter what name you give the Infinite Absolute you worship, no matter what theology you ascribe to, the results of believing in God are the same.[16]

What is the basis for this claim? The historical roots here actually go back to the arguments of certain new Christian movements that emerged in the United States in the late nineteenth century, and that placed a great emphasis on the healing ministry dimension of the original gospel message. For these movements—sometimes called "mind cure," sometimes "new thought," sometimes "Christian science," and sometimes "practical Christianity"—healing was one of the promised fruits of faith. Again and again, they recalled, the Jesus of the Gospels says to those who seek him out, "Your faith has healed you."[17] Followers of "mind cure" thus aimed to deliberately cultivate their faith (through chanting, visualizations, refusing to entertain negative thoughts, etc.) in the service of health. William James, observing the movements at the turn of the twentieth century, described them in the following way:

> The blind have been made to see, the halt to walk; lifelong invalids have had their health restored. . . . One hears of the "Gospel of Relaxation," of the "Don't Worry Movement," of people who repeat to themselves, "Youth, health, vigor!"[18]

Not yet taken seriously by medicine, nevertheless the message of mind-cure broadened its audience enormously when it was incorporated into the popular ministry of the unorthodox Methodist minister Norman Vincent Peale, who taught millions of Americans to believe in the "power of positive thinking."[19] In every one of the many books he published on positive thinking over the years, Peale promised his followers the gifts of renewed health and vitality. Here is a typical passage from one of them:

> Smith has never again had need to revert to the habit of taking tablets. He learned the amazing power of positive thinking to heal. Let me repeat. The technique is to believe that you are going to be better, believe that positive thinking is going to work for you, and remedial forces actually will be set in motion.[20]

Ironically, given his stated commitment to framing the power of positive thinking as fundamental to the Christian message, Peale actually probably spent more time than any other twentieth-century figure in the mind-cure movement downplaying the need to commit to any specific Christian or other specific faith tradition in order to enjoy the healing fruits of faith. This quasi-secularization of the healing power of faith would be completed some twenty years later, in the early 1970s, when the editor of *The New Republic*, Norman Cousins, wrote in *The New England Journal of Medicine* about his remarkable experiment in self-healing from a potentially fatal illness. His method involved deliberate cultivation of positive attitude, and his description of his experimental treatment—written for a medical audience—represented "faith" as a potent mental state with specific health-enhancing biochemistry.[21]

The combined legacies of Peale and Cousins have in our own time created conditions in which it seems natural to think of faith—religious or otherwise—as a key that unlocks the body's "natural" pharmacology cabinet. Today, there is a growing tendency to conceptualize the specific healing effects of belief—any kind of belief—through reference to what is known about the physiological changes associated with a *particular* kind of belief: not in God but in medicine and its treatments. This is the kind of belief that results in perceived and measurable changes in bodily functioning known as the "placebo effect."

For a long time, the placebo effect was defined as the subjective (but not truly curative) response that gullible patients have to inactive "sugar pills." In this understanding, evoking the placebo effect was tolerated (just barely) as a form of very occasional benevolent deception that doctors might practice on patients who couldn't be otherwise helped or didn't really have anything wrong with them.[22] Since the late 1970s, however, the placebo effect has been slowly rehabilitated as a true physiological phenomenon. The new ruling wisdom is that those infamous sugar pills—or, rather, the patient's faith in those pills—triggers changes in biochemistry that in turn lead to true healing processes. New brain imaging studies are being published that show, for example, startling similarities between the brain changes seen in patients given morphine and those seen in patients who received plain saline solution but believed they had been given morphine.[23]

The collective effect of the placebo-effect work has been to turn the healing power of belief—including and perhaps especially religious belief—into an entity that has nothing to do with God's compassion or Providence, and everything to do with certain intriguing realities of human psychology and physiology. There is an innate capacity for our bodies to try to bring into being, to the best of their ability, the optimistic scenarios in which we fervently believe. And nothing has contributed more to facilitating this innate capacity, some people have gone on to say, than belief in God's capacity to heal us. Indeed, it is not unlikely that we specifically evolved with the "wiring" (the term was originally used by Herbert Benson) to believe in some kind of beneficent divine power that can heal us, because such wiring kept our ancestors healthy in a time before there were many, if any, truly effective medical treatments available.[24]

Prayer Works

The idea that one might be able to explain religious faith healings by reference to the secular power of the placebo effect stands in striking tension to the final piece of the argument that religion is good for one's health. In fact, the last claim stands in tension with all three of the claims I have reviewed so far. This is because this last claim, a priori, rejects the relevance of all naturalistic explanations for the health benefits of religion. This is what this last claim says: prayer works.

Prayer works, not just because it provides a sense of social connection, or reduces stress, or evokes the body's own endogenous healing capacities through the psychobiology of the placebo effect. No, prayer itself changes people's health in ways that are independent of all of those other factors—indeed, in ways that seem to operate independently of all known psychological or psychobiological human mechanisms in general.

How do we know this? We know this because, when seriously ill patients are randomized into a "prayer group" and a "control group," there is some evidence that the sick people who are prayed by for by others ("intercessory prayer") improve more quickly or have fewer complications associated with their recovery than those in the control group. This happens even when the prayed-for people allegedly do not know whether or not they are in the "active treatment" group, and even (in at least one study) when they do not know they are being prayed for at all.

Like the other three claims I have briefly reviewed, there is a larger history to this one. It goes back to the rise of a vision of statistics as a powerful new tool in a position to resolve long-standing questions of a policy and social nature.[25] Specifically, back in the 1870s, Darwin's cousin, Francis Galton, rather cheekily proposed to use statistics to address a theological question: did God continue to answer prayers in the modern world? Noting that the Anglican liturgy included formal prayers for the long life of the reigning monarch, Galton's basic idea was to compare the longevity of members of the British royal family to that of other people of privilege, to see whether the outpouring of prayers to God on behalf of the former actually made a difference to their life span. What he found was that the royals were "literally the shortest-lived of all who have the advantage of affluence," even when deaths by accident or violence were excluded. Taking his investigations further revealed that, when the life spans of eminent members of the clergy were compared to those of eminent lawyers and physicians, the clergy—assumed by him to be the most prayerful group—also turned out to be "the shortest lived of the three" (see Table 14.1).[26]

For Galton and the circle of naturalistic thinkers with which he was associated, these results were effectively all a good joke. The clergy of the time objected that one cannot test God in this way, or reduce prayer's degree of

TABLE 14.1 Mean Age Attained by Males of Various Classes Who Had Survived Their 30th Year, from 1758 to 1843

	In Number	Average	Eminent Men
Members of Royal houses	97	64.04	
Clergy	945	69.49	66.42
Lawyers	294	68.14	66.51
Medical Profession	244	67.31	67.07
English aristocracy	1,179	67.31	
Gentry	1,632	70.22	
Trade and commerce	513	68.74	
Officers in the Royal Navy	366	68.40	
English literature and science	395	67.55	65.22
Officers of the Army	659	67.07	
Fine Arts	239	65.96	64.74

Note: Deaths by accident are excluded.

Source: Galton, Francis. "Statistical inquiries into the efficacy of prayer." Fortnightly Review, 12 (1872): 125–135.

efficacy to a number. Whatever the validity of this theological objection, the idea that prayer's efficacy should in principle be scientifically testable has persisted in our own time. Today, however, it is most vigorously defended, *not* by those with a secular agenda or an anticlerical ax to grind, but by people who see themselves as working on behalf of God and faith. God's reality and power will be vindicated by the very same scientific methodologies that, for so long, have had the effect of undermining faith in both.

The specific scientific methodology that is used is one that was originally designed to control for the influence of unwanted psychological factors when testing for the efficacy of drugs: the randomized placebo-controlled clinical trial, The hope is that this method will allow researchers to distinguish all known natural factors that might broadly cause religion to be good for one's health from the supernatural effects of prayer.

The best-known study in this vein is that of Randolph Byrd, who studied 393 patients admitted to the coronary care unit of the San Francisco General Hospital.[27] The patients were randomly assigned into two groups, one of which was prayed for and another that was not (there was no attempt to stop family members and others from praying for the people in the control group, leading to rather odd discussions about the effects of "background" prayer and "prayer dosage"). The so-called intercessors or "pray-ers" were all self-identified born-again Christians who already claimed to pray daily and to go to church. Their assignment was to pray daily for a speedy recovery of "their" patients with no complications.

The results showed no difference in the speed of recovery between the two groups, but Byrd found that, on 6 out of 26 kinds of possible complications, the prayed-for patients did better on a statistically significant level than the controls, and the controls did not do better than the prayed-for groups on any of the measures.[28]

In 1999, a Kansas-based researcher, William Harris, claimed to have replicated Byrd's findings with a larger population sample. Significantly, perhaps, the Harris replication actually did not find improvement on any of the specific measures of improvement identified by Byrd, but rather found improvement on other measures.[29] Currently, Herbert Benson's lab at Harvard University is attempting what is being touted as a definitive replication of the Byrd study, using multiple sites.

It should be said that this final piece of the larger argument for the health benefits of religion does share with the first three pieces a clear pragmatic orientation, at least in some of its renderings. Some insist that the most important thing to take from the research is the alleged fact that prayer works; the theological and metaphysical implications of this fact, they say, can all be worked out later. Thus, one of the scientists involved in the studies, Dale Matthews, exhorted a 1997 graduating class of medical students to get ready, because—he said—"the medicine of the future is going to be prayer and Prozac."[30]

Most people, though, clearly see that much more is at stake than a change in clinical practices, and some are not prepared to defer the larger discussion. Again, the specific issues that are at stake set this final piece of the larger argument for the health benefits of religion in a distinctly uneasy relationship to the first three claims. Proponents of the other three claims are always careful to leave open the *option* of God's reality, but the force of their arguments does not inherently depend on whether or not God really exists. Matters here are different. If prayer works—works in a way that cannot be reduced to the placebo effect, social support, or stress reduction—then God, or at least some kind of divine energy, as Larry Dossey has qualified it,[31] must both exist and be active in the world. This is why one finds the prayer studies being discussed, not just within medicine, but within forums concerned to document ways in which science is finding evidence for the existence of God. There it sits beside reviews of the anthropic principle from physics (the idea that the universe was deliberately constructed to support intelligent life), alleged fundamental problems with evolutionary theory and evidence for Creation, and presentations of the evidence for near-death and out-of-body experiences.[32]

There is another important way in which this final claim for the health benefits of religion differs from the other three. The other three, implicitly at least, have adopted a view of religion or spirituality that sees itself as theologically neutral. It is a view that assumes that a distinction can be made between the personal experiences that people have of the divine—what is generally called "spirituality"—and the specific theological systems within which they interpret those experiences. It then goes on to insist that none of those systems can be judged better than the others, because all of them work equally well in giving people the health benefits they want. Though the argument rarely is so explicit as to actually say so, what we are meant to understand is that, when religion becomes medicine, it is no longer about truth; it is about utility.

Matters are different when it comes to discussions about the efficacy of prayer. The fact that most of the most widely publicized studies to date have tested the efficacy of *Christian* prayer has not been lost on at least some people (not withstanding that one prominent 1998 study that claimed to find positive results was self-consciously interfaith in its study design).[33] One Christian fundamentalist Web site devoted to posting evidence from science for the reality of the Judeo-Christian God has crowed: "No other religion has succeeded in scientifically demonstrating that prayer to their God has any efficacy in healing." The Web site authors go on:

> Obviously, science has demonstrated in three separate studies the efficacy of Christian prayer in medical studies. There is no "scientific" (non-spiritual) explanation for the *cause* of the medical effects demonstrated in these studies. The only logical, but not testable, explanation is that God exists and answers the prayers of Christians.[34]

Better Health through Religion: What Kind of Alliance Is This?

The claim that religion is good for one's health is itself neither good news nor bad; neither to be celebrated nor rejected out of hand. My aim here has been to be analytical rather than polemical (there is enough polemic in this field already). In the first instance, I have wanted to insist that the four working parts of the argument actually add up to a far more unwieldy whole than its more uncritical advocates generally realize. In the course of this essay, I have already reviewed some of the specific instabilities and largely unanalyzed agendas lurking in one or another of the individual pieces.

Let me see what I can now say about the effort nevertheless to promote these four different arguments in the service of the common, larger claim for better health through religion. What should we think? In asking this question, I do not mean, what should we think of the argument as *medical science* (i.e., what do we think of the data, how good do we find the study designs);[35] nor what should we think of it as *theology* (i.e., how consistent is the vision of religion as good medicine with other understandings of the value of religion),[36] but rather what should we think of it as a *cultural vision of a new sort of alliance* between religion and medicine. What are we signing on to, if we sign on to this alliance?

I began this essay by observing that there already exist in our society several important ways of conceptualizing relations between religion and medicine in the modern world. These other perspectives are grounded, not in the authority of scientific data but in authority that draws on the force of certain ethical and existential commitments. Is the claim that religion is good for one's health compatible with an ongoing commitment to those ethical and existential commitments? If not—if the new perspective on the health benefits of religion is as likely as not to eclipse older perspectives on proper relations between medicine and religion—then what has been gained and what lost?

Many of the advocates for the health benefits of religion suggest that the new scientific findings simply add further weight to the ethical and existential concerns that have been the more traditional focus of dialogue between medicine and religion. The authors of the recent (2002) *Handbook of Religion and Health* (a review of more than 1,600 studies on the religion-health connection) explicitly identify the moral timeliness of all this work by noting that

> Patients are caught . . . wishing to have their diseases diagnosed and treated competently with the latest technology, yet having social, psychological, and spiritual needs that are being ignored because of an increasingly streamlined health care system that overemphasizes the physical over the spiritual. . . . Scientific medicine has been magnificently successful but is challenged to figure out how the ancient and venerable tradition of "doctor as healer" fits in and how to connect practically at the bedside with the way most human beings deal psychologically with life-threatening disease, which is broadly spiritual/religious.[37]

These authors believe that these new data from scientific medicine can be used to overcome the current ethical and existential limitations of clinical practice. Is the claim credible? I am skeptical. I am skeptical, not because I resist inherently the project of investigating the health benefits of religion, but simply because in the end that project is all still about more research and more therapy. Those people who have seen in religion a source of values and practices capable of responding to the spiritual inadequacies of modern medicine have consistently done so first by pointing out that Western medicine falls short existentially and ethically because it judges all things according to a utilitarian calculus of health; one that has little if any room for other issues that matter to sick people. In fact, Anatole Broyard did not want his doctor to tell him he should pray because it might help his cancer, or that he should consider going to church for his health (even assuming—as in fact was not the case—that he was a religious man). What he wanted was for his doctor to stop trying to fix him and instead to spend a little time beholding him as he was—listening to what was in his soul, listening to his efforts to make meaning of his experience.

Historically, as we know, the pastoral act of listening and finding sense in suffering has been seen as the job of the clergy. In the proposed new alliance between medicine and religion whose contours we are just glimpsing, however, it is not clear that the clergy will still have any unique domain of expertise.

What seems instead more likely is that the same utilitarian therapeutic criteria will be used to judge the value of practices for the soul (such as listening to confession) and practices for the body. To hold their own in this new alliance, clergy may feel compelled to learn the language of t-cell counts and brain biochemistry—and, indeed, at least some of them are beginning to do this.

I entitled this essay "Uneasy Alliances." The remarks I have made above should make clear why clergy or other kinds of religious practitioners might have grounds to feel uneasy about the call for a new kind of alliance between medicine and religion. I also think, however, that there is reason for medical science to feel uneasy about it. Its authority and values may triumph, but it runs the risk that both it and society as a whole will look back in time and judge that victory a pyrrhic one.

The reason is that there is surely something wrongheaded about supposing that the ethical and existential limitations of modern medicine can be met by it simply becoming an even more expansive version of what it has always been; by extending its "therapeutic ethos"[38] into areas that had not previously been conceived as "medical." There is really no reason to suppose that the human institution of medical science will become more "spiritual" if we ask it to assess the value of spiritual and religious human experiences using methodologies that were developed for quite different ends. There is every reason instead to suppose that those human experiences will simply become "medicalized"; translated into terms that—ironically enough—are likely in the end to feel every bit as alienating to patients as the high-tech and impersonal medical practices that previously left no room for the needs of the soul. Even *if* there is merit to the claim that certain kinds of religious practices can enhance one's health, the needs of what we call the soul will never be identical with the needs of the body.

The hard ethical and existential conversation about modern medicine and how it can best act to serve human flourishing and human values remains unfinished. It would be tragic if, in our pursuit of yet another health-enhancing elixir, it were to be prematurely cut off. To continue to pursue that conversation well, however, our society needs to insist on its right to continue to test the robustness of other perspectives on the most fruitful relations between medicine and religion. Above all, we do not want to foreclose for ourselves, even implicitly, the almost certain possibility that there are values in life worth protecting beyond the utilitarian, and perspectives worth defending that cannot be translated into the language of the laboratory and statistics.

NOTES

1. Norman Autton, *Pastoral Care in Hospitals* (London: Society for Promoting Christian Knowledge, 1968). Raymond Carey, *Hospital Chaplains: Who Needs Them?* (St. Louis: Colorado Health & Hospital Association, 1972).

2. A lot of the scholarly arguments in this vein over the past two decades have come from medical anthropology. One early classic work making this argument is Arthur Kleinman's *The Illness Narratives: Suffering, Healing, and the Human Condition* (New York: Basic Books, 1988). Also influential and persuasive in its approach is Arthur Frank's *The Wounded Storyteller: Body, Illness, and Ethics* (Chicago: University of Chicago Press, 1995).

3. Anatole Broyard, *Intoxicated by My Illness and Other Writings on Life and Death* (Greenwich, Conn.: Fawcett Books, 1993).

4. For an exhaustive overview of data-based articles on this topic, see Harold G. Koenig, Michael E. McCullough, and David B. Larson, *Handbook of Religion and Health* (New York: Oxford University Press, 2000). While I was revising this essay for publication, a colleague sent me a special January 2003 section of *American Psychologist*, with three densely referenced articles devoted to "Spirituality, Religion, and Health" as an "emerging research field": see *American Psychologist* 58 (January 2003): 24–74. A sampling of recent editorials in the medical press (both arguing for the relevance of the research for clinical practice, and warning against premature or unwarranted conclusions) includes A. J. Slomski, "Should Doctors Prescribe Religion?" *Med Econ* 7.1 (2000), 145–59; C. Marwick, "Should Physicians Prescribe Prayer for Health? Spiritual Aspects of Well-Being Considered," *JAMA* (1995): 273; 1561–1562; H. G. Koenig, E. Idler, S. Kasl, et al., "Religion, Spirituality, and Medicine: A Rebuttal to Skeptics," *International Journal Psychiatry Medicine* 29 (1999): 123–131; R. Sloan, E. Bagiella, L. Van de Creek, et al., "Should Physicians Prescribe Religious Activities?" *New England Journal of Medicine* (2000); L. Gundersen, "Faith and Healing," *Annual International Medicine* 132 (2000): 169–172.

5. Dale Matthews (with Connie Clark), *The Faith Factor: Proof of the Healing Power of Prayer* (New York: Penguin, 1999); Herbert Benson (with Marg Stark), *Timeless Healing: The Power and Biology of Belief* (New York: Scribner, 1996); Harold G. Koenig, *The Healing Power of Faith* (New York: Simon and Schuster, 1999); Jeff Levin, *God, Faith and Health: Exploring the Spirituality-Healing Connection* (New York: John Wiley and Sons, 2001).

6. Herbert Benson's version at Harvard University, which began in 1995 and has regularly attracted upwards of one thousand people, is probably the best known of these. The most recent description of the syllabus for his course can be viewed online at http://cme.med.harvard.edu/syl/benson.htm.

7. Some classic reference points in this literature include: L. F. Berkman and S. L. Syme, "Social Networks, Host Resistance and Mortality: A Nine Year Follow-Up Study of Alameda County Residents," *American Journal of Epidemiology* 109 (1979): 186–204; J. G. Bruhn and S. Wolf, *The Roseto Story* (Norman, Okla.: University of Oklahoma Press, 1979); S. Wolf, "Predictors of Myocardial Infarction over a Span of 30 years in Roseto, Pennsylvania," *Integrative Physiological and Behavioral Science*, 27.3 (1992): 246–257; K. R. Landis et al., "Social Relationships and Health," *Science* 241.4865 (1998): 540–545.

8. See, among others, James J. Lynch, *Broken Heart: The Medical Consequences of Loneliness* (New York: Basic Books, 1985).

9. For example, W. J. Strawbridge, R. D. Cohen, and G. A. Kaplan, "Frequent Attendance at Religious Services and Mortality over 28 Years," *AJPH* 87 (1997): 957–961.

10. "Mortality in 11 secular kibbutzim between 1970 and 1985 was nearly twice that of 11 matched religious kibbutzim. . . . There was no difference in social support or frequency of social contact between religious and secular kibbutzim." J. D. Kark, S. Carmel, R. Sinnreich, N. Goldberger, and Y. Friedlander, "Psychosocial Factors among Members of Religious and Secular Kibbutzim," *Israeli Journal of Medical Science* 32.3–4 (March–April 1996): 185–194.

11. The development and popularization of the concept of "stress" as we today understand it was led after World War II by the Viennese-born physiologist Hans Selye, who came to Canada (the University of Montreal) in the 1930s. See, for example, Hans Selye, "The Evolution of the Stress Concept,"*American Scientist* 61 (1973): 692–699. For more on the history of stress, see John W. Mason, "A Historical View of the Stress Field," *Journal of Human Stress* 1 (June 1975): 22–36.

12. For an introduction to Benson's early research in this area, see R. K. Wallace, H. Benson, and A. F. Wilson, "A Wakeful Hypometabolic State," *American Journal of Physiology* 221 (1971): 795–799; R. K. Wallace and H. Benson, "The Physiology of Meditation," *Scientific American* 226.2 (1972): 84–90, J. F. Beary and H. Benson, "A Simple Physiologic Technique which Elicits the Hypometabolic Changes of the Relaxation Response," *Psychosomatic Medicine* 36 (1974): 115–120; Benson's bestselling book popularizing his technique and its health-promoting effects was published in 1975: *The Relaxation Response* (New York: Avon Books, 1975).

13. In a 1993 interview with television presenter Bill Moyers, J. Kabat-Zinn was quite explicit on this point: "We're not going to make your stress go away at all. . . . You're not trying to make it go away. This is a fundamental point. People think 'I'll come here and it'll make all my stress go away.' We're not saying it'll make your stress go away at all." Kabat-Zinn, interview by Bill Moyers, *Healing and the Mind*, Public Affairs TV, 1993.

14. "An outpatient program in behavioral medicine for chronic pain patients based on the practice of mindfulness meditation: Theoretical considerations and preliminary results," J. Kabat-Zinn, *General Hospital Psychiatry* 4 (1982): 33–47; "The clinical use of mindfulness meditation for the self-regulation of chronic pain," Kabat-Zinn, L. Lipworth, and R. Burney, *Journal of Behavioral Medicine* 8.2 (1985): 63–190; Kabat-Zinn, *Full Catastrophe Living: Using the Wisdom of Your Body and Mind to Face Stress, Pain, and Illness* (New York: Delacorte, 1991); "Influence of a mindfulness meditation-based stress reduction intervention on rates of skin clearing in patients with moderate to severe psoriasis undergoing phototherapy (UBV) and photochemotherapy (PUVA)," Kabat-Zinn, E. Wheeler, T. Light, A. Skillings, M. J. Scharf, T. G. Cropley, et al., *Psychosomatic Medicine* 60.5 (1998): 625–632; and, most recently, R. Davidson et al., "Alterations in Brain and Immune Function Produced by Mindfulness Meditation," *Psychosomatic Medicine* 65 (2003): 564–570.

15. *Psychology Today* (October 1989).

16. Herbert Benson (with Marg Stark), *Timeless Healing: The Power and Biology of Belief* (New York: Scribner, 1996), 200.

17. Luke 8:48; Mark 10:51–52; Luke 17:19; Matthew 9:29–30.

18. See William James, "The Religion of Healthy-Mindedness," in *The Varieties of Religious Experience: A Study in Human Nature* (New York: Penguin Books, [1902] 1987).

19. For a good biography of Peale, see Carol V. R. George, *God's Salesman: Norman Vincent Peale and the Power of Positive Thinking* (New York: Oxford University Press, 1993). Peale's original bestseller, *The Power of Positive Thinking* (he wrote multiple variations on that original formula) has sold some 20 million copies to date, and continues to sell about 3,000 copies weekly.

20. Norman Vincent Peale, *The Amazing Results of Positive Thinking* (New York: Prentice Hall, 1959), 214 (in a chapter entitled "Better Health through Positive Thinking").

21. Norman Cousins, "Anatomy of an Illness (as Perceived by the Patient)," *New England Journal of Medicine* 296.26 (December 23, 1976): 1458–1463, quote on 1459.

22. See O. H. Pepper, "A Note on the Placebo," *American Journal of Pharmacy* 117 (1945): 409–412. See also R. P. C. Handfield-Jones, "A Bottle of Medicine from the Doctor," *The Lancet*, October 17, 1953, 823–825. For more on this history, see my " 'Seeing' the Placebo Effect: Historical Legacies and Present Opportunities," in *The Science of the Placebo: Toward an Interdisciplinary Research Agenda*, ed. A. Kleinman, H. Guess, L. Engel, and J. Kusek (London: British Medical Association, 2001).

23. P. Petrovic et al., "Placebo and Opioid Analgesia: Imaging a Shared Neuronal Network," *Science* 295 (2002): 1737–1740.

24. Cf. Andrew Newberg and Eugene Aquili, *Why God Won't Go Away: Brain Science and the Biology of Belief* (New York: Ballantine Books, 2002); Patrick Glynn's *God: The Evidence* (Rocklin, Calif.: Prima Publishing, 1997). Although not specifically concerned with religion, Nicholas Humphrey's recent work on the evolution and possible biological function of the placebo effect makes some of the same kinds of moves as these other works: see N. Humphrey, "Great Expectations: The Evolutionary Psychology of Faith-Healing and the Placebo Response," in *Proceedings of the 27th International Congress of Psychology*, ed. Lars Backman and Claes von Hosfsten (Psychology Press, 2000).

25. Ted Porter, *Trust in Numbers: The Pursuit of Objectivity in Science and Public Life* (Princeton, N.J.: Princeton University Press, 1997).

26. Francis Galton, "Statistical Inquiries into the Efficacy of Prayer," *Fortnightly Review* 11 (1872): 125–135.

27. Before Byrd, there were one or two other studies—all with negative results—that have received less attention: C. R. B. Joyce and R. M. C. Welldon, "The Objective Efficacy of Prayer: A Double-Blind Clinical Trail," *Journal of Chronic Diseases* 18 (1965): 367–377; P. J. Collipp, "The Efficacy of Prayer: A Triple-Blind Study," *Medical Times* 97 (1969): 201–204.

28. R. J. Byrd, "Positive Therapeutic Effects of Intercessory Prayer in a Coronary Care Unit Population," *Southern Medical Journal* 81 (1988): 826–829.

29. W. S. Harris, M. Gowda, J. W. Kolb, et al., "A Randomized, Controlled Trial of the Effects of Remote, Intercessory Prayer on Outcomes in Patients Admitted to the Coronary Care Unit," *Archive International Medicine* 159 (1999): 2273–2278. For the transcript of a March 13, 2001, debate between Harris and a skeptic, Irwin Tessman, see http://www.csicop.org/articles/20010810-prayer.

30. H. Sides, "The Calibration of Belief," *New York Times Magazine*, December 7, 1997, 92–95, reprinted as "Prescription: Prayer," *St. Petersburg Times*, December 29,

1997, D1–2. Ironically, Dale Matthews's own widely anticipated study investigating the power of intercessory prayer at a distance proved disappointing. See Gary P. Posner, "Study Yields No Evidence for Medical Efficacy of Distant Intercessory Prayer: A Follow-up Commentary," *The Scientific Review of Alternative Medicine* 6.1 (Winter 2002). Also online at http://members.aol.com/garypos/prayerstudyafterpub.html.

31. Larry Dossey, *Healing Words: The Power of Prayer and the Practice of Medicine* (New York: HarperCollins, 1993).

32. A prime example of work in this style is Patrick Glynn's *God: The Evidence* (Rocklin, Calif.: Prima Publishing, 1997).

33. Targ's was a six-month double-blind study that aimed to test the effects of spiritual healing on forty AIDS patients in the San Francisco Bay Area that took a consciously ecumenical approach to the healing process: the interveners consisted of forty practicing healers that self-identified variously as Christians, Jews, Buddhists, Native American shamans, and graduates of bioenergetic schools. The healers were given photographs of the AIDS victims, their first names, and their blood counts. Rather than ask God for help, the healers were directed to send positive healing energy, to direct an intention for health and well-being to the subject. The authors claim that the twenty AIDS patients who received the healing energy (without knowing they had been selected for such treatment) had "fewer and less severe new illnesses, fewer doctor visits, fewer hospitalizations, and improved mood" than the twenty patients in the control group who did not receive the energy. Fred Sicher, Elizabeth Targ, Daniel Moore, Helene S. Smith. "A Randomized, Double-Blind Study of the Effects of Distant Healing in a Population with Advanced AIDS," *Western Journal of Medicine* 169.6 (1998): 356–363.

34. "Evidence for God from Science: Harmony between the Bible and Science," online at http://www.godandscience.org/index.html.

35. Opinion within the research community on all these matters is sharply divided. See, for example, "Evidence behind Claim of Religion-Health Link Is Shaky, Researchers Say," a report of an article published in the March 2002 issue of the *Annals of Behavioral Medicine*, online at http://hbns.org/newsrelease/religion3-11-02.cfm. Compare that to the cautiously encouraging note sounded in the previously referenced 2003 special edition of *American Psychologist* on "Spirituality, Religion, and Health" as an "emerging research field."

36. Cf. Joel James Shuman and Keith G. Meador, *Heal Thyself: Spirituality, Medicine, and the Distortion of Christianity* (New York: Oxford University Press, 2003), 40–43.

37. Harold G. Koenig, Michael E. McCullough, and David B. Larson, *Handbook of Religion and Health* (New York: Oxford University Press, 2000), 5.

38. Cf. Philip Rieff, *The Triumph of the Therapeutic: Uses of Faith after Freud* (Chicago: University of Chicago Press, [1966], 1987).

BIBLIOGRAPHY

Autton, Norman. *Pastoral Care in Hospitals.* London: Society for Promoting Christian Knowledge, 1968.
Beary, J. F., and H. Benson. "A Simple Physiologic Technique which Elicits the Hypo-

metabolic Changes of the Relaxation Response." *Psychosomatic Medicine* 36 (1974): 115–120.

Benson, Herbert (with Marion Z. Klipper). *The Relaxation Response.* New York: Avon Books, 1975.

Benson, Herbert (with Marg Stark). *Timeless Healing: The Power and Biology of Belief.* New York: Scribner, 1996.

Berkman, L. F., and S. L. Syme. "Social Networks, Host Resistance and Mortality: A Nine Year Follow-Up Study of Alameda County Residents." *American Journal of Epidemiology* 109 (1979): 186–204.

Broyard, Anatole. *Intoxicated by My Illness and Other Writings on Life and Death.* Greenwich, Conn.: Fawcett Books, 1993.

Bruhn, J. G., and S. Wolf. *The Roseto Story.* Norman, Okla.: University of Oklahoma Press, 1979.

Byrd, R. J. "Positive Therapeutic Effects of Intercessory Prayer in a Coronary Care Unit Population." *Southern Medical Journal* 81 (1988): 826–829.

Carey, Raymond. *Hospital Chaplains: Who Needs Them?* St. Louis: Colorado Health & Hospital Association, 1972.

Collipp, P. J. "The Efficacy of Prayer: A Triple-Blind Study." *Medical Times* 97 (1969): 201–204.

Cousins, Norman. "Anatomy of an Illness (as Perceived by the Patient)." *New England Journal of Medicine* 296 (December 23, 1976): 1458–1463.

Davidson, R. J., et al. "Alterations in Brain and Immune Function Produced by Mindfulness Meditation." *Psychosomatic Medicine* 65 (2003): 564–570.

Dossey, Larry. *Healing Words: The Power of Prayer and the Practice of Medicine.* New York: HarperCollins, 1993.

Frank, Arthur. *The Wounded Storyteller: Body, Illness, and Ethics.* Chicago: University of Chicago Press, 1995.

Galton, Francis. "Statistical Inquiries into the Efficacy of Prayer." *Fortnightly Review* 12 (1872): 125–135.

George, Carol V. R. *God's Salesman: Norman Vincent Peale and the Power of Positive Thinking.* New York: Oxford University Press, 1993.

Glynn, Patrick. *God: The Evidence.* Rocklin, Calif.: Prima Publishing, 1997.

Gundersen, L. "Faith and Healing." *Annual International Medicine* 132 (2000): 169–172.

Handfield-Jones, R. P. C. "A Bottle of Medicine from the Doctor." *The Lancet,* October 17, 1953, 823–825.

Harrington, Anne. " 'Seeing' the Placebo Effect: Historical Legacies and Present Opportunities." In *The Science of the Placebo: Toward an Interdisciplinary Research Agenda,* edited by A. Kleinman, H. Guess, L. Engel, J. Kusek. London: British Medical Association, 2001.

Harris, W. S., et al. "A Randomized, Controlled Trial of the Effects of Remote, Intercessory Prayer on Outcomes in Patients Admitted to the Coronary Care Unit." *Archives International Medicine* 159 (1999): 2273–2278.

House, J. S., K. R. Landis, and D. Umberson. "Social Relationships and Health." *Science* 241 (1988): 540–545.

Humphrey, N. "Great Expectations: The Evolutionary Psychology of Faith-Healing and the Placebo Response." *Proceedings of the 27th International Congress of Psychology*, edited by Lars Backman and Claes von Hosfsten. London: Psychology Press, 2000.

James, William. *The Varieties of Religious Experience: A Study in Human Nature*. New York: Penguin Books, [1902] 1987.

Joyce, C. R. B., and R. M. C. Welldon. "The Objective Efficacy of Prayer: A Double-Blind Clinical Trial." *Journal of Chronic Diseases* 18 (1965): 367–377.

Kabat-Zinn, J. "An Outpatient Program in Behavioral Medicine for Chronic Pain Patients Based on the Practice of Mindfulness Meditation: Theoretical Considerations and Preliminary Results." *General Hospital Psychiatry* 4 (1982): 33–47.

———. *Full Catastrophe Living: Using the Wisdom of Your Body and Mind to Face Stress, Pain, and Illness*. New York: Delacorte. 1991.

Kabat-Zinn, J., L. Lipworth, and R. Burney. "The Clinical Use of Mindfulness Meditation for the Self-Regulation of Chronic Pain." *Journal of Behavioral Medicine* 8 (1985): 163–190.

Kabat-Zinn, J., et al. "Influence of a Mindfulness Meditation-Based Stress Reduction Intervention on Rates of Skin Clearing in Patients with Moderate to Severe Psoriasis Undergoing Phototherapy (UBV) and Photochemotherapy (PUVA)." *Psychosomatice Medicine* 60 (1998): 625–632.

Kark, J. D., et al. "Psychosocial Factors among Members of Religious and Secular Kibbutzim." *Israeli Journal of Medical Science* 32 (1996): 185–194.

Kleinman, Arthur. *The Illness Narratives: Suffering, Healing, and the Human Condition*. New York: Basic Books, 1988.

Koenig, Harold G. *The Healing Power of Faith*. New York: Simon and Schuster, 1999.

Koenig, Harold G., et al. "Religion, Spirituality, and Medicine: A Rebuttal to Skeptics." *International Journal Psychiatry Medicine* 29 (1999): 123–131.

Koenig, Harold G., Michael E. McCullough, and David B. Larson. *Handbook of Religion and Health*. New York: Oxford University Press, 2000.

Levin, Jeff. *God, Faith and Health: Exploring the Spirituality-Healing Connection*. New York: John Wiley and Sons, 2001.

Lynch, James J. *Broken Heart: The Medical Consequences of Loneliness*. New York: Basic Books, 1985.

Marwick, C. "Should Physicians Prescribe Prayer for Health? Spiritual Aspects of Well-Being Considered." *Journal of American Medical Association* 273 (1995): 1561–1562.

Mason, J. W. "A Historical View of the Stress Field: Part II." *Journal of Human Stress* 1 (June 1975): 22–36.

Matthews, Dale (with Connie Clark). *The Faith Factor: Proof of the Healing Power of Prayer*. New York: Penguin, 1999

Moyers, Bill. "Healing from Within." Vol. 3 of *Healing and the Mind*. Public Affairs TV, 1993.

Newberg, Andrew, and Eugene Aquili. *Why God Won't Go Away: Brain Science and the Biology of Belief*. New York: Ballantine Books, 2002.

Peale, Norman Vincent. *The Power of Positive Thinking*. New York: Prentice-Hall, 1952.

———. *The Amazing Results of Positive Thinking*. New York: Prentice Hall, 1959.

Pepper, O. H. "A Note on the Placebo." *American Journal of Pharmacy* 117 (1945): 409–412.

Petrovic, Predag, Eija Kalso, Karl Magnus Petersson, and Martin Ingvar. "Placebo and Opioid Analgesia: Imaging a Shared Neuronal Network." *Science* 295 (2002): 1737–1740.

Porter, Ted. *Trust in Numbers: The Pursuit of Objectivity in Science and Public Life.* Princeton, N.J.: Princeton University Press, 1997.

Posner, G. P. "Study Yields No Evidence for Medical Efficacy of Distant Intercessory Prayer: A Follow-Up Commentary." *The Scientific Review of Alternative Medicine* 6 (Winter 2002). Online at http://members.aol.com/garypos/prayerstudyafterpub .html.

Rieff, Philip. *The Triumph of the Therapeutic: Uses of Faith after Freud.* Chicago: University of Chicago Press, 1966.

Selye, Hans. "The Evolution of the Stress Concept." *American Scientist* 61 (1973): 692–699.

Shuman, Joel James, and Keith G. Meador. *Heal Thyself: Spirituality, Medicine, and the Distortion of Christianity.* New York: Oxford University Press, 2003.

Sicher, Fred, et al. "A Randomized, Double-Blind Study of the Effects of Distant Healing in a Population with Advanced AIDS." *Western Journal of Medicine* 169 (1998): 356–363.

Sides, H. "The Calibration of Belief." *New York Times Magazine,* December 7, 1997, 92–95.

Sloan, R., et al. "Should Physicians Prescribe Religious Activities?" *New England Journal of Medicine* 342 (2000): 1913–1916.

Slomski, A. J. "Should Doctors Prescribe Religion?" *Medical Economist* 77 (2000): 145–159.

Strawbridge, W. J., R. D. Cohen, and G. A. Kaplan. "Frequent Attendance at Religious Services and Mortality over 28 Years." *American Journal of Physiology Handbook* 87 (1997): 957–961.

Wallace, R. K., and H. Benson. "The Physiology of Meditation." *Scientific American* 226 (1972): 84–90.

Wallace, R. K., H. Benson, and A. F. Wilson. "A Wakeful Hypometabolic State." *American Journal of Physiology* 221 (1971): 795–799.

Wolf, S. "Predictors of Myocardial Infarction over a Span of 30 Years in Roseto, Pennsylvania." *Integrative Physiological and Behavioral Science* 27 (1992): 246–257.

15

The Intersubjective Worlds
of Science and Religion

B. Alan Wallace

In this paper I shall present a radical alternative to metaphysical realism, a view that underlies most literature on science and religion, and yet may also set science and religion in fundamental opposition to each other. Those who advocate metaphysical realism maintain that (1) the real world consists of mind-independent objects, (2) there is exactly one true and complete description of the way the world is, and (3) truth involves some sort of correspondence between an independently existent world and our descriptions of it.[1] Various sorts of cultural relativism and constructivism have been advocated as alternatives to metaphysical realism, but while they have proven appealing to many philosophers, they are generally found to be inadequate by practicing scientists and theologians alike.[2] In this paper, I propose a third alternative that emphasizes the intersubjective nature of both scientific and religious truth-claims, one which rejects the leap of faith required for metaphysical realism and equally shuns the nihilism that is implicit in so many versions of relativism. The central theme of this intersubjective view is that science and religion express truths arrayed along a spectrum of "invariance" among diverse cognitive frameworks. All truth-claims are embedded in experience, and their validity is put to the test within the "lived world" of human experience. They are neither confirmed nor refuted in relation to some hypothetical "real, objective world" that exists independently of experience.

The Trajectory of Metaphysical Realism Since
the Scientific Revolution

Since the time of Copernicus, natural philosophers have commonly assumed
there is a real, physical world that exists prior to and independent of the human
mind, and they have set themselves the task of penetrating "beyond the veil"
of subjective appearances to that external, objective world. Thus, the real world
has been viewed as something devoid of subjective experience, and as natural
philosophy evolved into modern science, many Christian theologians and scientists have believed that all *natural* phenomena can be reduced to physics,
but not the soul or God. The implication here is that not only God, but human
consciousness, is somehow supernatural, or at least "unnatural." And this is
precisely where scientific materialists break away from this Cartesian mind/
matter dualism and insist that the human mind, soul, and consciousness can
all be reduced to physics. Biologists, such as Richard Dawkins, Stephen Jay
Gould, and Edward O. Wilson, are particularly vehement on this point, declaring that evolution has clearly demonstrated that nonconscious, inorganic
matter evolved into primitive living organisms, some of which eventually
evolved into primates, including humans. Thus, the human soul, or consciousness, is an emergent property of the human organism, and is therefore a natural phenomenon that *can* be understood solely in terms of physics, chemistry,
and biology.

We shall return to the question of the emergent status of consciousness
in a moment, but now let's briefly review the course of the scientific study of
the external world of matter and the internal world of the mind. Throughout
the centuries, from ancient Greece and Rome on through medieval Europe,
generations of astronomers turned their attention to the skies, precisely observing the appearances and relative movements of celestial bodies. Such firsthand observations provided Copernicus with the empirical basis for his heliocentric model of the universe. The even more precise observations by the
Danish astronomer Tycho Brahe gave Kepler the data needed to discover the
elliptical orbits of the planets. Likewise, the precise observations of both celestial and terrestrial phenomena by Galileo and other early natural philosophers
gave Newton the empirical basis for devising the laws of classical mechanics.

These early natural philosophers were well aware of the fact that the phenomena they were observing were not external entities in themselves, but appearances of the physical world to the human senses. But this did not deter
them from taking these appearances seriously, thus establishing a science of
dynamics that paved the way for the science of mechanics. Over the centuries,
as progress in technology increased the precision and scope of observations
and experimentation, more and more sophisticated types of explanations of

physical phenomena could be devised. This same progression—from precise, increasingly sophisticated observations of physical phenomena, to theory construction—has characterized both the physical sciences and the life sciences throughout history.

The scientific treatment of mental phenomena, on the other hand, has followed a radically different historical trajectory. For centuries, philosophers have observed mental phenomena firsthand, but they have devised no sophisticated, rigorous methods comparable to those of natural philosophers for observing physical phenomena firsthand. And, unlike natural philosophers, their understanding of mental phenomena did not result in a rigorous science of "mental dynamics," or a phenomenology of the mind. They have not arrived at any consensus concerning the "mechanics" of mental phenomena, nor has their research yielded pragmatic benefits for society as a whole.

During the first three centuries since the Scientific Revolution, scientific attention was focused on external physical phenomena, while internal mental phenomena were largely ignored. When a science of the mind was finally initiated in the closing decades of the nineteenth century, psychologists did briefly devise a number of relatively crude and unsatisfactory methods for observing mental phenomena firsthand. But since the early twentieth century, introspection has been largely ignored in the field of psychology, which has tended to focus more on behavior and, more recently, brain function.

It is worth noting that by the time the science of psychology was taking its first baby steps, many physicists were confident that their understanding of the natural world was largely complete. Only details remained to be filled in. What has been the impact of this three-hundred-year failure on the part of natural scientists to attend to mental phenomena in general, and consciousness in particular, as elements of the natural world? In his classic work *The Principles of Psychology*, the American psychologist and philosopher William James presents an idea that sheds brilliant light on this issue:[3]

> The subjects adhered to become real subjects, attributes adhered to real attributes, the existence adhered to real existence; whilst the subjects disregarded become imaginary subjects, the attributes disregarded erroneous attributes, and the existence disregarded an existence in no man's land, in the limbo "where footless fancies dwell."
> ... Habitually and practically we do not *count* these disregarded things as existents at all ... they are not even treated as appearances; they are treated as if they were mere waste, equivalent to nothing at all.

By the late nineteenth century, natural scientists had for so long ignored the role of consciousness in the universe, they attributed to it an existence in "no man's land," which presumably played no significant role whatsoever in nature as a whole. And mental phenomena, which can be directly detected only by introspective observation, have come to be treated by many cognitive scientists as "mere waste, equivalent to nothing at all."

Contemporary cognitive scientific theories concerning the nature of the mind and its relation to the brain are not based on centuries of increasingly sophisticated introspective observations of mental phenomena. Instead of proceeding from the *dynamics* of the mind to the *mechanics* of mental processes, modern cognitive science has largely sought to bypass the dynamics of the mind and go straight to the dynamics and mechanics of the brain and behavior. As a result of the dissimilarity in the development of the physical sciences and the cognitive sciences, the modern West remains in a prescientific era when it comes to understanding the nature and origins of consciousness and its role in nature. There is no objective, scientific definition of consciousness and no objective, scientific means of detecting the presence, absence, or degree of consciousness in anything whatsoever, including minerals, plants, animals, human fetuses, or human adults. Scientific materialists, such as Harvard sociobiologist Edward O. Wilson, assure us that a balanced view of the universe has in no way been impaired by the dissimilarity in the development of the physical and cognitive sciences. It is only natural, they claim, that consciousness was so long ignored, for it is produced by the human brain, which is the most complex organism we know of in the whole of nature.

An unquestioned assumption in this materialist view is that all mental phenomena, including every form of consciousness, are emergent properties or functions of the brain and its physical interactions with the rest of the body and the environment. Given the scientific understanding of the history of the cosmos and the evolution of life, this conclusion seems inescapable. Where is there any scientific evidence of a nonmaterial soul, as imagined by Descartes? As the materialist neurophilosopher Patricia Churchland comments:[4]

> Western cosmologists would say that we don't have any evidence whatever that there was any non-material stuff. We can see the development of life on our planet starting with amino acids, RNA, and very simple single-celled organisms that didn't have anything like awareness, and the development of multi-celled organisms, and finally organisms with nervous systems. By then you find organisms that can see and move and interact. So the conclusion seems to be that the ability to perceive and have awareness and to think, arises out of nervous systems rather than out of some force that preceded the development of nervous systems.

This would be a very informative statement if cosmologists, or any other scientists, had any means of detecting the presence of nonmaterial stuff in the universe. But they don't. All their technological means of observation are physical instruments designed to measure physical phenomena. If scientists had observed all the physical phenomena in the universe and devised a complete explanation of them solely in terms of matter, they could indirectly infer that there is no nonmaterial stuff in the universe. But they haven't. And even though we know perfectly well—on the basis of nonscientific, subjective awareness—that consciousness exists in the natural world, there are no scientific means of detecting consciousness. In other words, there is no strictly scientific evidence for the existence of consciousness or any other subjective mental phenomena at all!

Is Consciousness an Emergent Property of Matter?

Given the historical lack of parity between the scientific study of physical and mental phenomena, by the twentieth century, what conclusion could cognitive scientists draw except that the mind is a mere epiphenomenon of the brain? They were trapped in an ideological straightjacket that seemed to allow them no alternative to scientific materialism other than to revert to the prescientific speculations of Descartes. And that is simply unacceptable. Modern advances in the neurosciences have made it abundantly clear that there are very specific correlations between mental processes and brain functions. More than a century ago, William James proposed three feasible theories to account for such correlations: (1) the brain produces thoughts, as an electric circuit produces light; (2) the brain releases, or permits, mental events, as the trigger of a crossbow releases an arrow by removing the obstacle that holds the string; and (3) the brain transmits thoughts, as light hits a prism, thereby transmitting a surprising spectrum of colors.[5] Among these various theories, the latter two allow for the continuity of consciousness beyond death. James, who believed in the third theory, hypothesized:[6]

> when finally a brain stops acting altogether, or decays, that special
> stream of consciousness which it subserved will vanish entirely
> from this natural world. But the sphere of being that supplied the
> consciousness would still be intact; and in that more real world with
> which, even whilst here, it was continuous, the consciousness
> might, in ways unknown to us, continue still.

If the brain simply permits or transmits mental events, making it more a conduit than a producer, James speculated that the stream of consciousness may be (1) a different type of phenomenon than the brain, which (2) interacts with the brain while we are alive, (3) which absorbs and retains the identity, personality, and memories constitutive in this interaction, and (4) which can continue to go on without the brain. Remarkably, empirical neuroscientific research thus far is compatible *with all three hypotheses* proposed by James, but the neuroscientific community on the whole has *chosen* to consider only the first hypothesis, which is the only one compatible with the principles of scientific materialism. Thus, instead of letting empirical evidence guide scientific theorizing, a metaphysical dogma is predetermining what kinds of theories can even be considered, and therefore, what kinds of empirical research are to be promoted.

James approached the question of the origins of human consciousness from a scientific perspective, free of the ideological constraints of scientific materialism. Fifteen hundred years earlier, Augustine approached this same question from the perspective of scriptural authority. After careful biblical research, he presented the following four hypotheses: (1) an individual's soul derives from those of one's parents, (2) individual souls are newly created from individual conditions at the time of conception, (3) souls exist elsewhere and are sent by God to inhabit human bodies, and (4) souls descend to the level of human existence by their own choice.[7] After asserting that all these hypotheses may be consonant with the Christian faith, he declared, "It is fitting that no one of the four be affirmed without good reason."[8] This subject, he claimed, had not been studied sufficiently by Christians to be able to decide the issue, or if it had, such writings had not come into his hands. While he suspected that individual souls are created due to individual conditions present at the time of conception, he acknowledged that, as far as he knew, the truth of this hypothesis had not been demonstrated. Instead of seeking compelling empirical evidence concerning the origins of consciousness, the Christian tradition has drawn its conclusions concerning this issue on purely doctrinal grounds. But, according to Augustine, it is an error to mistake mere conjecture for knowledge.

The hypothesis that all conscious states emerge from complex configurations of matter is so widely accepted among contemporary cognitive scientists that it is commonly treated as if it were an empirically confirmed scientific fact. This is a prime example of what historian Daniel J. Boorstin refers to an "illusion of knowledge," and such conflation of assumption and fact, he says, has throughout history acted as the principal obstacle to discovery.[9] In a similar vein, the Nobel Prize–winning physicist Murray Gell-Mann comments, "In my field an important new idea . . . almost always includes a negative statement, that some previously accepted principle is unnecessary intellectual baggage and it is now necessary to jettison that baggage."[10]

Is it so outlandish or unscientific to consider that states of consciousness originate essentially from prior states of consciousness? When considering the origins of the universe, MIT physicist Alan Guth speculates that perhaps our universe is not a singular event, but is more like a biological process of cell division. In that case, the universe may never have started and will almost certainly never stop. This eternally self-reproducing universe could even explain in a natural way where our universe came from: its parent universe. Guth presents the analogy of coming across a new species of rabbit in the forest. If you had to figure out where it came from, you could speculate that it spontaneously emerged out of a random configuration of molecules or was created by some other mysterious cosmic event. But the more plausible explanation is that the rabbit was produced by other rabbits. The same inference, he suggests, may be applied to the origination of our known universe.[11] This same notion could also be applied to the origination of known states of consciousness. It is perfectly feasible that all known human states of consciousness originated from a more fundamental realm, or realms, of consciousness, rather than insisting that they emerged out of a random configuration of molecules.

Descartes set forth a "cogito-centric" hypothesis that all mental processes and all possible bodily correlates "revolve around" a supernatural, immortal soul that was infused by God into the human organism and that functions autonomously from matter. Contemporary scientific materialism, on the other hand, has replaced this discredited notion with its "neurocentric" hypothesis that all mental processes "revolve around" the brain. But this view not only leaves unanswered, but obstructs empirical scientific inquiry into, many crucial features of the mind/body problem. With its fixation on the brain as the source of all mental phenomena, it impedes understanding of the complex ways in which subjective mental states influence brain states and the rest of the body. In order for scientific inquiry to progress in illuminating the relation between subjective mental events and objective neural events, it is necessary to treat both as equally "real," arising as interdependently related events, with neither playing an absolutely primary role.

What Is the Matter with Scientific Materialism?

The scientific view of the universe is based on human perceptions, refined and extended with the aid of technology. Great lengths are taken to ensure that scientific observations are truly objective, free of subjective biases. At the same time, scientific theories and models are themselves products of the human imagination. So what is the relation between our perceptions of the world and imagination? Cognitive neuroscience informs us that the capacities in the brain that are related to perception are largely the same as those related to imagination. Thus, perception, including scientific observations, is essentially sensorimotor-constrained imagination. In the words of neuroscientist Francisco Varela, "Perception is demonstrably constrained and shaped by the concurrent higher cognitive memories, expectations, and preparation for action . . . what is endogenous (self-activated memories and predispositions, for example) and hence the manifestation of the imaginary dimensions, is always a part of perception."[12] The same is said of the distinction between perception and dreaming: the primary difference is that the former is constrained by stimuli from the external environment, whereas the latter is not.[13]

What, then, is the nature of this "real, external, material world," which constrains perception and which physics ostensibly describes? Modern physics has its historical roots in the fundamental hypothesis of the Ionian thinker Democritus in the fourth century B.C.E., namely, that the real world consists essentially of atoms in space. Nobel Prize–winning physicist Richard Feynman presents the basic belief of scientific materialism when he declares, "there is nothing that living things do that cannot be understood from the point of view that they are made of atoms acting according to the laws of physics."[14] What is the current understanding of the nature of these atoms, or the elementary particles that constitute all the matter in the universe? All particles of matter and energy are now believed to consist of oscillations of immaterial, abstract quantities, known as "fields," existing in empty space. Steven Weinberg, another Nobel laureate in physics, comments, "In the physicist's recipe for the world, the list of ingredients no longer includes particles. Matter thus loses its central role in physics. All that is left are principles of symmetry."[15]

What has become of "real matter," existing independently of the human mind in the objective universe? Like the God of Moses being reduced to the abstraction of contemporary deism, the matter of Democritus seems also to have been reduced to a conceptual abstraction in contemporary physics. What is the real ideological commitment of scientific materialists? Is it to matter as "oscillations of immaterial, abstract quantities in empty space"? Or is it to "principles of symmetry"? I would argue that the real ideological commitment of scientific materialists is not to matter itself, but to the methods of the natural sciences, which they believe provide us with our only knowledge of the real world. This is a form of dogma, by which I mean a coherent, universally applied worldview consisting of a collection of beliefs and attitudes that call for a person's intellectual and emotional allegiance. A dogma, therefore, has a power over individuals and communities that is far greater than the power of mere facts and fact-related theories. Indeed, a dogma may prevail despite the most obvious contrary evidence, and commitment to a dogma may grow all the more zealous when obstacles are met. Thus, dogmatists often appear to be incapable of learning from any kind of experience that is not authorized by the dictates of their creed.[16] There are many factors that contribute to such allegiance to a dogma, including personal, social, political, and economic concerns. These influenced the Roman Catholic Church at the time of Galileo, and they now influence the dominant institutions of scientific materialism, such as the public educational system in the United States.

Apart from a dogmatic allegiance to scientific materialism, are there any compelling grounds for believing that oscillations of immaterial mathematical constructs or principles of symmetry exist in the objective world, independent of the human mind that conceives them? Since all measurements entail interactions of the system of measurement and the phenomena being measured, we never have any direct access to an objective world existing independently of all measurements. Werner Heisenberg comments in this regard, "What we observe is not nature in itself but nature exposed to our method of questioning."[17] Einstein comments in a similar vein, "on principle, it is quite wrong to try founding a theory on observable magnitudes alone. In reality the very opposite happens. It is the theory which decides what we can observe."[18]

Much as the principles of Newtonian mechanics are based on the presumed existence of absolute space and time, so are the principles of scientific materialism based on the presumed existence of a real, objective, physical universe that is reconstituted in our heads, based upon sensory input and the self-assembly of concepts. But Edward O. Wilson, who strongly supports this view (maintaining that only madmen and a few misguided philosophers reject it), acknowledges that there is no body of external objective truth by which scientific theories can be corroborated.[19] Werner Heisenberg, Max Born, and other physicists who took an instrumental role in formulating quantum mechanics came to the conclusion that it is futile to attribute existence to that which cannot be known even in principle. Let us bear this principle in mind as we consider that all scientific measurements are made within the context of the intersubjective world of practicing scientists. Likewise, all scientific theories are formulated in the minds of scientists, and they are tested by observations and experiments within the intersubjective world of scientists. And this specialized intersubjective world is a subset of the intersubjective world of humanity as a whole. Without in any way detracting from the value or validity of scientific knowledge, it appears that little, if anything, is lost by acknowledging that science illuminates facets of *the world of experience*, not *the world independent of experience*. As soon as this point is accepted, it becomes obvious that science is not the only, or even the best, means of exploring all aspects of this world. But then it was never designed to do so.

The Intersubjective Spectrum of Truths

The roots of the scientific exclusion of subjective phenomena from nature are to be found in the aspiration of early natural philosophers, many of whom were also theologians, to view the universe from a God's-eye perspective, which implied to them a purely objective perspective. This was their strategy for coming to know the mind of the Creator by way of His Creation. The problem with this approach, however, is that the objective world, independent of experience, is just as removed from scientists as God is to theologians.

The pioneers of the Scientific Revolution were influenced, of course, not only by the Judeo-Christian tradition, but by ancient Greek philosophers, such as Democritus and Aristotle. And this does indeed seem to be a reasonable assumption. What accounts for the commonality of experience among difference subjects, if not an independent, external, physical world? On the other hand, what are the grounds for concluding that the world that exists independently of the human mind consists solely of a kind of stuff that corresponds to our human concepts of matter? If consciousness is as fundamental to the universe as are space-time and mass-energy, then the world independent of the human mind may be comprised of both subjective and objective phenomena. Or it may transcend human concepts altogether, including those of subject and object, mind and matter, and even existence and nonexistence.

If one considers this alternative hypothesis, subjective experience need no longer be banned from the natural world, and the scientific taboo against the firsthand exploration of consciousness and its relation to the objective world may be discarded. This move also encourages us to reappraise our categories of "subjective" versus "objective," and of "convention" versus "reality." In the words of Harvard philosopher Hilary Putnam, "What is factual and what is conventional is a matter of degree; we cannot say, 'These and these elements of the world are the raw facts; the rest is convention, or a mixture of these raw facts with convention.' "[20] The existence of a concrete object like a tree, he argues, is also a matter of convention; and our observation of a tree is possible only in dependence on a conceptual scheme. The reason for this is that "elements of what we call 'language' or 'mind' *penetrate so deeply into what we call 'reality' that the very project of representing ourselves as being 'mappers' of something 'language-independent' is fatally compromised from the very start.*"[21]

The very distinction between the terms "subjective" and "objective" is itself embedded in a conceptual framework, and there is no way to justify the assertion that any truth-claim is purely objective or purely subjective. For example, the assertion that the pizzas I bake are the tastiest ones in town may be objectively true for one person—myself. Perhaps another example of a similarly localized truth is the statement that all the points made in this paper are perfectly clear and utterly compelling. The truth of such claims may be limited to one subject! Moving along the spectrum of intersubjective truths, other claims may be valid solely within the context of a single family, a community, a nation, an ethnic group, or a species. The validity of such statements is tested not with respect to an objective reality, independent of all experience, but with respect to the concentric rings of intersubjective experience. None of these assertions is purely subjective or purely objective, but there is a gradation in terms of their invariance across multiple, cognitive frames of reference. Some statements may be valid only locally, in terms of specific individuals or societies at a certain time and place; while others may be more universally valid, in the sense that they are true for a broad range of individuals and even species. Errors commonly arise when one assumes that a statement that is true for one limited frame of cognitive reference is equally true outside that context.

One truth that *is* invariable across all perceptual frames of reference is that perceived objects exist in relation to the perceptual faculties by which they are apprehended. For example, perceived colors exist in relation to the visual faculty that sees them, and perceived sounds exist relative to the auditory faculty that hears them. There is no reason to believe that such perceptual phenomena exist in the objective world, independent of all sense perception. Nevertheless, in our intersubjective world of experience, multiple subjects may apprehend colors and sounds in similar ways, which allows for true statements to be made about them that are independent of any specific subject. Another truth that is invariable across all cognitive frames of reference is that conceptual objects exist in relation to the conceptual faculties and frameworks by which they are apprehended. However, when these concepts are reified, we may be led to believe that they exist in the objective world, independent of any thinking mind or conceptual framework. This theory does not reduce all concepts to mere artifacts of specific individuals or societies. As Hilary Putnam comments, "the stars are indeed independent of our minds in the sense of being causally independent; we did not make the stars. . . . The fact that there is no one metaphysically privileged description of the universe does not mean that the universe depends on our minds."[22]

The Pursuit of the Universal Truths

Scientists and religious people alike make truth-claims based on extraordinary experiences that may be accessed by only a select group of highly trained individuals, yet they maintain these truths are universal, throughout space and time and for all possible subjects. For example, when probing the quantum mechanical nature of elementary particles, the relativistic curvature of space-time, or the multiple dimensions of string theory, physicists must resort to pure mathematics. The more physicists probe into the nature of phenomena existing in external space, the more they describe them in terms of quantitative abstractions that are experienced in the internal space of the mind. When they try to explain their insights to nonmathematicians, they can do so only roughly and by using metaphors. Likewise, the more contemplatives probe into the nature of phenomena existing in the internal space of the mind, the more they describe them in terms of qualitative abstractions, which also exist in the internal space of the mind. In their writings one finds theories of multiple dimensions of consciousness,[23] but when they try to explain their insights to noncontemplatives, they must also resort to metaphors, which convey only rough approximations of their discoveries.

The language of mathematicians is untranslatable into any other language, and the same is true of the language of contemplatives. Although one mathematical system may be translated into the equations of another system, none can be translated into the experiences or concepts of the general lay public. The same is true of contemplative writings. In some cases one contemplative system may translate well into the language of another, but a sophisticated contemplative theory can never be adequately translated into the language of common, everyday experiences and ideas. The only way one can truly understand mathematics is by practicing it, not just reading about it; and the same is true of contemplation. The chief difference between mathematical and contemplative discourse is that noncontemplatives can easily draw the conclusion that they are thoroughly fathoming contemplative writings, when in fact they are reducing such accounts to their own, more prosaic experiences and ideas. Here is one more case of an illusion of knowledge, for the contemplatives are using ordinary language in extraordinary ways, and only an experienced contemplative knows the referents of the words and phrases used in contemplative writings. Noncontemplatives reduce those ideas to experiences that are familiar to them, but in so doing, they give themselves the false impression that they have fathomed what the contemplatives were writing about.

Steven Katz, a contemporary scholar of comparative mysticism, for example, insists that experienced contemplatives are in no better a position to evaluate their experiences than are noncontemplatives.[24] This notion is just as implausible as the idea that a nonmathematician could evaluate the relation between Heisenberg's matrix equations and Schrödinger's wave equation describing quantum mechanical phenomena. But the misconception that one can evaluate contemplative truth-claims solely on the basis of reading books about mysticism is widespread both among scholars and the lay public. Edward O. Wilson, for example, falls into this trap when he suggests that all mystical experiences are basically the same, and that they have all yielded no insights whatsoever into the nature of reality.[25] Scientists and scholars who try to evaluate one or more contemplative system without acquiring any contemplative experience of their own are thus confined to the echo chambers of their own preconceptions.

A fundamental problem facing both mathematicians and contemplatives is the ineffability of their insights to outsiders. In this regard, three types of ineffability may be posited. First, something may be deemed ineffable if it lies outside of anyone's experience. The objective world with all its contents, existing independently of all experience, fits that description.[26] Secondly, that which lies within the scope of one person's experience is ineffable to those who lack that experience or anything like it. This is true of many mathematical and contemplative insights. Thirdly, an insight may transcend all concepts, so even if one has experienced it directly, it may not be verbally conveyed to anyone, regardless of the range of their experience. A prime example of such an ineffable experience is that of pure, conceptually unstructured consciousness, which figures prominently in many contemplative traditions of the world.[27]

This brings us back to the status of consciousness in nature, and a kind of hierarchy among the physical sciences, life sciences, and cognitive sciences. By probing the nature of inorganic phenomena, one may fathom all the laws of physics, but knowledge of physics alone has not predicted or explained the emergence of life in the universe. By probing the nature of organic phenomena, using all the tools of the physical and life sciences, one may discover the laws of physics and biology, but they alone have not predicted or explained the emergence of consciousness in the universe. Continuing along this spectrum, by probing the nature of the mind and its relation to the brain, using all the tools of the physical sciences, life sciences, and cognitive sciences, one may discover the laws of physics, biology, and psychology. But they have not predicted or explained the possibility of pure consciousness that transcends all conceptual constructs, including those of subject and object. Modern science has no way of testing the hypothesis of pure consciousness or its implications. Indeed, as mentioned previously, there is presently no scientific definition of consciousness of any sort, there are no scientific means of objectively measuring consciousness, and there is no scientific knowledge of the necessary and sufficient causes for its emergence. However, the fact that we presently lack a science of consciousness does not necessarily mean that no other civilization, either in our own cultural past or elsewhere, is equally deficient. Indeed, many contemplatives, from the West and the East, have claimed knowledge of pure consciousness, and many have asserted that such insight yields knowledge of the nature of reality as a whole.[28]

Evaluating Scientific and Religious Truth-Claims

This brings us to the crucial problem of evaluating both scientific and religious truth-claims. When it comes to scientific and mathematical assertions about the nature of reality, a certain degree of consensus has been established as to how to evaluate such claims. But there is no such consensus regarding the alleged discoveries of contemplatives of different religious traditions. Are contemplative writings simply creations of overactive imaginations, or are they based on authentic, personal experiences? At first glance, it may seem that the difference between scientific and contemplative claims is that the former can be verified by third-person criteria, whereas the latter cannot. But upon closer inspection, this distinction does not hold in such a straightforward way.

Ever since the early days of the Royal Society of London, scientific discoveries, which ostensibly occur in the "public domain" of third-person experience, have been corroborated or repudiated by select groups of professional scientists who share a great deal of assumptions and expertise. The validity of sophisticated scientific discoveries has never been established on the basis of the experiences or ideas of the general public. Rather, subsets of the scientific community form their own elite, intersubjective groups, who alone can authoritatively judge the value of their peers' theories and discoveries.

Unlike scientific discoveries that may be witnessed firsthand by multiple "third persons" in an intersubjective domain of experience, the verification or refutation of a mathematical proof is a private, first-person event. The external manifestation of a sophisticated mathematical proof is unintelligible to the nonmathematician, so the evaluation of its validity is confined to professional mathematicians. Who is in a position to judge whether a student of mathematics has in fact understood a particular proof? This may not be done by a fellow student, let along a layperson, who represents a third-person perspective, nor can the student rely entirely on his or her own first-person judgment. Rather, the level of the student's understanding must be judged by a competent mathematician, serving in the role of mentor. Only if this mentor has already fathomed the proof in question can he or she authoritatively judge whether the student has done so. In this regard, mathematical discoveries are comparable to contemplative insights. According to many contemplative traditions, the student enters into formal training and regularly reports his or her experiential insights to a competent mentor, who then evaluates them and guides the student to yet deeper insights. Advanced contemplatives, on the other hand, may claim to have gained specific insights into certain facets of reality, and their claims are then subjected to sophisticated peer review by other senior contemplatives of their tradition.

Once a mathematical theorem has been logically proven to be internally consistent, one may move on to empirical criteria for evaluating whether or not it accurately describes or predicts certain phenomena in nature. There are also pragmatic criteria for evaluating such a theorem, testing whether it is useful for creating new technologies. Empirical and pragmatic criteria are also used in evaluating contemplative theories and practices. Empirically, one observes whether or not they correspond to or predict the types of experiences that emerge in the course of training. Pragmatically, one tests their usefulness in terms of their practical benefits in the life of the contemplative and those with whom he or she engages. The benefits are of course not technological in nature. Rather, they have to do with the attenuation of vices, the growth of virtues, and the enhancement of one's own and others' well-being, especially of the kind early Christianity called *eudaimonia*, or a "truth-given joy."

Contemplative experience is, of course, only one facet of religious experience at large. For some religious traditions it is regarded as being of central importance, while for others it is marginal or even absent altogether. How is one more generally to evaluate the truth-claims made by scientists and religious people? Such truth-claims may be based on one or more of three foundations. First, some scientific and religious assertions are purely dogmatic in nature, which is to say that they cannot be confirmed or refuted solely on the basis of logic or experience. The metaphysical principles of scientific materialism and religious claims based solely on divine authority fit into that category, and it is primarily these claims that form the basis of heated debate between believers of these different scientific and religious ideologies.[29] Second are truth-claims that are based on logical reasoning, and these are subject to rational analysis.

Third are truth-claims based on firsthand experience, be it scientific or religious.

William Christian, a scholar of religion, comments that in the context of inter-religious dialogue, as long as one is reporting on religious beliefs, speakers can be informative "when they define or explain doctrines of their traditions, but not when they are asserting them."[30] This same criterion should apply to advocates of the principles of scientific materialism when addressing audiences adhering to other belief systems. This is especially pertinent in institutions of public education, in which the articles of faith of scientific materialism are commonly conflated with scientific fact. Even Edward O. Wilson, who so ardently embraces scientific materialism, acknowledges that it "is a metaphysical worldview, and a minority one at that, shared by only a few scientists and philosophers. It cannot be proved with logic from first principles or grounded in any definitive set of empirical tests."[31] Nevertheless, advocates of this quasi-religious ideology commonly insist with impunity that their students in the American public education system accept its veracity, not only as a set of working hypotheses, but as established scientific fact. Proponents of other religious belief systems, in stark contrast, are strictly prohibited from promoting their beliefs in American public schools, let alone presenting them as scientifically verified truths. The tenets of scientific materialism or any other metaphysical creed may indeed be rationally accepted as working hypotheses, as long as they are not repudiated either by empirical evidence or logic. But one must not expect others to adopt one's own working hypotheses simply because one finds them very compelling and compatible with scientific evidence or with religious scriptures.

William Christian does acknowledge that adherents of a religion may make informative utterances about their own experiences "if they are relevant."[32] This leaves open the possibility that religious people may speak informatively of their own experiences; and such reports may be taken seriously by others who do not share their religious beliefs. In an inter-religious setting or in a science/religion dialogue, should religious people be confined to making truth-claims only on the basis of their *own* personal experience? May they not make such assertions on the basis of the experience of other religious people, even if they are no longer living? Such an allowance is obviously made for scientists and mathematicians—none of them are confined to making assertions based solely on their own personal experience. Progress in science and mathematics would grind to a halt if that were the case.

There is evidently no simple formula for evaluating truth-claims among the various religions and sciences, but there is one guiding principle that may be helpful, and that is to be on the constant lookout for illusions of knowledge, the conflation of assumptions with genuine knowledge. On this basis, one may evaluate a wide range of scientific and religious truth-claims rationally, empirically, and pragmatically. Regarding both scientific and religious theories and practices, we may first ask whether they are internally consistent. Then, what subjective and objective phenomena do they explain and predict? Finally, how does the adoption of those theories and practices affect the lives of individuals, societies, and their relation with the rest of the world?

If the fundamental aim of both science and religion is to reveal truths that enhance the well-being of humanity, what are the strengths and weaknesses of each of these fields of inquiry, and how might they complement each other? When we raise such questions, the discord between science and religion may give way to a collaborative pursuit of truth in the service of humanity. I believe this strategy accords with the spirit of empiricism proposed by William James when he wrote:[33]

> Let empiricism once become associated with religion, as hitherto, through some strange misunderstanding, it has been associated with irreligion, and I believe that a new era of religion as well as philosophy will be ready to begin. . . . I fully believe that such an empiricism is a more natural ally than dialectics ever were, or can be, of the religious life.

NOTES

1. Hilary Putnam, *Realism with a Human Face*, ed. James Conant (Cambridge, Mass.: Harvard University Press, 1990), 30.

2. Edward O. Wilson, *Consilience: The Unity of Knowledge* (New York: Knopf, 1998), 60–61.

3. William James, *The Principles of Psychology* (New York: Dover Publications, [1890] 1950), 290–291.

4. Zara Houshmand, Robert Livingston, and B. Alan Wallace, eds., *Consciousness at the Crossroads: Conversations with the Dalai Lama on Brain Science and Buddhism* (Ithaca, N.Y.: Snow Lion Publications, 1999), 48–49.

5. William James, *Essays in Religion and Morality* (Cambridge: Harvard University Press, 1989), 85–86.

6. Ibid., 87.

7. Augustine, *The Free Choice of the Will*, trans. Francis E. Tourscher (Philadelphia: The Peter Reilly Co., 1937).

8. Ibid., 379.

9. Daniel J. Boorstin, *The Discoverers: A History of Man's Search to Know His World and Himself* (New York: Vintage Books, 1985), xv.

10. Henning Genz, *Nothingness: The Science of Empty Space* (Cambridge, Mass.: Perseus Books, 1999), 310.

11. K. C. Cole, *The Hole in the Universe: How Scientists Peered Over the Edge of Emptiness and Found Everything* (New York: Harcourt, 2001), 185.

12. Francisco J. Varela and Natalie Depraz, "Imagining: Embodiment, Phenomenology, and Transformation," in *Buddhism and Science: Breaking New Ground*, ed. B. Alan Wallace (New York: Columbia University Press, 2003), 202.

13. Stephen LaBerge and Howard Rheingold, *Exploring the World of Lucid Dreaming* (New York: Ballantine, 1990).

14. Richard P. Feynman, R. B. Leighton, and M. Sands, eds., *The Feynman Lectures in Physics* (Reading, Mass.: Addison-Wesley, 1963), 1–9.

15. K. C. Cole, "In Patterns, Not Particles, Physicists Trust," *Los Angeles Times*, March 4, 1999.

16. Paul Feyerabend, "Quantum Theory and Our View of the World" in *Physics and Our View of the World*, ed. Jan Hilgevoord (Cambridge: Cambridge University Press, 1994), 149–168.

17. Werner Heisenberg, *Physics and Philosophy: The Revolution in Modern Science* (New York: Harper and Row, 1962), 58.

18. Ibid., 63.

19. Wilson, *Consilience*, 59.

20. Putnam, *Realism with a Human Face*, 28.

21. Ibid., 28.

22. Hilary Putnam, "Replies and Comments," *Erkenntnis* 34.3 (1991): 407.

23. B. Alan Wallace, *The Bridge of Quiescence: Experiencing Tibetan Buddhist Meditation* (Chicago: Open Court, 1998), 90–93; Henepola Gunaratana, *The Path of Serenity and Insight: An Explanation of the Buddhist Jhanas* (Columbia, Mo.: South Asia Books, 1985), 49–141.

24. Steven T. Katz, "The 'Conservative' Character of Mystical Experience," in *Mysticism and Religious Traditions*, ed. Steven T. Katz (Oxford: Oxford University Press, 1983), 5.

25. Wilson, *Consilience*, 46, 260.

26. B. Alan Wallace, *Choosing Reality: A Buddhist View of Physics and the Mind* (Ithaca, N.Y.: Snow Lion, 1996), 75–78.

27. Robert K. C. Forman, ed., *The Problem of Pure Consciousness: Mysticism and Philosophy* (New York: Oxford University Press, 1990); Wallace, *The Bridge of Quiescence*, 243–248; B. Alan Wallace, *The Taboo of Subjectivity: Toward a New Science of Consciousness* (New York: Oxford University Press), 112–120.

28. Dom Cuthbert Butler, *Western Mysticism: The Teaching of Augustine, Gregory and Bernard on Contemplation and the Contemplative Life*, 3rd ed. (London: Constable and Co., 1967), 49; Wallace, "The Buddhist Tradition of *Shamatha*: Methods for Refining and Examining Consciousness," *Journal of Consciousness Studies* 6.2–3 (1999): 176.

29. Wallace, *The Taboo of Subjectivity*, 21–37.

30. William A. Christian, *Oppositions of Religious Doctrines: A Study in the Logic of Dialogue among Religions* (London: Macmillan Press, 1972), 88.

31. Wilson, *Consilience*, 9.

32. Christian, *Oppositions of Religious Doctrines*, 88–89; Wallace, *The Bridge of Quiescence*, 6.

33. William James, *A Pluralistic Universe* (Cambridge: Harvard University Press, [1909] 1977), 142.

BIBLIOGRAPHY

Augustine. *The Free Choice of the Will.* Translated by Francis E. Tourscher. Philadel-
    phia: The Peter Reilly Co., 1937.
Boorstin, Daniel J. *The Discoverers: A History of Man's Search to Know His World and
    Himself.* New York: Vintage Books, 1985.
Butler, Dom Cuthbert. *Western Mysticism: The Teaching of Augustine, Gregory and Ber-
    nard on Contemplation and the Contemplative Life.* 3rd ed. London: Constable and
    Co., 1967.
Christian, William A. *Oppositions of Religious Doctrines: A Study in the Logic of Dialogue
    among Religions.* London: Macmillan Press, 1972.
Cole, K. C. "In Patterns, Not Particles, Physicists Trust." *Los Angeles Times,* March 4,
    1999.
————. *The Hole in the Universe: How Scientists Peered Over the Edge of Emptiness and
    Found Everything.* New York: Harcourt, 2001.
Feyerabend, Paul. "Quantum Theory and Our View of the World." In *Physics and Our
    View of the World,* ed. Jan Hilgevoord. Cambridge: Cambridge University Press,
    1994.
Feynman, Richard P., R. B. Leighton, and M. Sands, eds. *The Feynman Lectures in
    Physics.* Reading, Mass.: Addison-Wesley Publishing, 1963.
Forman, Robert K. C., ed. *The Problem of Pure Consciousness: Mysticism and Philosophy.*
    New York: Oxford University Press, 1990.
Genz, Henning. *Nothingness: The Science of Empty Space.* Cambridge, Mass.: Perseus
    Books, 1999.
Gunaratana, Henepola. *The Path of Serenity and Insight: An Explanation of the Bud-
    dhist Jhanas.* Columbia, Mo.: South Asia Books, 1995.
Heisenberg, Werner. *Physics and Philosophy: The Revolution in Modern Science.* New
    York: Harper and Row, 1962.
————. *Physics and Beyond: Encounters and Conversations.* New York: Harper and Row,
    1971.
Houshmand, Zara, Robert Livingston, and B. Alan Wallace, eds. *Consciousness at the
    Crossroads: Conversations with the Dalai Lama on Brain Science and Buddhism.* Ith-
    aca, N.Y.: Snow Lion Publications, 1999.
James, William. *The Principles of Psychology.* New York: Dover Publications, [1890]
    1950.
————. *A Pluralistic Universe.* Cambridge: Harvard University Press, [1909] 1977.
————. *Essays in Religion and Morality.* Cambridge: Harvard University Press, 1989.
Katz, Steven T. "The 'Conservative' Character of Mystical Experience." In *Mysticism
    and Religious Traditions,* ed. Steven T. Katz. Oxford: Oxford University Press,
    1983.
LaBerge, Stephen, and Howard Rheingold. *Exploring the World of Lucid Dreaming.*
    New York: Ballantine, 1990.
Putnam, Hilary. *Realism with a Human Face,* ed. James Conant. Cambridge: Harvard
    University Press, 1990.
————. "Replies and Comments." *Erkenntnis* 34.3 (1991): 401–424.
Varela, Francisco J., and Natalie Depraz. "Imagining: Embodiment, Phenomenology,

and Transformation." In *Buddhism and Science: Breaking New Ground*, ed. B. Alan Wallace, 195–230. New York: Columbia University Press, 2003.

Wallace, B. Alan. *Choosing Reality: A Buddhist View of Physics and the Mind*. Ithaca, N.Y.: Snow Lion Publications, 1996.

———. *The Bridge of Quiescence: Experiencing Tibetan Buddhist Meditation*. Chicago: Open Court, 1998.

———. "The Buddhist Tradition of *Shamatha*: Methods for Refining and Examining Consciousness." *Journal of Consciousness Studies* 6.2–3 (1999): 175–187.

———. *The Taboo of Subjectivity: Toward a New Science of Consciousness*. New York: Oxford University Press, 2000.

Wilson, E. O. *Consilience: The Unity of Knowledge*. New York: Knopf, 1998.

Index